FO

FROM CRITICAL THINKING to ARGUMENT

A Portable Guide

Sylvan Barnet
Tufts University

Hugo Bedau
Tufts University

Bedford/St. Martin's   BOSTON • NEW YORK

For Bedford / St. Martin's
Senior Developmental Editor: Adam Whitehurst
Senior Production Editor: Harold Chester
Senior Production Supervisor: Jennifer Peterson
Marketing Manager: Emily Rowin
Copy Editor: Virginia Perrin
Indexer: Melanie Belkin
Photo Researcher: Connie Gardner
Art Director: Lucy Krikorian
Text Design: Linda M. Robertson
Cover Design: Donna Dennison
Cover Photo: Igloo with Electricity © Thomas Roepke/Corbis
Composition: Cenveo
Printing and Binding: RR Donnelley-Harrisonburg

President, Bedford/St. Martin's: Denise B. Wydra
Editorial Director for English and Music: Karen S. Henry
Director of Development: Erica T. Appel
Director of Marketing: Karen R. Soeltz
Production Director: Susan W. Brown
Director of Rights and Permissions: Hilary Newman

Manufactured in the United States of America.

8 7 6 5 4 3
f e d c b a

For information, write: Bedford/St. Martin's, 75 Arlington Street, Boston, MA 02116   (617-399-4000)

ISBN: 978-1-4576-4995-0

Acknowledgments

Preface

This brief book is about reading other people's arguments and writing your own. Before we describe the sorts of essays we include here, we first want to mention our chief assumptions about the aims of a course that might use *From Critical Thinking to Argument: A Portable Guide.*

Probably most students and instructors would agree that, as *critical readers,* students should be able to

- Summarize accurately an argument they have read;
- Locate the thesis (the claim) of an argument;
- Locate the assumptions, stated and unstated, of an argument;
- Analyze and evaluate the strength of the evidence and the soundness of the reasoning offered in support of the thesis; and
- Analyze, evaluate, and account for discrepancies among various readings on a topic (for example, explain why certain facts are used, why probable consequences of a proposed action are examined or are ignored, or why two sources might interpret the same facts differently).

Probably, too, students and instructors would agree that, as *thoughtful writers,* students should be able to

- Imagine an audience and write effectively for it (for instance, by using the appropriate tone and providing the appropriate amount of detail);

- Present information in an orderly and coherent way;
- Be aware of their own assumptions;
- Locate sources and incorporate them into their own writing, not simply by quoting extensively or by paraphrasing but also by having digested material so that they can present it in their own words;
- Properly document all borrowings—not merely quotations and paraphrases but also borrowed ideas; and
- Do all these things in the course of developing a thoughtful argument of their own.

In the first edition of this book we quoted Edmund Burke and John Stuart Mill. Burke said,

He that wrestles with us strengthens our nerves, and sharpens our skill. Our antagonist is our helper.

Mill said,

He who knows only his own side of the cause knows little.

These two quotations continue to reflect the view of argument that underlies this text: In writing an essay one is engaging in a serious effort to know what one's own ideas are and, having found them, to contribute to a multisided conversation. One is not setting out to trounce an opponent, and that is partly why such expressions as "marshaling evidence," "attacking an opponent," and "defending a thesis" are misleading. True, on television talk shows we see right-wingers and left-wingers who have made up their minds and who are concerned only with pushing their own views and brushing aside all others. But in an academic community, and indeed in our daily lives, we learn by listening to others and also by listening to ourselves.

We draft a response to something we have read, and in the very act of drafting we may find—if we think critically about the words we are putting down on paper—we are changing (perhaps slightly, perhaps radically) our own position. In short, one reason that we write is so that we can improve our ideas. And even if we do not drastically change our views, we and our readers at least come to a better understanding of why we hold the views we do.

FEATURES

In Part One, the first four chapters deal with recognizing and evaluating assumptions—in both texts and images—as a way to start annotating, summarizing, and analyzing arguments. Among the topics discussed are critical thinking, analysis, summary and paraphrase, reasoning, and the uses of humor, emotion, and images. Chapter 4, Visual Rhetoric: Images as Arguments, not only helps students to analyze advertisements but also offers suggestions about using visuals such as maps, graphs, tables, and pie charts in their own arguments.

Chapters 5 and 6 focus principally on writing. Students are expected to apply the critical thinking and reading skills they have learned to writing analytical and argumentative papers. We include sample student papers as models. Chapter 7, on research, includes information on finding, evaluating, and documenting electronic and other sources and discusses ways to choose topics for research, take notes, avoid plagiarism, and integrate quotations. Two annotated student papers—one in MLA style and one in APA style—provide models for reading and reference.

Part Two, a kid of appendix, presents alternative perspectives on argument: the Toulmin model, logical reasoning (a detailed discussion of induction, deduction, and fallacies), a description of Rogerian argument (named for the psychologist Carl Rogers), and a new chapter on the rhetorical analysis of artifacts of popular culture.

We trust that this book is brief enough and affordable enough to be assigned as an accompaniment to a separate anthology of readings or as a supplement to a selection of individual longer works that do not include necessary instruction in critical thinking and argument.

WHAT'S NEW IN THE FOURTH EDITION

We have made some significant changes in the fourth edition that we believe enrich the book and make the content more accessible.

A new chapter on rhetorical analysis of popular culture gives students a framework for making arguments about popular culture, from public service announcements to *Here Comes Honey Boo Boo*.

More help for research. This edition includes a new MLA research paper on corporate social responsibility and additional material about working with sources, including a heavily revised section on summary, paraphrase, and patchwriting (the practice of copying and pasting material from sources without appropriate integration or attribution).

More help with writing strategies. Three new Idea Prompts, or templates, offer strategies for establishing *ethos*, varying tone, and constructing Toulmin arguments. Three new checklists break down strategies for considering audience and conducting sound rhetorical analysis.

ACKNOWLEDGMENTS

Finally, it is our pleasant duty to thank those who have strengthened this book by their comments and advice on the third edition: Elizabeth Bowman, Northern Illinois University; Brooke Champagne, University of Alabama; William Duffy, Francis Marion University; Michael Geary, Bristol Community College; Alan Goldman, Massachusetts Bay Community College; Gregory Hagan, Madisonville Community College; Philip Hart, Plymouth State University; Jackie Herbers, Viterbo University; Jessica Kidd, University of Alabama; Alison Langdon, Western Kentucky University; Quincy Lieskse, Craven Community College; Ellen Novotny, Adams State College; Tom Miner, Sacramento City College; Zach Petrea, Heartland Community College; Wendy Secrist, Lewis-Clark State College; Jennifer Swartout, Heartland Community College; and Jenara Turman, University of Nebraska at Kearney.

We would also like to thank Anthony Atkins, who graciously provided his feedback on the text and contributed a new chapter on rhetorical analysis and popular culture, and Martha Friedman, Connie Gardner, Linda Winters, and Margaret Gorenstein, who adeptly managed art research and text permissions.

We are also deeply indebted to the people at Bedford/St. Martin's, especially to our editor, Adam Whitehurst, who is wise, patient, supportive, and unfailingly helpful. Steve Scipione, Maura Shea, and John Sullivan, our editors for all of the preceding editions, have left a lasting impression on us and on the book; without their work on the first three editions, there probably would not be a fourth. Others at Bedford/St. Martin's to whom we are deeply indebted include Charles H. Christensen, Joan E. Feinberg,

Denise Wydra, Shuli Traub, and Harold Chester, all of whom have offered countless valuable (and invaluable) suggestions. Intelligent, informed, firm yet courteous, persuasive—all of these folks know how to think and how to argue.

YOU GET MORE DIGITAL CHOICES FOR *FROM CRITICAL THINKING TO ARGUMENT*

From Critical Thinking to Argument doesn't stop with a book. Online, you'll find both free and affordable premium resources to help students get even more out of the book and your course. You'll also find convenient instructor resources, such as downloadable sample syllabi, classroom activities, and even a nationwide community of teachers. To learn more about or order any of the products below, contact your Bedford/St. Martin's sales representative, e-mail sales support (sales_support@bedfordstmartins.com), or visit the Web site at **bedfordstmartins.com**.

Student Resources

ReWriting **3.0, bedfordstmartins.com/rewriting** The best collection of open writing resources on the Web, *Re:Writing* 3.0 gives you and your students even more ways to think, watch, practice, and learn about writing concepts. Listen to Nancy Sommers on using a teacher's comments to revise. Try a logic puzzle. Consult our resources for writing centers. Send your students to free and open resources, choose flexible premium resources to supplement your print text, or upgrade to an expanding collection of innovative digital content.

VideoCentral is a growing collection of videos for the writing class that captures real-world, academic, and student writers talking about how and why they write. VideoCentral can be packaged for free with *From Critical Thinking to Argument*. An activation code is required. To order VideoCentral packaged with the print book, use **ISBN 978-1-4576-7679-6**.

i-series

Add more value to your text by choosing one of the following tutorial series, free when packaged with *From Critical Thinking to Argument*. This popular series presents multimedia tutorials in a flexible format—because there are things you can't do in a book. To learn more about package options or any of the products below, contact your Bedford/St. Martin's sales representative or visit **bedfordstmartins.com**.

ix visualizing composition 2.0 (available online) helps students put into practice key rhetorical and visual concepts. To order *ix visualizing composition* packaged with the print book, use **ISBN 978-1-4576-7678-9**.

i-claim: visualizing argument 2.0 (available online) shows students how to analyze and compose arguments in words, images, and sounds with six tutorials, an illustrated glossary, and over seventy multimedia arguments. To order *i-claim: visualizing argument* packaged with the print book, use **ISBN 978-1-4576-7677-2**.

Instructor Resources

You have a lot to do in your course. Bedford/St. Martin's wants to make it easy for you to find the support you need—and to get it quickly.

TeachingCentral **(bedfordstmartins.com/teachingcentral)** offers the entire list of Bedford/St. Martin's print and online professional resources in one place. You'll find landmark reference works, sourcebooks on pedagogical issues, award-winning collections, and practical advice for the classroom—all free for instructors.

Bits **(bedfordbits.com)** collects creative ideas for teaching a range of composition topics in an easily searchable blog. A community of teachers—leading scholars, authors, and editors—discusses revision, research, grammar and style, technology, peer review, and much more. Take, use, adapt, and pass the ideas around. Then, come back to the site to comment or share your own suggestions.

Brief Contents

Contents

3 Critical Reading: Getting Deeper into Arguments   70

PART ONE

FROM CRITICAL THINKING to ARGUMENT and RESEARCH

1

Critical Thinking

What is the hardest task in the world? To think.

— RALPH WALDO EMERSON

I write entirely to find out what I'm thinking, what I'm looking at, what I see and what it means. What I want and what I fear.

— JOAN DIDION

In all affairs it's a healthy thing now and then to hang a question mark on the things you have long taken for granted.

— BERTRAND RUSSELL

Although Emerson said simply "to think," he clearly was using the word *think* in the sense of *critical thinking*. By itself, *thinking* can mean almost any sort of mental activity, from idle daydreaming ("During the chemistry lecture I kept thinking about how I'd like to go camping") to careful analysis ("I'm thinking about whether I can afford more than one week—say two weeks—of camping in the Rockies," or even "I'm thinking about whether Emerson's comment is true").

In short, when we add the adjective *critical* to the noun *thinking*, we eliminate reveries, just as we also eliminate snap judgments. We are talking about searching for hidden assumptions, noticing various facets, unraveling different strands, and evaluating what is most significant. The word *critical* comes from a Greek word, *krinein*, meaning "to separate," "to choose"; it implies conscious, deliberate inquiry, and especially it implies adopting a skeptical state of mind. To say that it implies a skeptical state of mind is by no means to say that it implies a self-satisfied fault-finding state of mind. Quite the reverse: Because critical thinkers seek to draw

"He saves all his critical thinking for my behavior."

intelligent conclusions, they are sufficiently open-minded that they can adopt a skeptical attitude

- Toward *their own* ideas,
- Toward *their own* assumptions, and
- Toward the evidence *they themselves* tentatively offer,

as well as toward the assumptions and evidence offered by others. When they reread a draft they have written, they read it with a skeptical frame of mind, seeking to improve the thinking that has gone into it.

THINKING ABOUT DRIVERS' LICENSES AND PHOTOGRAPHIC IDENTIFICATION

By way of illustration, let's think about a case that was in the news in 2003. When Sultaana Freeman, an American Muslim woman in Florida, first applied for a driver's license, she refused on religious grounds to unveil her face for the photograph that Florida requires. She was allowed to remain veiled for the photo, with only her eyes showing. Probably in a response to the terrorist attacks of September 11, 2001, she was informed in 2002 that her license would be revoked if she refused to allow the Department of Motor Vehicles to photograph her face. She sued the state of Florida, saying that unveiling would violate her Islamic beliefs. "I'm fighting for the principle and the religious freedom of all people in the country," she said. "It's not about me."

Well, let's think about this—let's think critically, and, to do this, we will use a simple aid that is equal to the best word processor, a pencil. Your own experience has already taught you that thinking is largely a matter of association; one thought leads to another, as when you jot down "peanut butter" on a shopping list and then add "bread," and "bread" somehow reminds you—you don't know why—that you also need paper napkins. As the humorist Finley Peter Dunne observed, philosophers and cows have the gift of meditation, but "others don't begin to think till they begin to talk or write." So what are some thoughts that come to mind when we begin to talk or write about this Florida case?

Critical thinking means questioning not only the assumptions of others but also questioning *your own* assumptions. We will discuss this point at some length later in this chapter, but here we want to say only that when you write an argument, you ought to be *thinking*, evaluating evidence and assumptions, not merely collecting evidence to support a preestablished conclusion.

Back to the Florida case: Page 6 shows what we came up with in a few minutes, using a process called *clustering*. (We illustrate clustering again on page 170.)

In the center of a sheet of paper, we jotted down a phrase summarizing the basic issue, and then we began jotting down what must be the most obvious justification for demanding the picture—national safety. (We might equally well have begun with the most obvious justifications for refusing to be photographed—religious belief and perhaps privacy, to think of arguments that Sultaana Freeman—or, more likely, her lawyer—might set forth.) Then we let our minds work, and one thought led to another. Sometimes almost as soon as we jotted down an idea we saw that it wasn't very good, but we made considerable progress.

In the illustration, we have added numbers to the ideas, simply so that you can see how our minds worked, which is to say how we jumped around. Notice, for instance, that our fifth point—our fifth idea—is connected to our first point. When we were rereading our first four jottings, the fifth idea—that she is not being discriminated against as a Muslim—came to mind, and we saw that it should be linked with the first point. Our sixth point—a modification

4. Not the point: She believes her face ought not to be seen by a cop who might ask for her license.

3. Compromise: Maybe have a woman photographer take the picture in private.

1. National security is more important than private beliefs.

2. Infringement on one's religious beliefs.

5. She is *not* being discriminated against, as a Muslim. All people who want a Florida license need a photo.

6. Not quite true. Temporary licenses are issued without a photo.

of our fifth, occurred to us even before we finished writing the fifth. The sixth point, that temporary licenses in Florida are issued without photographs, prompted us to start thinking more vigorously about the arguments that Ms. Freeman, or her lawyer, might offer.

A very brief digression: A legal case is usually a matter of guilty or not guilty, right or wrong, yes or no. Of course in some trials a defendant can be found guilty of certain charges and innocent of others, but, again, it is usually an either/or situation: The prosecution wins, or the defense wins. But in many other aspects of life, there is room for compromise, and it may well be that *both* sides win—by seeing what ground they share and by developing additional common ground. We go into this topic at greater length on page 357, where we discuss Rogerian argument (named for Carl Rogers, a psychotherapist).

Now back to *Freeman v. State of Florida, Department of Highway Safety and Motor Vehicles*, where we began by trying to list arguments on one side versus arguments on the other.

- After making our seventh note, which goes back to the issue of religious liberty (hence we connected it with a line to the

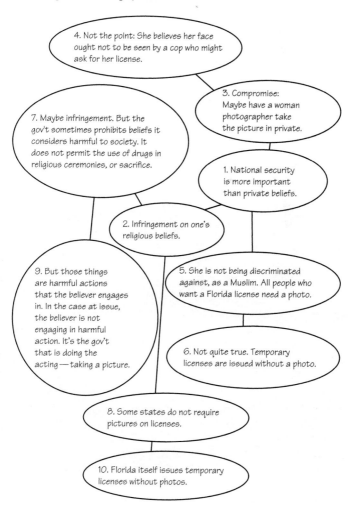

central issue) and which turned out to be an argument that the government rather than the plaintiff might make, we decided to keep thinking about government positions and wrote the eighth note—that some states do not require pictures on drivers' licenses.

- The ninth note—that the government is prohibiting a belief, not a harmful action—in some degree refutes our seventh note, so we connected it to the seventh.

Again, if you think with a pencil and a sheet of paper and let your mind make associations, you will find, perhaps to your surprise, that you have plenty of interesting ideas. Doubtless you will also have some not-so-interesting ones. We confess that we have slightly edited our notes; originally they included two points that we are ashamed we thought of:

- "What is she complaining about? In some strict Islamic countries they don't even let women drive, period."
- "Being deprived of a license isn't a big deal. She can take the bus."

It will take only a moment of reflection to decide that these thoughts can scarcely be offered as serious arguments: What people

Plaintiff in *Freeman v. State of Florida, Department of Highway Safety and Motor Vehicles.* (Peter Cosgrove/© AP/Worldwide Photos.)

do in strict Islamic countries has nothing to do with what we should do in ours, and that bus service is available is utterly irrelevant to the issue of whether this woman's rights are being infringed. Still, if a fear of making fools of ourselves had prevented us from jotting down ideas, we would not have jotted down any decent ideas, and the page would not have gotten written.

The outcome of the driver's license photo case? Judge Janet C. Thorpe ruled against the plaintiff, explaining that "the State has always had a compelling interest in promoting public safety. That interest is served by having the means to accurately and swiftly determine identities in given circumstances." (You can read Judge Thorpe's entire decision online—sixteen highly readable double-spaced pages—by going to Google and typing in "Sultaana Lakiana.")

> **A RULE FOR WRITERS:** One good way to start writing an essay is to start generating ideas—and at this point don't worry that some of them may be nonsense. Just get ideas down on paper, and evaluate them later.

TOPICS FOR CRITICAL THINKING AND WRITING

1. Think about Judge Thorpe's comment, quoted in the preceding paragraph. Even if we agree that a photograph establishes identity—itself a debatable point—one might raise a question: Given the fact that Florida has not passed a law requiring a photo ID, why should it say that the driver of a vehicle must provide a photo ID? Isn't a driver's license a mere certification of permission to drive?

2. Judge Thorpe wrote the following as part of her explanation for her decision:

   > Although the Court acknowledges that Plaintiff herself most likely poses no threat to national security, there likely are people who would be willing to use a ruling permitting the wearing of fullface cloaks in driver's license photos by pretending to ascribe to religious beliefs in order to carry out activities that would threaten lives.

   Is the judge in effect saying that we should infringe on Sultaana Freeman's religious beliefs because someone else might do something wicked?

3. In England in 2006 a Muslim woman—a British citizen—was removed from her job as a schoolteacher because she wore a veil.

The stated reason was that the veil prevented her from effectively communicating with children. What do you think of the view that a woman has a right to wear a veil, but when she enters the marketplace she may rightly be denied certain jobs? What are your reasons?

THINKING ABOUT ANOTHER ISSUE CONCERNING DRIVERS' LICENSES: ANALYZING AND EVALUATING MULTIPLE PERSPECTIVES

Let's think critically about a law passed in West Virginia in 1989. The law provides that although students may drop out of school at the age of sixteen, no dropout younger than eighteen can hold a driver's license. (Several states now have comparable laws.)

What ought we to think of such a law?

- Is it fair?
- What is its purpose?
- Is it likely to accomplish its purpose?
- Might it unintentionally cause some harm?
- If so, can we weigh the potential harm against the potential good? Who gains something and who loses something?

Suppose you had been a member of the West Virginia state legislature in 1989: How would you have voted? Why?

In thinking critically about a topic, we try to see it from all sides before we come to our conclusion. We conduct an argument with ourselves, advancing and then questioning opinions:

- What can be said *for* the proposition, and
- What can be said *against* it?

Our first reaction may be quite uncritical, quite unthinking: "What a good idea!" or "That's outrageous!" But critical thinking requires us to reflect further, trying to support our position *and also* trying to see the other side. One can almost say that the heart of critical thinking is a *willingness to face objections to one's own beliefs,* a willingness to adopt a skeptical attitude not only toward authority and toward views opposed to our own but also toward common sense—that is, toward the views that seem obviously right to us. If we assume we have a monopoly on the truth and we dismiss as bigots those who oppose us, or if we say our opponents are acting merely out of self-interest and we do not in fact analyze their views, we are being critical but we are not engaged in critical thinking.

> **A RULE FOR WRITERS:** Early in the process of jotting down your ideas on a topic, stop to ask yourself, "What might reasonably be offered as an *objection* to my view?"

In short, as we will say several times (because we think the point is basic, *argument is an instrument of learning* as well as of persuasion.

Critical thinking requires us to see things from perspectives other than our own and to envision the likely consequences of our positions. (This sort of imaginative thinking—grasping a perspective other than our own and considering the possible consequences of positions—is imperative if we want others to take our positions seriously.)

Thinking critically involves a twofold activity:

analysis, finding the parts of the problem and then separating them, trying to see how things fit together; and

evaluation, judging the merit of our claims and assumptions and the weight of the evidence in their favor.

If we engage in imaginative, analytic, and evaluative thought, we will have second and third ideas; almost to our surprise we may find ourselves adopting a position that we initially couldn't imagine we would hold. As we think about the West Virginia law, we might find ourselves coming up with a fairly wide variety of ideas, each triggered by the preceding idea but not necessarily carrying it a step further. For instance, we may think X and then immediately think, "No, that's not quite right. In fact, come to think of it, the opposite of X is probably true." We haven't carried X further, but we have progressed in our thinking.

Critical Thinking at Work: From Jottings to a Short Essay

We have already seen examples of **clustering** or **mapping** on pages 6 and 7, which is to say we have seen examples of *thinking* or, more specifically, generating ideas by imagining responses—

counterthoughts—to first thoughts. Here is another example, this time showing a student's thoughts about the issue of whether homeschooled students should be permitted to participate in extra-curricular activities, especially varsity sports, in public schools.

IDEA PROMPT 1.1 MAPPING PROS AND CONS

Should homeschooled students be allowed to play on public school sports teams?

Yes	No
1. Parents of homeschoolers pay taxes that support public schools.	2. But so what? They have chosen homeschooling. They have rejected the ideas of the public school.
3. Homeschooling is officially approved. These aren't truant students. It's just that they or their parents think they can do a better job on some things—not all things—than the public schools.	4. But it is unfair to deprive a public school student of the shot to play on the high school football team because an outside kid gets the spot.
5. Speaking of unfairness, is it fair to deprive a talented homeschooler of the possibility of an athletic scholarship? Or of participating in a National Academy of Science project?	6. Yes, it is fair. The public school students get the opportunity because they have competed under conditions that are monitored. They have their coursework standardized and their grades are monitored according to the same criteria as other students.
	7. By the way, I have learned that some homeschool proponents oppose the idea of kids participating in public school activities. They say it weakens the homeschool program.

A first reaction might be, "Yes, of course. Their parents pay taxes, so the schools should be available, even if the parents have chosen not to make full use of them," or, on the other hand, a first reaction might be, "Certainly not. The parents have opted out of the system. School is not a cafeteria where one chooses the things one likes, and rejects the rest."

One of our students, Steve Jeffries, began by jotting down his first thoughts—and also the counterresponses that he himself generated. He numbered his notes so that we could easily see their sequence.

A STUDENT'S ESSAY, DEVELOPED FROM A CLUSTER AND A LIST

Steve Jeffries, the student who submitted the cluster or preliminary map of ideas concerning homeschooling, transformed the material into a list and ultimately wrote a short essay (the assigned essay was to be "250–500 words") on the topic. Notice that in the essay—the product of several revised drafts—the student introduced points he had *not* thought of when he was mapping, notably the material about the football player Tim Tebow. The cluster, in short, was a *first* step, not a road map of the final essay.

Play Ball! Why Homeschoolers Should Be Allowed to Play on Public School Teams

Perhaps the most famous homeschooler is Tim Tebow, now a star quarterback with the New York Jets, but how can a homeschooler have much chance to play high school football? How can a young person, however talented in a sport that is a team sport, further develop this talent if there is no team on which he or she can play? Fortunately for Tebow—and for football fans throughout the country—Tebow was raised in Florida, a state that allows homeschoolers to play on teams in their school districts. Most states are not so enlightened.

The chief arguments against homeschoolers playing on public school teams seem to be three: First, they (or their parents) have chosen *not* to participate in the public school system; second, if they do get on the team, they may deprive a public school student of his or her place on the team; and, third, public school students are eligible to play on a team only if they meet certain standards concerning grades and the number of courses they are taking, but homeschoolers sometimes are not evaluated in this way. A fourth argument comes, surprisingly, from some homeschool parents themselves: Some of these parents say they do *not* want their children to participate in the extracurricular activities of the public school because such participation undermines the very idea of homeschooling. We do not need to consider this last objection, since if the parents don't want their children to participate in any of the activities, there is no problem for the public school, no question about whether the students are eligible.

The first argument is correct in saying that the parents have chosen to homeschool the children, but this does not mean, or should not mean, that the parents have also chosen to prevent the children from participating in extracurricular activities. It merely means that for various reasons the parents think they can do a better job of *teaching* their children than the public school system does — and the plan of the parents has been officially approved by the local school board. The plan concerns reading, writing, and 'rithmetic, not sports, or, for that matter, the chess team or the band. The second argument, about depriving a public school student of a place on the team, perhaps has some merit, but surely all members of a team want — for their *own* sake — all of the players to be the best available players, and if a homeschooler is (say) a better quarterback than any present student in the public school, almost surely the members of the team want the homeschooler. Chess players and musicians similarly want to play with the best players, knowing that their own skills are improved when they are teamed with superior players. Third, although homeschoolers are not always evaluated in terms of numbers of courses they are taking, everyone knows that homeschoolers (or at least their parents!) are very serious, and that homeschooled children are being well-educated.

Not every homeschooler is a Tim Tebow, who brought fame to his Florida high school, but every talented homeschooler ought to be given the opportunity to participate in extracurricular affairs in the local school if their parents are willing to let them. It's good for *all* of the people concerned and, what's more, it is fair, and fairness is part of what American education is about.

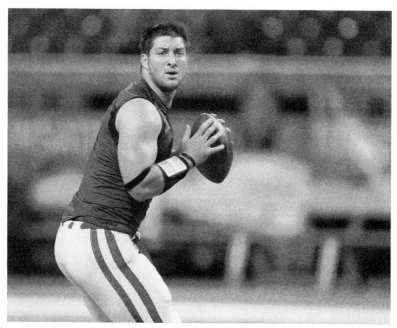

Tim Tebow

The Essay Analyzed

The title, by its first two words, immediately engages a reader's attention, and the subtitle states the thesis. This introductory material—a paper begins with its title, not with its first paragraph—lets the readers know where they will be going.

The first paragraph mentions a name familiar to many—probably to most—readers, and reminds them that Tebow was a homeschooler who was allowed to play on the team of a public high school. The writer's implication presumably is this: If Tebow, an American hero, did it, it must be OK.

The second paragraph draws heavily on the student's preliminary map. It sets forth pretty much all of the objections, and, at the end of this paragraph, the writer explains to the readers why only three of the four points will be discussed. Again, the writer is keeping the readers informed of where they are going. And presumably the readers are interested in hearing more from this thoughtful writer.

The third paragraph fulfills the expectations that the second paragraph set up. Ordinarily a writer would not attempt to cover three objections in one paragraph—probably each objection would get a paragraph to itself—but the assignment limited the student to 250–500 words. The second and third paragraphs are in effect the central body of this essay. By the end of the third paragraph the author has argued his case—offered his evidence in support of his thesis—and now the writer merely has to wrap things up, to make an effective exit.

The fourth paragraph employs a time-tested formula for ending: It returns to a point made at the beginning—Tebow—and thus the wheel comes full circle. This paragraph, in addition to providing a sense of completeness or finality, also appeals to the reader's sense of fairness—normally an effective gesture, though in this instance a reader may wonder if the writer has convincingly demonstrated that fairness requires public schools to admit home-schoolers to extracurricular activities. Are *you* convinced that it is *unfair* to deny homeschoolers access to a public school's extracurricular activities? Why, or why not?

WRITING AS A WAY OF THINKING

We have already seen, in the clusters that students have written, concise examples of how the act of writing helps thinkers to think. "To learn to write," Robert Frost said, "is to learn to have ideas." But how do you "learn to have ideas"? Often we discover ideas while we are in the process of talking with others. A friend says X about some issue, and we—who have never really thought much about the matter—say,

- "Well, yes, I see what you are saying, but, come to think of it, I'm not of your opinion. I see it differently—*not* X *but* Y." Or maybe we say,

- "*Yes,* X, *sure, and also* a bit of *Y,* too."

Mere chance—the comment of a friend—has led us to an idea that we didn't know we had. This sort of discovery may at first seem something like the discovery we make when we reach under the couch to retrieve a ball that the dog has pushed and we find a ten-dollar bill instead. "How it got there, I'll never know, but I'm glad I found it."

In fact, learning to have ideas is not largely a matter of chance. Or if chance *is* involved, well, as Louis Pasteur put it, "Chance favors the prepared mind." What does this mean? It means that somehow, lurking in the mind, are some bits of information or hints or maybe hunches that in the unexpected circumstance—when talking, or when listening to a lecture or a classroom discussion, or especially when reading—are triggered and result in useful thoughts. A sort of seat-of-the-pants knowledge that, when brought to the surface, when worked on, when thought about, produces good results.

Consider the famous episode of Archimedes, the ancient Greek mathematician, who discovered a method to determine the volume of an irregularly shaped object. The problem: A king gave a goldsmith a specific weight of gold with which to make a crown in the shape of laurel leaves. When the job was finished the king weighed the crown, found that it was the weight of the gold he had provided, but he nevertheless suspected that the goldsmith might have substituted some silver for the gold. How could Archimedes find out (without melting or in any other way damaging the crown) if the crown was pure gold? Meditating produced no ideas, but when he entered a bathtub Archimedes noticed that the level of water rose as he immersed his body. He suddenly realized that he could thus determine the volume of the crown—by measuring the amount of displaced water. Since silver is less dense than gold, it takes a greater volume of silver to equal a given weight of gold. That is, a given weight of gold will displace less water than the same weight of silver. Archimedes then immersed the given weight of gold, measured the water it displaced, and found that indeed the crown displaced more water than the gold did. In his excitement at hitting upon his idea, Archimedes is said to have leaped out of the tub and run naked through the street, shouting "Eureka" (Greek for "I have found [it]").

Getting Ideas

Why do we tell this story? Partly because we like it, but chiefly because the word *eureka* comes from the same Greek word that has given our language the word **heuristic** (pronounced hyooRIStik), a method or process of discovering ideas, in short, of thinking. In this method, one thing triggers another. (Note: In computer science *heuristic* has a more specialized meaning.) Now, one of the best ways of getting ideas is to hear what is going on around you—and what is going on around you is talk, in and out of the classroom, and talk in the world of books. You will find, as we said at the beginning of this discussion, that your response may be, "Well, yes, I see what you are saying, but, come to think of it, I don't see it quite that way.

I see it differently—not *X* but *Y*." As we said earlier, argument is an instrument of learning as well as of persuasion. For instance,

> *Yes*, solar power is a way of conserving energy, *but* do we need to despoil the Mojave Desert and endanger desert life with—literally—fifty thousand solar mirrors, so that folks in Los Angeles can heat their pools? Doesn't it make sense to reduce our use of energy, rather than merely to develop sources of renewable energy that violate the environment? Some sites should be off-limits.

Or maybe your response to the proposal (now at least ten years old) that wind turbines be placed in Cape Cod, Massachusetts, is,

> *Given our need* for wind power, *how can a reasonable person object* to the proposal that we put 130 wind turbines in Cape Cod, Massachusetts? *Yes*, the view will be changed, *but* in fact the turbines are quite attractive. No one thinks that windmills in Holland spoil the landscape. So the view will be changed, but not spoiled, *and furthermore* wind turbines do not endanger birds or aquatic life.

When you are asked to write about something you have read in this book, if your first response is that you have no ideas, remember the responses that we have mentioned—"No, I don't see it that way," or "Yes, but," or "Yes, and moreover"—and see if one of them helps you to respond to the work—helps you, in short, to get ideas.

A related way of getting ideas practiced by the ancient Greeks and Romans and still regarded as among the best ways, is to consider what the ancients called **topics,** from the Greek word *topos*, meaning "place," as in our word *topography* (a description or representation of a place). For the ancients, certain topics, put into the form of questions, were in effect places where one went to find ideas. Among the classical topics were definition, comparison, relationship, and testimony. By prompting oneself with questions about these topics, one finds oneself moving toward answers (see Idea Prompt 1.2).

If you think you are at a loss for ideas when confronted with an issue (and when confronted with an assignment to write about it), you probably will find ideas coming to you if you turn to the relevant classical topics and begin jotting down your responses. (In classical terminology, you are engaged in the process of invention, from the Latin *invenire*, "to come upon," "to find.") Seeing your ideas on paper—even in the briefest form—will help bring other ideas to mind and will also help you to evaluate them. For instance, after jotting down ideas as they come and responses to them,

IDEA PROMPT 1.2 UNDERSTANDING CLASSICAL TOPICS

Definition	*What is it?*	"The West Virginia law defines a high school dropout as . . ."
Comparison	*What is it like or unlike?*	"Compared with the national rate of teenagers involved in fatal accidents, teenagers from West Virginia . . ."
Relationship	*What caused it, and what will it cause?*	"The chief cause of teenage fatal driving accidents is alcohol. Admittedly, there are no statistics on whether high school dropouts have a higher rate of alcoholism than teenagers who remain in school, but nevertheless . . ."
Testimony	*What is said about it, for instance, by experts?*	"Judge Smith, in sentencing the youth, said that in all of his long experience . . ."

1. You might go on to organize them into two lists, pro and con;
2. Next, you might delete ideas that, when you come to think about them, strike you as simply wrong or irrelevant; and
3. Then you might develop those ideas that strike you as pretty good.

You probably won't know where you stand until you have gone through some such process. It would be nice if we could make a quick decision, immediately justify it with three excellent reasons, and then give three further reasons showing why the opposing view is inadequate. In fact, however, we almost never can come to a reasoned decision without a good deal of preliminary thinking.

Consider again the West Virginia law we discussed earlier in this chapter. Here is a kind of inner dialogue that you might engage in as you think critically about it:

The purpose is to give students an incentive to stay in school by making them pay a price if they choose to drop out.

Adolescents will get the message that education really is important.

But come to think of it, *will* they? Maybe they will see this as just another example of adults bullying young people.

According to a newspaper article, the dropout rate in West Virginia decreased by 30 percent in the year after the bill was passed.

Well, that sounds good, but is there any reason to think that kids who are pressured into staying really learn anything? The *assumption* behind the bill is that if would-be dropouts stay in school, they—and society—will gain. But is the assumption sound? Maybe such students will become resentful, will not learn anything, and may even be so disruptive that they will interfere with the learning of other students.

Notice how part of the job is *analytic,* recognizing the elements or complexities of the whole, and part is *evaluative,* judging the adequacy of all of these ideas, one by one. Both tasks require critical thinking in the form of analyzing and evaluating, and those processes themselves require a disciplined *imagination.*

So far we have jotted down a few thoughts and then immediately given some second thoughts contrary to the first. Of course, the counterthoughts might not immediately come to mind. For instance, they might not occur until we reread our notes or try to explain the law to a friend, or until we sit down and begin drafting an essay aimed at supporting or undermining the law. Most likely, in fact, some good ideas won't occur until a second or third or fourth draft.

Here are some further thoughts on the West Virginia law. We list them more or less as they arose and as we typed them into a computer—not sorted out neatly into two groups, pro and con, or evaluated as you would want to do in further critical thinking of your own. And, of course, a later step would be to organize the material into some useful pattern. As you read, you might write your own responses in the margin.

Education is *not* optional, something left for the individual to take or not to take—like going to a concert, jogging, getting annual health checkups, or getting eight hours of sleep each night. Society has determined that it is *for the public good* that citizens have a substantial education, so we require education up to a certain age.

Come to think about it, maybe the criterion of age doesn't make much sense. If we want an educated citizenry, it would make more sense to require people to attend school until they demonstrated competence in certain matters rather than until they reached a certain age. Exceptions, of course, would be made for mentally challenged persons and perhaps for certain other groups with special needs.

What is needed is not legal pressure to keep teenagers in school but schools that hold the interest of teenagers.

A sixteen-year-old usually is not mature enough to make a decision of this importance.

Still, a sixteen-year-old who finds school unsatisfying and who therefore drops out may become a perfectly useful citizen.

Denying a sixteen-year-old a driver's license may work in West Virginia, but it would scarcely work in a state with great urban areas, where most high school students rely on public transportation.

We earn a driver's license by demonstrating certain skills. The state has no right to take away such a license unless we have demonstrated that we are unsafe drivers.

To prevent a person of sixteen from having a driver's license prevents that person from holding certain kinds of jobs, and that's unfair.

A law of this sort deceives adults into thinking that they have really done something constructive for teenage education, but it may work *against* improving the schools. It may be *counterproductive:* If we are really serious about educating youngsters, we have to examine the curriculum and the quality of our teachers.

Doubtless there is much that we haven't said, on both sides, but we hope you will agree that the issue deserves thought. In fact, several states now revoke the driver's license of a teenager who drops out of school, and four of these states go even further and revoke the licenses of students whose academic work does not reach a given standard. On the other hand, Louisiana, which for a while had a law like West Virginia's, dropped it in 1997.

✔ A CHECKLIST FOR CRITICAL THINKING

Attitudes

☐ Does my thinking show imaginative open-mindedness and intellectual curiosity?

☐ Am I willing to examine my assumptions?

☐ Am I willing to entertain new ideas—both those that I
encounter while reading and those that come to mind while
writing?

☐ Am I willing to exert myself—for instance, to do research—
to acquire information and to evaluate evidence?

Skills

☐ Can I summarize an argument accurately?

☐ Can I evaluate assumptions, evidence, and inferences?

☐ Can I present my ideas effectively—for instance, by organizing and by writing in a manner appropriate to my imagined
audience?

If you were a member of a state legislature voting on this
proposal, you would *have* to think about the issue. But just as a
thought experiment, try to put into writing your tentative views.

One other point about this issue. If you had to think about
the matter *today,* you might also want to know whether the West
Virginia legislation of 1989 is considered a success and on what
basis. That is, you would want to get answers to such questions as
the following:

- What sort of evidence tends to support the law or tends to
  suggest that the law is a poor idea?

- Did the reduction in the dropout rate continue, or did the
  reduction occur only in the first year following the passage
  of the law?

- If indeed students who wanted to drop out did not, was their
  presence in school a good thing, both for them and for their
  classmates?

- Have some people emerged as authorities on this topic? What
  makes them authorities, and what do they have to say?

- Has the constitutionality of the bill been tested? With what
  results?

Some of these questions require you to do **research** on the topic. The questions raise issues of fact, and some relevant evidence probably is available. If you are to arrive at a conclusion in which you can have confidence, you will have to do some research to find out what the facts—the objective data—are. Merely explaining your position, without giving the evidence, will not be very convincing.

Even without doing any research, however, you might want to look over the ideas, pro and con, perhaps adding some totally new thoughts or perhaps modifying or even rejecting (for reasons that you can specify) some of those already given. If you do think a bit further about this issue, and we hope that you will, notice an interesting point about *your own* thinking: It probably is not *linear* (moving in a straight line from A to B to C) but *recursive,* moving from A to C and back to B or starting over at C and then back to A and B. By zigging and zagging almost despite yourself, you'll get to a conclusion that may finally seem correct. In retrospect it seems obvious; *now* you can chart a nice line from A to B to C—but that was not at all evident to you at the start.

A SHORT ESSAY ILLUSTRATING CRITICAL THINKING

When we read an essay, we expect the writer to have thought things through, at least to a considerable degree. We do not want to read every false start, every fuzzy thought, every ill-organized paragraph that the writer knocked off. Yes, writers make false starts, put down fuzzy thoughts, write ill-organized paragraphs, but then they revise and revise yet again, and they end by giving us a readable essay that seems effortlessly written. Still—and here we get to our real point—in argumentative essays, writers need to show their readers that they have made some effort; they need to show us *how* they got to their final (for the moment) views. It is not enough for the writer to say, "I believe *X*"; rather, the writer must in effect say, "I believe *X*—and I hope you will believe it also—because *Y* and *Z*, though attractive, just don't stand up to inquiry as well as *X* does. *Y* is superficially plausible, but . . . , and *Z*, which is an attractive alternative to *Y,* nevertheless fails because . . ."

Notice in the following short essay—on parents putting spyware into the computers of their children—that Harlan Coben frequently brings up objections to his own position; that is, he shows his awareness of other views and then tries to show why he thinks his position is preferable. Presumably he thus communicates to his readers a sense that he is thoughtful, well-informed, and fair-minded.

Harlan Coben

Harlan Coben (b. 1962) is the author of Hold Tight *(2009). Reprinted here is an essay published in the* New York Times *on March 16, 2008. Following is a letter that was written in response and was later published in the* Times.

The Undercover Parent

Not long ago, friends of mine confessed over dinner that they had put spyware on their fifteen-year-old son's computer so they could monitor all he did online. At first I was repelled at this invasion of privacy. Now, after doing a fair amount of research, I get it.

Make no mistake: If you put spyware on your computer, you have the ability to log every keystroke your child makes and thus a good portion of his or her private world. That's what spyware is—at least the parental monitoring kind. You don't have to be an expert to put it on your computer. You just download the software from a vendor and you will receive reports—weekly, daily, whatever—showing you everything your child is doing on the machine.

Scary. But a good idea. Most parents won't even consider it.

Maybe it's the word: spyware. It brings up associations of Dick Cheney sitting in a dark room, rubbing his hands together and reading your most private thoughts. But this isn't the government we are talking about—this is your family. It's a mistake to confuse the two. Loving parents are doing the surveillance here, not faceless bureaucrats. And most parents already monitor their children, watching over their home environment, their school.

Today's overprotective parents fight their kids' battles on the 5 playground, berate coaches about playing time and fill out college applications—yet when it comes to chatting with pedophiles or watching beheadings or gambling away their entire life savings, then . . . then their children deserve independence?

Some will say that you should simply trust your child, that if he is old enough to go on the Internet he is old enough to know the dangers. Trust is one thing, but surrendering parental responsibility to a machine that allows the entire world access to your home borders on negligence.

Some will say that it's better just to use parental blocks that deny access to risky sites. I have found that they don't work. Children know how to get around them. But more than that—and this is where it gets tough—I want to know what's being said in e-mail and instant messages and in chat rooms.

There are two reasons for this. First, we've all read about the young boy unknowingly conversing with a pedophile or the girl who was cyberbullied to the point where she committed suicide. Would a watchful eye have helped? We rely in the real world on teachers and parents to guard against bullies—do we just dismiss bullying on the Internet and all it entails because we are entering difficult ethical ground?

Second, everything your child types can already be seen by the world—teachers, potential employers, friends, neighbors, future dates. Shouldn't he learn now that the Internet is not a haven of privacy?

One of the most popular arguments against spyware is the claim 10 that you are reading your teenager's every thought, that in today's world, a computer is the little key-locked diary of the past. But posting thoughts on the Internet isn't the same thing as hiding them under your mattress. Maybe you should buy your children one of those little key-locked diaries so that they too can understand the difference.

Am I suggesting eavesdropping on every conversation? No. With new technology comes new responsibility. That works both ways. There is a fine line between being responsibly protective and irresponsibly nosy. You shouldn't monitor to find out if your daughter's friend has a crush on Kevin next door or that Mrs. Peterson gives too much homework or what schoolmate snubbed your son. You are there to start conversations and to be a safety net. To borrow from the national intelligence lexicon—and yes, that's uncomfortable— you're listening for dangerous chatter.

Will your teenagers find other ways of communicating to their friends when they realize you may be watching? Yes. But text messages and cell phones don't offer the anonymity and danger of the Internet. They are usually one-on-one with someone you know. It is far easier for a predator to troll chat rooms and MySpace and Facebook.

There will be tough calls. If your sixteen-year-old son, for example, is visiting hardcore pornography sites, what do you do? When I was sixteen, we looked at *Playboy* centerfolds and read *Penthouse Forum*. You may argue that's not the same thing, that Internet pornography makes that stuff seem about as harmful as "SpongeBob."

And you're probably right. But in my day, that's all you could get. If something more graphic had been out there, we probably would have gone for it. Interest in those, um, topics is natural. So start a dialogue based on that knowledge. You should have that talk anyway, but now you can have it with some kind of context.

Parenting has never been for the faint of heart. One friend of mine, using spyware to monitor his college-bound, straight-A daughter, found out that not only was she using drugs but she was sleeping with her dealer. He wisely took a deep breath before confronting her. Then he decided to come clean, to let her know how he had found out, to speak with her about the dangers inherent in her behavior. He'd had these conversations before, of course, but this time he had context. She listened. There was no anger. Things seem better now. `15`

Our knee-jerk reaction as freedom-loving Americans is to be suspicious of anything that hints at invasion of privacy. That's a good and noble thing. But it's not an absolute, particularly in the face of the new and evolving challenges presented by the Internet. And particularly when it comes to our children.

Do you tell your children that the spyware is on the computer? I side with yes, but it might be enough to show them this article, have a discussion about your concerns and let them know the possibility is there.

Overall View of the Essay

Before we comment in some detail on Coben's essay, we need to say that in terms of the length of its paragraphs, this essay is not a model for you to imitate. Material in newspapers customarily is given in very short paragraphs, partly because readers are reading it while eating breakfast or while commuting to work, and partly because the columns are narrow; a paragraph of only two or three sentences may still be an inch or two deep.

The title, "The Undercover Parent" is provocative, attention-getting.

Paragraph 1 contains cues that telegraph the reader that there will be a change ("Not long ago," "At first," and "Now"). These cues set up expectations, and then Coben to some degree fulfills the expectations. We say "to some degree" because the essay still has a number of paragraphs to go.

Paragraph 2 presses the point, almost aggressively ("Make no mistake").

Paragraph 3 pretty much does the same. The writer is clearly reassuring the readers that he knows how most of them feel. The idea is "scary," yes—and then comes a crucial word, "but," signaling to the reader that Coben takes a different view. We then expect him to tell us why. And—who knows?—he may even convince us.

Paragraph 4 reassures us that Coben does have some idea of why the idea is "scary," and it goes on—with another "but"—to clarify the point. We may not agree with Coben, but it is evident that he is *thinking*, inching along from one idea to the next, frequently to an opposing idea.

Paragraph 5 shows that again Coben has a sense of what is going on in the world ("Today's overprotective parents"), or, rather, he has two senses, because he adds "yet," equivalent to "but." In effect he says, "Yes *A*, but also *B*."

Paragraph 6 begins "Some will say," another indication that the writer knows what is going on. And we can expect that "some will say" will, sooner or later, lead into another "but" (or other comparable word), indicating that although some say *X*, he says *Y*.

Paragraph 7 again begins "Some will say." *We* will say that again the reader knows Coben's report of what "some" say will lead to a report that what *Coben* says (i.e., thought) is different.

Paragraph 8 begins, "There are two reasons." OK, we as readers know where we will be going: We will hear two reasons. Now, when Coben drafted this paragraph he may—who knows?—have first written "There are three reasons," or "There is one reason." Whatever he wrote as a prompt, it got him moving, got him thinking, and then, in the course of writing, of finding ideas, he revised when he found out exactly how many reasons he could offer. In any case, in the paragraph as we have it, he promises to give two reasons, and in this paragraph he gives the first, nicely labeled "First." Notice too, that he provides *evidence*, and he draws in the reader: "we've all read." In short, he establishes a cozy relationship with his reader.

Paragraph 9 begins, helpfully, "Second." Fine, we know exactly where Coben is taking us: He is giving us the second of the two reasons that he discovered, and that he implicitly promised to give when in the previous paragraph he said, "There are two reasons."

Paragraph 10 begins, "One of the most popular arguments against spying is," and so we know, again, where Coben will be taking us: He will, in effect, be telling us what some folks—but not Coben—say. Very simple, very obvious—Coben will be summarizing one of the most popular arguments against spying—and we are grateful to him for letting us know at the beginning of the paragraph what his intentions are.

Paragraph 11 continues his intimate relation with the reader ("Am I suggesting eavesdropping . . . ?") He thus lets us know that he has a good sense of how the reader probably is responding. As we will say several times in this book, good writers are able to put themselves into their readers' shoes. Because they have a sense of how the reader is responding, they offer whatever the reader needs at the moment, for instance a definition, or an example.

Paragraph 12 begins with a question ("Will your teenagers find other ways of communicating . . . ?"), and this question again indicates that Coben is walking in the shoes of his readers; he knows that this question is on their minds. His answer is twofold, "Yes," and "But." Again the "but" is a sign of critical thinking, a sign that Coben has a clear sense of position *A* but wants to move his reader from *A* to *B*.

Paragraph 13, beginning "There will be tough calls," is yet another example of Coben's demonstration to his readers that he is aware of their doubts, aware that they may be thinking Coben has simplified things.

Paragraph 14 (beginning "And you're probably right") continues his demonstration that he is aware of how his readers may respond—but it is immediately followed with a "But." Again, he is nudging us from position *A* to his position, position *B*.

Paragraph 15, like several of the earlier paragraphs, shows Coben is sympathetic to the real-world problems of his readers ("Parenting has never been for the faint of heart"), and it also shows that he is a person of experience. In this paragraph, where he refers to the problem of a friend, he tells us of the happy solution. In short, he tells us that life is tough, but experience shows that there is hope. (The letter-writer, Carol Weston, strongly implies that this bit of experience Coben offers in this paragraph is *not* at all typical.)

Paragraph 16 again indicates the writer's sense of the reader ("Our knee-jerk reaction"), and it again evokes a "But."

Paragraph 17, the final paragraph, pretty directly addresses the reader ("Do you tell your children that the spyware is on the computer?"), and it offers a mixed answer: "I side with yes, but . . . ." Again Coben is showing not only his awareness of the reader but also his awareness that the problem is complicated: There is something to be said for *A* but also something to be said for *B*. He ends by suggesting that indeed this article might be discussed by parents with their children, thereby conveying to his readers the suggestion that he is a fair-minded guy, willing to have his ideas put up for discussion.

Since this essay was published, smartphones have become increasingly popular, complicating Coben's point that "text messages and cell phones don't offer the anonymity and danger of the Internet." Many students' phones are now their primary means of accessing the Internet. How does this trend invite you to reconsider Coben's argument?

Following is Carol Weston's response to Coben's essay that the *Times* later published (March 23, 2008).

Letter of Response by Carol Weston

To the Editor:

In "The Undercover Parent" (Op-Ed, March 16), the novelist Harlan Coben writes that putting spyware on a child's computer is a "good idea."

✓ A CHECKLIST FOR EVALUATING LETTERS
OF RESPONSE

After reading the letters responding to an editorial or to a previous letter, go back and read each letter. Have you asked yourself the following questions?

☐ What assumption(s) does the letter-writer make? Do you share the assumption(s)?

☐ What is the writer's claim?

☐ In what ways does the writer consider the audience?

☐ What evidence, if any, does the writer offer to support the claim?

☐ Is there anything about the style of the letter—the distinctive use of language, the tone—that makes the letter especially engaging or especially annoying?

As a mother and advice columnist for girls, I disagree. For most families, spyware is not only unnecessary, but it also sends the unfortunate message, "I don't trust you."

Mr. Coben said a friend of his "using spyware to monitor his college-bound, straight-A daughter, found out that not only was she using drugs but she was sleeping with her dealer." He confronted her about her behavior. "She listened. There was no anger. Things seem better now."

Huh?! No anger? No tears or shouting or slammed doors? C'mon. If only raising teenagers were that simple.

Parenting is both a job and a joy. It does not require spyware, but it does require love, respect, time, trust, money, and being as available as possible 24/7. Luck helps, too.

CAROL WESTON
New York, March 16, 2008

The writer is an advice columnist for Girls' Life *magazine.*

TOPICS FOR CRITICAL THINKING AND WRITING

1. How important is the distinction (para. 4) between government invasion of privacy and parental invasion of privacy?

2. Complete the following sentence: An invasion of privacy is permissible if and only if . . .

3. Identify the constructive steps a normal parent might consider taking before going so far as to install spyware.

4. Do you agree with Weston's statement that installing spyware translates to "I don't trust you"? Would you feel differently (or not) if you were a parent?

5. How does Weston effectively use her audience when responding to Coben?

6. Write your own letter to the editor, indicating your reasons for supporting or rejecting Coben's argument.

EXAMINING ASSUMPTIONS

In Chapter 3 we will discuss **assumptions** in some detail, but here we want to introduce the topic by emphasizing the importance of *identifying* and *examining* assumptions—the assumptions you will encounter in the writings of others and the assumptions you will rely on in your own essays.

With this in mind, let's return again to considering the West Virginia driver's license law. What assumptions did the legislature make in enacting this statute? We mentioned earlier one such assumption: If the law helped to keep teenagers from dropping out of school, then that was a good thing for them and for society in general. For all we know, the advocates of this legislation may have made this assumption *explicit* in the course of their argument in favor of the statute. Perhaps they left this assumption *tacit*, believing that the point was obvious and that everyone shared this assumption. The assumption may be obvious, but it was not universally shared; the many teenagers who wanted to drop out of school at sixteen and keep their drivers' licenses did not share it.

Another assumption that the advocates of this legislation may have made is this:

> The provisions of this statute are the most efficient way to keep teenagers in high school.

Defending such an assumption is no easy task because it requires identifying other possible legislative strategies and evaluating their merits against those of the proposed legislation.

✓ A CHECKLIST FOR EXAMINING ASSUMPTIONS

☐ What assumptions does the writer's argument presuppose?

☐ Are these assumptions explicit or implicit?

☐ Are these assumptions important to the author's argument or only incidental?

☐ Does the author give any evidence of being aware of the hidden assumptions in her or his argument?

☐ Would a critic be likely to share these assumptions, or are they exactly what a critic would challenge?

☐ What sort of evidence would be relevant to supporting or rejecting these assumptions?

☐ Am I willing to grant the author's assumptions? Would most readers grant them?

☐ If not, why not?

Consider now two of the assumptions involved in the Sultaana Freeman case. Thanks to the "clustering" exercise (pp. 4–9), these and other assumptions are already on display. Perhaps the most important and fundamental assumption Ms. Freeman made is this:

> Where private religious beliefs conflict with duly enacted laws, the former should prevail.

This assumption is widely shared in our society and is by no means unique to Muslim women seeking drivers' licenses in Florida after September 11, 2001. Freeman's opponents, however, probably assumed a very different but equally fundamental proposition:

> Private religious practices and beliefs must yield to the demands of national security.

Obviously these two assumptions were on a collision course and neither side could hope to prevail so long as the key assumptions of the other side were ignored.

Jena McGregor

Jena McGregor, a graduate of the University of Georgia, writes a daily blog for the Washington Post. *We reprint a piece that she published on May 25, 2012, when women in the military forces were still prohibited from serving in combat positions. On January 24, 2013, Defense Secretary Leon Panetta, acting on a recommendation from the Joint Chiefs of Staff, lifted the ban on women in combat roles, but opposition remains. For example, a group called Concerned Women for America immediately protested that "our military cannot continue to choose social experimentation and political correctness over combat readiness." Other topics for discussion are printed below, after the essay.*

Military Women in Combat: Why Making It Official Matters

It's been a big couple of weeks for women in the military.

Last week, female soldiers began formally moving into jobs in previously all-male battalions, a program that will later go Army-wide. The move is a result of rule changes following a February report that opened some 14,000 new positions to women in critical jobs much closer to the front lines. However, some 250,000 combat jobs still remain officially closed to them.

The same week, Rep. Loretta Sanchez (D, Calif.) and Sen. Kirsten Gillibrand (D, N.Y.) introduced legislation in both houses of Congress that would encourage the "repeal of the Ground Combat Exclusion policy" for women in the armed forces. Then this Wednesday, two female U.S. Army reservists filed a lawsuit that seeks to overturn the remaining restrictions on women in combat, saying they limit "their current and future earnings, their potential for promotion and advancement, and their future retirement benefits." (A Pentagon spokesperson told Bloomberg News that Defense Secretary Leon Panetta "is strongly committed to examining the expansion of roles for women in the U.S. military, as evidenced by the recent step of opening up thousands of more assignments to women.")

One of the arguments behind both the lawsuit and the new legislation is that the remaining restrictions hurt women's opportunities for advancement. Advocates for women in the military say that even if women like Gen. Ann Dunwoody have reached four-star general status, she and women like her without official frontline combat experience apparently haven't been considered for the military's very highest posts. "If women remain restricted to combat service and combat service support specialties, we will not see a woman as Commandant of the Marine Corps, or CENTCOM commander, or Chairman of the Joint Chiefs of Staff," writes

Greg Jacob, policy director for the Service Women's Action Network. "Thus women in the military are being held back simply because they are women. Such an idea is not only completely at odds with military ethics, but is distinctly un-American."

Women have been temporarily "attached" to battalions for the last decade; still, allowing women to formally serve in combat operations could help to break down the so-called brass ceiling.

Another way to break down the ceiling would be to consider talented women for top military leadership positions, whether or not they've officially held certain combat posts. Presidents have chosen less-senior officers for Joint Chiefs roles, which are technically staff jobs, wrote Laura Conley and Lawrence Korb, a former assistant defense secretary in the Reagan administration and a senior fellow at the Center for American Progress, in the *Armed Forces Journal* last year. They argue that putting a woman on the Joint Chiefs would help the military grapple with rising sexual harassment issues, bring nontraditional expertise (which women have developed because of some of their role exclusions) at a time when that's increasingly critical, and send the signal that the military is not only open to women, but puts no barriers in their way.

Yes, putting women in combat roles beyond those that have been recently formalized would require many adjustments, both logistical and psychological, for the military and for its male troops. There are plenty of women who may not be interested in these jobs, or who do not meet the physical demands required of them. And gradual change may be prudent. The recent openings are a start; Army Chief of Staff Ray Odierno's acknowledgment last week that if women are allowed into infantry, they will at some point probably go through Ranger School, is encouraging.

But at a time when experience like the infantry is reportedly crucial for getting top posts, it's easy to see how official and sizable policy changes are needed in order to create a system that lets talented women advance to the military's highest echelons. In any field where there are real or perceived limitations for women's advancement, it's that much harder to attract the best and brightest. Indeed, the Military Leadership Diversity Commission recommended last March that the services end combat exclusion policies for women, along with other "barriers and inconsistencies, to create a level playing field for all qualified service members." As the commission chairman, Retired Air Force Gen. Lester L. Lyles, told the American Forces Press Service at the time, "we know that [the exclusion] hinders women from promotion."

For the military to achieve the diverse workforce it seeks, interested and capable women should either not face exclusions, or the culture of the armed forces needs to change so that women without that particular experience can still reach the very top. Both changes may be difficult, but the latter is extraordinarily so. Ending the restrictions is the shortest route to giving the military the best pool of talent possible and the most diverse viewpoints for leading it.

Topics for Critical Thinking and Writing

1. How would you characterize McGregor's tone (her manner)? Thoughtful? Pushy? Point to passages that support your view.

2. Explain the term *brass ceiling* (para. 5).

3. One argument *against* sending women onto an actual battlefield, as infantry or as members of a tank crew, is that if they are captured they might be gang-raped. In your view, how significant is this as an argument?

4. Here is a second argument that has been made against sending women into direct combat: Speaking generally, women do not have the upper-body strength that men have, and a female soldier (again, we are speaking generally, not about a particular individual) would thus be less able to pull a wounded companion out of a burning tank or off a battlefield. To put the matter strongly: Male soldiers might feel that they could not count on their female comrades in a time of need. What is your reply?

5. In her final paragraph, McGregor suggests that if the armed forces changed their policy and did not in effect require battlefield experience for the very highest jobs, the military thus would achieve diversity at the top and women would have an opportunity for top pay. What are your thoughts? For instance, is the idea that the top officers should have experienced hand-to-hand combat out of date, romantic, hopelessly *macho*, or irrelevant to modern warfare? Explain.

6. What do you make of the following argument? If women in the military should be treated exactly the way men are, why, if there is a national draft, should the draft be limited to males? If a national emergency requires conscription, why shouldn't women be drafted, just like men?

FIVE EXERCISES IN CRITICAL THINKING

As you are drafting your essays for one or more of the assignments, consider typing your notes in a Google document and writing your essay in a blog so that you can easily share your thoughts on your topic. As always, submit and complete assignments the way that your teacher directs. However, free online venues can serve as good places for you to maintain copies of your notes and essays for later consultation.

1. Think further about the 1989 West Virginia law that prohibits high school dropouts younger than eighteen from holding a driver's license. Jot down pros and cons, and then write a balanced dialogue between two imagined speakers who hold opposing views on the merits of the law. You'll doubtless have to revise your dialogue several times, and in revising your drafts you will find that further ideas come to you. Present *both* sides as strongly as possible. (You may want to give the two speakers distinct characters; for instance, one may be a student who has dropped out and the other a concerned teacher, or one a parent—who perhaps argues that he or she needs the youngster to work full-time driving a delivery truck—and one a legislator. But do not write as if the speakers must present the arguments they might be expected to hold. A student might argue *for* the law, and a teacher *against* it.)

2. Take one of the following topics and write down all the pro and con arguments you can think of in, say, ten minutes. Then, at least an hour or two later, return to your notes and see whether you can add to them. Finally, as in Exercise 1, write a balanced dialogue, presenting each idea as strongly as possible. (If none of these topics interests you, talk with your instructor about the possibility of choosing a topic of your own.) Suggested topics:

   a. Colleges should not award athletic scholarships.
   b. Bicyclists and motorcyclists should be required by law to wear helmets.
   c. High school teachers should have the right to search students for drugs on school grounds.
   d. Smoking should be prohibited in all parts of all college buildings.
   e. College administrators should take no punitive action against students who use racist language or language that offends any minority.
   f. Students should have the right to drop out of school at any age.
   g. In rape trials, the names of the alleged victims should not be released to the public.
   h. The United States ought to require a national identity card.

3. On the evening of July 31, 2001, after court employees had left the Alabama Judicial Building in Montgomery, Chief Justice Roy S. Moore of the Alabama Supreme Court and his supporters installed in the lobby of the courthouse a four-foot-high, 5,200-pound granite block bearing the text of the Ten Commandments. Moore had not discussed his plan with other justices. Civil liberties groups complained that the monument was an unconstitutional attempt to endorse a specific religion (the First Amendment to the U.S. Constitution says, "Congress shall make no law respecting an establishment of religion"), and in 2002 a federal judge ordered Moore to remove the monument. He refused, saying that the monument is a symbol of the roots of American law. He also said, "To do my duty, I must obey God." His supporters have offered several arguments on his behalf, notably that (a) the Founding Fathers often spoke of God; (b) every courtroom has a Bible to swear in witnesses and jurors; (c) the U.S. Supreme Court has a frieze of lawgivers, including Moses with the Ten Commandments, Hammurabi, Confucius, and Muhammad. In August 2003, Moore was suspended from his position on the court, and the monument was removed from view. Your views?

4. Since 1937, when San Francisco's Golden Gate Bridge opened, some 1,200 people have leaped from it to their deaths. The board of the Golden Gate Bridge, Highway and Transportation District periodically contemplates plans to make it suicide-proof. It discusses the kinds of devices proposed (railings, nets, or a combination), the cost (an estimated $15.25 million, which could be used for other civic purposes), the aesthetic factor (the devices may spoil the appearance of this renowned art deco work), and the engineering uncertainties (some engineers express reservations about the aerodynamic drag the barrier may create). And now consider these additional arguments against altering the bridge: (a) the government has no business paternalistically interfering with the free will of persons who wish to commit suicide; (b) if the Golden Gate Bridge is made suicide-proof, persons who wish to commit suicide will easily find some other site, such as the nearby Bay Bridge; (c) only 3 percent of the persons who commit suicide in the Bay Area do so by leaping from the bridge.

   The assignment: You are on the board of the Golden Gate Bridge. Suicides on the bridge are now averaging two a month, and a proposal to make the bridge suicide-proof has come up. Taking account of the arguments just mentioned, and any others—pro and con—that you can think of, what is your well-reasoned 500-word response?

5. In September 2004, the year of a presidential election, the Bush-Cheney campaign approached Allegheny College (in northwest Pennsylvania), asking to rent for October 13 the college's gymnasium, the largest enclosed space in the area. Because the electoral votes of Pennsylvania were uncertain, Vice President Cheney's appearance at Allegheny was likely to get national attention, at least briefly. The college did *not* have in place a policy against renting space to a political organization, so refusal to rent the gymnasium might seem like discrimination against the Republican Party. Further, the college faculty and administrators involved in making the decision concluded that the event would strengthen town–gown relationships and energize the students to participate in the political process. The gymnasium was therefore rented to the Bush-Cheney campaign, so that the vice president could appear.

   The event was a sort of town-hall-style presentation, but tickets were limited: The campaign personnel distributed most of the six hundred tickets to local Republican activists; forty tickets were given to a group called College Republicans, who could distribute the tickets as they saw fit. Obviously the idea was to keep out hecklers and demonstrators, an entirely reasonable plan from the Republican point of view. Why should Republicans rent a hall and stage an event that might get national coverage if the opposing party could use it to get TV attention?

   The issue: Should a college—supposedly a site where inquiry is open, where ideas are exchanged freely in robust debate—allow its facilities to be used by those who would stifle debate? Professor Daniel M. Shea, who initially favored the decision to rent the gymnasium, ultimately concluded that he was mistaken. In an essay in the *Chronicle of Higher Education* (August 4, 2006), Shea discusses the affair, and he suggests that colleges and universities ought to band together to "form an open-event alliance." Candidates might have at their disposal half of the available seats, but the other half would be for the college to distribute through some sort of open procedure, perhaps a lottery.

   The assignment: Assume that a political party wanted to rent your institution's gymnasium or a large lecture hall. What would your position be? Why? In a letter of about 500 words addressed to the college paper, set forth your views.

2

Critical Reading: Getting Started

Some books are to be tasted, others to be swallowed, and some few to be chewed and digested.

—FRANCIS BACON

ACTIVE READING

In the passage that we quote at the top of this page, Bacon makes at least two good points. One is that books are of varying worth; the second is that a taste of some books may be enough.

But even a book (or an essay) that you will chew and digest is one that you first may want to taste. How can you get a taste—that is, how can you get some sense of a piece of writing *before* you sit down to read it carefully?

Previewing

Even before you read a work, you may have some ideas about it, perhaps because you already know something about the **author.** You know, for example, that a work by Martin Luther King Jr. will probably deal with civil rights. You know, too, that it will be serious and eloquent. On the other hand, if you pick up an essay by Woody Allen, you will probably expect it to be amusing. It may be serious—Allen has written earnestly about many topics, especially those concerned with the media—but it's your hunch that the essay will be at least somewhat entertaining and probably will not be terribly difficult to understand. In short, a reader who has some knowledge of the author probably has some idea of what the writing will be like, and so the reader reads it in a certain mood.

Admittedly, most of the authors represented in this book are not widely known, but we give biographical notes that may provide you with some sense of what to expect.

The **place of publication** may also tell you something about the essay. For instance, the *National Review* is a conservative journal. If you notice that an essay on affirmative action was published in the *National Review,* you are probably safe in tentatively assuming that the essay will not endorse affirmative action. On the other hand, *Ms. Magazine* is a liberal publication, and an essay on affirmative action published in *Ms.* will probably be an endorsement. You often can learn a good deal about a journal or magazine simply by flipping through it and looking at the kinds of advertisements in it.

The **title** of an essay, too, may give you an idea of what to expect. Of course, a title may announce only the subject and not the author's thesis or point of view ("On Gun Control," "Should Drugs Be Legal?"), but fairly often it will indicate the thesis too, as in "Give Children the Vote" and "Gay Marriages: Make Them Legal." Knowing more or less what to expect, you can probably take in some of the major points even on a quick reading.

Skimming: Finding the Thesis

Although most of the material in this book is too closely argued to be fully understood by merely skimming, still, skimming can tell you a good deal. Read the first paragraph of an essay carefully because it may announce the author's **thesis** (chief point, major claim), and it may give you some sense of how the argument for that thesis will be conducted. (What we call the *thesis* can also be called the *main idea,* the *point,* or even the *argument,* but in this book we use *argument* to refer not only to the thesis statement but also to the entire development of the thesis in the essay.) Run your eye over the rest, looking for key expressions that indicate the author's conclusions, such as "It follows, then, that . . ." Passages of this sort often occur as the first or last sentence in a paragraph. And of course, pay attention to any headings within the text. Finally, pay special attention to the last paragraph because it probably will offer a summary and a brief restatement of the writer's thesis.

Having skimmed the work, you probably know the author's thesis, and you may detect the author's methods—for instance, whether the author supports the thesis chiefly by personal experience, by statistics, or by ridiculing the opposition. You also have a clear idea of the length and some idea of the difficulty of the piece.

You know, then, whether you can read it carefully now before dinner or whether you had better put off a careful reading until you have more time.

Reading with a Careful Eye: Underlining, Highlighting, Annotating

Once you have a general idea of the work—not only an idea of its topic and thesis but also a sense of the way in which the thesis is argued—you can then go back and start reading it carefully.

As you read, **underline** or **highlight** key passages, and make **annotations** in the margins. Because you are reading actively, or interacting with the text, you will not simply let your eye rove across the page.

- You will highlight what seem to be the chief points, so that later when you review the essay you can easily locate the main passages.

- But don't overdo a good thing. If you find yourself highlighting most of a page, you are probably not thinking carefully enough about what the key points are.

- Similarly, your marginal annotations should be brief and selective. They will probably consist of hints or clues, things like "really?" "doesn't follow," "good," "compare with Jones," and "check this."

- In short, in a paragraph you might highlight a key definition, and in the margin you might write "good," or "on the other hand," or "?" if you think the definition is fuzzy or wrong.

- With many electronic formats you can use tools to highlight or annotate. Also consider copying and pasting passages you would normally highlight in a Google document. Include a link to the piece and create an RSS feed to the journal's Web site. Having your notes in an electronic format makes it easy to access and use them later.

You are interacting with the text and laying the groundwork for eventually writing your own essay on what you have read.

What you annotate will depend largely on your **purpose.** If you are reading an essay in order to see the ways in which the writer organizes an argument, you will annotate one sort of thing. If you are reading in order to challenge the thesis, you will annotate other things. Here is a passage from an essay entitled "On

Racist Speech," with a student's rather skeptical, even aggressive annotations. But notice that at least one of the annotations — "Definition of 'fighting words'" — apparently was made chiefly in order to remind the reader of where an important term appears in the essay. The essay is by Charles R. Lawrence III, a professor of law at Georgetown University. It originally appeared in the *Chronicle of Higher Education* (October 25, 1989), a publication read chiefly by college and university faculty members and administrators.

Example of such a policy?

University officials who have formulated policies to respond to incidents of racial harassment have been characterized in the press as "thought police," but such policies generally do nothing more than impose sanctions against intentional face-to-face insults. When racist speech takes the form of face-to-face insults, catcalls, or other assaultive speech aimed at an individual or small group of persons, it falls directly within the "fighting words" exception to First Amendment protection. The Supreme Court has held that words which "by their very utterance inflict injury or tend to incite an immediate breach of the peace" are not protected by the First Amendment.

*? [margin]*

*Example? [margin]*

What about sexist spee[margin]

*Definition o "fighting words" [margin]*

If the purpose of the First Amendment is to foster the greatest amount of speech, racial insults disserve that purpose. Assaultive racist speech functions as a preemptive strike. The invective is experienced as a blow, not as a proffered idea, and once the blow is struck, it is unlikely that a dialogue will follow. Racial insults are particularly undeserving of First Amendment protection because the perpetrator's intention is not to discover truth or initiate dialogue but to injure the victim. In most situations, members of minority groups realize that they are likely to lose if they respond to epithets by fighting and are forced to remain silent and submissive.

Really? Prob ably depend on the indi-vidual. [margin]

Why must speech always seek "to discover truth"? [margin]

*How does h know? [margin]*

"This; Therefore, That"

To arrive at a coherent thought or a coherent series of thoughts that will lead to a reasonable conclusion, a writer has to go through a good deal of preliminary effort. On page 16 we talked about patterns of thought that stimulate the generation of specific ideas. The path to sound conclusions involves similar thought patterns that carry forward the arguments presented in the essay:

- While these arguments are convincing, they fail to consider . . .

- While these arguments are convincing, they must also consider . . .

- These arguments, rather than being convincing, instead prove . . .
- While these authors agree, in my opinion . . .
- Although it is often true that . . .

And consider also

- What sort of audience would agree with such an argument?
- What sort of audience would be opposed?
- What are the differences in values between these two kinds of audiences?

All of these patterns can serve as heuristics or prompts—that is, they can stimulate the creation of ideas.

And if the writer is to convince the reader that the conclusion is sound, the reasoning that led to the conclusion must be set forth in detail, with a good deal of "This; therefore, that"; "If this, then that"; and "It might be objected at this point that . . ." The arguments in this book require more comment than President Calvin Coolidge provided when his wife, who hadn't been able to go to church on a Sunday, asked him what the preacher's sermon was about. "Sin," he said. His wife persisted: "What did the preacher say about it?" Coolidge's response: "He was against it."

But, again, when we say that most of the arguments in this book are presented at length and require careful reading, we do not mean that they are obscure; we mean, rather, that the reader has to take the sentences thoughtfully, one by one. And speaking of one by one, we are reminded of an episode in Lewis Carroll's *Through the Looking-Glass:*

> "Can you do Addition?" the White Queen asked. "What's one and one and one and one and one and one and one and one and one and one?"
> "I don't know," said Alice. "I lost count."
> "She can't do Addition," the Red Queen said.

It's easy enough to add one and one and one and so on, and Alice can, of course, do addition, but not at the pace that the White Queen sets. Fortunately, you can set your own pace in reading the cumulative thinking set forth in the essays we reprint. Skimming won't work, but slow reading—and thinking about what you are reading—will.

When you first pick up an essay, you may indeed want to skim it, for some of the reasons mentioned on page 40, but sooner or later you have to settle down to read it and to think about it. The effort will be worthwhile. John Locke, the seventeenth-century English philosopher, said,

> *Reading* furnishes the mind with materials of knowledge; it is *thinking* [that] makes what we read ours. We are of the ruminating kind, and it is not enough to cram ourselves with a great load of collections; unless we chew them over again they will not give us strength and nourishment.

First, Second, and Third Thoughts

Suppose you are reading an argument about pornographic pictures. For the present purpose, it doesn't matter whether the argument favors or opposes censorship. As you read the argument, ask yourself whether *pornography* has been adequately defined. Has the writer taken the trouble to make sure that the reader and the writer are thinking about the same thing? If not, the very topic under discussion has not been adequately fixed; and therefore further debate over the issue may well be so unclear as to be futile. How, then, ought a topic such as this be defined for effective critical thinking?

It goes without saying that pornography can't be defined simply as pictures of nude figures or even of nude figures copulating, for such a definition would include not only photographs taken for medical, sociological, and scientific purposes but also some of the world's great art. Nobody seriously thinks that such images should be called pornography.

Is it enough, then, to say that pornography "stirs lustful thoughts" or "appeals to prurient interests"? No, because pictures of shoes probably stir lustful thoughts in shoe fetishists, and pictures of children in ads for underwear probably stir lustful thoughts in pedophiles. Perhaps, then, the definition must be amended to "material that stirs lustful thoughts in the average person." But will this restatement do? First, it may be hard to agree on the characteristics of "the average person." In other matters, the law often does assume that there is such a creature as "the reasonable person," and most people would agree that in a given situation there might be a reasonable response—for almost everyone. But we cannot be so sure that the same is true about the emotional responses of this "average person." In any case, far from stimulating sexual impulses, sadomasochistic pictures of booted men wielding whips on naked women probably turn off "the average person," yet this is the sort of material that most people would agree is pornographic.

Something must be wrong, then, with the definition that pornography is material that "stirs lustful thoughts in the average person." We began with a definition that was too broad ("pictures of nude figures"), but now we have a definition that is too narrow. We must go back to the drawing board. This is not nitpicking. The label "average person" was found to be inadequate in a pornography case argued before the Supreme Court; because the materials in question were aimed at a homosexual audience, it was agreed that the average person would not find them sexually stimulating.

One difficulty has been that pornography is often defined according to its effect on the viewer ("genital commotion," Father Harold Gardiner, S.J., called it, in *Catholic Viewpoint on Censorship*), but different people, we know, may respond differently. In the first half of the twentieth century, in an effort to distinguish between pornography and art—after all, most people don't want to regard Botticelli's *Venus* or Michelangelo's *David* as "dirty"—it was commonly said that a true work of art does not stimulate in the spectator ideas or desires that the real object might stimulate. But in 1956, Kenneth Clark, probably the most influential English-speaking art critic of the twentieth century, changed all that; in a book called *The Nude* he announced that "no nude, however abstract, should fail to arouse in the spectator some vestige of erotic feeling."

SUMMARIZING AND PARAPHRASING

Perhaps the best approach to a fairly difficult essay is, after first reading, to reread it and simultaneously to take notes on a sheet of paper, perhaps summarizing each paragraph in a sentence or two. Writing a summary will help you to

- understand the contents and
- see the strengths and weaknesses of the piece.

Don't confuse a summary with a paraphrase. A paraphrase is a word-by-word or phrase-by-phrase rewording of a text, a sort of translation of the author's language into your own. A paraphrase is therefore as long as the original or even longer; a summary is much shorter. A book may be summarized in a page, or even in a paragraph or a sentence. Obviously the summary will leave out all detail, but—if the summary is a true summary—it accurately states the gist, the essential thesis or claim or point of the original.

Why would anyone ever summarize, and why would anyone ever paraphrase? Because, as we have already said, these two activities—in different ways—help readers follow the original author's ideas. But, again, summarizing and paraphrasing are not the same.

- **When you summarize,** you are standing back, saying very briefly what the whole adds up to; you are seeing the forest, not the individual trees.

- **When you paraphrase,** you are inching through the forest, scrutinizing each tree—that is, finding a synonym for almost every word in the original, in an effort to make sure that you know exactly what you are dealing with. (*Caution:* Do not incorporate a summary or a paraphrase into your own essay without acknowledging your source and stating that you are summarizing or paraphrasing.)

Let's examine the distinction between summary and paraphrase in connection with the first two paragraphs of Paul Goodman's essay, "A Proposal to Abolish Grading," which is excerpted from Goodman's book, *Compulsory Miseducation and the Community of Scholars* (1966). The two paragraphs run thus:

> Let half a dozen of the prestigious universities—Chicago, Stanford, the Ivy League—abolish grading, and use testing only and entirely for pedagogic purposes as teachers see fit.
>
> Anyone who knows the frantic temper of the present schools will understand the transvaluation of values that would be effected by this modest innovation. For most of the students, the competitive grade has come to be the essence. The naive teacher points to the beauty of the subject and the ingenuity of the research; the shrewd student asks if he is responsible for that on the final exam.

A **summary** of these two paragraphs might run thus:

> If some top universities used tests only to help students to learn, students would stop worrying about grades and might share the teacher's interest in the beauty of the subject.

We hope we have accurately summarized Goodman's point, though we know we have lost his flavor, his style—for instance, the wry tone in his pointed contrast between "the naive teacher" and "the shrewd student."

Now for a **paraphrase**. Suppose you are not quite sure what Goodman is getting at, maybe because you are uncertain about the meanings of some words (perhaps *pedagogic* and *transvaluation*?), or maybe just because the whole passage is making such a startling point that you want to make sure that you have understood it. In such a case, you may want to move slowly through the sentences, translating them (so to speak) into your own English. For instance, you might turn Goodman's "pedagogic purposes" into "goals in teaching" or "attempts to help students to learn" or something else. Here is a paraphrase—not a summary but an extensive rewording—of Goodman's paragraphs:

> Suppose some of the top universities—such as Chicago, Stanford, Harvard, and Yale, and whatever other schools are in the Ivy League—stopped using grades and used tests only in order to help students to learn.
>
> Everyone who is aware of the hysterical mood in schools today will understand the enormous change in views of what is good and bad that would come about by this small change. At present, instructors, unworldly folk, talk about how beautiful their subjects are, but smart students know that grades are what count, so they listen to instructors only if they know that the material the instructor is talking about will be on the exam.

In short, you may want to paraphrase an important text that your imagined reader may find obscure because it is written in specialized, technical language, for instance, the language of psychiatry or of sociology. You want the reader to see the passage itself—you don't want to give just the gist, just a summary—but you know that the full passage will puzzle the reader, so you offer help, giving a paraphrase before going on to make your own point about the author's point.

A second good reason to offer a paraphrase is if there is substantial disagreement about what the text says. The Second Amendment to the U.S. Constitution is a good example of this sort of text:

> A well regulated Militia being necessary to the security of a free State, the right of the people to keep and bear Arms shall not be infringed.

Exactly what, one might ask, is a "Militia"? And what does it mean for a militia to be "well regulated"? And does "the people" mean each individual, or does it mean—something very different—the citizenry as some sort of unified group? After all, elsewhere in the document, when the Constitution speaks of individuals, it speaks of a "man" or a "person," not "the people." To speak of "the people" is to use a term (some argue) that sounds like a reference to a unified group—perhaps the citizens of each of the thirteen states?—rather than a reference to individuals. On the other hand, if Congress did mean a unified group rather than individuals, why didn't it say "Congress shall not prohibit the states from organizing militias"?

In fact, thousands of pages have been written about this sentence, and if you are going to talk about it, you certainly have to let your reader know exactly what you make out of each word. In short, you almost surely will paraphrase it, going word by word, giving your reader your sense of what each word or phrase says. Here is one paraphrase:

> Because an independent society needs the protection of an armed force if it is to remain free, the government may not limit the right of the individuals (who may some day form the militia needed to keep the society free) to possess weapons.

In this interpretation, the Constitution grants individuals the right to possess weapons, and that is that. Other students of the Constitution, however, offer very different paraphrases, usually along these lines:

> Because each state that is now part of the United States may need to protect its freedom [from the new national government], the national government may not infringe on the right of each state to form its own disciplined militia.

This second paraphrase says that the federal government may not prevent each state from having a militia; it says nothing about every individual person having a right to possess weapons. The first of these two paraphrases, or something like it, is one that might be offered by the National Rifle Association or any other group that interprets the Constitution as guaranteeing individuals the right to own guns. The second paraphrase, or something like it, might be offered by groups that seek to limit the ownership of guns.

Why paraphrase? Here are two reasons (perhaps the *only* two reasons) why you might paraphrase a passage:

- To help yourself to understand it. In this case, the paraphrase does not appear in your essay.
- To help your reader to understand a passage that is especially important but that for one reason or another is not immediately clear. In this case, you paraphrase the passage to let the reader know exactly what it means. This paraphrase, of course, does appear in your essay.

PARAPHRASE, PATCHWRITING, AND PLAGIARISM

We have indicated that only on rare occasions will you have a reason to introduce a paraphrase into your essays, but in your preliminary work, when you take notes, you may find yourself sometimes
copying word for word, sometime paraphrasing (usually in an
effort to get the author's idea clearly into your mind), sometimes
summarizing, and—here we get to patchwriting—sometimes producing a medley of borrowed words and original words that, if submitted in the final essay, opens you to the charge of **plagiarism**
*even if you have rearranged the phrases and clauses, and even if you have
cited your source.*

Here is an example. First, we give the source, a paragraph from
Jena McGregor's essay on whether women serving in the armed
forces should be allowed to participate directly in combat. (The
entire essay is printed on pages 32–35.)

> Last week, female soldiers began formally moving into jobs in
> previously all-male battalions, a program that later will go Army-
> wide. The move is a result of rule changes following a February
> report that opened some 14,000 new positions to women in criti-
> cal jobs much closer to the front lines. However, some 250,000
> jobs still remain officially closed to them.

Now for a student's patchwriting version:

> Women in the army recently began to formally move into jobs in
> battalions that previously were all-male. This program later will go
> throughout the Army. According to author Jena McGregor, the move
> comes from changes in the rules following a February report that
> opened about 14,000 new jobs to women in critical jobs that are
> much closer to the front lines. About 250,000 jobs, however—as
> McGregor points out—continue to be officially closed to women.

As you can see, the writer has followed the source, pretty much
phrase by phrase—certainly sentence by sentence—making small
verbal changes, such as substituting

> Women in the army recently

for McGregor's

> Last week, female soldiers

and substituting

> the move comes from changes in the rules

for McGregor's

> The move is a result of rule changes. . . .

What the student should have done is either (a) *quote the passage exactly,* setting it off to indicate that it is a quotation and indicating the source, or (b) *summarize it briefly* and give credit to the source — maybe in a sentence such as

> Jena McGregor points out that although a recent change in army
> rules has resulted in new jobs being opened for women in the mili-
> tary, some 250,000 jobs continue to be off limits.

We think you will agree that patchwriting — as opposed to this example of a sentence frankly summarizing a source — is *not* essentially the student's writing but, rather, is the source material thinly disguised: In a given paragraph of patchwriting, usually some of the words are copied from the source, and all or almost all of the rest consists of synonyms substituted for the words of the source, sometimes with minor rearrangement of phrases and clauses. That is, the sequence of ideas and their arrangement, as well as most of the language, are entirely or almost entirely derived from the source, even if some of the words are different. **The fact that you may cite a source is not enough to protect you from the charge of plagiarism.** The citation of a source tells a reader that some fact or some idea — or some groups of words enclosed within quotation marks or set off by indentation — is derived from the named source; it does *not* tell the reader that almost everything in the paragraph is, in effect, the writing of someone else with a few words changed, a few words added, and a few phrases moved around.

The best way to prevent yourself from introducing patchwriting into your final essay is to make certain that when you take notes you indicate, *in the notes themselves,* what sorts of notes they are. For example:

- When you are quoting word for word, put the passage within quotation marks, and cite the page number(s) of the source.

- When you are paraphrasing—perhaps in an effort to make certain that you understand the writer's idea, or perhaps because the original uses highly technical language and you know that your reader will not understand the idea unless you put it into somewhat simpler nontechnical language—use some sign, perhaps *(par)*, to remind yourself later that this passage is a paraphrase and thus is not really *your* writing.

- When you are summarizing, again use some key, such as *(sum)*, and cite the page(s) of the source.

Make certain that in your notes you indicate the degree of indebtedness to your source, and, again, do *not* think that in a paraphrase if you name a source you are not plagiarizing. The reader assumes the name indicates the source of a fact or an idea—not that it indicates that the paragraph is essentially a rewriting of the original with perhaps an occasional original phrase inserted here and there.

If you have taken notes properly, with indications of the sort we have mentioned, when you write your paper you can say things like

> *X*'s first reason is simple. He says, " . . ." (and here you quote *X*'s words, putting them within quotation marks).

or

> *X*'s point can be summarized thus . . . . (and here too you will cite the page).

or

> *X*, writing for lawyers, not surprisingly uses some technical language, but we can paraphrase her conclusion thus: . . . . (here you give the citation).

In short,

- Avoid patchwriting; it is *not* acceptable.

- Enclose direct quotations within quotation marks, or, if the quotations are long, set them off.

- If you offer a paraphrase, tell your readers that you are paraphrasing and tell them *why* you are paraphrasing rather than quoting directly or summarizing.

For additional information about plagiarism, see page 232.

✓ A CHECKLIST FOR A PARAPHRASE

☐ Do I have a good reason offering a paraphrase rather than a summary?

☐ Is the paraphrase entirely in my own words—a sort of word-by-word translation—rather than a patchwork of the source's words and my own words with some of my own rearrangement of phrases and clauses?

☐ Do I not only cite the source but also explicitly say that the entire passage is a paraphrase?

A RULE FOR WRITERS: Your essay is *likely to include brief summaries* of points of view that you are agreeing or disagreeing with, but it will *rarely include a paraphrase* unless the original is obscure and you think you need to present a passage at length but in words that are clearer than those of the original. If you do paraphrase, explicitly identify the material as a paraphrase. Never submit patchwriting.

Last Words (Almost) about Summarizing

Summarizing each paragraph or each group of closely related para-graphs will help you to follow the thread of the discourse and, when you are finished, will provide you with a useful map of the essay. Then, when you reread the essay yet again, you may want to underline passages that you now understand are the author's key ideas—for instance, definitions, generalizations, summaries—and you may want to jot notes in the margins, questioning the logic, expressing your uncertainty, or calling attention to other writers who see the matter differently. Here is a paragraph from a 1973 decision of the U.S. Supreme Court, written by Chief Justice Warren Burger, setting forth reasons that the government may censor obscene material. We follow it with a sample summary.

> If we accept the unprovable assumption that a complete education requires the reading of certain books, and the well-nigh universal belief that good books, plays, and art lift the spirit, improve the mind, enrich the human personality, and develop character, can

we then say that a state legislature may not act on the corollary assumption that commerce in obscene books, or public exhibitions focused on obscene conduct, have a tendency to exert a corrupting and debasing impact leading to antisocial behavior? The sum of experience, including that of the past two decades, affords an ample basis for legislatures to conclude that a sensitive, key relationship of human existence, central to family life, community welfare, and the development of human personality, can be debased and distorted by crass commercial exploitation of sex. Nothing in the Constitution prohibits a State from reaching such a conclusion and acting on it legislatively simply because there is no conclusive empirical data.

Now for a student's summary. Notice that the summary does not include the reader's evaluation or any other sort of comment on the original; it is simply an attempt to condense the original. Notice too that, because its purpose is merely to assist the reader to grasp the ideas of the original by focusing on them, it is written in a sort of shorthand (not every sentence is a complete sentence), though, of course, if this summary were being presented in an essay, it would have to be grammatical.

> Unprovable but acceptable assumption that good books etc. shape character, so that legislature can assume obscene works debase character. Experience lets one conclude that exploitation of sex debases the individual, family, and community. Though "there is no conclusive empirical data" for this view, the Constitution lets states act on it legislatively.

Notice that

- A few words (in the last sentence of the summary) are quoted exactly as in the original. They are enclosed within quotation marks.
- For the most part, the original material is drastically reduced. The first sentence of the original, some eighty words, is reduced in the summary to nineteen words.

Of course, the summary loses much of the detail and flavor of the original: "Good books etc." is not the same as "good books, plays, and art"; and "shape character" is not the same as "lift the spirit, improve the mind, enrich the human personality, and develop character." But the statement in the summary will do as a rough approximation, useful for a quick review. More important, the act of writing a summary forces the reader to go slowly and to think about each sentence of the original. Such thinking may help the reader–writer to see the complexity—or the hollowness—of the original.

The sample summary in the preceding paragraph was just that, a summary; but when writing your own summaries, you will often find it useful to inject your own thoughts ("seems far-fetched," "strong point," "I don't get it"), enclosing them within square brackets or in some other way to keep these responses distinct from your summary of the writer's argument.

Review: If your instructor asks you to hand in a summary,

- It should not contain ideas other than those found in the original piece.
- You can rearrange these, add transitions as needed, and so forth, but the summary should give the reader nothing but a sense of the original piece.
- If the summary includes any of the original wording, these words should be enclosed within quotation marks.
- In your notes, keep a clear distinction between *your* writing and the writing of your *source.* For the most part you will summarize, but if you paraphrase, indicate that the words are a paraphrase, and if you quote directly, indicate that you are quoting.

We don't want to nag you, but we do want to emphasize the need to read with a close eye, taking notes as you go along using a pen or pencil or highlighter or a computer program, blog, or Google document. If you read slowly and take notes, you will find that what you read will give you the "strength and nourishment" that John Locke spoke of.

> **A RULE FOR WRITERS:** Remember that when you write a summary, you are putting yourself into the author's shoes.

Having insisted that the essays in this book need to be read slowly because the writers build one reason on another, we will now seem to contradict ourselves by presenting an essay that can almost be skimmed. Susan Jacoby's essay originally appeared in the

New York Times, a thoroughly respectable newspaper but not one that requires its readers to linger over every sentence. Still, compared with most of the news accounts, Jacoby's essay requires close reading. When you read the essay, you will notice that it zigs and zags, not because Jacoby is careless or wants to befuddle her readers but because she wants to build a strong case to support her point of view and must therefore look at some widely held views that she does *not* accept; she must set these forth and then give her reasons for rejecting them.

Susan Jacoby

Susan Jacoby (b. 1946), a journalist since the age of seventeen, is well known for her feminist writings. "A First Amendment Junkie" (our title) appeared in the Hers column in the New York Times *in 1978.*

A First Amendment Junkie

It is no news that many women are defecting from the ranks of civil libertarians on the issue of obscenity. The conviction of Larry Flynt, publisher of *Hustler* magazine—before his metamorphosis into a born-again Christian—was greeted with unabashed feminist approval. Harry Reems, the unknown actor who was convicted by a Memphis jury for conspiring to distribute the movie *Deep Throat,* has carried on his legal battles with almost no support from women who ordinarily regard themselves as supporters of the First Amendment. Feminist writers and scholars have even discussed the possibility of making common cause against pornography with adversaries of the women's movement—including opponents of the equal rights amendment and "right-to-life" forces.

All of this is deeply disturbing to a woman writer who believes, as I always have and still do, in an absolute interpretation of the First Amendment. Nothing in Larry Flynt's garbage convinces me that the late Justice Hugo L. Black was wrong in his opinion that "the Federal Government is without any power whatsoever under the Constitution to put any type of burden on free speech and expression of ideas of any kind (as distinguished from conduct)." Many women I like and respect tell me I am wrong; I cannot remember having become involved in so many heated discussions of a public issue since the end of the Vietnam War. A feminist writer described my views as those of a "First Amendment junkie."

Many feminist arguments for controls on pornography carry the implicit conviction that porn books, magazines, and movies pose a greater threat to women than similarly repulsive exercises of free speech pose to other offended groups. This conviction has, of course, been shared by everyone—regardless of race, creed, or sex—who has ever argued in favor of abridging the First Amendment. It is the argument used by some Jews who have withdrawn their support from the American Civil Liberties Union because it has defended the right of American Nazis to march through a community inhabited by survivors of Hitler's concentration camps.

If feminists want to argue that the protection of the Constitution should not be extended to *any* particularly odious or threatening form of speech, they have a reasonable argument (although I don't agree with it). But it is ridiculous to suggest that the porn shops on 42nd Street are more disgusting to women than a march of neo-Nazis is to survivors of the extermination camps.

The arguments over pornography also blur the vital distinction between expression of ideas and conduct. When I say I believe unreservedly in the First Amendment, someone always comes back at me with the issue of "kiddie porn." But kiddie porn is not a First Amendment issue. It is an issue of the abuse of power—the power adults have over children—and not of obscenity. Parents and promoters have no more right to use their children to make porn movies than they do to send them to work in coal mines. The responsible adults should be prosecuted, just as adults who use children for back-breaking farm labor should be prosecuted.

Susan Brownmiller, in *Against Our Will: Men, Women, and Rape*, has described pornography as "the undiluted essence of antifemale propaganda." I think this is a fair description of some types of pornography, especially of the brutish subspecies that equates sex with death and portrays women primarily as objects of violence.

The equation of sex and violence, personified by some glossy rock record album covers as well as by *Hustler,* has fed the illusion that censorship of pornography can be conducted on a more rational basis than other types of censorship. Are all pictures of naked women obscene? Clearly not, says a friend. A Renoir nude is art, she says, and *Hustler* is trash. "Any reasonable person" knows that.

But what about something between art and trash—something, say, along the lines of *Playboy* or *Penthouse* magazines? I asked five women for their reactions to one picture in *Penthouse* and got responses that ranged from "lovely" and "sensuous" to "revolting" and "demeaning." Feminists, like everyone else, seldom have rational reasons for their preferences in erotica. Like members of juries, they tend to disagree when confronted with something that falls short of 100 percent vulgarity.

In any case, feminists will not be the arbiters of good taste if it becomes easier to harass, prosecute, and convict people on obscenity charges. Most of the people who want to censor girlie magazines are equally opposed to open discussion of issues that are of vital concern to women: rape, abortion, menstruation, contraception, lesbianism—in fact, the entire range of sexual experience from a women's viewpoint.

Feminist writers and editors and filmmakers have limited   10
financial resources: Confronted by a determined prosecutor, Hugh Hefner[1] will fare better than Susan Brownmiller. Would the Memphis jurors who convicted Harry Reems for his role in *Deep Throat* be inclined to take a more positive view of paintings of the female genitalia done by sensitive feminist artists? *Ms.* magazine has printed color reproductions of some of those art works; *Ms.* is already banned from a number of high school libraries because someone considers it threatening and/or obscene.

Feminists who want to censor what they regard as harmful pornography have essentially the same motivation as other would-be censors: They want to use the power of the state to accomplish what they have been unable to achieve in the marketplace of ideas and images. The impulse to censor places no faith in the possibilities of democratic persuasion.

It isn't easy to persuade certain men that they have better uses for $1.95 each month than to spend it on a copy of *Hustler*? Well, then, give the men no choice in the matter.

I believe there is also a connection between the impulse toward censorship on the part of people who used to consider themselves civil libertarians and a more general desire to shift responsibility from individuals to institutions. When I saw the movie *Looking for Mr. Goodbar,* I was stunned by its series of visual images equating sex and violence, coupled with what seems to me the mindless message (a distortion of the fine Judith Rossner novel) that casual sex equals death. When I came out of the movie, I was even more shocked to see parents standing in line with children between the ages of ten and fourteen.

I simply don't know why a parent would take a child to see such a movie, any more than I understand why people feel they

[1]**Hugh Hefner** Founder and longtime publisher of *Playboy* magazine. [Editors' note.]

can't turn off a television set their child is watching. Whenever I
say that, my friends tell me I don't know how it is because I don't
have children. True, but I do have parents. When I was a child,
they did turn off the TV. They didn't expect the Federal Communications Commission to do their job for them.

I am a First Amendment junkie. You can't OD on the First   15
Amendment, because free speech is its own best antidote.

Summarizing Jacoby, Paragraph by Paragraph

Suppose we want to make a rough summary, more or less paragraph by paragraph, of Jacoby's essay. Such a summary might look
something like this (the numbers refer to Jacoby's paragraphs):

1. Although feminists usually support the First Amendment,
   when it comes to pornography, many feminists take pretty
   much the position of those who oppose ERA and abortion
   and other causes of the women's movement.
2. Larry Flynt produces garbage, but I think his conviction represents an unconstitutional limitation of freedom of speech.
3, 4. Feminists who want to control (censor) pornography
   argue that it poses a greater threat to women than similar
   repulsive speech poses to other groups. If feminists want to
   say that all offensive speech should be restricted, they can
   make a case, but it is absurd to say that pornography is a
   "greater threat" to women than a march of neo-Nazis is to
   survivors of concentration camps.
5. Trust in the First Amendment is not refuted by kiddie porn;
   kiddie porn is not a First Amendment issue but an issue of
   child abuse.
6, 7, 8. Some feminists think censorship of pornography can
   be more "rational" than other kinds of censorship, but a
   picture of a nude woman strikes some women as base and
   others as "lovely." There is no unanimity.
9, 10. If feminists censor girlie magazines, they will find that
   they are unwittingly helping opponents of the women's
   movement to censor discussions of rape, abortion, and so
   on. Some of the art in the feminist magazine *Ms.* would
   doubtless be censored.
11, 12. Like other would-be censors, feminists want to use the
   power of the state to achieve what they have not achieved
   in "the marketplace of ideas." They display a lack of faith in
   "democratic persuasion."

13, 14. This attempt at censorship reveals a desire to "shift responsibility from individuals to institutions." The responsibility—
for instance, to keep young people from equating sex with
violence—is properly the parents'.

15. We can't have too much of the First Amendment.

Jacoby's **thesis**, or major claim, or chief proposition—that
any form of censorship of pornography is wrong—is clear enough,
even as early as the end of her first paragraph, but it gets its life or
its force from the **reasons** offered throughout the essay. If we want
to reduce our summary even further, we might say that Jacoby
supports her thesis by arguing several subsidiary points. We will
merely assert them briefly, but Jacoby **argues** them—that is, she
gives reasons:

a. Pornography can scarcely be thought of as more offensive
than Nazism.
b. Women disagree about which pictures are pornographic.
c. Feminists who want to censor pornography will find that
they help antifeminists to censor discussions of issues advocated by the women's movement.
d. Feminists who favor censorship are in effect turning to the
government to achieve what they haven't achieved in the
free marketplace.
e. One sees this abdication of responsibility in the fact that
parents allow their children to watch unsuitable movies and
television programs.

If we want to present a brief summary in the form of one
coherent paragraph—perhaps as part of our own essay to show
the view we are arguing in behalf of or against—we might write
something like this summary. (The summary would, of course, be
prefaced by a **lead-in** along these lines: "Susan Jacoby, writing in
the *New York Times,* offers a forceful argument against censorship of
pornography. Jacoby's view, briefly, is . . .".)

When it comes to censorship of pornography, some feminists take
a position shared by opponents of the feminist movement. They
argue that pornography poses a greater threat to women than other
forms of offensive speech offer to other groups, but this interpretation is simply a mistake. Pointing to kiddie porn is also a mistake,
for kiddie porn is an issue involving not the First Amendment but

child abuse. Feminists who support censorship of pornography will inadvertently aid those who wish to censor discussions of abortion and rape or censor art that is published in magazines such as *Ms.* The solution is not for individuals to turn to institutions (that is, for the government to limit the First Amendment) but for individuals to accept the responsibility for teaching young people not to equate sex with violence.

Whether we agree or disagree with Jacoby's thesis, we must admit that the reasons she sets forth to support it are worth thinking about. Only a reader who closely follows the reasoning with which Jacoby buttresses her thesis is in a position to accept or reject it. Indeed, one might want to do research on some of her points to see if her interpretation is satisfactory.

TOPICS FOR CRITICAL THINKING AND WRITING

1. What does Jacoby mean when she says she is a "First Amendment junkie" (para. 15)?

2. The essay is primarily an argument against the desire of some feminists to try to censor pornography of the sort that appeals to some heterosexual adult males, but the next-to-last paragraph is about television and children. Is the paragraph connected to Jacoby's overall argument? If so, how?

3. Evaluate the final paragraph as a final paragraph. (Effective final paragraphs are not, of course, all of one sort. Some, for example, round off the essay by echoing something from the opening; others suggest that the reader, having now seen the problem, should think further about it or even act on it. But a good final paragraph, whatever else it does, should make the reader feel that the essay has come to an end, not just broken off.)

4. This essay originally appeared in the *New York Times*. If you are unfamiliar with this newspaper, consult an issue or two in your library. Next, in a paragraph, try to characterize the readers of the paper—that is, Jacoby's audience.

5. Jacoby claims in paragraph 2 that she "believes . . . in an absolute interpretation of the First Amendment." What does such an interpretation involve? Would it permit shouting "Fire!" in a crowded theater even though the shouter knows there is no fire? Would it permit shouting racist insults at blacks or immigrant Vietnamese? Spreading untruths about someone's past? If the "absolutist"

interpretation of the First Amendment does permit these statements, does that argument show that nothing is morally wrong with uttering them? (*Does* the First Amendment, as actually interpreted by the Supreme Court today, permit any or all of these claims? Consult your reference librarian for help in answering this question.)

6. Jacoby implies that permitting prosecution of persons on obscenity charges will lead eventually to censorship of "open discussion" of important issues such as "rape, abortion, menstruation, contraception, lesbianism" (para. 9). Do you find her fears convincing? Does she give any evidence to support her claim?

✓ A CHECKLIST FOR GETTING STARTED

☐ Have I adequately previewed the work?

☐ Can I state the thesis?

☐ If I have written a summary,

   ☐ Is the summary accurate?

   ☐ Does the summary mention all the chief points?

   ☐ If there are inconsistencies, are they in the summary or the original selection?

   ☐ Will the summary be clear and helpful?

   ☐ Have I considered the audience for whom the author is writing?

ESSAYS FOR ANALYSIS

Zachary Shemtob and David Lat

Zachary Shemtob teaches criminal justice at Central Connecticut State University; David Lat is a former federal prosecutor. We reprint an essay that originally appeared in the New York Times *in 2011.*

Executions Should Be Televised

Earlier this month, Georgia conducted its third execution this year. This would have passed relatively unnoticed if not for a controversy surrounding its videotaping. Lawyers for the condemned inmate, Andrew Grant DeYoung, had persuaded a judge to allow the recording of his last moments as part of an effort to obtain evidence on whether lethal injection caused unnecessary suffering.

Though he argued for videotaping, one of Mr. DeYoung's defense lawyers, Brian Kammer, spoke out against releasing the footage to the public. "It's a horrible thing that Andrew DeYoung had to go through," Mr. Kammer said, "and it's not for the public to see that."

We respectfully disagree. Executions in the United States ought to be made public.

Right now, executions are generally open only to the press and a few select witnesses. For the rest of us, the vague contours are provided in the morning paper. Yet a functioning democracy demands maximum accountability and transparency. As long as executions remain behind closed doors, those are impossible. The people should have the right to see what is being done in their name and with their tax dollars.

This is particularly relevant given the current debate on whether   5
specific methods of lethal injection constitute cruel and unusual punishment and therefore violate the Constitution.

There is a dramatic difference between reading or hearing of such an event and observing it through image and sound. (This is obvious to those who saw the footage of Saddam Hussein's hanging in 2006 or the death of Neda Agha-Soltan during the protests in Iran in 2009.) We are not calling for opening executions completely to the public—conducting them before a live crowd—but rather for broadcasting them live or recording them for future release, on the Web or TV.

When another Georgia inmate, Roy Blankenship, was executed in June, the prisoner jerked his head, grimaced, gasped, and lurched, according to a medical expert's affidavit. The *Atlanta Journal-Constitution* reported that Mr. DeYoung, executed in the same manner, "showed no violent signs in death." Voters should not have to rely on media accounts to understand what takes place when a man is put to death.

Cameras record legislative sessions and presidential debates, and courtrooms are allowing greater television access. When he was an Illinois state senator, President Obama successfully pressed for the videotaping of homicide interrogations and confessions. The most serious penalty of all surely demands equal if not greater scrutiny.

Opponents of our proposal offer many objections. State lawyers argued that making Mr. DeYoung's execution public raised safety concerns. While rioting and pickpocketing occasionally marred executions in the public square in the eighteenth and nineteenth centuries, modern security and technology obviate this concern. Little would change in the death chamber; the faces of witnesses and executioners could be edited out, for privacy reasons, before a video was released.

Of greater concern is the possibility that broadcasting execu-   10
tions could have a numbing effect. Douglas A. Berman, a law professor, fears that people might come to equate human executions with putting pets to sleep. Yet this seems overstated. While public indifference might result over time, the initial broadcasts would undoubtedly get attention and stir debate.

Still others say that broadcasting an execution would offer an unbalanced picture — making the condemned seem helpless and sympathetic, while keeping the victims of the crime out of the picture. But this is beside the point: the defendant is being executed precisely because a jury found that his crimes were so heinous that he deserved to die.

Ultimately the main opposition to our idea seems to flow from an unthinking disgust — a sense that public executions are archaic, noxious, even barbarous. Albert Camus related in his essay "Reflections on the Guillotine" that viewing executions turned him against capital punishment. The legal scholar John D. Bessler suggests that public executions might have the same effect on the public today; Sister Helen Prejean, the death penalty abolitionist, has urged just such a strategy.

That is not our view. We leave open the possibility that making executions public could strengthen support for them; undecided viewers might find them less disturbing than anticipated.

Like many of our fellow citizens, we are deeply conflicted about the death penalty and how it has been administered. Our focus is on accountability and openness. As Justice John Paul Stevens wrote in *Baze v. Rees*, a 2008 case involving a challenge to lethal injection, capital punishment is too often "the product of habit and inattention rather than an acceptable deliberative process that weighs the costs and risks of administering that penalty against its identifiable benefits."

A democracy demands a citizenry as informed as possible about   15
the costs and benefits of society's ultimate punishment.

TOPICS FOR CRITICAL THINKING AND WRITING

1. In paragraphs 9–13 the authors discuss objections to their position. Are you satisfied with their responses to the objections, or do you think the authors do not satisfactorily dispose of one or more of the objections. Explain.

2. In paragraph 4 the authors say that "the people should have the right to see what is being done in their name and with their tax dollars." But while we are on the subject of *rights*, might the person who is being executed not have a right to die in privacy? Articulate your view.

3. In their concluding paragraph the authors imply that their proposal, if enacted, will help to inform citizens "about the costs and benefits of society's ultimate punishment." Do you agree? What reasons do they offer to support their proposal?

4. In your view, what is the strongest argument the authors give on behalf of their proposal? What is the weakest? Explain why you made these choices.

"And now let's welcome, for the first and last time . . ."

Gwen Wilde

This essay was written for a composition course at Tufts University.

Why the Pledge of Allegiance Should Be Revised

(Student Essay)

All Americans are familiar with the Pledge of Allegiance, even if they cannot always recite it perfectly, but probably relatively few know that the *original* Pledge did *not* include the words "under God." The original Pledge of Allegiance, published in the September 8, 1892, issue of the *Youth's Companion,* ran thus:

> I pledge allegiance to my flag, and to the Republic for which it stands: one Nation indivisible, with Liberty and justice for all. (Djupe 329)

In 1923, at the first National Flag Conference in Washington, D.C., it was argued that immigrants might be confused by the words "my Flag," and it was proposed that the words be changed to "the Flag of the United States." The following year it was changed again, to "the Flag of the United States of America," and this wording became the official—or, rather, unofficial—wording, unofficial because no wording had ever been nationally adopted (Djupe 329).

In 1942, the United States Congress included the Pledge in the United States Flag Code (4 USC 4, 2006), thus for the first time officially sanctioning the Pledge. In 1954, President Dwight D. Eisenhower approved adding the words "under God." Thus, since 1954 the Pledge reads:

> I pledge allegiance to the flag of the United States of America, and to the Republic for which it stands: one nation under God, indivisible,with Liberty and Justice for all. (Djupe 329)

In my view, the addition of the words "under God" is inappropriate, and they are needlessly divisive—an odd addition indeed to a Nation that is said to be "indivisible."

Very simply put, the Pledge in its latest form requires all Americans to say something that some Americans do not believe. I say "requires" because although the courts have ruled that students may not be compelled to recite the Pledge, in effect peer pressure does compel all but the bravest to join in the recitation. When President Eisenhower authorized the change, he said,

> In this way we are reaffirming the transcendence of religious faith in America's heritage and future; in this way we shall constantly strengthen those spiritual weapons which forever will be our country's most powerful resource in peace and war. (Sterner)

Exactly what did Eisenhower mean when he spoke of "the transcendence of faith in America's heritage," and when he spoke of "spiritual weapons"? I am not sure what "the transcendence of faith in America's heritage" means. Of course many Americans have been and are deeply religious—no one doubts it—but the phrase certainly goes far beyond saying that many Americans have been devout. In any case, many Americans have *not* been devout, and many Americans have *not* believed in "spiritual weapons," but they have nevertheless been patriotic Americans. Some of them have fought and died to keep America free.

In short, the words "under God" cannot be uttered in good faith by many Americans. True, something like 70 or even 80% of Americans say they are affiliated with some form of Christianity, and approximately another 3% say they are Jewish. I don't have the figures for persons of other faiths, but in any case we can surely all agree that although a majority of Americans say they have a religious affiliation, nevertheless several million Americans do *not* believe in God.

If one remains silent while others are reciting the Pledge, 5 or even if one remains silent only while others are speaking the words "under God," one is open to the charge that one is unpatriotic, is "unwilling to recite the Pledge of Allegiance." In the Pledge, patriotism is connected with religious belief, and it is this connection that makes it divisive and (to be blunt) un-American. Admittedly the belief is not very specific: one is not required to say that one believes in the divinity of Jesus, or in the power of Jehovah, but the fact remains, one is required to express belief in a divine power, and if one doesn't express this belief one is—according to the Pledge—somehow not fully an American, maybe even un-American.

Please notice that I am not arguing that the Pledge is unconstitutional. I understand that the First Amendment to the Constitution says that "Congress shall make no law respecting an establishment of religion, or prohibiting the free exercise thereof." I am not arguing that the words "under God" in the Pledge add up to the "establishment of religion," but they certainly do assert a religious doctrine. Like the words "In God we trust," found on all American money, the words "under God" express an idea that many Americans do not hold, and there is no reason why these Americans—loyal people who may be called upon to defend the country with their lives—should be required to say that America is a nation "under God."

It has been argued, even by members of the Supreme Court, that the words "under God" are not to be taken terribly seriously, not to be taken to say what they seem to say. For instance, Chief Justice Rehnquist wrote,

> To give the parent of such a child a sort of "heckler's veto" over a patriotic ceremony willingly participated in by other students, simply because the Pledge of Allegiance contains the descriptive phrase "under God," is an unwarranted extension of the establishment clause, an extension which would have the unfortunate effect of prohibiting a commendable patriotic observance. (qtd. in Mears)

Chief Justice Rehnquist here calls "under God" a "descriptive phrase," but descriptive of *what*? If a phrase is a "descriptive phrase," it describes something, real or imagined. For many Americans, this phrase does *not* describe a reality. These Americans may perhaps be mistaken—if so, they may learn of their error at Judgment Day—but the fact is, millions of intelligent Americans do not believe in God.

Notice, too, that Chief Justice Rehnquist goes on to say that reciting the Pledge is "a commendable patriotic observance." Exactly. That is my point. It is a *patriotic* observance, and it should not be connected with religion. When we announce that we respect the flag—that we are loyal Americans—we should not also have to announce that we hold a particular religious belief, in this case a belief in monotheism, a belief that there is a God and that God rules.

One other argument defending the words "under God" is often heard: The words "In God We Trust" appear on our money. It is claimed that these words on American money are analogous to the words "under God" in the Pledge. But the situation really is very different. When we hand some coins over, or some paper money, we are concentrating on the business transaction, and we are not making any affirmation about God or our country. But when we recite the Pledge—even if we remain silent at the point when we are supposed to say "under God"—we are very conscious that we are supposed to make this affirmation, an affirmation that many Americans cannot in good faith make, even though they certainly can unthinkingly hand over (or accept) money with the words "In God We Trust."

Because I believe that *reciting* the Pledge is to be taken seriously, with a full awareness of the words that is quite different from when we hand over some money, I cannot understand the recent comment of Supreme Court Justice Souter, who in a case said that the phrase "under God" is "so tepid, so diluted, so far from compulsory prayer, that it should, in effect, be beneath the constitutional radar" (qtd. in "Guide"). I don't follow his reasoning that the phrase should be "beneath the constitutional radar," but in any case I am willing to put aside the issue of constitutionality. I am willing to grant that this phrase does not in any significant sense signify the "establishment of religion" (prohibited by the First Amendment) in the United States. I insist, nevertheless, that the phrase is neither "tepid" nor "diluted." It means what it says—it *must* and *should* mean what it says, to everyone who utters it—and, since millions of loyal Americans cannot say it, it should not be included in a statement in which Americans affirm their loyalty to our great country.

In short, the Pledge, which ought to unite all of us, is divisive; it includes a phrase that many patriotic Americans cannot bring themselves to utter. Yes, they can remain silent when others recite these two words, but, again, why should they have to remain silent? The Pledge of Allegiance should be something that *everyone* can say, say out loud, and say with pride. We hear much talk of returning to the ideas of the Founding Fathers. The Founding Fathers did not create the Pledge of Allegiance, but we do know that they never mentioned God in the Constitution. Indeed the only reference to religion, in the so-called establishment clause of the First Amendment, says, again, that "Congress shall make no law respecting an establishment of religion, or prohibiting the free exercise thereof." Those who wish to exercise religion are indeed free to do so, but the place to do so is not in a pledge that is required of all schoolchildren and of all new citizens.

WORKS CITED

Djupe, Paul A. "Pledge of Allegiance." *Encyclopedia of American Religion and Politics*. Ed. Paul A. Djupe and Laura R. Olson. New York: Facts on File, 2003. Print.
"Guide to Covering 'Under God' Pledge Decision." *ReligionLink*. Religion Newswriters Foundation, 17 Sept. 2005. Web. 9 Feb. 2007.

Mears, Bill. "Court Dismisses Pledge Case." *CNN.com* Cable News Network 15 June 2004. Web. 9 Feb. 2007.

Sterner, Doug. "The Pledge of Allegiance." *Home of Heroes.* N.p., n.d. Web. 9 Feb. 2007.

Topics for Critical Thinking and Writing

1. Summarize the essay in a paragraph.

2. Does the background material about the history of the pledge serve a useful purpose? Should it be deleted? Why, or why not?

3. Does the writer give enough weight to the fact that no one is compelled to recite the pledge? Explain your answer.

4. What arguments does the writer offer in support of her position?

5. Does the writer show an adequate awareness of other counterarguments?

6. Which is the writer's strongest argument? Is any argument notably weak, and, if so, how could it be strengthened?

7. What assumptions—tacit or explicit—does the author make? Do you agree or disagree with them? Please explain.

8. What do you take the words "under God" to mean? Do they mean "under God's special protection"? Or "acting in accordance with God's rules"? Or "accountable to God"?

9. Chief Justice Rehnquist wrote that the words "under God" are a "descriptive phrase." What do you think he meant by this?

10. What is the purpose of the Pledge of Allegiance? Does the phrase "under God" promote or defeat that purpose? Explain your answer.

11. What do you think about substituting "with religious freedom" for "under God"? Set forth your response, supported by reasons, in about 250 words.

12. Wilde makes a distinction between the reference to God on U.S. money and the reference to God in the Pledge. Do you agree with her that the two cases are not analogous? Explain.

13. What readers might *not* agree with Wilde's arguments? What values do they hold? How might you try to persuade an audience who disagrees with her to consider her proposal?

14. Putting aside your own views on the issue, what grade would you give this essay as a work of argumentative writing? Support your evaluation with reasons.

3

Critical Reading: Getting Deeper into Arguments

He that wrestles with us strengthens our nerves, and sharpens our skill. Our antagonist is our helper.

—EDMUND BURKE

PERSUASION, ARGUMENT, DISPUTE

When we think seriously about an argument (not name calling or mere rationalization), not only do we hear ideas that may be unfamiliar, but we are also forced to examine closely our own cherished opinions, and perhaps for the first time really come to see the strengths and weaknesses of what we believe. As John Stuart Mill put it, "He who knows only his own side of the case knows little."

It is customary, and useful, to distinguish between **persuasion** and **argument**. Persuasion has the broader meaning. To **persuade** is to win over—whether

- by giving reasons (that is, by argument, by logic),
- by appealing to the emotions, or, for that matter,
- by using torture.

Argument, one form of persuasion, relies on reason; *it offers statements as reasons for other statements*. Rhetoricians often use the Greek word *logos*, which merely means "word" or "reason," to denote this aspect of persuasive writing—the appeal to reason. An appeal to reason may by supported by

- physical evidence;
- the testimony of experts;
- common sense; and
- probability.

We can put it this way: The goal of *argument* is to convince by demonstrating the truth (or probable truth) of an assertion, whereas the goal of *persuasion* is to conquer, by one means or another.

The appeal to the emotions is known as **pathos.** Strictly speaking, *pathos* is Greek for "feeling," and especially for "suffering," but it now covers all sorts of emotional appeals—for instance, to one's sense of pity or sympathy (Greek for "feeling with") or one's sense of patriotism.

Notice that an argument, in the sense of statements that are offered as reasons for other statements, does not require two speakers or writers who represent opposed positions. The Declaration of Independence is an argument, setting forth the colonists' reasons for declaring their independence. In practice, of course, someone's argument usually advances reasons for a claim in opposition to someone else's position or belief. But even if one is writing only for oneself, trying to clarify one's thinking by setting forth reasons, the result is an argument. **Dispute,** however, is a special kind of argument in which two or more people express views that are at odds.

Most of this book is about argument in the sense of the presentation of reasons in support of claims, but of course, reason is not the whole story. If an argument is to be effective, it must be presented persuasively. For instance, the writer's **tone** (attitude toward self, topic, and audience) must be appropriate if the discourse is to persuade the reader. The careful presentation of the self is not something disreputable, nor is it something that publicity agents or advertising agencies invented. Aristotle (384–322 B.C.) emphasized the importance of impressing on the audience that the speaker is a person of good sense and high moral character. (He called this aspect of persuasion *ethos,* the Greek word for "character," a basis of persuasion different from *logos,* which we have noted is the word for persuasion by appealing to reason.)

Writers convey their trustworthiness by

- using language appropriate to the setting, avoiding vulgar language;

- showing an awareness of the complexity of the issue (for instance, by granting the goodwill of those offering other points of view and by recognizing that there may be some merit to contrary points of view); and

- showing attention to detail (for instance, by citing relevant statistics).

In short, writers who are concerned with *ethos*—and all writers should be—employ devices that persuade readers that the writers are trustworthy, are fair-minded, intelligent persons in whom the reader can have confidence.

We talk at length about tone, along with other matters such as the organization of an argument, in Chapter 5, Writing an Analysis of an Argument, but here we deal with some of the chief devices used in reasoning, and we glance at emotional appeals.

We should note at once, however, that an argument presupposes a fixed **topic.** Suppose we are arguing about Thomas Jefferson's assertion, in the Declaration of Independence, that "all men are created equal." Jones subscribes to this statement, but Smith says it is nonsense and argues that one has only to look around to see that some people are brighter than others, or healthier, or better coordinated, or whatever. Jones and Smith, if they intend to argue the point, will do well to examine what Jefferson actually wrote:

> We hold these truths to be self-evident, that all men are created equal: that they are endowed by their Creator with certain unalienable rights; and that among these are life, liberty, and the pursuit of happiness.

There is room for debate over what Jefferson really meant and about whether he is right, but clearly he was talking about *equality of rights.* If Smith and Jones wish to argue about Jefferson's view of equality—that is, if they wish to offer their reasons for accepting, rejecting, or modifying it—they will do well first to agree on what Jefferson said or what he probably meant to say. Jones and Smith may still hold different views; they may continue to disagree on whether Jefferson was right and proceed to offer arguments and counterarguments to settle the point. But only if they can agree on *what* they disagree about will their dispute get somewhere.

IDEA PROMPT 3.1 ESTABLISHING TRUSTWORTHINESS AND CREDIBILITY

Acknowledge weaknesses, exceptions, and complexities.	"Although the unemployment rate continues to decline, further investigation into under-employment and the loss of jobless benefits is necessary in order to truly understand the unemployment crisis in the United States."
Use personal experience when appropriate.	"As a student who works and attends school full time, I can speak firsthand about the impor- tance of increased availability of financial aid."
Use a tone that respects your audience.	When appropriate, use humor to connect to your readers. Avoid vulgarity or incendiary language that might alienate an audience.
Mention the quali- fications of any sources as a way to boost your own credibility.	"According to Deborah Tannen, author and noted professor of linguistics at Georgetown University . . ."

REASON VERSUS RATIONALIZATION

Reason may not be our only way of finding the truth, but it is a way we often rely on. The subway ran yesterday at 6:00 A.M. and the day before at 6:00 A.M. and the day before, and so I infer from this evidence that it will also run today at 6:00 A.M. (a form of reason-ing known as **induction**). Bus drivers require would-be passen-gers to present the exact change; I do not have the exact change; therefore, I infer I cannot ride on the bus (**deduction**). (The terms *deduction* and *induction* are discussed in more detail on pages 83–85 and 88–90.)

We also know that, if we set our minds to a problem, we can often find reasons (not necessarily sound ones but reasons nevertheless) for almost anything we want to justify. Here is an entertaining example from Benjamin Franklin's *Autobiography*:

> I believe I have omitted mentioning that in my first voyage from Boston, being becalmed off Block Island, our people set about

catching cod and hauled up a great many. Hitherto I had stuck
to my resolution of not eating animal food, and on this occasion,
I considered with my master Tryon the taking of every fish as a
kind of unprovoked murder, since none of them had or ever could
do us any injury that might justify the slaughter. All this seemed
very reasonable. But I had formerly been a great lover of fish,
and when this came hot out of the frying pan, it smelt admirably
well. I balanced some time between principle and inclination,
till I recollected that when the fish were opened I saw smaller
fish taken out of their stomachs. Then thought I, if you eat one
another, I don't see why we mayn't eat you. So I dined upon cod
very heartily and continued to eat with other people, returning
only now and then occasionally to a vegetable diet. So convenient
a thing it is to be a *reasonable creature,* since it enables one to find
or make a reason for everything one has a mind to do.

Franklin is being playful; he is *not* engaging in critical thinking.
He tells us that he loved fish, that this fish "smelt admirably well,"
and so we are prepared for him to find a reason (here one as weak
as "Fish eat fish, therefore people may eat fish") to abandon his
vegetarianism. (But think: Fish also eat their own young. May we
therefore eat ours?)

Still, Franklin touches on a truth: If necessary, we can find reasons to justify whatever we want. That is, instead of reasoning we
may *rationalize* (devise a self-serving but dishonest reason), like the
fox in Aesop's fables who, finding the grapes he desired were out of
his reach, consoled himself with the thought that they were probably sour.

Perhaps we can never be certain that we are not rationalizing,
except when, like Franklin, we are being playful—but we can seek
to think critically about our own beliefs, scrutinizing our assumptions, looking for counterevidence, and wondering if different conclusions can reasonably be drawn.

SOME PROCEDURES IN ARGUMENT

Definition

Definition, we mentioned in our first chapter, is one of the classical
topics, a "place" to which one goes with questions; in answering
the questions, one finds ideas. When we define, we are answering
the question "What is it?" and in answering this question as precisely as we can, we will find, clarify, and develop ideas.

We have already glanced at an argument over the proposition that "all men are created equal," and we saw that the words needed clarification. *Equal* meant, in the context, not physically or mentally equal but something like "equal in rights," equal politically and legally. (And of course, *men* meant "white men and women.") Words do not always mean exactly what they seem to: There is no lead in a lead pencil, and a standard 2-by-4 is currently 1⅝ inches in thickness and 3⅜ inches in width.

Definition by Synonym   Let's return, for a moment, to *pornography*, a word that, we saw, is not easily defined. One way to define a word is to offer a **synonym.** Thus, pornography can be defined, at least roughly, as "obscenity" (something indecent). But definition by synonym is usually only a start because we find that we will have to define the synonym and, besides, that very few words have exact synonyms. (In fact, *pornography* and *obscenity* are not exact synonyms.)

Definition by Example   A second way to define something is to point to an example (this is often called **ostensive definition,** from the Latin *ostendere*, "to show"). This method can be very helpful, ensuring that both writer and reader are talking about the same

"It all depends on how you define 'chop.'"

thing, but it also has its limitations. A few decades ago many people pointed to James Joyce's *Ulysses* and D. H. Lawrence's *Lady Chatterley's Lover* as examples of obscene novels, but today these books are regarded as literary masterpieces. Possibly they can be obscene and also be literary masterpieces. (Joyce's wife is reported to have said of her husband, "He may have been a great writer, but . . . he had a very dirty mind.")

One of the difficulties of using an example, however, is that the example is richer and more complex than the term it is being used to define, and this richness and complexity get in the way of achieving a clear definition. Thus, if one cites Lawrence's *Lady Chatterley's Lover* as an example of pornography, a reader may erroneously think that pornography has something to do with British novels or with heterosexual relationships outside of marriage. Yet neither of these ideas is part of the concept of pornography.

We are not trying here to formulate a satisfactory definition of *pornography*. Our object is to show that:

- An argument will be most fruitful if the participants first agree on what they are talking about.
- One way to secure such agreement is to define the topic ostensively.
- Choosing the right example, one that has all the central or typical characteristics, can make a topic not only clear but also vivid.

Definition by Stipulation   Arguments frequently involve matters of definition: In a discussion of gun control, for instance, you probably will hear one side speak of *assault weapons* and the other side reject the term and speak of *so-called assault weapons*. In arguing, you can hope to get agreement—at least on what the topic of argument is—by offering a **stipulative definition** (from a Latin verb, "to bargain"). You and a representative of the other side can agree, for instance, that by *assault weapon* you both mean (and this was the meaning of the term in the ban approved by Congress in 1994, which expired in 2004, and which President Obama in 2013 asked Congress to renew) a semiautomatic firearm (the spent cartridge case is automatically extracted and a new round is automatically reloaded into the chamber but is not fired until the trigger is pulled again) with a detachable magazine *and at least two of the following five characteristics:*

- collapsible or folding stock
- pistol grip (thus allowing the weapon to be fired from the hip)
- bayonet mount
- grenade launcher
- flash suppressor (to keep the shooter from being blinded by muzzle flashes).

Again, this is an agreed-upon definition. Congress put *fully* automatic weapons into an entirely different category, and the legislatures of California and of New York each agreed on a stipulation different from that of Congress: In these two states, an assault weapon is a semiautomatic firearm with a detachable magazine and with any *one* (not two) of the five bulleted items.

Let's now look at stipulative definitions in other contexts. Who is a *Native American*? In discussing this issue, you might stipulate that by *Native American* you mean any person with any Native American blood; or you might say, "For the purpose of the present discussion, I mean by a *Native American* any person who has at least one grandparent of pure Native American blood." A stipulative definition is appropriate where

- no fixed or standard definition is available, and
- some arbitrary specification is necessary to fix the meaning of a key term in the argument.

Not everyone may be willing to accept your stipulative definition, and alternatives can probably be defended. In any case, when you stipulate a definition, your audience knows what *you* mean by the term thus defined.

It would *not* be reasonable, of course, to stipulate that by *Native American* you mean anyone with a deep interest in North American aborigines. That's just too idiosyncratic to be useful. Similarly, an essay on Jews in America will have to rely on some definition of the key idea. Perhaps the writer will stipulate the definition used in Israel: A Jew is a person who has a Jewish mother or, if not born of a Jewish mother, a person who has formally adopted the Jewish faith. Or perhaps the writer will stipulate another meaning: Jews are people who consider themselves to be Jews. Some sort of reasonable definition must be offered.

To stipulate, however, that by *Jews* you mean "persons who believe that the area formerly called Palestine rightfully belongs to the Jews" would hopelessly confuse matters. Remember the old riddle and the answer: If you call a dog's tail a leg, how many legs does a dog have? Answer: Four. Calling a tail a leg doesn't make it a leg.

In an essay called "When 'Identity' Politics Is Rational," Stanley Fish begins by stipulating a definition. His first paragraph begins thus:

> If there's anything everyone is against in these election times, it's "identity politics," a phrase that covers a multitude of sins. Let me start with a definition. (It may not be yours, but it will at least allow the discussion to be framed.) You're practicing identity politics when you vote for or against someone because of his or her skin color, ethnicity, religion, gender, sexual orientation, or any other marker that leads you to say yes or no independently of a candidates' ideas or policies.

Fish will go on to argue, in later paragraphs, that sometimes identity politics makes very good sense, that it is *not* irrational, is *not* logically indefensible, but here we simply want to make two points—one about how a definition helps the writer, the second about how it helps the reader:

- A definition is a good way to get yourself started when you are drafting an essay, a useful stimulus (idea prompt, pattern, template, heuristic) that will help *you* to think about the issue, a device that will stimulate your further thinking.

- A definition lets readers be certain that they are clear about what the author means by a crucial word.

Readers may disagree with Fish, but at least they know what he means when he speaks of identity politics.

A stipulation may be helpful and legitimate. Here is the opening paragraph of an essay by Richard B. Brandt titled "The Morality and Rationality of Suicide" (from *A Handbook for the Study of Suicide*, edited by Seymour Perlin). Notice that

- the author first stipulates a definition, and

- then, aware that the definition may strike some readers as too broad and therefore unreasonable or odd, he offers a reason on behalf of his definition.

"Suicide" is conveniently defined, for our purposes, as doing something which results in one's death, either from the intention of ending one's life or the intention to bring about some other state of affairs (such as relief from pain) which one thinks it certain or highly probable can be achieved only by means of death or will produce death. It may seem odd to classify an act of heroic self-sacrifice on the part of a soldier as suicide. It is simpler, however, not to try to define "suicide" so that an act of suicide is always irrational or immoral in some way; if we adopt a neutral definition like the above we can still proceed to ask when an act of suicide in that sense is rational, morally justifiable, and so on, so that all evaluations anyone might wish to make can still be made.

Sometimes a definition that at first seems extremely odd can be made acceptable, if strong reasons are offered in its support. Sometimes, in fact, an odd definition marks a great intellectual step forward. For instance, in 1990 the U.S. Supreme Court recognized that *speech* includes symbolic nonverbal expression such as protesting against a war by wearing armbands or by flying the American flag upside down. Such actions, because they express ideas or emotions, are now protected by the First Amendment. Few people today would disagree that *speech* should include symbolic gestures. Indeed, the definition of speech continues to evolve as more of our public discourse takes place online. It is important to offer strong context for definitions in your arguments.

A definition that seems notably eccentric to many readers and thus far has not gained much support is from page 94 of Peter Singer's *Practical Ethics,* in which the author suggests that a nonhuman being can be a *person.* He admits that "it sounds odd to call an animal a person" but says that it seems so only because of our bad habit of sharply separating ourselves from other species. For Singer, *persons* are "rational and self-conscious beings, aware of themselves as distinct entities with a past and a future." Thus, although a newborn infant is a human being, it is not a person; on the other hand, an adult chimpanzee is not a human being but probably is a person. You don't have to agree with Singer to know exactly what he means and where he stands. Moreover, if you read his essay, you may even find that his reasons are plausible and that by means of his unusual definition he has enlarged your thinking.

The Importance of Definitions   Trying to decide on the best way to define a key idea or a central concept is often difficult as well as controversial. *Death,* for example, has been redefined in recent years. Traditionally, a person was dead when there was no longer any heartbeat. But with advancing medical technology, the medical profession has persuaded legislatures to redefine death as cessation of cerebral and cortical functions—so-called brain death.

Some scholars have hoped to bring clarity into the abortion debate by redefining *life.* Traditionally, human life begins at birth or perhaps at viability (the capacity of a fetus to live independently of the uterine environment). However, some have proposed a *brain birth* definition, in the hope of resolving the abortion controversy. Some thinkers want abortion to be prohibited by law at the point where "integrated brain functioning begins to emerge," allegedly about seventy days after conception. Whatever the merits of such a redefinition, the debate is convincing evidence of just how important the definition of certain terms can be.

Last Words about Definition   Since Plato's time, in the fourth century B.C., it has often been argued that the best way to give a definition is to state the *essence* of the thing being defined. Thus, the classic example defines *man* as "a rational animal." (Today, to avoid sexist implications, instead of *man* we would say *human being* or *person.*) That is, the property of *rational animality* is taken to be the essence of every human creature, and so it must be mentioned in the definition of *man.* This statement guarantees that the definition is neither too broad nor too narrow. But philosophers have long criticized this alleged ideal type of definition, on several grounds, one of which is that no one can propose such definitions without assuming that the thing being defined has an essence in the first place—an assumption that is not necessary. Thus, we may want to define *causality,* or *explanation,* or even *definition* itself, but it is doubtful whether it is sound to assume that any of these things has an essence.

A much better way to provide a definition is to offer a set of **sufficient and necessary conditions.** Suppose we want to define the word *circle* and are conscious of the need to keep circles distinct from other geometrical figures such as rectangles and spheres. We might express our definition by citing sufficient and necessary conditions as follows: "Anything is a circle *if and only if* it is a closed plane figure and all points on the circumference are equidistant from the center." Using the connective "if and only if" (called the *biconditional*) between the definition and what is being defined helps to force into our consciousness the need to make the definition neither too exclusive (too narrow) nor too inclusive (too broad). Of course, for most ordinary purposes we don't require such a formally precise and explicit definition. Nevertheless, perhaps the best criterion to keep in mind when assessing a proposed definition is whether it can be stated in the "if and only if" form, and whether, if it is so stated, it is true; that is, if it truly specifies *all and only* the things covered by the word being defined. Idea Prompt 3.2 provides examples.

We are not saying that the four sentences in the table are incontestable. They are arguable. We offer them merely to show ways of defining, and the act of defining is one way of helping you to get your own thoughts going. Notice, too, that the fourth of these examples, a "statement of necessary and sufficient conditions" (indicated by "if and only if") is a bit stiff for ordinary writing. An informal prompt along this line might begin, "Essentially, something can be called *pornography* if it presents. . . ."

Assumptions

In Chapter 1, Critical Thinking, we discussed the **assumptions** made by the authors of two essays on campus discipline. But we have more to say about assumptions. We have already said that in the form of discourse known as argument certain statements are offered as reasons for other statements. But even the longest and most complex chain of reasoning or proof is fastened to assumptions—one or more *unexamined beliefs.* (Even if such a belief is

---

IDEA PROMPT 3.2 WAYS TO GIVE DEFINITIONS

Synonym	"Pornography, simply stated, is obscenity."
Example	"Pornography is easily seen in D. H. Lawrence's *Lady Chatterley's Lover* in the scene where . . ."
Stipulation	"For the purposes of this essay, pornography refers to . . ."
Statement of necessary and sufficient conditions	"Something can be called pornography if and only if it presents sexually stimulating material without offering anything of redeeming social value."

shared by writer and reader, it is no less an assumption.) Benjamin Franklin argued against paying salaries to the holders of executive offices in the federal government on the grounds that men are moved by ambition (love of power) and by avarice (love of money) and that powerful positions conferring wealth incite men to do their worst. These assumptions he stated, though he felt no need to argue them at length because he assumed that his readers shared them.

An assumption may be unstated. A writer, painstakingly arguing specific points, may choose to keep one or more of the argument's assumptions tacit. Or the writer may be as unaware of some underlying assumption as of the surrounding air. For example, Franklin didn't even bother to state another assumption. He must have assumed that persons of wealth who accept an unpaying job (after all, only persons of wealth could afford to hold unpaid government jobs) will have at heart the interests of all classes of people, not only the interests of their own class. Probably Franklin did not state this assumption because he thought it was perfectly obvious, but if you think critically about the assumption, you may find reasons to doubt it. Surely one reason we pay our legislators is to make certain that the legislature does not consist only of people whose incomes may give them an inadequate view of the needs of others.

An Example: Assumptions in the Argument Permitting Abortion

1. Ours is a pluralistic society, in which we believe that the religious beliefs of one group should not be imposed on others.
2. Personal privacy is a right, and a woman's body is hers, not to be violated by laws that tell her she may not do certain things to her body.

But these (and other) arguments *assume* that a fetus is not—or not yet—a person and therefore is not entitled to the same protection against assaults that we are. Virtually all of us assume that it is usually wrong to kill a human being. Granted, we may find instances in which we believe it is acceptable to take a human life, such as self-defense against a would-be murderer. But even here we find a shared assumption that persons are ordinarily entitled not to be killed.

The argument about abortion, then, usually depends on opposed assumptions: For one group, the fetus is a human being and a potential person—and this potentiality is decisive. But for the other group it is not. Persons arguing one side or the other of the abortion issue ought to be aware that opponents may not share their assumptions.

Premises and Syllogisms

Premises are stated assumptions used as reasons in an argument. (The word comes from a Latin word meaning "to send before" or "to set in front.") A premise thus is a statement set down—assumed—before the argument is begun. The joining of two premises—two statements taken to be true—to produce a conclusion, a third statement, is called a **syllogism** (Greek for "a reckoning together"). The classic example is this:

Major premise:	All human beings are mortal.
Minor premise:	Socrates is a human being.
Conclusion:	Socrates is mortal.

Deduction

The mental process of moving from one statement ("All human beings are mortal") through another ("Socrates is a human being") to yet a further statement ("Socrates is mortal") is called **deduction,** from Latin for "lead down from." In this sense, deductive reasoning does not give us any new knowledge, although it is easy to construct examples that have so many premises, or premises that are so complex, that the conclusion really does come as news to most who examine the argument. Thus, the great detective Sherlock Holmes was credited by his admiring colleague, Dr. Watson, with unusual powers of deduction. Watson meant in part that Holmes could see the logical consequences of apparently disconnected reasons, the number and complexity of which left others at a loss. What is common in all cases of deduction is that the reasons or premises offered are supposed to contain within themselves, so to speak, the conclusion extracted from them.

Often a syllogism is abbreviated. Martin Luther King Jr., defending a protest march, wrote in "Letter from Birmingham Jail":

> You assert that our actions, even though peaceful, must be condemned because they precipitate violence.

Fully expressed, the argument that King attributes to his critics would be stated thus:

Society must condemn actions (even if peaceful) that precipitate violence.

This action (though peaceful) will precipitate violence.

Therefore, society must condemn this action.

An incomplete or abbreviated syllogism in which one of the premises is left unstated, of the sort found in King's original quotation, is called an **enthymeme** (Greek for "in the mind").

Here is another, more whimsical example of an enthymeme, in which both a premise and the conclusion are left implicit. Henry David Thoreau remarked that "circumstantial evidence can be very strong, as when you find a trout in the milk." The joke, perhaps intelligible only to people born before 1930 or so, depends on the fact that milk used to be sold "in bulk"—that is, ladled out of a big can directly to the customer by the farmer or grocer. This practice was finally prohibited in the 1930s because for centuries the sellers, in order to increase their profit, were diluting the milk with water. Thoreau's enthymeme can be fully expressed thus:

Trout live only in water.

This milk has a trout in it.

Therefore, this milk has water in it.

(© The New Yorker Collection 2003: Robert Mankoff from cartoonbank.com. All rights reserved.)

These enthymemes have three important properties: Their premises are *true,* the form of their argument is *valid,* and they leave *implicit* either the conclusion or one of the premises.

Sound Arguments

The purpose of a syllogism is to present reasons that establish its conclusion. This is done by making sure that the argument satisfies both of two independent criteria:

- First, all of the premises must be *true.*
- Second, the syllogism must be *valid.*

Once these criteria are satisfied, the conclusion of the syllogism is guaranteed. Any such argument is said to establish or to prove its conclusion, or to use another term, it is said to be **sound.** Here's an example of a sound argument, a syllogism that proves its conclusion:

Extracting oil from the Arctic Wildlife Refuge would adversely affect the local ecology.

Adversely affecting the local ecology is undesirable, unless there is no better alternative fuel source.

Therefore, extracting oil from the Arctic Wildlife Refuge is undesirable, unless there is no better alternative fuel source.

Each premise is **true,** and the syllogism is **valid,** so it establishes its conclusion.

But how do we tell in any given case that an argument is sound? We perform two different tests, one for the truth of each of the premises and another for the validity of the argument.

The basic test for the **truth** of a premise is to determine whether what it asserts corresponds with reality; if it does, then it is true, and if it doesn't, then it is false. Everything depends on the content of the premise—what it asserts—and the evidence for it. (In the preceding syllogism, the truth of the premises can be tested by checking the views of experts and interested parties, such as policymakers, environmental groups, and experts on energy.)

The test for **validity** is quite different. We define a valid argument as one in which the conclusion follows from the premises, so that if all the premises are true then the conclusion *must* be true, too. The general test for validity, then, is this: If one grants the premises, one must also grant the conclusion. Or to put it another way, if one grants the premises but denies the conclusion, is one caught in a self-contradiction? If so, the argument is valid; if not, the argument is invalid.

The preceding syllogism passes this test. If you grant the information given in the premises but deny the conclusion, you have contradicted yourself. Even if the information were in error, the conclusion in this syllogism would still follow from the premises— the hallmark of a valid argument! The conclusion follows because the validity of an argument is a purely formal matter concerning the *relation* between premises and conclusion based on what they mean.

This relationship can be seen more clearly by examining an argument that is valid but that, because one or both of the premises are false, does *not* establish its conclusion. Here is an example of such a syllogism:

> The whale is a large fish.
>
> All large fish have scales.
>
> Therefore, whales have scales.

We know that the premises and the conclusion are false: Whales are mammals, not fish, and not all large fish have scales (sharks have no scales, for instance). But when the validity of the argument is being determined, the truth of the premises and the conclusion is beside the point. Just a little reflection assures us that *if* both of these premises were true, then the conclusion would have to be true as well. That is, anyone who grants the premises of this syllogism and yet denies the conclusion has contradicted herself. So the validity of an argument does not in any way depend on the truth of the premises or the conclusion.

A sound argument, as we said, is an argument that passes both the test of true premises and the test of valid inference. To put it another way, a sound argument

- passes the test of content (the premises are true, as a matter of fact) and it
- passes the test of form (its premises and conclusion, by virtue of their very meanings, are so related that it is impossible for the premises to be true and the conclusion false).

Accordingly, an unsound argument, an argument that fails to prove its conclusion, suffers from one or both of two defects.

- First, not all of the premises are true.
- Second, the argument is invalid.

Usually, we have in mind one or both of these defects when we object to someone's argument as "illogical." In evaluating someone's deductive argument, therefore, you must always ask: Is it vulnerable to criticism on the ground that one (or more) of its premises is false? Or is the inference itself vulnerable because even if all the premises are all true, the conclusion still wouldn't follow?

A deductive argument *proves* its conclusion if and only if *two conditions* are satisfied: (1) All the premises are *true,* and (2) it would be *inconsistent to assert the premises and deny the conclusions.*

A Word about False Premises
Suppose that one or more of the premises of a syllogism are false but the syllogism itself is valid. What does that tell us about the truth of the conclusion? Consider this example:

> All Americans prefer vanilla ice cream to other flavors.
>
> Tiger Woods is an American.
>
> Therefore, Tiger Woods prefers vanilla ice cream to other flavors.

The first (or major) premise in this syllogism is false. Yet the argument passes our formal test for validity; it is clear that if one grants both premises, then one must accept the conclusion. So we can say that the conclusion *follows from* its premises, even though the premises *do not prove* the conclusion. This is not as paradoxical as it may sound. For all we know, the conclusion of this argument may in fact be true; Tiger Woods may indeed prefer vanilla ice cream, and the odds are that he does because consumption statistics show that a majority of Americans prefer vanilla. Nevertheless, if the conclusion in this syllogism is true, it is not because this argument proved it.

A Word about Invalid Syllogisms
Usually, one can detect a false premise in an argument, especially when the suspect premise appears in someone else's argument. A trickier business is the invalid syllogism. Consider this argument:

> All terrorists seek publicity for their violent acts.
>
> John Doe seeks publicity for his violent acts.
>
> Therefore, John Doe is a terrorist.

In the preceding syllogism, let us grant that the first (major) premise is true. Let us also grant that the conclusion may well be true. Finally, the person mentioned in the second (minor) premise could indeed be a terrorist. But it is also possible that the conclusion is false; terrorists are not the only ones who seek publicity for their violent acts; think, for example, of the violence committed against doctors, clinic workers, and patients at clinics where abortions are performed. In short, the truth of the two premises is no guarantee that the conclusion is also true. It is possible to assert both premises and deny the conclusion without self-contradiction.

How do we tell, in general and in particular cases, whether a syllogism is valid? Chemists use litmus paper to enable them to tell instantly whether the liquid in a test tube is an acid or a base. Unfortunately, logic has no litmus test to tell us instantly whether an argument is valid or invalid. Logicians beginning with Aristotle have developed techniques that enable them to test any given argument, no matter how complex or subtle, to determine its validity. But the results of their labors cannot be expressed in a paragraph or even a few pages; not for nothing are semester-long courses devoted to teaching formal deductive logic. Apart from advising you to consult Chapter 9, A Logician's View: Deduction, Induction, Fallacies, all we can do here is repeat two basic points.

First, validity of deductive arguments is a matter of their *form* or *structure*. Even syllogisms like the one on the Arctic Wildlife Refuge on page 85 come in a large variety of forms (256 different ones, to be precise), and only some of these forms are valid. Second, all valid deductive arguments (and only such arguments) pass this test: If one accepts all the premises, then one must accept the conclusion as well. Hence, if it is possible to accept the premises but reject the conclusion (without self-contradiction, of course), then the argument is invalid.

Let us exit from further discussion of this important but difficult subject on a lighter note. Many illogical arguments masquerade as logical. Consider this example: If it takes a horse and carriage four hours to go from Pinsk to Chelm, does it follow that a carriage with two horses will get there in two hours?

Note: In Chapter 9, we discuss at some length other kinds of deductive arguments, as well as **fallacies,** which are kinds of invalid reasoning.

Induction

Whereas deduction takes our beliefs and assumptions and extracts their hidden consequences, **induction** uses information about observed cases to reach a conclusion about unobserved cases. (The word comes from the Latin *in ducere,* "to lead into" or "to lead up to.") If we observe that the bite of a certain snake is poisonous, we may conclude on this evidence that another snake of the same general type is also poisonous. Our inference might be even broader. If we observe that snake after snake of a certain type has a poisonous bite and that these snakes are all rattlesnakes, we are tempted to **generalize** that all rattlesnakes are poisonous.

By far the most common way to test the adequacy of a generalization is to confront it with one or more **counterexamples.** If the counterexamples are genuine and reliable, then the generalization must be false. For example, an essay by Ronald Takaki on the "myth" of Asian racial superiority is full of examples that contradict the alleged superiority of Asians; they are counterexamples to that thesis, and they help to expose it as a "myth." What is true of Takaki's reasoning is true generally in argumentative writing. We are constantly testing our generalizations against actual or possible counterexamples, or by doing research on the issue.

Unlike deduction, induction gives us conclusions that go beyond the information contained in the premises used in their support. Not surprisingly, the conclusions of inductive reasoning are not always true, even when all the premises are true. On page 73, we gave as an example our observation that on previous days a subway has run at 6:00 A.M. and that therefore we believe that it runs at 6:00 A.M. every day. Suppose, following this reasoning, we arrive at the subway platform just before 6:00 A.M. on a given day and wait an hour without a train. What inference should we draw to explain this? Possibly today is Sunday, and the subway doesn't run before 7:00 A.M. Or possibly there was a breakdown earlier this morning. Whatever the explanation, we relied on a sample that was not large enough (a larger sample might have included some early morning breakdowns) or not representative enough (a more representative sample would have included the later starts on holidays).

A Word about Samples   When we reason inductively, much depends on the size and the quality of the sample—"sample" because a writer probably cannot examine every instance. If, for example, we are offering an argument concerning the politics of members of sororities and fraternities, we probably cannot interview *every* member. Rather, we select a sample. But is the sample a fair sample? Is it representative of the larger group? We may interview five members of Alpha Tau Omega and find that all five are Republicans, yet we cannot legitimately conclude that all members of ATO are Republicans. The problem is not always one of failing to interview large numbers. A poll of ten thousand college students tells us very little about "college students" if all ten thousand are white males at the University of Texas. Such a sample, because it leaves out women and minority males, obviously is not sufficiently *representative* of "college students" as a group. Further, though not all of the students at the University of Texas are from Texas or even from the Southwest, it is quite likely that the student body is not fully representative (for instance, in race and in income) of American college students. If this conjecture is correct, even a truly representative sample of University of Texas students would not allow one to draw firm conclusions about American college students.

In short: An argument that uses samples ought to tell the reader how the samples were chosen. If it does not provide this information, the argument may rightly be treated with suspicion.

Evidence: Experimentation, Examples, Authoritative Testimony, Statistics

Different disciplines use different kinds of evidence:

- In literary studies, the texts are usually the chief evidence.
- In the social sciences, field research (interviews, surveys) usually provides evidence.

In the sciences, reports of experiments are the usual evidence; if an assertion cannot be tested—if an assertion is not capable of being shown to be false—it is a *belief*, an *opinion*, not a scientific hypothesis.

Experimentation   Induction is obviously useful in arguing. If, for example, one is arguing that handguns should be controlled, one will point to specific cases in which handguns caused accidents or were used to commit crimes. If one is arguing that abortion has a traumatic effect on women, one will point to women who testify to that effect. Each instance constitutes **evidence** for the relevant generalization.

In a courtroom, evidence bearing on the guilt of the accused is introduced by the prosecution, and evidence to the contrary is introduced by the defense. Not all evidence is admissible (hearsay, for example, is not, even if it is true), and the law of evidence is a highly developed subject in jurisprudence. In the forum of daily life, the sources of evidence are less disciplined. Daily experience, a particularly memorable observation, an unusual event we witnessed—any or all of these may be used as evidence for (or against) some belief, theory, hypothesis, or explanation. The systematic study of what experience can yield is what science does, and one of the most distinctive features of the evidence that scientists can marshal on behalf of their claims is that it is the result of **experimentation.** Experiments are deliberately contrived situations that are often complex in their technology and designed to yield particular observations. What the ordinary person does with unaided eye and ear, the scientist does, much more carefully and thoroughly, with the help of laboratory instruments.

The variety, extent, and reliability of the evidence obtained in daily life and in the laboratory are quite different. It is hardly a surprise that in our civilization much more weight is attached to the "findings" of scientists than to the corroborative (much less the contrary) experiences of the ordinary person. No one today would seriously argue that the sun really does go around the earth just because it looks that way; nor would we argue that because viruses are invisible to the naked eye they cannot cause symptoms such as swellings and fevers, which are quite plainly visible.

Examples   One form of evidence is the **example.** Suppose that we argue that a candidate is untrustworthy and should not be elected to public office. We point to episodes in his career—his misuse of funds in 1998 and the false charges he made against an opponent in 2002—as examples of his untrustworthiness. Or if we are arguing that President Truman ordered the atom bomb dropped to save American (and, for that matter, Japanese) lives that otherwise would have been lost in a hard-fought invasion of Japan, we point to the stubbornness of the Japanese defenders in battles on the islands of Saipan, Iwo Jima, and Okinawa, where Japanese soldiers fought to the death rather than surrender.

These examples, we say, show us that the Japanese defenders of the main islands would have fought to their deaths without surrendering, even though they knew they would be defeated. Or if we argue that the war was nearly won when Truman dropped the bomb, we can cite secret peace feelers as examples of the Japanese willingness to end the war.

An example is a sample; these two words come from the same Old French word, *essample,* from the Latin *exemplum,* which means "something taken out"—that is, a selection from the group. A Yiddish proverb shrewdly says that "'For example' is no proof," but the evidence of well-chosen examples can go a long way toward helping a writer to convince an audience.

In arguments, three sorts of examples are especially common:

- real events,
- invented instances (artificial or hypothetical cases), and
- analogies.

We will treat each of these briefly.

REAL EVENTS   In referring to Truman's decision to drop the atom bomb, we have already touched on examples drawn from real events—the battles at Saipan and elsewhere. And we have also seen Ben Franklin pointing to an allegedly real happening, a fish that had consumed a smaller fish. The advantage of an example drawn from real life, whether a great historical event or a local incident, is that its reality gives it weight. It can't simply be brushed off.

On the other hand, an example drawn from reality may not provide as clear-cut an instance as could be wished for. Suppose, for instance, that someone cites the Japanese army's behavior on Saipan and on Iwo Jima as evidence that the Japanese later would have fought to the death in an American invasion of Japan and would therefore have inflicted terrible losses on themselves and on the Americans. This example is open to the response that in June and July 1945, Japanese diplomats sent out secret peace feelers, so that in August 1945, when Truman authorized dropping the bomb, the situation was very different.

Similarly, in support of the argument that nations will no longer resort to atomic weapons, some people have offered as evidence the fact that since World War I the great powers have not used poison gas. But the argument needs more support than this fact provides. Poison gas was not decisive or even highly effective in World War I. Moreover, the invention of gas masks made it obsolete.

In short, any *real* event is so entangled in its historical circumstances that it might not be adequate or even relevant evidence in the case being argued. In using a real event as an example (and real events certainly can be used), the writer ordinarily must

demonstrate that the event can be taken out of its historical context and be used in the new context of argument. Thus, in an argument against using atomic weapons in warfare, the many deaths
and horrible injuries inflicted on the Japanese at Hiroshima and
Nagasaki can be cited as effects of nuclear weapons that would
invariably occur and did not depend on any special circumstances
of their use in Japan in 1945.

INVENTED INSTANCES **Artificial** or **hypothetical cases —
invented instances** — have the great advantage of being protected
from objections of the sort just given. Recall Thoreau's trout in the
milk; that was a colorful hypothetical case that nicely illustrated his
point. An invented instance ("Let's assume that a burglar promises not to shoot a householder if the householder swears not to
identify him. Is the householder bound by the oath?") is something
like a drawing of a flower in a botany textbook or a diagram of the
folds of a mountain in a geology textbook. It is admittedly false,
but by virtue of its simplifications it sets forth the relevant details
very clearly. Thus, in a discussion of rights, the philosopher Charles
Frankel says,

> Strictly speaking, when we assert a right for X, we assert that Y
> has a duty. Strictly speaking, that Y has such a duty presupposes
> that Y has the capacity to perform this duty. It would be nonsense
> to say, for example, that a nonswimmer has a moral duty to swim
> to the help of a drowning man.

This invented example is admirably clear, and it is immune to
charges that might muddy the issue if Frankel, instead of referring to a wholly abstract person, Y, talked about some real person,
Jones, who did not rescue a drowning man. For then he would
get bogged down over arguing about whether Jones *really* couldn't
swim well enough to help, and so on.

Yet invented cases have their drawbacks. First and foremost,
they cannot be used as evidence. A purely hypothetical example
can illustrate a point or provoke reconsideration of a generalization,
but it cannot substitute for actual events as evidence supporting an
inductive inference. Sometimes such examples are so fanciful, so
remote from life that they fail to carry conviction with the reader.
Thus the philosopher Judith Jarvis Thomson, in the course of her
argument entitled "A Defense of Abortion," asks you to imagine
that you wake up one day and find that against your will a cel-
ebrated violinist whose body is not adequately functioning has

been hooked up into your body for life support. Do you have the right to unplug the violinist? Readers of the essays in this book will have to decide for themselves whether the invented cases proposed by various authors are helpful or whether they are so remote that they hinder thought. Readers will have to decide, too, about when they can use invented cases to advance their own arguments.

But we add one point: Even a highly fanciful invented case can have the valuable effect of forcing us to see where we stand. We may say that we are, in all circumstances, against vivisection—the practice of performing operations on live animals for the purpose of research. But what would we say if we thought that an experiment on one mouse would save the life of someone we love? Or conversely, if one approves of vivisection, would one also approve of sacrificing the last giant panda to save the life of a senile stranger, a person who in any case probably would not live longer than another year? Artificial cases of this sort can help us to see that, well, no, we didn't really mean to say such-and-such when we said so-and-so.

ANALOGIES   The third sort of example, **analogy,** is a kind of comparison. An analogy asserts that things that are alike in some ways are alike in yet another way. Example: "Before the Roman Empire declined as a world power, it exhibited a decline in morals and in physical stamina; our culture today shows a decline in morals (look at the high divorce rate, and look at the crime rate) and we also show a decline in physical culture (just read about obesity in children). America, like Rome, will decline as a world power."

Strictly, an analogy is an extended comparison in which different things are shown to be similar in several ways. Thus, if one wants to argue that a head of state should have extraordinary power during wartime, one can argue that the state at such a time is like a ship in a storm: The crew is needed to lend its help, but the decisions are best left to the captain. (Notice that an analogy compares things that are relatively *un*like. Comparing the plight of one ship to another or of one government to another is not an analogy; it is an inductive inference from one case of the same sort to another such case.)

Or take another analogy: We have already glanced at Judith Thomson's hypothetical case in which the reader wakes up to find himself or herself hooked up to a violinist. Thomson uses this situation as an analogy in an argument about abortion. The reader stands for the mother, the violinist for the unwanted fetus.

Whether this analogy is close enough to pregnancy to help illuminate our thinking about abortion is something that you may want
to think about.

The problem with argument by analogy is this: Two admittedly different things are agreed to be similar in several ways, and
the arguer goes on to assert or imply that they are also similar in
another way—the point that is being argued. (That is why Thomson argues that if something is true of the reader-hooked-up-to-
a-violinist, it is also true of the pregnant mother-hooked-up-to-a-
fetus.) But the two things that are said to be analogous and that are
indeed similar in characteristics *A, B,* and *C* are also different—let's
say in characteristics *D* and *E*. As Bishop Butler is said to have
remarked in the early eighteenth century, "Everything is what it is,
and not another thing."

Analogies can be convincing, especially because they can make
complex issues simple. "Don't change horses in midstream," of
course, is not a statement about riding horses across a river but
about choosing leaders in critical times. Still, in the end, analogies
do not necessarily prove anything. What may be true about riding
horses across a stream may not be true about choosing leaders in
troubled times or about deciding on a given change of leadership.
Riding horses across a stream and choosing leaders are, at bottom,
different things, and however much these activities may be said to
resemble one another, they remain different, and what is true for
one need not be true for the other.

Analogies can be helpful in developing our thoughts and in
helping listeners or readers to understand a point we are trying
to make. It is sometimes argued, for instance—on the analogy of
the doctor–patient or the lawyer–client or the priest–penitent relationship—that newspaper and television reporters should not be
required to reveal their confidential sources. That is worth thinking
about: Do the similarities run deep enough, or are there fundamental differences? Or take another example: Some writers who support abortion argue that the fetus is not a person any more than the
acorn is an oak. That is also worth thinking about. But one should
also think about this response: A fetus is not a person, just as an
acorn is not an oak, but an acorn is a potential oak, and a fetus is
a potential person, a potential adult human being. Children, even
newborn infants, have rights, and one way to explain this claim is
to call attention to their potentiality to become mature adults. And
so some people argue that the fetus, by analogy, has the rights of an
infant, for the fetus, like the infant, is a potential adult.

Three analogies for consideration: First, let's examine a brief comparison made by Jill Knight, a member of the British Parliament, speaking about abortion:

> Babies are not like bad teeth, to be jerked out because they cause suffering.

Her point is effectively put; it remains for the reader to decide whether or not fetuses are *babies* and if a fetus is not a baby, *why* it can or can't be treated like a bad tooth.

Now, a second bit of analogical reasoning, again about abortion: Thomas Sowell, an economist at the Hoover Institute, grants that women have a legal right to abortion, but he objects to a requirement that the government pay for abortions:

> Because the courts have ruled that women have a legal right to
> an abortion, some people have jumped to the conclusion that
> the government has to pay for it. You have a constitutional right
> to privacy, but the government has no obligation to pay for your
> window shades. (*Pink and Brown People*, 1981, p. 57)

We leave it to the reader to decide whether the analogy is compelling — that is, if the points of resemblance are sufficiently significant to allow one to conclude that what is true of people wanting window shades should be true of people wanting abortions.

And one more: A common argument on behalf of legalizing gay marriage draws an analogy between gay marriage and interracial marriage, a practice that was banned in sixteen states until 1967, when the Supreme Court declared miscegenation statutes unconstitutional. The gist of the analogy is this: Racism and discrimination against gay and lesbian people are the same. If marriage is a fundamental right — as the Supreme Court held in its 1967 decision when it struck down bans on miscegenation — then it is a fundamental right for gay people as well as heterosexual people.

Authoritative Testimony   Another form of evidence is **testimony,** the citation or quotation of authorities. In daily life we rely heavily on authorities of all sorts: We get a doctor's opinion about our health, we read a book because an intelligent friend recommends it, we see a movie because a critic gave it a good review, and we pay at least a little attention to the weather forecaster.

In setting forth an argument, one often tries to show that one's view is supported by notable figures, perhaps Jefferson, Lincoln, Martin Luther King Jr., or scientists who won the Nobel Prize. You may recall that in the second chapter, in talking about definitions of pornography, we referred to Kenneth Clark. To make certain that you were impressed by his testimony even if you had never heard of him, we described him as "probably the most influential English-speaking art critic of the twentieth century." But heed some words of caution:

- Be sure that the authority, however notable, is an authority on the topic in question (a well-known biologist might be an authority on vitamins but not on the justice of a war).
- Be sure that the authority is not biased. A chemist employed by the tobacco industry isn't likely to admit that smoking may be harmful, and a "director of publications" (that means a press agent) for a hockey team isn't likely to admit that watching or even playing ice hockey stimulates violence.
- Beware of nameless authorities: "a thousand doctors," "leading educators," "researchers at a major medical school."
- Be careful when using authorities who indeed were great authorities in their day but who now may be out of date (Adam Smith on economics, Julius Caesar on the art of war, Louis Pasteur on medicine).
- Cite authorities whose opinions your readers will value. William F. Buckley Jr.'s conservative/libertarian opinions mean a good deal to readers of the magazine that he founded, the *National Review*, but probably not to most liberal thinkers. Gloria Steinem's liberal/feminist opinions carry weight with the readers of the magazines that she cofounded, *New York* and *Ms.* magazine, but probably not to most conservative thinkers. If you are writing for the general reader, your usual audience, cite authorities who are likely to be accepted by the general reader.

One other point: *You* may be an authority. You probably aren't nationally known, but on some topics you perhaps can speak with the authority of personal experience. You may have been injured on a motorcycle while riding without wearing a helmet, or you may have escaped injury because you wore a helmet; you may have dropped out of school and then returned; you may have tutored a student whose native language is not English, or you may be such a student and you may have received tutoring. You may have attended a school with a bilingual education program. In short, your personal testimony on topics relating to these issues may be invaluable, and a reader will probably consider it seriously.

Statistics   The last sort of evidence we discuss here is quantitative
or statistical. The maxim "More is better" captures a basic idea of
quantitative evidence. Because we know that 90 percent is greater
than 75 percent, we are usually ready to grant that any claim supported by experience in 90 percent of the cases is more likely to
be true than an alternative claim supported by experience only
75 percent of the time. The greater the difference, the greater
our confidence. Consider an example. Honors at graduation from
college are often computed on a student's cumulative grade-point
average (GPA). The undisputed assumption is that the nearer a
student's GPA is to a perfect record (4.0), the better scholar he or
she is and therefore the more deserving of highest honors. Consequently, a student with a GPA of 3.9 at the end of her senior year is
a stronger candidate for graduating summa cum laude than another
student with a GPA of 3.6. When faculty members on the honors
committee argue over the relative academic merits of graduating
seniors, we know that these quantitative, statistical differences in
student GPAs will be the basic (even if not the only) kind of evidence under discussion.

GRAPHS, TABLES, NUMBERS   Statistical information can be
marshaled and presented in many forms, but it tends to fall into
two main types: the graphic and the numerical. Graphs, tables, and
pie charts are familiar ways of presenting quantitative data in an
eye-catching manner. (See pages 142–45.) To prepare the graphics, however, one first has to get the numbers themselves under
control, and for some purposes it may be acceptable simply to stick
with the numbers themselves.

But should the numbers be presented in percentages or in frac-
tions? Should one report, say, that the federal budget underwent
a twofold increase over the decade, that it increased by 100 percent, that it doubled, or that the budget at the beginning of the
decade was one-half what it was at the end? Taken strictly, these
are equivalent ways of saying the same thing. Choice among them,
therefore, in an example like this perhaps will rest on whether
one's aim is to dramatize the increase (a 100 percent increase looks
larger than a doubling) or to play down the size of the increase.

THINKING ABOUT STATISTICAL EVIDENCE   Statistics often get a
bad name because it is so easy to misuse them, unintentionally or

not, and so difficult to be sure that they have been correctly gathered in the first place. (We remind you of the old saw "There are lies, damned lies, and statistics.") Every branch of social science and natural science needs statistical information, and countless decisions in public and private life are based on quantitative data in statistical form. It is important, therefore, to be sensitive to the sources and reliability of the statistics and to develop a healthy skepticism when confronted with statistics whose parentage is not fully explained.

Consider, for instance, statistics that kept popping up during the baseball strike of 1994. The owners of the clubs said that the average salary of a major-league player was $1.2 million. (The **average** in this case—technically the **mean**—is the result of dividing the total number of salary dollars by the number of players.) The players' union, however, did not talk about the average; rather, the union talked about the **median,** which was less than half of the average, a mere $500,000. (The *median* is the middle value in a distribution. Thus, of the 746 players, 363 earned less than $500,000, 361 earned more, and 22 earned exactly $500,000.) The union said, correctly, that *most* players earned a good deal less than the $1.2 million figure that the owners kept citing; but the $1.2 million average sounded more impressive to the general public, and that is the figure that the guy in the street mentioned when asked for an opinion about the strike.

Consider this statistic: In Smithville in 2011, 1 percent of the victims in fatal automobile accidents were bicyclists. In 2012 the percentage of bicyclists killed in automobile accidents was 2 percent. Was the increase 1 percent (not an alarming figure), or was it 100 percent (a staggering figure)? The answer is both, depending on whether we are comparing (a) bicycle deaths in automobile accidents with *all* deaths in automobile accidents (that's an increase of 1 percent), or (b) bicycle deaths in automobile accidents *only with other bicycle deaths* in automobile accidents (an increase of 100 percent). An honest statement would say that bicycle deaths due to automobile accidents doubled in 2012, increasing from 1 to 2 percent. But here's another point: Although every such death is lamentable, if there was one such death in 2009 and two in 2010, the increase from one death to two (an increase of 100 percent!) hardly suggests that there is a growing problem that needs attention. No one would be surprised to learn that in the next year there were no deaths, or only one or even two.

If it is sometimes difficult to interpret statistics, it is often at least equally difficult to establish accurate statistics. Consider this example:

> Advertisements are the most prevalent and toxic of the mental pollutants. From the moment your radio alarm sounds in the morning to the wee hours of late-night TV, microjolts of com-mercial pollution flood into your brain at the rate of about three thousand marketing messages per day. (Kalle Lasn, *Culture Jam,* 1999, pp. 18–19)

Lasn's book includes endnotes as documentation, so, curious about the statistics, we turn to the appropriate page and we find this information concerning the source of his data:

> "three thousand marketing messages per day." Mark Landler, Walecia Konrad, Zachary Schiller, and Lois Therrien, "What Happened to Advertising?" *BusinessWeek,* September 23, 1991, page 66. Leslie Savan in *The Sponsored Life* (Temple University Press, 1994), page 1, estimated that "16,000 ads flicker across an individual's consciousness daily." I did an informal survey in March 1995 and found the number to be closer to 1,500 (this included all marketing messages, corporate images, logos, ads, brand names, on TV, radio, billboards, buildings, signs, clothing, appliances, in cyberspace, etc., over a typical twenty-four hour period in my life). (219)

Well, this endnote is odd. In the earlier passage, you will recall, the author asserted that "about three thousand marketing messages per day" flood into a person's brain. Now, in the documentation, he helpfully cites a source for that statistic, from *BusinessWeek*— though we have not the faintest idea of how the authors of the article in *BusinessWeek* came up with that figure. Oddly, he goes on to offer a very different figure (16,000 ads), and then, to our utter confusion, he offers yet a third figure, 1,500, based on his own "informal survey."

Probably the one thing we can safely say about all three figures is that none of them means very much. Even if the com-pilers of the statistics told us exactly how they counted—let's say that among countless other criteria they assumed that the average person reads one magazine per day and that the average magazine contains 124 advertisements—it would be hard to take them seri-ously. After all, in leafing through a magazine, some people may read many ads, some may read none. Some people may read some ads carefully—but perhaps to enjoy their absurdity. Our point: Although the author in his text said, without implying any uncertainty, that "about three thousand marketing messages per day" reach an individual, it is evident (if one checks the endnote) that even he is confused about the figure he gives.

Some last words about the unreliability of some statistical information, stuff that looks impressive but that is, in fact, insubstantial. Marilyn Jager Adams studied the number of hours that families read to their children in the five or so years before the children go to school. In her book on the topic, *Beginning to Read: Thinking*

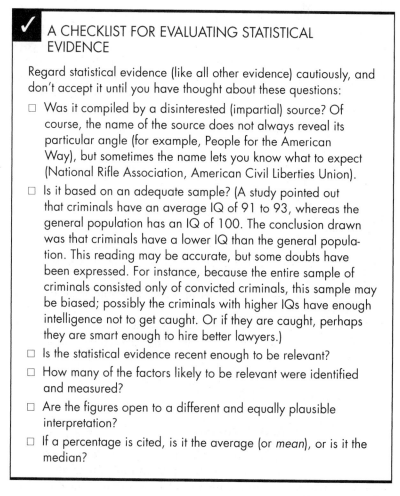

✓ A CHECKLIST FOR EVALUATING STATISTICAL EVIDENCE

Regard statistical evidence (like all other evidence) cautiously, and don't accept it until you have thought about these questions:

☐ Was it compiled by a disinterested (impartial) source? Of course, the name of the source does not always reveal its particular angle (for example, People for the American Way), but sometimes the name lets you know what to expect (National Rifle Association, American Civil Liberties Union).

☐ Is it based on an adequate sample? (A study pointed out that criminals have an average IQ of 91 to 93, whereas the general population has an IQ of 100. The conclusion drawn was that criminals have a lower IQ than the general population. This reading may be accurate, but some doubts have been expressed. For instance, because the entire sample of criminals consisted only of convicted criminals, this sample may be biased; possibly the criminals with higher IQs have enough intelligence not to get caught. Or if they are caught, perhaps they are smart enough to hire better lawyers.)

☐ Is the statistical evidence recent enough to be relevant?

☐ How many of the factors likely to be relevant were identified and measured?

☐ Are the figures open to a different and equally plausible interpretation?

☐ If a percentage is cited, is it the average (or *mean*), or is it the median?

and Learning about Print, she pointed out that in all those preschool years, poor families read to their children only twenty-five hours, whereas in the same period middle-income families read 1,000 to 1,700 hours. The figures were much quoted in newspapers and by children's advocacy groups. Dr. Adams could not, of course, interview every family in these two groups; she had to rely on samples. What were her samples? For poor families, she selected twenty-four children in twenty families, all in Southern California. One might wonder if families from only one geographic area can provide an adequate sample, but let's think about Dr. Adams's sample of middle-class families. How many families constituted the sample? Exactly one, her own. We leave it to you to decide how much value her findings—again, they were much cited—have.

We are not suggesting that everyone who uses statistics is trying to deceive or even that many who use statistics are unconsciously deceived by them. We mean to suggest only that statistics are open to widely different interpretations and that often those columns of numbers, so precise with their decimal points, are in fact imprecise and possibly even worthless because they may be based on insufficient or biased samples.

Quiz

What is wrong with the following statistical proof that children do not have time for school?

> One-third of the time they are sleeping (about 122 days);
>
> One-eighth of the time they are eating (three hours a day, totaling 45 days);
>
> One-fourth of the time is taken up by summer and other vacations (91 days);
>
> Two-sevenths of the year is weekends (104 days).
>
> Total: 362 days—so how can a kid have time for school?

NONRATIONAL APPEALS

Satire, Irony, Sarcasm, Humor

In talking about definition, deduction, and evidence, we have been talking about means of rational persuasion. But as mentioned earlier, there are also other means of persuasion. Take force, for example. If *X* kicks *Y*, threatens to destroy *Y*'s means of livelihood, or threatens *Y*'s life, *X* may persuade *Y* to cooperate. One form of irrational but sometimes highly effective persuasion is **satire**—that is, witty ridicule. A cartoonist may persuade viewers that a politician's views are unsound by caricaturing (and thus ridiculing) the politician's appearance or by presenting a grotesquely distorted (funny, but unfair) picture of the issue.

Satiric artists often use caricature; satiric writers, also seeking to persuade by means of ridicule, often use **verbal irony.** Irony of this sort contrasts what is said and what is meant. For instance, words of praise may be meant to imply blame (when Shakespeare's Cassius says, "Brutus is an honorable man," he means his hearers to think that Brutus is dishonorable), and words of modesty may be meant to imply superiority ("Of course, I'm too dumb to understand this problem"). Such language, when heavy-handed, is called **sarcasm** ("You're a great guy," said to someone who will not lend the speaker ten dollars). If it is witty—if the jeering is in some degree clever—it is called irony rather than sarcasm.

Although ridicule is not a form of argument (because it is not a form of reasoning), passages of ridicule, especially verbal irony, sometimes appear in essays that are arguments. These passages, like reasons, or for that matter like appeals to the emotions, are efforts to persuade the hearer to accept the speaker's point of view. The great trick in using humor in an argument is, on the one hand, to avoid mere wisecracking, which makes the writer seem like a smart aleck, and, on the other hand, to avoid mere clownishness, which makes the writer seem like a fool. Later in this chapter (p. 109) we print an essay by George F. Will that is (or seeks to be?) humorous in places. You be the judge.

Emotional Appeals

It is sometimes said that good argumentative writing appeals only to reason, never to emotion, and that any sort of emotional appeal is illegitimate, irrelevant. "Tears are not arguments," the Brazilian writer Machado de Assis said. Logic textbooks may even stigmatize with Latin labels the various sorts of emotional appeal—for instance, *argumentum ad populum* (appeal to the prejudices of the mob, as in "Come on, we all know that schools don't teach anything anymore") and *argumentum ad misericordiam* (appeal to pity, as in "No one ought to blame this poor kid for stabbing a classmate because his mother was often institutionalized for alcoholism and his father beat him").

True, appeals to emotion may get in the way of the facts of the case; they may blind the audience by, in effect, throwing dust in its eyes or by stimulating tears.

Learning from Shakespeare   A classic example is found in Shakespeare's *Julius Caesar,* when Marc Antony addresses the Roman populace after Brutus, Cassius, and others have assassinated Caesar. The real issue is whether Caesar was becoming tyrannical (as the assassins claim) and would therefore curtail the freedom of the people. Antony turns from the evidence and stirs the mob against the assassins by appealing to its emotions. In the ancient Roman biographical writing that Shakespeare drew on, Sir Thomas North's translation of Plutarch's *Lives of the Noble Grecians and Romans,* Plutarch says that Antony,

> perceiving that his words moved the common people to compassion, . . . framed his eloquence to make their hearts yearn [that is, grieve] the more, and, taking Caesar's gown all bloody in his hand, he laid it open to the sight of them all, showing what a number of cuts and holes it had upon it. Therewithal the people fell presently into such a rage and mutiny that there was no more order kept.

Here are a few extracts from Antony's speeches in Shakespeare's play. Antony begins by asserting that he will speak only briefly:

> Friends, Romans, countrymen, lend me your ears;
> I come to bury Caesar, not to praise him.

After briefly offering some rather insubstantial evidence that Caesar gave no signs of behaving tyrannically (for example, "When that the poor have cried, Caesar hath wept"), Antony begins to play directly on the emotions of his hearers. Descending from the platform so that he may be in closer contact with his audience (like a modern politician, he wants to work the crowd), he calls attention to Caesar's bloody toga:

> If you have tears, prepare to shed them now.
> You all do know this mantle; I remember
> The first time ever Caesar put it on:
> 'Twas on a summer's evening, in his tent,
> That day he overcame the Nervii.
> Look, in this place ran Cassius' dagger through;
> See what a rent the envious Casca made;
> Through this, the well-belovèd Brutus stabbed. . . .

In these few lines Antony

- first prepares the audience by suggesting to them how they should respond ("If you have tears, prepare to shed them now"),

- then flatters them by implying that they, like Antony, were intimates of Caesar (he credits them with being familiar with Caesar's garment),

- then evokes a personal memory of a specific time ("a summer's evening")—not just any old specific time but a very important one, the day that Caesar won a battle against the Nervii (a particularly fierce tribe in what is now France).

In fact, Antony was not at the battle, and he did not join Caesar until three years later.

Antony does not mind being free with the facts; his point here is not to set the record straight but to stir the mob against the assassins. He goes on, daringly but successfully, to identify one particular slit in the garment with Cassius's dagger, another with Casca's, and a third with Brutus's. Antony cannot know which slit was made by which dagger, but his rhetorical trick works.

Notice, too, that Antony arranges the three assassins in climactic order, since Brutus (Antony claims) was especially beloved by Caesar:

> Judge, O you gods, how dearly Caesar loved him!
> This was the most unkindest cut of all;
> For when the noble Caesar saw him stab,
> Ingratitude, more strong than traitor's arms,
> Quite vanquished him. Then burst his mighty heart. . . .

Nice. According to Antony, the noble-minded Caesar—Antony's words have erased all thought of the tyrannical Caesar—died not from the wounds inflicted by daggers but from the heartbreaking perception of Brutus's ingratitude. Doubtless there was not a dry eye in the house. We can all hope that if we are ever put on trial, we have a lawyer as skilled in evoking sympathy as Antony.

Are Emotional Appeals Fallacious?   The oration is obviously successful in the play and apparently was successful in real life, but it is the sort of speech that prompts logicians to write disapprovingly of attempts to stir feeling in an audience. (As mentioned earlier in this chapter, the evocation of emotion in an audience is called *pathos,* from the Greek word for "emotion" or "suffering.") There is nothing inherently wrong in stimulating our audience's emotions when attempting to establish a claim, but when an emotional appeal confuses the issue that is being argued about or shifts the attention away from the facts of the issue, we can reasonably speak of the fallacy of emotional appeal.

No fallacy is involved, however, when an emotional appeal heightens the facts, bringing them home to the audience rather than masking them. If we are talking about legislation that would govern police actions, it is legitimate to show a photograph of the battered, bloodied face of an alleged victim of police brutality. True, such a photograph cannot tell the whole truth; it cannot tell us if the subject threatened the officer with a gun or repeatedly resisted an order to surrender. But it can tell us that the victim was severely beaten and (like a comparable description in words) evoke in us emotions that may properly enter into our decision about the permissible use of police evidence. Similarly, an animal rights activist who is arguing that calves are cruelly confined might reasonably tell us about the size of the pen in which the beast—unable to turn around or even to lie down—is kept. Others may argue that calves don't much care about turning around or have no right to turn around, but the verbal description, which unquestionably makes an emotional appeal, can hardly be called fallacious or irrelevant.

In appealing to emotions then, the important things are

- not to falsify (especially by oversimplifying) the issue,
- not to distract attention from the facts of the case,
- to think ethically about how emotions may affect the audience.

Focus on the facts and concentrate on offering reasons (essentially, statements linked with "because"), but you may also legitimately bring the facts home to your readers by seeking to induce in them the appropriate emotions. Your words will be fallacious only if you stimulate emotions that are not rightly connected with the facts of the case.

DOES ALL WRITING CONTAIN ARGUMENTS?

Our answer to the question we have just posed is no—but probably *most* writing *does* contain an argument of sorts. Or put it this way: The writer wants to persuade the reader to see things the way the writer sees them—at least until the end of the essay. After all, even a recipe for a cherry pie in a food magazine—a piece of writing that is primarily expository (how to do it) rather than argumentative (how a reasonable person ought to think about this topic)—probably includes, near the beginning, a sentence with a hint of an argument in it, such as "*Because* [a sign that a *reason* will be offered] this pie can be made quickly and with ingredients (canned cherries) that are always available, give it a try, and it will surely become one of your favorites." Clearly, such a statement cannot stand as a formal argument—a discussion that takes account of possible counterarguments, that relies chiefly on logic and little if at all on emotional appeal, and that draws a conclusion that seems irrefutable.

Still, the statement is something of an argument on behalf of making a pie with canned cherries. In this case, a claim is made (the pie will become a favorite), and two *reasons* are offered in support of this claim:

- It can be made quickly, and
- the chief ingredient—because it is canned—can always be at hand.

The underlying *assumptions* are

- You don't have a great deal of time to waste in the kitchen.
- Canned cherries are just as tasty as fresh cherries—and even if they aren't, well, you wouldn't know the difference.

When we read a lead-in to a recipe, then, we won't find a formal argument, but we probably will get a few words that seek to persuade us to keep reading. And most writing does contain such material—sentences that give us a reason to keep reading, that engage our interests, and that make us want to stay with the writer for at least a little longer. If the recipe happens to be difficult and time-consuming, the lead-in may say,

> Although this recipe for a cherry pie, using fresh cherries that you will have to pit, is a bit more time-consuming than the usual recipe that calls for canned cherries, once you have tasted it you will never go back to canned cherries.

Again, although the logic is scarcely compelling, the persuasive element is evident. The assumption here is that you have a discriminating palate; once you have tasted a pie made with fresh cherries,

---

✓   A CHECKLIST FOR ANALYZING AN ARGUMENT

NOTE: See also Chapter 11, A Rhetorician's View, pages 371–88.

☐ What is the writer's claim or thesis? Ask yourself:
  ☐ What claim is being asserted?
  ☐ What evidence is imagined?
  ☐ What assumptions are being made—and are they acceptable?
  ☐ Are important terms satisfactorily defined?

☐ What support (evidence) is offered on behalf of the claim? Ask yourself:
  ☐ Are the examples relevant, and are they convincing?
  ☐ Are the statistics (if any) relevant, accurate, and complete? Do they allow only the interpretation that is offered in the argument?
  ☐ If authorities are cited, are they indeed authorities on this topic, and can they be regarded as impartial?
  ☐ Is the logic—deductive and inductive—valid?
  ☐ If there is an appeal to emotion—for instance, if satire is used to ridicule the opposing view—is this appeal acceptable?

☐ Does the writer seem to you to be fair? Ask yourself:
  ☐ Are counterarguments adequately considered?
  ☐ Is there any evidence of dishonesty or of a discreditable attempt to manipulate the reader?
  ☐ How does the writer establish the image of himself or herself that we sense in the essay? What is the writer's tone, and is it appropriate?

---

you will never again enjoy the canned stuff. The writer is not giving us a formal argument, with abundant evidence and with a detailed refutation of counterarguments, but we do know where the writer stands and how the writer wishes us to respond.

In short, almost all writers are trying to persuade readers to see things *their* way.

AN EXAMPLE: AN ARGUMENT AND A LOOK AT THE WRITER'S STRATEGIES

This essay concerns President George W. Bush's proposal that drilling be allowed in part of the Arctic National Wildlife Refuge (ANWR, pronounced "An-war"). The section of the ANWR that is proposed for drilling is called the "1002 area," as defined by Section 1002 of the Alaska National Interest Lands Conservation Act of 1980. In March 2003, the Senate rejected the Bush proposal, but the issue remains alive.

We follow George F. Will's essay with some comments about the ways in which he constructs his argument.

George F. Will

George F. Will (b. 1941), a syndicated columnist whose writing appears in 460 newspapers, was born in Champaign, Illinois, and educated at Trinity College (Hartford), Oxford University, and Princeton University. Will has served as the Washington, D.C., editor of the National Review *and now writes a regular column for* Newsweek. *His essays have been collected in several books.*

This essay was originally published in 2002, and therefore it is in some respects dated—for instance in its reference to the price of gasoline—but we think you can still learn from it a great deal about certain ways to argue.

Being Green at Ben and Jerry's

Some Environmental Policies Are Feel-Good Indulgences for an Era of Energy Abundance

If you have an average-size dinner table, four feet by six feet, put a dime on the edge of it. Think of the surface of the table as the Arctic National Wildlife Refuge in Alaska. The dime is larger than the piece of the coastal plain that would have been opened to drilling for oil and natural gas. The House of Representatives voted for drilling, but the Senate voted against access to what Sen. John Kerry, Massachusetts Democrat and presidential aspirant, calls "a few drops of oil." ANWR could produce, for twenty-five years, at least as much oil as America currently imports from Saudi Arabia.

Six weeks of desultory Senate debate about the energy bill reached an almost comic culmination in . . . yet another agriculture subsidy. The subsidy is a requirement that will triple the amount of ethanol, which is made from corn, that must be put in gasoline, ostensibly to clean America's air, actually to buy farmers' votes.

Over the last three decades, energy use has risen about 30 percent. But so has population, which means per capita energy use is unchanged. And per capita GDP has risen substantially, so we are using 40 percent less energy per dollar output. Which is one reason there is no energy crisis, at least none as most Americans understand such things—a shortage of, and therefore high prices of, gasoline for cars, heating oil for furnaces and electricity for air conditioners.

In the absence of a crisis to concentrate the attention of the inattentive American majority, an intense faction—full-time environmentalists—goes to work. Spencer Abraham, the secretary of Energy, says "the previous administration . . . simply drew up a list of fuels it *didn't* like—nuclear energy, coal, hydropower, and oil—which together account for 73 percent of America's energy supply." Well, there are always windmills.

Sometimes lofty environmentalism is a cover for crude poli- 5 tics. The United States has the world's largest proven reserves of coal. But Mike Oliver, a retired physicist and engineer, and John Hospers, professor emeritus of philosophy at USC, note that in 1996 President Clinton put 68 billion tons of America's cleanest-burning coal, located in Utah, off-limits for mining, ostensibly for environmental reasons. If every existing U.S. electric power plant burned coal, the 68 billion tons could fuel them for forty-five years at the current rate of consumption. Now power companies must import clean-burning coal, some from mines owned by Indonesia's Lippo Group, the heavy contributor to Clinton, whose decision about Utah's coal vastly increased the value of Lippo's coal.

The United States has just 2.14 percent of the world's proven reserves of oil, so some people say it is pointless to drill in places like ANWR because "energy independence" is a chimera. Indeed it is. But domestic supplies can provide important insurance against uncertain foreign supplies. And domestic supplies can mean exporting hundreds of billions of dollars less to oil-producing nations, such as Iraq.

Besides, when considering proven reserves, note the adjective. In 1930 the United States had proven reserves of 13 billion barrels. We then fought the Second World War and fueled the most fabulous economic expansion in human history, including the electricity-driven "New Economy." (Manufacturing and running computers consume 15 percent of U.S. electricity. Internet use alone accounts for half of the growth in demand for electricity.) So by 1990 proven reserves were . . . 17 billion barrels, not counting any in Alaska or Hawaii.

In 1975 proven reserves in the Persian Gulf were 74 billion barrels. In 1993 they were 663 billion, a ninefold increase. At the current rate of consumption, today's proven reserves would last 150 years. New discoveries will be made, some by vastly improved techniques of deep-water drilling. But environmental policies will define opportunities. The government estimates that beneath the U.S. outer continental shelf, which the government owns, there are at least 46 billion barrels of oil. But only 2 percent of the shelf has been leased for energy development.

Opponents of increased energy production usually argue for decreased consumption. But they flinch from conservation measures. A new $1 gasoline tax would dampen demand for gasoline, but it would stimulate demands for the heads of the tax increasers. After all, Americans get irritable when impersonal market forces add 25 cents to the cost of a gallon. Tougher fuel-efficiency requirements for vehicles would save a lot of energy. But who would save the legislators who passed those requirements? Beware the wrath of Americans who like to drive, and autoworkers who like to make cars that are large, heavy, and safer than the gasoline-sippers that environmentalists prefer.

Some environmentalism is a feel-good indulgence for an era 10 of energy abundance, which means an era of avoided choices. Or ignored choices—ignored because if acknowledged, they would not make the choosers feel good. Karl Zinsmeister, editor in chief of the *American Enterprise* magazine, imagines an oh-so-green environmentalist enjoying the most politically correct product on the planet—Ben & Jerry's ice cream. Made in a factory that depends on electricity-guzzling refrigeration, a gallon of ice cream requires four gallons of milk. While making that much milk, a cow produces eight gallons of manure, and flatulence with another eight gallons of methane, a potent "greenhouse" gas. And the cow consumes lots of water plus three pounds of grain and hay, which is produced with tractor fuel, chemical fertilizers, herbicides and insecticides, and is transported with truck or train fuel:

"So every time he digs into his Cherry Garcia, the conscientious environmentalist should visualize (in addition to world peace) a pile of grain, water, farm chemicals, and energy inputs much bigger than his ice cream bowl on one side of the table, and, on the other side of the table, a mound of manure eight times the size of his bowl, plus a balloon of methane that would barely fit under the dining room table."

Cherry Garcia. It's a choice. *Bon appétit.*

George F. Will's Strategies

Now let's look at Will's essay, to see some of the techniques that he uses, techniques that enable him to engage a reader's interest and perhaps enable him to convince the reader, or at least make the reader think, that Will probably is on to something.

We need hardly add that if you think some or all of his techniques—his methods, his strategies—are effective, you will consider adapting them for use in your own essays.

The title, "Being Green at Ben and Jerry's," does not at all prepare the reader for an argument about drilling in the National Arctic Wildlife Refuge, but if you have read any of Will's other columns in *Newsweek*, you probably know that he is conservative and that he will be poking some fun at the green folk—the environmentalists. Will can get away with using a title that is not focused because he has a body of loyal readers—people who will read him because they want to read him, whatever the topic is—but the rest of us writers have to give our readers some idea of what we will be talking about. In short, let your readers know early, perhaps in the title, where you will be taking them.

The subtitle, "Some Environmental Policies Are Feel-Good Indulgences for an Era of Energy Abundance," perhaps added by an editor of the magazine, does suggest that the piece will concern energy, and the words "feel-good indulgence" pretty clearly tell readers that Will believes the environmentalists are indulging themselves.

Paragraph 1 offers a striking comparison. Will wants us to believe that the area proposed for drilling is tiny, so he says that if we imagine the entire Arctic National Wildlife Refuge as a dinner table, the area proposed for drilling is the size of a dime. We think you will agree that this opening seizes a reader's attention. Assuming the truth of the figure—but there seems to be some dispute, since opponents have said that the area would be more like the size of a dinner plate—the image is highly effective. A dime is so small! And is worth so little! Still, one might ask (but probably

WILL / BEING GREEN AT BEN AND JERRY'S

one doesn't, because Will's figure is so striking) if the tininess of the area really is decisive. One might easily, and apparently with reason, dismiss as absurd the idea that a minuscule tsetse fly could kill a human being, or that the plague is spread by fleas that have bitten rats, because these proposals sound ridiculous—but they are true.

One other point about the first paragraph: Will's voice sounds like a voice you might hear in your living room: "If you have an average-size dinner table," "the dime is larger," "at least as much oil." Don't think that in your own essays you need to adopt a highly formal style. Your reader should think of you as serious but not solemn.

Will goes on to say that Senator John Kerry, an opponent of drilling and therefore on the side that Will opposes, dismisses the oil in the refuge as "a few drops." Will replies that it "could produce, for twenty-five years, at least as much oil as America currently imports from Saudi Arabia." Kerry's "a few drops" is, of course, not to be taken literally; he means, in effect, that the oil is a drop in the bucket. But when one looks into the issue, one finds that estimates by responsible sources vary considerably, from 3.2 billion barrels to 11.5 billion barrels.

Paragraph 2 dismisses the Senate's debate ("almost comic . . . actually to buy farmers' votes").

Paragraph 3 offers statistics to make the point that "there is no energy crisis." Here, as in the first paragraph (where he showed his awareness of Kerry's view), Will indicates that he is familiar with views other than his own. In arguing a case, it is important for the writer to let readers know that indeed there are other views—which the writer then goes on to show are less substantial than the writer's. Will is correct in saying that "per capita energy use is unchanged," but those on the other side might say, "Yes, per capita consumption has not increased, but given the population increase, the annual amount has vastly increased, which means that resources are being depleted and that pollution is increasing."

Paragraph 4 asserts again that there is no energy crisis, pokes fun at "full-time environmentalists" (perhaps there is a suggestion that such people really ought to get a respectable job), and ends with a bit of whimsy: These folks probably think we should go back to using windmills.

Paragraph 5, in support of the assertion that "Sometimes lofty environmentalism is a cover for crude politics," cites an authority (often an effective technique), and, since readers are not likely to recognize the name, it also identifies him ("professor emeritus of philosophy at USC"), and it then offers further statistics (again effective). The paragraph begins by talking about "crude politics" and ends with the assertion that "Now power companies must import clean-burning coal, some from mines owned by Indonesia's Lippo Group, the heavy contributor to Clinton." In short, Will does what he can to suggest that the views of at least some environmentalists are rooted in money and politics.

Paragraph 6 offers another statistic ("The United States has just 2.14 percent of the world's proven reserves of oil"), and he turns it against those who argue that therefore it is pointless for us to drill in Alaska. In effect, Will is replying to people like Senator Kerry who say that the Arctic refuge provides only "a few drops of oil." The point, Will suggests, is not that we can't achieve independence; the point is that "domestic supplies can provide important insurance against uncertain foreign supplies."

Paragraph 7 begins nicely with a transition, "Besides," and then offers additional statistics concerning the large amount of oil that we have. It was, for instance, enough to fuel "the most fabulous economic expansion in human history."

Paragraph 8 offers additional statistics, first about "proven reserves" in the Persian Gulf and then about an estimate—but it is only an estimate—of oil "beneath the U.S. outer continental shelf." We are not certain of Will's point, but in any case the statistics suggest to a reader that the author has done his homework.

Paragraph 9 summarizes the chief position (as Will sees it) of those on the other side: They usually argue for decreased consumption, but they are afraid to argue for the sort of tax on gasoline that might indeed decrease consumption because they know that many Americans want to drive large, heavy cars. Further, the larger, heavier cars that the environmentalists object to are in fact "safer than the gasoline-sippers that environmentalists prefer."

Paragraph 10 uses the term "feel-good indulgence," which is also found in the subtitle of the essay, and now, in the third sentence of the paragraph, we hear again of Ben and Jerry, who have not been in our minds since the title of the essay, "Being Green at Ben and Jerry's." Perhaps we have been wondering all this while why Ben and Jerry are in the title. Almost surely the reader knows that Ben and Jerry are associated with ice cream and therefore with cows and meadows, and probably many readers know, at least vaguely, that Ben and Jerry are somehow associated with environmentalism and with other causes often thought to be on the left.

Will (drawing on an article by Karl Zinsmeister, editor of the *American Enterprise*) writes what we consider an extremely amusing paragraph in which he points out that the process of making ice cream "depends on electricity-guzzling refrigeration" and that the cows are, so to speak, supported by fuel that transports fertilizers, herbicides, and insecticides. Further, in the course of producing the four gallons of milk that are required for one gallon of ice cream, the cows themselves—those darlings of environmentalists—contribute "eight gallons of manure, and flatulence with another eight gallons of methane, a potent 'greenhouse' gas." As we see when we read Will's next paragraph, the present paragraph is in large measure a lead-in for the following quotation. Will knows it is is not enough to give a quotation; a writer has to make use of the quotation—has to lead in to it or, after quoting, has to comment on it, or do both.

Paragraph 11 is entirely devoted to quoting Zinsmeister, who imagines an environmentalist digging into a dish of one of Ben and Jerry's most popular flavors, Cherry Garcia. We are invited to see the bowl of ice cream on one side of the table—here Will effectively evokes the table of his first paragraph—and a pile of manure on the other side, "plus a balloon of methane that would barely fit under the dining room table." Vulgar, no doubt, but funny too. George Will knows that humor as well as logic (and statistics and other kinds of evidence) can be among the tools a writer uses in getting an audience to accept or at least to consider an argument.

Paragraph 12 consists of three short sentences, adding up to less than a single line of type: "Cherry Garcia. It's a choice. *Bon appétit.*" None of the sentences mentions oil or the Arctic Refuge or statistics, and therefore this ending might seem utterly irrelevant to the topic, but we think Will is very effectively saying, "Sure, you have a choice about drilling in the Arctic Refuge; any sensible person will choose the ice cream (drilling) rather than the manure and the gas (not drilling)."

Topics for Critical Thinking and Writing

1. What, if anything, makes Will's essay interesting? What, if anything, makes it highly persuasive? How might it be made more persuasive?

2. In paragraph 10, Will clowns a bit about the gas that cows emit, but apparently this gas, which contributes to global warming, is no

laughing matter. The government of New Zealand, in an effort to reduce livestock emissions of methane and nitrous oxide, proposed a tax that would subsidize future research on the emissions. The tax would cost the average farmer $300 a year. Imagine that you are a New Zealand farmer. Write a letter to your representative, arguing for or against the tax.

3. Senator Barbara Boxer, campaigning against the proposal to drill in ANWR, spoke of the refuge as "God's gift to us" (*New York Times*, March 20, 2002). How strong an argument is she offering? Some opponents of drilling have said that drilling in ANWR is as unthinkable as drilling in Yosemite or the Grand Canyon. Again, how strong is this argument? Can you imagine circumstances in which you would support drilling in these places? Do we have a moral duty to preserve certain unspoiled areas?

4. The Inupiat (Eskimo) who live in and near ANWR by a large majority favor drilling, seeing it as a source of jobs and a source of funding for schools, hospitals, and police. But the Ketchikan Indians, who speak of themselves as the "Caribou People," see drilling as a threat to the herds that they depend on for food and hides. How does one balance the conflicting needs of these two groups?

5. Opponents of drilling in ANWR argue that over its lifetime of fifty years, the area would produce less than 1 percent of the fuel we need during the period and that therefore we should not risk disturbing the area. Further, they argue that drilling in ANWR is an attempt at a quick fix to U.S. energy needs, whereas what is needed are sustainable solutions, such as the development of renewable energy sources (e.g., wind and sun) and fuel-efficient automobiles. How convincing do you find these arguments?

6. Proponents of drilling include a large majority—something like 75 percent—of the people of Alaska, including its governor and its two senators. How much attention should be paid to their voices?

7. Analyze the essay in terms of its use of *ethos*, *pathos*, and *logos*.

8. What sort of audience do you think Will is addressing? What values do his readers probably share? What makes you think so?

4

Visual Rhetoric: Images as Arguments

A picture is worth a thousand words.

—PROVERB

"What is the use of a book," thought Alice, "without pictures or conversations?"

—LEWIS CARROLL

SOME USES OF IMAGES

Most visual materials that accompany written arguments serve one of two functions—they appeal to the emotions (e.g., a photograph of a calf in a pen so narrow that the calf cannot turn, in an essay on animal liberation) or they clarify numerical data (e.g., a graph showing five decades of male and female law school enrollments). There are of course additional uses for pictures, for example, cartoons may add a welcome touch of humor or satire, but in this chapter we concentrate on appeals to emotion and briefly on graphs and related images.

APPEALS TO THE EYE

We began the preceding chapter by distinguishing between *argument,* which we said relies on reason (*logos*), and *persuasion,* which we said is a broad term that can include appeals to the emotions (*pathos*) — for example, an appeal to pity. Threats, too, can be persuasive. As Al Capone famously said, "You can get a lot more done with a kind word and a gun than with a kind word alone." Indeed, most of the remarks that we can think of link persuasion not with the power of reason but with the power of emotional appeals, of flattery, of threats, and of appeals to self-interest. We have in mind passages spoken not only by the likes of the racketeer Al Capone, but by more significant figures. Consider these two remarks, which both use the word *interest* in the sense of "self-interest":

> Would you persuade, speak of Interest, not Reason.
> —Ben Franklin

> There are two levers for moving men—interest and fear.
> —Napoleon Bonaparte

An appeal to self-interest is obviously at the heart of most advertisements: "Buy *X* automobile, and members of the opposite sex will find you irresistible," "Use *Y* instant soup, and your family will love you more," "Try *Z* cereal and enjoy regularity." We will look at advertisements later in this chapter, but first let's talk a bit more about the use and abuse of visual material in persuasion.

When we discussed the appeal to emotion (p. 103), we quoted from Mark Antony's speech to the Roman populace in Shakespeare's *Julius Caesar.* You will recall that Antony stirred the mob by displaying Caesar's blood-stained mantle, that is, by supplementing his words with visual material:

> Look, in this place ran Cassius' dagger through;
> See what a rent the envious Casca made;
> Through this, the well-belovèd Brutus stabbed. . . .

In courtrooms today, trial lawyers and prosecutors still do this sort of thing when

- they exhibit photos of a bloody corpse, or
- they introduce as witnesses small children who sob as they describe the murder of their parents.

The appeal clearly is not to reason but to the jurors' emotions—and yet, can we confidently say that this sort of visual evidence—this attempt to stir anger at the alleged perpetrator of the crime and pity for the victims—is irrelevant? Why shouldn't jurors vicariously experience the assault?

Martin Luther King Jr. delivering his "I Have a Dream" speech on August 28, 1963, from the steps of the Lincoln Memorial. The visual aspects—the setting (the Lincoln Memorial with the Washington Monument and the Capitol in the distance) and King's gestures—are part of the persuasive rhetoric of the speech.

When we think about it—and it takes only a moment of thinking—the appeal in the courtroom to the eye and then to the heart or mind is evident even in smaller things, such as the clothing that the lawyers wear and the clothing that they advise their clients to wear. To take the most obvious, classic example: The mugger who normally wears jeans, a T-shirt, and a leather jacket appears in court in a three-piece suit, dress shirt, and necktie. Lawyers know that in arguing a case, visuals make statements—perhaps not logical arguments but nevertheless meaningful statements that will attract or repel jurors.

Another sort of visual appeal connected with some arguments should be mentioned briefly—the visual appeal of the specific setting in which the argument occurs. Martin Luther King Jr.'s great speech of August 28, 1963, "I Have a Dream" (p. 119), still reads very well on the page, but part of its immense appeal when it was first given

(Edvard Munch, *The Scream.* © 2007 The Munch Museum/ The Munch-Ellingsen Group/Artists Rights Society [ARS], NY. Digital Image ©/The Museum of Modern Art, NY. Licensed by SCALA/Art Resource. Reproduction, including downloading, of Munch works is prohibited by copyright laws and international conventions without the express written permission of Artists Rights Society [ARS], New York.)

Images played an important role in the activities of the antislavery movement in the nineteenth century. On the top left is a diagram that shows how human cargo was packed into a slave ship; it was distributed with Thomas Clarkson's *Essay on the Slavery and Commerce of the Human Species* (1804). On the top right is Frederick W. Mercer's photograph (April 2, 1863) of Gordon, a "badly lacerated" runaway slave. Images such as the slave ship and Gordon were used against the claims of slaveowners that slavery was a humane institution—claims that also were supported by illustrations, such as the woodcut at the bottom, titled *Attention Paid to a Poor Sick Negro, from Josiah Priest's In Defense of Slavery* (1843).

was due to its setting: King spoke to some 200,000 people in Washington, D.C., as he stood on the steps of the Lincoln Memorial. That setting, rich with associations of slavery and of freedom, was part of King's argument.

Pictures—and here we get to our chief subject—are also sometimes used as parts of arguments because pictures make statements.
Some pictures, like Edvard Munch's *The Scream* (p. 120), make obvious statements: The swiftly receding diagonal lines of the fence and
the walkway, the wavy sky, and the vibrating vertical lines to the
right of the figure all convey the great agitation experienced by the
figure in the woodcut.

Some pictures, like the photographs shown to members of
Congress during the debate over whether permission should be
given to drill in the Arctic National Wildlife Refuge are a bit less
obvious:

- *Opponents* of drilling showed beautiful pictures of polar bears
  frolicking, wildflowers in bloom, and caribou on the move.

- *Proponents* of drilling showed bleak pictures of what they
  called "barren land" and "a frozen wasteland."

Both sides knew very well that images are powerful persuaders,
and they did not hesitate to use images as supplements to words.

We again invite you to think about the appropriateness of
using images in arguments. Should argument be entirely a matter
of reason, of logic (*logos*), without appeals to the emotions (*pathos*)?
Or can images of the sort that we have already mentioned provide
visual (and emotional) support for reasons that are offered? The
statement that "the Arctic National Wildlife Refuge is a home for
abundant wildlife, notably polar bears, caribou, and wildflowers"
may not mean much until it is reinforced with breathtaking images.
(And, similarly, the statement that "most of the ANWR land is barren" may not mean much until it is corroborated by images of the
vast bleakness.)

> **A RULE FOR WRITERS:** If you think that pictures will help you to make
> the point you are arguing, include them with captions explaining
> sources and relevance.

ARE SOME IMAGES NOT FIT TO BE SHOWN?

Images of suffering—human or, as animal rights activists have
made us see, animal—can be immensely persuasive. In the nineteenth century, for instance, the antislavery movement made

extremely effective use of images in its campaign. We reproduce two antislavery images here, as well as a counterimage that sought to assure viewers that slavery is a beneficent system (p. 121). But are there some images not fit to print?

Until recently, many newspapers did not print pictures of lynched African Americans, hanged and burned and maimed. The reasons for not printing such images probably differed in the South and North: Southern papers may have considered the images to be discreditable to whites, while Northern papers may have deemed the images too revolting. Even today, when it is commonplace to see in newspapers and on television screens pictures of dead victims of war, or famine, or traffic accidents, one rarely sees bodies that are horribly maimed. (For traffic accidents, the body is usually covered, and we see only the smashed car.) The U.S. government has refused to release photographs showing the bodies of American soldiers killed in the war in Iraq, and it has been most reluctant to show pictures of dead Iraqi soldiers and civilians. Only after many Iraqis refused to believe that Saddam Hussein's two sons had been killed did the U.S. government reluctantly release pictures showing

Huynh Cong (Nick) Ut, *The Terror of War: Children on Route 1 near Trang Bang*

Eddie Adams, *Execution of Viet Cong prisoner, Saigon,* 1968

the blood-spattered faces of the two men—and some American newspapers and television programs refused to use the images.

There have been notable exceptions to this practice, such as Huynh Cong (Nick) Ut's 1972 photograph of children fleeing a napalm attack in Vietnam (p. 123), which was widely reproduced in the United States and won the photographer a Pulitzer Prize in 1973. The influence of this particular photograph cannot be measured, but it is widely felt to have played a substantial role in increasing public pressure to end the Vietnam War. Another widely reproduced picture of horrifying violence is Eddie Adams's picture (1968, above) of a South Vietnamese chief of police firing a pistol into the head of a Viet Cong prisoner.

The issue remains: Are some images unacceptable? For instance, although capital punishment is legal in parts of the United States—by methods including lethal injection, hanging, shooting, and electrocution—every state in the Union prohibits the publication of pictures showing a criminal being executed. (On this topic, see Wendy Lesser, *Pictures at an Execution* [1993].)

The most famous recent example of an image widely thought to be unprintable concerns the murder of Daniel Pearl, a Jewish reporter for the *Wall Street Journal.* Pearl was captured and murdered in June 2002 by Islamic terrorists in Pakistan. His killers videotaped Pearl reading a statement denouncing American policy and being decapitated. The video also shows a man's arm holding Pearl's head. The video ends with the killers making demands (such as the release of the Muslim prisoners being held by the United States in Guantánamo Bay, Cuba) and asserting that "if our demands are not met, this scene will be repeated again and again."

The chief arguments against reproducing in newspapers material from this video were that

- the video and even still images from it are unbearably gruesome;
- showing the video would traumatize the Pearl family; and
- the video is propaganda by an enemy.

Those who favored broadcasting the video on television and printing still images from it in newspapers tended to argue that

- the photo will show the world what sort of enemy the United States is fighting;
- newspapers have published pictures of other terrifying sights (notably, people leaping out of windows of New York's twin towers and endless pictures of the space shuttle *Challenger* exploding); and
- no one was worried about protecting the families of these other victims from seeing painful images.

But ask yourself if the comparison of the Daniel Pearl video to the photos of the twin towers and of the *Challenger* is valid. You may respond that the individuals in the twin towers pictures are not specifically identifiable and that the images of the *Challenger*, though horrifying, are not as visually revolting as the picture of a severed head held up for view.

The *Boston Phoenix,* a weekly newspaper, published some images from the Daniel Pearl video and also put a link to the video (with a warning that the footage is "extremely graphic") on its Web site. The editor of the *Phoenix* justified publication on the three grounds we list. Pearl's wife, Mariane Pearl, was quoted in various newspapers as condemning the "heartless decision to air this despicable video," and a spokeswoman for the Pearl family, when asked for comment, referred reporters to a statement issued earlier, which said that broadcasters who show the video

> fall without shame into the terrorists' plan. . . . Danny believed that journalism was a tool to report the truth and foster

understanding—not perpetuate propaganda and sensationalize tragedy. We had hoped that no part of this tape would ever see the light of day. . . . We urge all networks and news outlets to exercise responsibility and not aid the terrorists in spreading their message of hate and murder.[1]

Although some journalists expressed regret that Pearl's family was distressed, they insisted that journalists have a right to reproduce such material and that the images can serve the valuable purpose of shocking viewers into awareness.

Politics and Pictures

Consider, too, the controversy that erupted in 1991, during the Persian Gulf War, when the U.S. government decided that newspapers would not be allowed to photograph coffins returning with the bodies of military personnel killed during the war. In later years the policy was sometimes ignored, but in 2003 the George W. Bush administration decreed that there would be "no arrival ceremony for, or media coverage of, deceased military personnel returning [from Iraq or Afghanistan] . . . to the Dover (Delaware) base." The government enforced the policy strictly.

Members of the news media strongly protested, as did many others, chiefly arguing that

- The administration was trying to sanitize the war, i.e., was depriving the public of important information—images—that showed the real cost of the war.

- Grief for the deaths of military personnel is not a matter only for the families of the deceased. The sacrifices were made for the nation, and the nation should be allowed to grieve. Canada and Britain have no such ban, and when the coffins are transported the public lines the streets to pay honor to the fallen warriors. In fact, in Canada a portion of the highway near the Canadian base has been renamed, "Highway of Heroes."

- The coffins at Dover Air Force base are not identified by name, so there is no issue about intruding on the privacy of grieving families.

---

[1]Quoted in the *Hartford Courant,* June 5, 2002, and reproduced on the Internet by the Freedom of Information Center, under the heading "Boston Paper Creates Controversy."

Coffins at Dover Air Force Base, Delaware

The chief arguments in defense of the ban were

- Photographs violate the privacy of the families.
- If the arrival of the coffins at Dover is given publicity, some grieving families will think they should go to Dover to be present when the bodies arrive, and this may cause a financial hardship on the families.

Alexander Gardner, *Home of a Rebel Sharpshooter*

- If the families give their consent, the press is *not* barred from individual graveside ceremonies at hometown burials. The ban extends only to the arrival of the coffins at Dover Air Force Base.

In February 2009, President Obama changed the policy and permitted coverage of the transfer of bodily remains. In his Address to the Joint Session of Congress, February 24, 2009, he said, "For seven years we have been a nation at war. No longer will we hide its price." On February 27, Defense Secretary Robert M. Gates announced that the government ban was lifted and that families will decide whether to allow photographs and videos of the "dignified transfer process at Dover."

EXERCISE

In an argumentative essay of about 250 words—perhaps two or three paragraphs—give your view of the issue of permitting photos of military coffins. In an opening paragraph you may want to explain the issue, and in this same paragraph you may want to summarize the arguments that you reject. The second (and perhaps final) paragraph of a two-paragraph essay may give the reasons you reject those arguments. Additionally, you may want to devote a third paragraph to a more general reflection.

TOPIC FOR CRITICAL THINKING AND WRITING

Marvin Kalb, a distinguished journalist, was quoted as saying that the public has a right to see the tape of Daniel Pearl's murder but that "common sense, decency, [and] humanity would encourage editors . . . to say 'no, it is not necessary to put this out.' There is no urgent demand on the part of the American people to see Daniel Pearl's death." What is your view?

Query In June 2006 two American soldiers were captured in Iraq. Later their bodies were found, dismembered and beheaded. Should newspapers have shown photographs of the mutilated bodies? Why, or why not? (In July 2006, insurgents in Iraq posted images on the Internet, showing a soldier's severed head beside his body.)

Another issue concerning the appropriateness or inappropriateness of showing images occurred early in 2006. In September 2005 a Danish newspaper, accused of being afraid to show political cartoons that were hostile to Muslim terrorists, responded by publishing twelve cartoons. One cartoon, for instance, showed the Prophet Muhammad wearing a turban that looked like a bomb. The images at first did not arouse much attention, but when in January 2006 they were reprinted in Norway, they attracted worldwide attention and outraged Muslims, most of whom regard any depiction of the Prophet as blasphemous. The upshot is that some Muslims in various Islamic nations burned Danish embassies and engaged in other acts of violence. Most non-Muslims agreed that the images were in bad taste, and apparently in deference to Islamic sensibilities (but possibly also out of fear of reprisals) very few Western newspapers reprinted the cartoons when they covered the news events. Most newspapers (including the *New York Times*) were content merely to describe the images. These papers believed that readers had to be told the news but because the drawings were so offensive to some persons they should be described rather than reprinted. A controversy then arose: Do readers of a newspaper deserve to *see* the evidence for themselves, or can a newspaper adequately fulfill its function by offering only a verbal description?

Persons who argued that the images should be reproduced generally made these points:

- Newspapers should yield neither to the delicate sensibilities of some readers nor to threats of violence.

- Jews for the most part do not believe that God should be depicted (the prohibition against "graven images" is found in Exodus 20.3), but they raise no objections to such Christian images as Michelangelo's painting of God awakening Adam, depicted on the ceiling of the Sistine Chapel. Further, when Andres Serrano (a Christian) in 1989 exhibited a photograph of a small plastic crucifix submerged in urine, it outraged a wider public—several U.S. senators condemned it because the artist had received federal funds—but virtually all newspapers showed the image, and many even printed its title, *Piss Christ*. That is, the subject was judged to be newsworthy, and the fact that some viewers would regard the image as blasphemous was not considered highly relevant.

- We value freedom of speech, and newspapers should not be intimidated. When certain pictures are a matter of news, the pictures should be shown to readers.

On the other hand, opposing voices were heard:

- Newspapers should—must—recognize deep-seated religious beliefs. They should indeed report the news, but there is no reason to *show* images that some people regard as blasphemous. The images can be adequately *described* in words.

- The Jewish response to Christian images of God and even the tolerant Christian's response to Serrano's image of Christ immersed in urine are simply irrelevant to the issue of whether images of the Prophet Muhammad should be represented in a Western newspaper. Virtually all Muslims regard depictions of the Prophet as blasphemous, and that is what counts.

- Despite all the Western talk about freedom of the press, the press does *not* reproduce all images that become matters of news. For instance, news items about the sale of child pornography do not include images of the pornographic photos.

EXERCISES: THINKING ABOUT IMAGES

1. Does the display of the cartoons constitute an argument? If so, what is the conclusion, and what are the premises? If not, then

what sort of statement, if any, does publishing these cartoons constitute?

2. Hugh Hewitt, an evangelical Christian, offered a comparison to the cartoon of Muhammad with a bomblike turban. Suppose, he asked, an abortion clinic had been bombed by someone who said he was an Evangelical Christian. Would newspapers publish "a cartoon of Christ's crown of thorns transformed into sticks of TNT?" Do you think they would? If you were the editor of a paper, would you? Why, or why not?

3. One American newspaper, the *Boston Phoenix,* did not publish any of the cartoons "out of fear of retaliation from the international brotherhood of radical and bloodthirsty Islamists who seek to impose their will on those who do not believe as they do. . . . We could not in good conscience place the men and women who work at the *Phoenix* and its related companies in physical jeopardy." Evaluate this position.

READING ADVERTISEMENTS

Advertising is one of the most common forms of visual persuasion we encounter in everyday life. None of us is so unsophisticated these days as to believe everything we see in an ad, yet the influence of advertising in our culture is pervasive and subtle. Consider, for example, a much-reproduced poster sponsored by Gatorade and featuring Michael Jordan. Such an image costs an enormous amount to produce and disseminate, and nothing in it is left to chance. The photograph of Jordan is typical, his attitude simultaneously strained and graceful, his face exultant, as he performs the feat for which he is so well known and about which most of us could only dream. We are aware of a crowd watching him, but the people in this crowd appear tiny, blurred, and indistinct compared to the huge image in the foreground; the photograph, like the crowd, focuses solely on Jordan. He is a legend, an icon of American culture. He is dressed not in his Chicago Bulls uniform but in a USA jersey, connecting his act of gravity-defying athleticism with the entire nation and with our sense of patriotism. The red, white, and blue of the uniform strengthens this impression in the original color photograph of the advertisement.

What do we make of the verbal message boldly written along the left-hand margin of the poster, "Be like Mike"? We are certainly not foolish enough to believe that drinking Gatorade will enable us to perform like Michael Jordan on the basketball court.

But who among us wouldn't like to "Be like Mike" in some small way, to enjoy even a glancing association with his athletic grace and power—to say nothing of his fame, wealth, and sex appeal? Though the makers of Gatorade surely know we will not all rush out to buy their drink to improve our game, they are banking on the expectation that the association of their name with Jordan, and our memory of their logo in association with Jordan's picture, will create a positive impression of their product. If Mike drinks Gatorade—well, why shouldn't I give it a try? The good feelings and impressions created by the ad will, the advertisers hope, travel with us the next time we consider buying a sports drink.

As we discuss the power of advertising, it is appropriate to say a few words about the corporate logos that appear everywhere these days—on billboards, in newspapers and magazines, on television, on Web sites, and on T-shirts. It is useful to think of a logo as a sort of advertisement in shorthand. It is a single, usually simple, image that carries with it a world of associations and impressions. (The makers of Gatorade would certainly hope that we will be reminded of Michael Jordan and his slam dunk when we see their product name superimposed over the orange lightning bolt.)

Let's look at two additional advertisements, each of which relies almost entirely on an image rather than on words. The first, an ad for a TV comedy that made its debut in 2009 (p. 133), boldly gives the title of the show and the name of the network, but the most interesting words are in tiny print:

Funny. On so many levels.

These words flatter the readers, thus making the readers highly susceptible to the implicit message, "Look at this program." Why do we say the words are flattering? For three reasons:

- The small size of the type implies that the reader is not someone whose attention can be caught only by headlines.
- The pun on "levels" (physical levels, and levels of humor) is a witty way of telling us that the show offers not only the low comedy of physical actions but also the high comedy of witty talk—talk that, for instance, may involve puns.
- The two terse incomplete sentences assume that the sophisticated reader does not need to have things explained at length.

Funny. On so many levels.

modern family

abc

The picture itself is attractive, showing what seems to be a wide variety of people (though of course we are not shown any faces or bodies that in real life might cause us some uneasiness) posed in the style of a family portrait. Indeed, these wholesome figures, standing in affectionate poses, are all dressed in white (without any ketchup stains) and are neatly framed (except for the patriarch, at the extreme right) by a pair of seated youngsters whose legs dangle down from the levels. The modern family, we are told, is large and varied (this one includes a gay son and his partner, and their

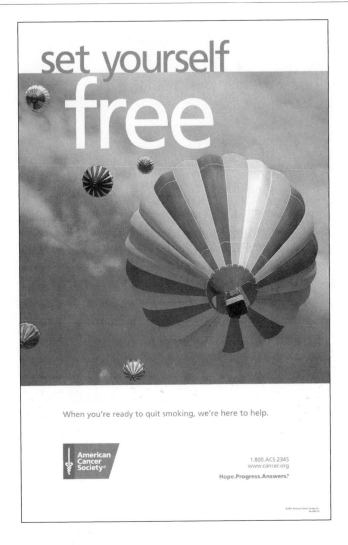

adopted Vietnamese baby), smart and warm. And best of all, it is "Funny. On so many levels."

The second ad (above) features two lines of text that are also short and sweet: "Set yourself free" and "When you're ready to quit smoking, we're here to help." The first of these lines—with "free" in large letters—is reinforced by the image of free-floating balloons, which in this context almost seem to be giant lungs. The implication is that once the viewer decides to quit smoking, the air will be purer, lungs will fully distend, and there will be a great sense of freedom; one

✓ A CHECKLIST FOR ANALYZING IMAGES
(ESPECIALLY ADVERTISEMENTS)

☐ What is the overall effect of the design? Colorful and busy (suggesting activity)? Quiet and understated (for instance, chiefly white and grays, with lots of empty space)? Old-fashioned or cutting edge?

☐ What about the image immediately gets your attention? Size? Position on the page? Beauty of the image? Grotesqueness of the image? Humor?

☐ Who is the audience for the image? Affluent young men? Housewives? Retired persons?

☐ What is the argument?

☐ Does the text make a rational appeal (*logos*) ("Tests at a leading university prove that . . . ," "If you believe X, you should vote 'No' on this referendum")?

☐ Does the image appeal to the emotions, to dearly held values (*pathos*)? Examples: Images of starving children or maltreated animals appeal to our sense of pity; images of military valor may appeal to our patriotism; images of luxury may appeal to our envy; images of sexually attractive people may appeal to our desire to be like them; images of violence or of extraordinary ugliness (as, for instance, in some ads showing a human fetus being destroyed) may seek to shock us.

☐ Does the image make an ethical appeal — that is, does it appeal to our character as a good human being (*ethos*)? Ads by charitable organizations often appeal to our sense of decency, fairness, and pity, but ads that appeal to our sense of prudence (ads for insurance companies or for investment houses) also essentially are making an ethical appeal.

☐ What is the relation of print to image? Does the image do most of the work, or does it serve to attract us and to lead us on to read the text?

will no longer be tied down in the way that an addiction to tobacco ties one down or restrains one's freedom. The second sentence, beneath the picture—on ground level, so to speak—assures the reader that when the addict is "ready to quit smoking, we're here to help." Who, after all, wouldn't want to be "set . . . free" (especially into the wonderful world of the floating balloons that soar in the tobacco-free air), and who wouldn't want the assurance that, if the experience is a bit risky, someone is there to help?

TOPICS FOR CRITICAL THINKING AND WRITING

1. Imagine that you work for a business that advertises in a publication such as *Time* or *Newsweek,* for instance, a vacation resort, a manufacturer of clothes, or an automaker. Design an advertisement: Describe the picture and write the text, and then, in an essay of 500 words, explain who your target audience is (college students? young couples about to buy their first home? retired persons?) and explain why you use the sorts of appeals (for instance, to reason, to the emotions, to a sense of humor) that you do.

2. It is often said that colleges, like businesses, are selling a product. Examine a brochure or catalog that is sent to prospective applicants to a college, and analyze the kinds of appeals that some of the images make.

WRITING ABOUT A POLITICAL CARTOON

Most editorial pages print political cartoons as well as editorials. Like the writers of editorials, cartoonists seek to persuade, but they rarely use words to *argue* a point. True, they may use a few words in speech balloons or in captions, but generally the drawing does most of the work. Because their aim usually is to convince the viewer that some person's action or proposal is ridiculous, cartoonists almost always **caricature** their subjects:

- They exaggerate the subject's distinctive features to the point where
- The subject becomes grotesque and ridiculous—absurd, laughable, contemptible.

True, it is scarcely fair to suggest that because, say, the politician who proposes such-and-such is short, fat, and bald his proposal is ridiculous, but that is the way cartoonists work. Further, cartoonists are concerned with producing a striking image, not with exploring an issue, so they almost always oversimplify, implying that there really is no other sane view.

In the course of saying that (a) the figures in the cartoon are ridiculous and *therefore* their ideas are contemptible, and (b) there is only one side to the issue, cartoonists often use **symbolism**, for instance:

- symbolic figures (Uncle Sam),
- animals (the Democratic donkey and the Republican elephant),
- buildings (the White House stands symbolically for the president of the United States),
- things (a bag with a dollar sign on it usually symbolizes a bribe).

For anyone brought up in our culture, these symbols (like the human figures who are represented) are obvious, and cartoonists assume that viewers will instantly recognize the symbols and figures, will get the joke, and will see the absurdity of whatever it is that the cartoonist is seeking to demolish.

In writing about the argument presented in a cartoon, normally you will discuss the ways in which the cartoon makes its point. Caricature, we have said, usually implies, "This is ridiculous, as you can

---

✔ **A CHECKLIST FOR EVALUATING AN ANALYSIS OF POLITICAL CARTOONS**

☐ Is a lead-in provided?

☐ Is a brief but accurate description of the drawing provided?

☐ Is the source of the cartoon cited (and perhaps commented on)?

☐ Is a brief report of the event or issue that the cartoon is dealing with and an explanation of all of the symbols included?

☐ Is there a statement of the cartoonist's claim (point, thesis)?

☐ Is there an analysis of the evidence, if any, that the image offers in support of the claim?

☐ Is there an analysis of the ways in which the content and style of the drawing help to convey the message?

☐ Is there adequate evaluation of the effectiveness of the drawing?

☐ Is there adequate evaluation of the effectiveness of the text (caption or speech balloons) and of the fairness of the cartoon?

IDEA PROMPT 4.1 ANALYSIS OF A POLITICAL CARTOON

Context	*Who is the artist? Where and when was it published?*	"This cartoon by Walt Handelsman was originally published in *Newsday* on September 12, 2009. Handelsman, a Pulitzer Prize–winning cartoonist, drew this cartoon in response to recent breaches of political decorum."
Description	*What does the cartoon look like?*	"It depicts a group of Washington, D.C., tourists being driven past what the guide calls 'The Museum of Modern American Political Discourse,' a building in the shape of a giant toilet."
Analysis	*How does the cartoon make its point? Is it effective?*	"The toilet as a symbol of the level of political discussion dominates the cartoon, effectively driving home the point that as Americans we are watching our leaders sink to new lows as they debate the future of our nation. Seen on a scale similar to familiar monuments in Washington, Handelsman may be in fact pointing out that today's politicians, rather than being remembered for great achievements like those of George Washington or Abraham Lincoln, will instead be remembered for their rudeness and aggression."

plainly see by the absurdity of the figures depicted" or "What *X*'s proposal adds up to, despite its apparent complexity, is nothing more than . . ." As we have already said, this sort of persuasion, chiefly by ridicule, probably is unfair: A funny-looking person *can offer* a thoughtful political proposal, and almost certainly the issue is more complicated than the cartoonist indicates. But this is largely the way cartoons work, by ridicule and by omitting counterarguments, and we should not reject the possibility that the cartoonist has indeed put his or her finger on the absurdity of the issue.

Probably your essay will include an *evaluation* of the cartoon; indeed, the *thesis* underlying your analytic/argumentative essay may be (for instance) that the cartoon is effective (persuasive) for such-and-such reasons, but it is also unfair for such-and-such reasons.

In analyzing the cartoon—in grasping the attitude of the cartoonist—consider such things as

- the relative size of the figures in the image;
- the quality of the lines—thin and spidery, or thick and seemingly aggressive;
- the amount of empty space in comparison with the amount of heavily inked space (a drawing with lots of inky areas will convey a more oppressive sense than a drawing that is largely open);
- the degree to which text is important, and what the text says—is it witty? Heavy-handed?

Caution: If your instructor lets you choose a cartoon, be sure to choose one with sufficient complexity to make the exercise worthwhile. (See also Idea Prompt 4.1.)

Let's look at an example. Jackson Smith wrote this essay in a composition course at Tufts University.

Jackson Smith

Pledging Nothing?

(Student Essay)

Gary Markstein's cartoon about the Pledge of Allegiance is one of dozens that can be retrieved by a search engine. It happens that every one of the cartoons that I retrieved mocked the courts for ruling that schools cannot require students to recite the Pledge of Allegiance in its present form, which includes the words "under God." I personally object to these words, so the cartoons certainly do not speak for me, but I'll try as impartially as possible to analyze the strength of Markstein's cartoon.

Markstein shows us, in the cartoon, four school children reciting the Pledge. Coming out of all four mouths is a speech balloon with the words, "One nation under nothing in particular." The children are facing a furled American flag, and to the right of the flag is a middle-aged female teacher, whose speech balloon is in the form of a cloud, indicating that she is *thinking* rather than saying the words, "God help us."

Certainly the image grabs us: Little kids lined up reciting the Pledge of Allegiance, an American flag, a maternal-looking teacher, and, in fact, if one examines the cartoon closely, one sees an apple on the teacher's desk. It's almost a Norman Rockwell scene, except, of course, it is a cartoon, so the figures are all a bit grotesque—but, still, they are nice folks. What is *not* nice, Markstein says, is what these kids must recite, "One nation under nothing in particular." In fact the cartoon is far from telling the truth. Children who recite the Pledge without the words "under God" will still be saying that they are pledging allegiance to something quite specific—the United States:

> I pledge allegiance to the flag of the United States of America, and to the Republic for which it stands: one nation indivisible, with Liberty and Justice for all.

That's really quite a lot, very far from Markstein's "under nothing in particular." But no one, I suppose, expects fairness in a political cartoon—and of course this cartoon *is* political, because the issue of the Pledge has become a political football, with liberals on the whole wanting the words "under God" removed and conservatives on the whole wanting the words retained.

Let's now look at some of the subtleties of the cartoon. First, although, as I have said, cartoons present grotesque caricatures, the figures here are all affectionately presented. None of these figures is menacing. The teacher, with her spectacles and her rather dumpy figure, is clearly a benevolent figure, someone who in the eyes of the cartoonist rightly is disturbed about the fate of these little kids who are not allowed to say the words "under God." (Nothing, of course, prevents the children from speaking about God when they are not in the classroom. Those who believe in God can say grace at mealtime, can go to Sunday School, can go to church regularly, can pray before they go to bed, etc.) Markstein suggests that the absence of these words makes the entire Pledge meaningless ("under nothing in particular"), and in a master stroke he has conveyed this idea of impoverishment by showing a tightly furled flag, a flag that is presented as minimally as possible. After all, the flag could have been shown more fully, perhaps hanging from a pole that extended from a wall into the classroom, or the flag could have been displayed extended against a wall. Instead we get the narrowest of flags, something that is not much more than a furled umbrella, identifiable as the American flag by its stripes and a few stars in the upper third. Markstein thus cleverly suggests that with the loss of the words "under God," the flag itself is reduced to almost nothing.

Fair? No. Effective? Yes, and that's the job of a cartoonist. 5 Readers probably give cartoons no more than three or four seconds, and Markstein has made the most of those few seconds. The reader gets his point, and if the reader already holds this view, he or she probably says, "Hey, here's a great cartoon." I don't hold that view, but I am willing to grant that it is a pretty good cartoon, effectively making a point that I think is wrong-headed.

VISUALS AS AIDS TO CLARITY: MAPS, GRAPHS, TABLES, AND PIE CHARTS

Maps were obviously part of the argument in the debate over drilling in the Arctic National Wildlife Refuge.

- Advocates of drilling argued that drilling would take place only in a tiny area. Their map showed Alaska, with an indication (in gray) of the much smaller part of Alaska that was the Refuge, and a further indication (cross-hatched) of what these advocates of drilling emphasized was a minuscule part of the Refuge.

- Opponents, however, showed maps indicating the path of migrating caribou and the roads that would have to be constructed across the refuge to get to the area where the drilling would take place.

Graphs, tables, and pie charts usually present quantitative data in visual form, helping writers clarify mind-numbing statistical assertions. For instance, a line graph may tell us how many immigrants came to the United States in each decade of the last century.

A bar graph (the bars can run either horizontally or vertically) offers similar information; we can see at a glance that, say, the second bar is almost double the length of the first, indicating that the number is almost double.

A pie chart is a circle divided into wedges so that we can see—literally—how a whole is divided into its parts. We can see, for instance, that of the entire pie—which may represent registered voters in a certain state—one-fourth are registered Democrats,

> ✓ A CHECKLIST FOR CHARTS AND GRAPHS
>
> ☐ Is the source authoritative?
> ☐ Is the source cited?
> ☐ Will the chart or graph be intelligible to the imagined audience?
> ☐ Is the caption, if any, clear and helpful?

one-fifth are registered Republicans, and the remainder do not give a party affiliation.

A NOTE ON USING VISUALS IN YOUR OWN PAPER

Every paper uses some degree of visual persuasion, merely in its appearance: perhaps a title page, certainly margins (ample—but not so wide that they tell the reader that the writer is unable to write a paper of the assigned length), double-spacing for the convenience of the reader, paragraphing (again for the convenience of the reader), and so on. But you may also want to use images—for example, pictures, graphs, or pie charts. Keep a few guidelines in mind as you begin to work with images, "writing" visuals into your own argument with at least as much care as you would read them in others':

- Consider the needs and attitudes of your audience, and select the type of visuals—graphs, drawings, photographs—likely to be most persuasive to that audience.

- Consider the effect of color, composition, and placement within your document. Because images are most effective when they appear near the text that supplements them, do not group all of your images at the end of the paper.

Remember especially that images are almost never self-supporting or self-explanatory. They may be evidence for your argument (Ut's photograph of napalm victims is *very* compelling evidence of suffering), but they are not arguments themselves.

COMING TO AMERICA . . .

Both the percentage and number of foreign-born people in the United States dropped during much of the twentieth century, but after 1970, the tide was turning again.

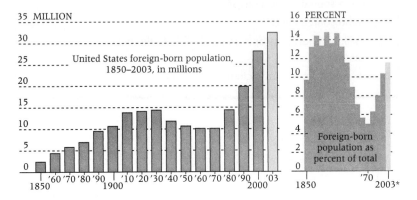

. . . FROM NEAR AND FAR

Central America, Mexico, and Asia contribute most to the foreign-born population.

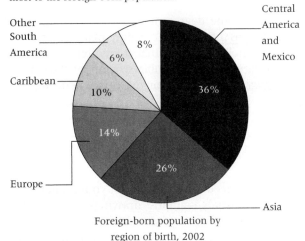

Foreign-born population by
region of birth, 2002

*Most recent estimate
Source: United States Census Bureau

- Be sure to explain each image that you use, integrating it into the verbal text that provides the logic and principal support of your thesis.

- Be sure to cite the source of any image, for instance, a graph or a pie chart, that you paste into your argument.

(DILBERT © Scott Adams. Distributed by permission of United Features Syndicate, Inc.)

A NOTE ON FORMATTING YOUR PAPER: DOCUMENT DESIGN

Even if you do not use pictures or graphs or charts, the format you use—the margins, the font, the headings and subheadings, if any, will still give your paper a visual aspect. NoonewantstoreadapaperthatlookslikethisORLIKETHIS*ORLIKETHIS*ANDCERTAINLYNOT **LIKETHIS**ORLIKETHIS. For academic papers, margins (one inch on each side), spacing (double-spaced), and font and size (Times New Roman, 12 point) are pretty well standardized, and it is usually agreed that the text should be justified at the left rather than centered (to avoid rivers of white down the page), but you are still in charge of some things, notably headings and bulleted or numbered lists—as well as, of course, the lengths of your paragraphs.

Headings in a long paper (more than five pages) are functional, helping to guide the reader from unit to unit, but the extra white space—a decorative element—is also functional, giving the reader's eye a moment of rest. Longish academic papers often use one, two, or even three levels of headings, normally distinguished by type size, position, and highlighting ("highlighting" includes the use of CAPITALS, **boldface**, and *italic*). Here are examples of three levels:

FIRST-LEVEL HEADING

Second-Level Heading

Third-Level Heading

If you use headings, you must be consistent in the form. For instance, if you use a noun phrase such as "the present system"

printed in CAPITAL LETTERS for the first of your first-level headings, you must use noun phrases and caps for the rest of your first-
level headings, thus:

THE PRESENT SYSTEM
THE NEED TO CHANGE

But you need not use noun phases and you need not use capitals.
You may use, for instance, -*ing* headings (gerund phrases), and you
may decide to capitalize only the first letter of each word other
than prepositions and articles, thus:

Thinking about Immigration

Reviewing the Past

Thinking about the Future

Reconsidering Legislation

And here are headings that use a single word:

Problems

Answers

Strengths

Weaknesses

Finally, headings that consist of questions can be effective:

What Are We Now Doing?
Why Should We Change?

Caution: Although headings can be useful in a paper of moder-
ate or considerable length, they almost never are useful in a paper
of five or fewer pages.

5

Writing an Analysis of an Argument

This is what we can all do to nourish and strengthen one another: listen to one another very hard, ask questions, too, send one another away to work again, and laugh in all the right places.

—NANCY MAIRS

I don't wait for moods. You accomplish nothing if you do that. Your mind must know it has got to get down to work.

—PEARL S. BUCK

Fear not those who argue but those who dodge.

—MARIE VON EBNER-ESCHENBACH

ANALYZING AN ARGUMENT

Examining the Author's Thesis

Most of your writing in other courses will require you to write an analysis of someone else's writing. In a course in political science you may have to analyze, say, an essay first published in *Foreign Affairs,* perhaps reprinted in your textbook, that argues against raising tariff barriers to foreign trade. Or a course in sociology may require you to analyze a report on the correlation between fatal accidents and drunk drivers under the age of twenty-one. Much of your writing, in short, will set forth reasoned responses to your reading as preparation for making an argument of your own.

Obviously you must understand an essay before you can analyze it thoughtfully. You must read it several times—not just skim it—and (the hard part) you must think critically about it. Again, you'll find that your thinking is stimulated if you take notes and if you ask yourself questions about the material. Are there any Web sites or organizations dedicated to the material you are analyzing? If there are, visit some to see what others are saying about the material you are reviewing. Notes will help you to keep track of the writer's thoughts and also of your own responses to the writer's thesis. The writer probably *does* have a thesis, a claim, a point, and if so, you must try to locate it. Perhaps the thesis is explicitly stated in the title or in a sentence or two near the beginning of the essay or in a concluding paragraph, but perhaps you will have to infer it from the essay as a whole.

Notice that we said the writer *probably* has a thesis. Much of what you read will indeed be primarily an argument; the writer explicitly or implicitly is trying to support some thesis and to convince you to agree with it. But some of what you read will be relatively neutral, with the argument just faintly discernible—or even with no argument at all. A work may, for instance, chiefly be a report: Here are the data, or here is what X, Y, and Z said; make of it what you will. A report might simply state how various ethnic groups voted in an election. In a report of this sort, of course, the writer hopes to persuade readers that the facts are correct, but no thesis is advanced, at least not explicitly or perhaps even consciously; the writer is not evidently arguing a point and trying to change our minds. Such a document differs greatly from an essay by a political analyst who presents similar findings to persuade a candidate to sacrifice the votes of this ethnic bloc and thereby get more votes from other blocs.

Examining the Author's Purpose

While reading an argument, try to form a clear idea of the author's **purpose.** Judging from the essay or the book, was the purpose to persuade, or was it to report? An analysis of a pure report (a work apparently without a thesis or argumentative angle) on ethnic voting will deal chiefly with the accuracy of the report. It will, for example, consider whether the sample poll was representative.

Much material that poses as a report really has a thesis built into it, consciously or unconsciously. The best evidence that the prose you are reading is argumentative is the presence of two kinds of key terms: transitions that imply the drawing of a conclusion and verbs that imply proof (see Idea Prompt 5.1). Keep your eye out for

IDEA PROMPT 5.1 DRAWING CONCLUSIONS AND IMPLYING PROOF

Transitions that imply the drawing of a conclusion	*therefore, because, for the reason that, consequently*
Verbs that imply proof	*confirms, verifies, accounts for, implies, proves, disproves, is (in)consistent with, refutes, it follows that*

such terms, and scrutinize their precise role whenever they appear. If the essay does not advance a thesis, think of one that it might support or some conventional belief that it might undermine.

Examining the Author's Methods

If the essay advances a thesis, you will want to analyze the strategies or methods of argument that allegedly support the thesis.

- Does the writer quote authorities? Are these authorities competent in this field? Are equally competent authorities who take a different view considered?

- Does the writer use statistics? If so, who compiled them, and are they appropriate to the point being argued? Can they be interpreted differently?

- Does the writer build the argument by using examples or analogies? Are they satisfactory?

- Are the writer's assumptions acceptable?

- Does the writer consider all relevant factors? Has he or she omitted some points that you think should be discussed? For instance, should the author recognize certain opposing positions and perhaps concede something to them?

- Does the writer seek to persuade by means of ridicule? If so, is the ridicule fair: Is it supported also by rational argument?

- Is the argument aimed at a particular audience?

In writing your analysis, you will want to tell your reader something about the author's purpose and something about the author's **methods.** It is usually a good idea at the start of your analysis—if not in the first paragraph, then in the second or third—to let the reader know the purpose (and thesis, if there is one) of the work you are analyzing and then to summarize the work briefly.

Next you will probably find it useful (your reader will certainly find it helpful) to write out *your* thesis (your evaluation or judgment). You might say, for instance, that the essay is impressive but not conclusive, or is undermined by convincing contrary evidence, or relies too much on unsupported generalizations, or is wholly admirable. Remember, because your paper is itself an argument, it needs its own thesis.

And then, of course, comes the job of setting forth your analysis and the support for your thesis. There is no one way of going about this work. If, say, your author gives four arguments (for example, an appeal to common sense, the testimony of authorities, the evidence of comparisons, and an appeal to self-interest), you might want to do one of the following:

- Take up these four arguments in sequence.
- Discuss the simplest of the four and then go on to the more difficult ones.
- Discuss the author's two arguments that you think are sound and then turn to the two that you think are not sound (or perhaps the reverse).
- Take one of these approaches and then clinch your case by constructing a fifth argument that is absent from the work under scrutiny but in your view highly important.

In short, the organization of your analysis may or may not follow the organization of the work you are analyzing.

Examining the Author's Persona

You will probably also want to analyze something a bit more elusive than the author's explicit arguments: the author's self-presentation. Does the author seek to persuade readers partly by presenting himself or herself as conscientious, friendly, self-effacing, authoritative, tentative, or in some other light? Most writers do two things:

- They present evidence.
- They present themselves (or, more precisely, they present the image of themselves that they wish us to behold).

In some persuasive writing this **persona** or **voice** or presentation of the self may be no less important than the presentation of evidence. In other cases, the persona may not much matter, but our point is that you should spend a little time looking at the author's self-presentation to consider if it's significant.

In establishing a persona, writers adopt various rhetorical strategies, ranging from the use of characteristic words to the use of a particular form of organization. For instance,

- The writer who speaks of an opponent's "gimmicks" instead of "strategy" probably is trying to downgrade the opponent and also to convey the self-image of a streetwise person.

- On a larger scale, consider the way in which evidence is presented and the kind of evidence offered. One writer may first bombard the reader with facts and then spend relatively little time drawing conclusions. Another may rely chiefly on generalizations, waiting until the end of the essay to bring the thesis home with a few details. Another may begin with a few facts and spend most of the space reflecting on these. One writer may seem professorial or pedantic, offering examples of an academic sort; another, whose examples are drawn from ordinary life, may seem like a regular guy.

All such devices deserve comment in your analysis.

The writer's persona, then, may color the thesis and help it develop in a distinctive way. If we accept the thesis, it is partly because the writer has won our goodwill by persuading us of his or her good character (*ethos,* in Aristotle's terms). Later we talk more about the appeal to the character of the speaker—the so-called *ethical appeal,* but here we may say that good writers present themselves not as wise-guys, bullies, or pompous asses but as decent people whom the reader would like to invite to dinner.

The author of an essay may, for example, seem fair-minded and open-minded, treating the opposition with great courtesy and expressing interest in hearing other views. Such a tactic is itself a persuasive device. Or take an author who appears to rely on hard evidence such as statistics. This reliance on seemingly objective truths is itself a way of seeking to persuade—a rational way, to be sure, but a mode of persuasion nonetheless.

Especially in analyzing a work in which the author's persona and ideas are blended, you will want to spend some time commenting on the persona. Whether you discuss it near the beginning of your analysis or near the end will depend on your own sense of how you want to construct your essay, and this decision will partly depend on the work you are analyzing. For example, if the author's persona is kept in the background and is thus relatively invisible, you may want to make that point fairly early to get it out of the way and then concentrate on more interesting matters. If, however, the persona is interesting—and perhaps seductive, whether because it seems so scrupulously objective or so engagingly subjective—you may want to hint at this quality early in your essay and then develop the point while you consider the arguments.

In short, the author's self-presentation usually matters. Reorganize its effect, whether positive or negative.

Examining Persona and Intended Audience

A key element in understanding an argument lies in thinking about the intended audience—how the author perceives the audience and what strategies the author uses to connect to it. We have already said something about the creation of the author's persona. An author with a loyal following is, almost by definition, someone who in earlier writings has presented an engaging persona, a persona with a trustworthy *ethos*. A trusted author can sometimes cut corners and can perhaps adopt a colloquial tone that would be unacceptable in the writing of an unknown author.

Authors who want to win the assent of their audiences need to think about how they present information and how they present *themselves*. Think about how you prefer people to talk to you or address you. What sorts of language do you find engaging? Much of course depends on the circumstances, notably the topic, the audience, and the place. A joke may be useful in an argument about whether the government should regulate junk food, but almost surely a joke will be inappropriate—will backfire, will alienate the audience—in an argument about abortion. The *way* an author addresses the reader (through an invented persona) can have a significant impact on the reader's perception of the author, which is to say perception of the author's *views*, the author's *argument*. A slip in tone or an error of fact, however small, may be enough for the audience to dismiss the author's argument. Understanding audience means thinking about all of the possible audiences that may come into contact with your writing or your message, and thinking about the consequences of what you write and where it is published.

You may recall a tweet by Lebron James, who formerly played basketball for the Cleveland Cavaliers but who now plays for the

Miami Heat. After James left the Cavaliers (and his home state of Ohio), the Los Angeles Lakers beat the Cavaliers by fifty-five points, and James tweeted: "Crazy. Karma is a b****. Gets you every time. It's not good to wish bad on anybody. God sees everything!" Cleveland fans not surprisingly perceived his tweet as a slap in the face. The broader audience, too, outside of Cleveland, perceived it as uncalled for. Lebron James clearly did not think about his audience(s). To put it in rhetorical terms, Lebron James vastly diminished his *ethos*. Doubtless he wishes he could retract the tweet, but, as the ancient Roman poet Horace said, *"Nescit vox missa reverti"* ("The word once spoken can never be recalled"), or, in plain proverbial English, "Think twice before you speak."

Consider Facebook status updates. Have you ever posted a status update and wished you could take it back only to find out it was too late? People you did not want to see it saw it before you could remove it. Have you ever tweeted or even texted something you wished you hadn't? When reading and writing more formal essays, it is equally important to think about who wrote what you are reading, and who will read what you are writing.

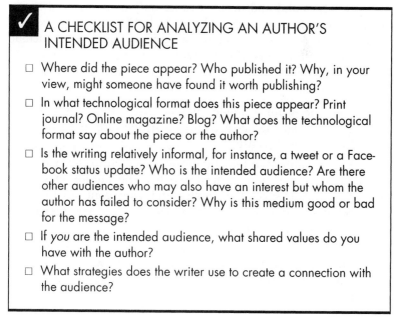

✔ A CHECKLIST FOR ANALYZING AN AUTHOR'S INTENDED AUDIENCE

- ☐ Where did the piece appear? Who published it? Why, in your view, might someone have found it worth publishing?

- ☐ In what technological format does this piece appear? Print journal? Online magazine? Blog? What does the technological format say about the piece or the author?

- ☐ Is the writing relatively informal, for instance, a tweet or a Facebook status update? Who is the intended audience? Are there other audiences who may also have an interest but whom the author has failed to consider? Why is this medium good or bad for the message?

- ☐ If *you* are the intended audience, what shared values do you have with the author?

- ☐ What strategies does the writer use to create a connection with the audience?

Summary

In the last few pages we have tried to persuade you that, in writing an analysis of your reading, you must do the following:

- Read and reread thoughtfully. Composing and keeping notes will help you to think about what you are reading.
- Be aware of the purpose of the material to which you are responding.

We have also tried to point out these facts:

- Most of the nonliterary material that you will read is designed to argue, to report, or to do both.
- Most of this material also presents the writer's personality, or voice, and this voice usually merits attention in an analysis. An essay on, say, nuclear war, in a journal devoted to political science may include a voice that moves from an objective tone to a mildly ironic tone to a hortatory tone, and this voice is worth commenting on.

Possibly all this explanation is obvious. There is yet another point, equally obvious but often neglected by students who begin by writing an analysis and end up by writing only a summary, a shortened version of the work they have read: Although your essay is an analysis of someone else's writing, and you may have to include a summary of the work you are writing about, your essay is *your* essay, your analysis, not a mere summary. The thesis, the organization, and the tone are yours.

- Your thesis, for example, may be that, although the author is convinced she has presented a strong case, her case is far from proved because, . . .
- Your organization may be deeply indebted to the work you are analyzing, but it need not be. The author may have begun with specific examples and then gone on to make generalizations and to draw conclusions, but you may begin with the conclusions.
- Your tone, similarly, may resemble your subject's (let's say the voice is courteous academic), but it will nevertheless have its own ring, its own tone of, say, urgency, caution, or coolness.

Most of the essays that we have included thus far are more or less in an academic style, and indeed several are by students and by professors. But argumentative writing is not limited to academicians—if it were, your college would not be requiring you to take a course in the subject. The following essay, in a breezy style, comes from a columnist who writes for the *New York Times*.

✓ A CHECKLIST FOR ANALYZING A TEXT

Have I considered all of the following matters?

- ☐ Who is the author? What stake might he or she have in writing this piece?
- ☐ Is the piece aimed at a particular audience? A neutral audience? What is your evidence? Persons who are already sympathetic to the author's point of view? A hostile audience?
- ☐ What is the author's thesis (argument, main point, claim)?
- ☐ What assumptions does the author make? Do I share them? If not, why not?
- ☐ Does the author ever confuse facts with beliefs or opinions?
- ☐ What appeals does the author make? To reason (*logos*), for instance, with statistics, the testimony of authorities, and personal experience? To the emotions (*pathos*), for instance, by an appeal to "our better nature," or to widely shared values? To our sense that the speaker is trustworthy (*ethos*)?
- ☐ How convincing is the evidence? Why do you think so?
- ☐ Are significant objections and counterevidence adequately discussed?
- ☐ How is the text organized, and is the organization effective? Are the title, the opening paragraphs, and the concluding paragraphs effective? In what ways?
- ☐ If visual materials such as graphs, pie charts, or pictures are used, how persuasive are they? Do they make a logical appeal? (Charts and graphs presumably make a logical appeal.) Do they make an emotional appeal? An ethical appeal?
- ☐ What is the author's tone? Is it appropriate?
- ☐ To what extent has the author convinced me? Why?

AN ARGUMENT, ITS ELEMENTS, AND A STUDENT'S ANALYSIS OF THE ARGUMENT

Nicholas D. Kristof

Nicholas D. Kristof (b. 1959) grew up on a farm in Oregon. After graduating from Harvard, he was awarded a Rhodes scholarship to Oxford, where he studied law. In 1984 he joined the New York Times *as a correspondent, and since 2001 he has written as a columnist. He has won two Pulitzer Prizes.*

For Environmental Balance, Pick Up a Rifle

Here's a quick quiz: Which large American mammal kills the most humans each year?

It's not the bear, which kills about two people a year in North America. Nor is it the wolf, which in modern times hasn't killed anyone in this country. It's not the cougar, which kills one person every year or two.

Rather, it's the deer. Unchecked by predators, deer populations are exploding in a way that is profoundly unnatural and that is destroying the ecosystem in many parts of the country. In a wilderness, there might be ten deer per square mile; in parts of New Jersey, there are up to 200 per square mile.

One result is ticks and Lyme disease, but deer also kill people more directly. A study for the insurance industry estimated that deer kill about 150 people a year in car crashes nationwide and cause $1 billion in damage. Granted, deer aren't stalking us, and they come out worse in these collisions—but it's still true that in a typical year, an American is less likely to be killed by Osama bin Laden than by Bambi.

If the symbol of the environment's being out of whack in the 5 1960s was the Cuyahoga River in Cleveland catching fire, one such symbol today is deer congregating around what they think of as salad bars and what we think of as suburbs.

So what do we do? Let's bring back hunting.

Now, you've probably just spilled your coffee. These days, among the university-educated crowd in the cities, hunting is viewed as barbaric.

The upshot is that towns in New York and New Jersey are talking about using birth control to keep deer populations down. (Liberals presumably support free condoms, while conservatives back abstinence education.) Deer contraception hasn't been very successful, though.

Meanwhile, the same population bomb has spread to bears. A bear hunt has been scheduled for this week in New Jersey—prompting outrage from some animal rights groups (there's also talk of bear contraception: make love, not cubs).

As for deer, partly because hunting is perceived as brutal and 10 vaguely psychopathic, towns are taking out contracts on deer through discreet private companies. Greenwich, Connecticut, budgeted $47,000 this year to pay a company to shoot eighty deer from raised platforms over four nights—as well as $8,000 for deer birth control.

Look, this is ridiculous.

We have an environmental imbalance caused in part by the decline of hunting. Humans first wiped out certain predators—like wolves and cougars—but then expanded their own role as predators to sustain a rough ecological balance. These days, though, hunters are on the decline.

According to "Families Afield: An Initiative for the Future of Hunting," a report by an alliance of shooting organizations, for every hundred hunters who die or stop hunting, only sixty-nine hunters take their place.

I was raised on *Bambi*—but also, as an Oregon farm boy, on venison and elk meat. But deer are not pets, and dead deer are as natural as live deer. To wring one's hands over them, perhaps after polishing off a hamburger, is soggy sentimentality.

What's the alternative to hunting? Is it preferable that deer die 15 of disease and hunger? Or, as the editor of *Adirondack Explorer* magazine suggested, do we introduce wolves into the burbs?

To their credit, many environmentalists agree that hunting can be green. The New Jersey Audubon Society this year advocated deer hunting as an ecological necessity.

There's another reason to encourage hunting: it connects people with the outdoors and creates a broader constituency for wilderness preservation. At a time when America's wilderness is being gobbled away for logging, mining, or oil drilling, that's a huge boon.

Granted, hunting isn't advisable in suburban backyards, and I don't expect many soccer moms to install gun racks in their minivans. But it's an abdication of environmental responsibility to

eliminate other predators and then refuse to assume the job ourselves. In that case, the collisions with humans will simply get
worse.

In October, for example, Wayne Goldsberry was sitting in a
home in northwestern Arkansas when he heard glass breaking in
the next room. It was a home invasion—by a buck.

Mr. Goldsberry, who is six feet one inch and weighs two hun-   20
dred pounds, wrestled with the intruder for forty minutes. Blood
spattered the walls before he managed to break the buck's neck.

So it's time to reestablish a balance in the natural world—by
accepting the idea that hunting is as natural as bird-watching.

Topics for Critical Thinking and Writing

1. What is Kristof's chief thesis? (State it in one sentence.)

2. Does Kristof make any assumptions—tacit or explicit—with
    which you disagree? With which you agree? Write them down.

3. Is the slightly humorous tone of Kristof's essay inappropriate for a
    discussion of deliberately killing wild animals? Why, or why not?

4. If you are familiar with *Bambi,* does the story make any *argument*
    against killing deer, or does the story appeal only to our emotions?

5. Do you agree that "hunting is as natural as bird-watching" (para.
    21)? In any case, do you think that an appeal to what is "natural"
    is a good argument for expanding the use of hunting?

6. To whom is Kristof talking? How do you know?

The Essay Analyzed

OK, time's up. Let's examine Kristof's essay with an eye to
identifying those elements we mentioned earlier in this chapter
(pp. 147–55) that deserve notice when examining *any* argument:
the author's *thesis, purpose, methods, persona,* and *audience.* And while
we're at it, let's also notice some other features of Kristof's essay
that will help us appreciate its effects and evaluate it. We will thus
be in a good position to write an evaluation or an argument that
confirms, extends, or even rebuts Kristof's argument.

But first, a caution: Kristof's essay appeared in a newspaper
where paragraphs are customarily very short, partly to allow for
easy reading and partly because the columns are narrow and even

short paragraphs may extend for an inch or two. If his essay were to appear in a book, doubtless the author would join many of the paragraphs, making longer units. In analyzing a work, think about where it originally appeared. A blog, a print journal, an online magazine? Does the format in some measure influence the piece?

Title   By combining "Environmental Balance" with "Rifle"—terms that don't seem to go together—Kristof starts off with a bang. He gives a hint of his *topic* (something about the environment) and of his thesis (some sort of way of introducing ecological balance). He also conveys something of his persona by introducing a rifle into the environment. He is, the title suggests, a no-nonsense, hard-hitting guy.

Opening Paragraphs   Kristof immediately grabs hold of us ("Here's a quick quiz") and asks a simple question, but one that we probably have not thought much about: "Which large American mammal kills the most humans each year?" In his second paragraph he tells us it is *not* the bear—the answer most readers probably come up with—nor is it the cougar. Not until the third paragraph does Kristof give us the answer, the deer. But remember, Kristof is writing in a newspaper, where paragraphs customarily are very short. It takes us only a few seconds to get to the third paragraph and the answer.

Thesis   What is the basic thesis Kristof is arguing? Somewhat unusually, Kristof does *not* announce it in its full form until his sixth paragraph ("Let's bring back hunting"), but, again, his paragraphs are very short, and if the essay were published in a book, Kristof's first two paragraphs probably would be combined, as would the third and fourth.

Purpose   Kristof's purpose is clear: He wants to *persuade* readers to adopt his view. This amounts to trying to persuade us that his thesis (stated above) is *true*. Kristof, however, does not show that his essay is argumentative or persuasive by using many of the key terms that normally mark argumentative prose. He doesn't call anything his *conclusion*, none of his statements is labeled *my premises*, and he doesn't connect clauses or sentences with *therefore* or *because*. Almost the only traces of the language of argument are "Granted" (para. 18) and "So" (that is, *therefore*) in his final paragraph.

Despite the lack of argumentative language, the argumentative nature of his essay is clear. He has a thesis—one that will strike many readers as highly unusual—and he wants readers to accept it, so he must go on to *support* it; accordingly, after his introductory paragraphs, in which he calls attention to a problem and offers a solution (his thesis), he must offer evidence, and that is what much of the rest of the essay seeks to do.

Methods   Although Kristof will have to offer evidence, he begins by recognizing the folks on the other side, "the university-educated crowd in the cities, [for whom] hunting is viewed as barbaric" (para. 7). He goes on to spoof this "crowd" when, speaking of methods of keeping the deer population down, he says in paragraph 8, "Liberals presumably support free condoms, while conservatives back abstinence education." Ordinarily it is a bad idea to make fun of persons who hold views other than your own—after all, they just may be on to something, they just might know something you don't know, and, in any case, impartial readers rarely want to align themselves with someone who mocks others. In the essay we are looking at, however, Kristof gets away with this smart-guy tone because he (a) has loyal readers and (b) has written the entire essay in a highly informal or playful manner. Think again about the first paragraph, which begins "Here's a quick quiz." The informality is not only in the contraction (*Here's* versus *Here is*), but in the very idea of beginning by grabbing the readers and thrusting a quiz at them. The playfulness is evident throughout: For instance, immediately after Kristof announces his thesis, "Let's bring back hunting," he begins a new paragraph (7) with, "Now, you've probably just spilled your coffee."

Kristof's methods of presenting evidence include providing *statistics* (paras. 3, 4, 10, and 13), giving *examples* (paras. 10, 19–20), and citing *authorities* (paras. 13 and 16).

Persona   Kristof presents himself as a confident, no-nonsense fellow, a persona that not many writers can get away with, but that probably is acceptable in a journalist who regularly writes a newspaper column. His readers know what to expect, and they read him with pleasure. But it probably would be inadvisable for an unknown writer to adopt this persona, unless perhaps he or she were writing for an audience that could be counted on to be friendly (in this instance, an audience of hunters). If this essay appeared in a hunting magazine, doubtless it would please and entertain its audience. It would not convert anybody, but conversion would not be its point if it were published in a magazine read by hunters. In the *New York Times,* where the essay originally appeared, Kristof could count on a moderately sympathetic audience because he has a large number of faithful readers, but one can guess that many of these readers—chiefly city dwellers—read him for entertainment rather than for information about how they should actually behave.

By the way, when we speak of "faithful readers" we are in effect saying that the author has established good *ethos,* has convinced those readers that he or she is *worth* reading.

Closing Paragraphs   The first two of the last three paragraphs report an episode (the 200-pound buck inside the house) that Kristof presumably thinks is pretty conclusive evidence. The final paragraph begins with "So," strongly implying a logical conclusion to the essay.

Let's now turn to a student's analysis of Kristof's essay and then to our analysis of the student's analysis. (We should say that the analysis of Kristof's essay that you have just read is partly indebted to the student's essay that you are about to read.)

Betsy Swinton

Professor Knowles

English 101B

March 12, 2013

Tracking Kristof

Nicholas D. Kristof's "For Environmental Balance, Pick
Up a Rifle" is an engaging piece of writing, but whether it is
convincing is something I am not sure about. And I am not
sure about it for two reasons: (1) I don't know much about the
deer problem, and that's my fault; (2) I don't know much about
the deer problem, and that's Kristof's fault. The first point
needs no explanation, but let me explain the second.

Kristof is making an argument, offering a thesis: Deer are
causing destruction, and the best way to reduce the destruction
is to hunt deer. For all that I know, he may be correct both in
his comment about what deer are doing and also in his comment
about what must be done about deer. My ignorance of the
situation is regrettable, but I don't think that I am the only
reader from Chicago who doesn't know much about the deer
problems in New Jersey, Connecticut, and Arkansas, the states
that Kristof specifically mentions in connection with the deer
problem. He announces his thesis early enough, in his sixth
paragraph, and he is entertaining throughout his essay, but does
he make a convincing case? To ask "Does he make a convincing
case?" is to ask "Does he offer adequate evidence?" and "Does he
show that his solution is better than other possible solutions?"

To take the first question: In a short essay Kristof can
hardly give overwhelming evidence, but he does convince me

that there is a problem. The most convincing evidence he gives appears in paragraph 16, where he says that the New Jersey Audubon Society "advocated deer hunting as an ecological necessity." I don't really know anything about the New Jersey Audubon Society, but I suppose that they are people with a deep interest in nature and in conservation, and if even such a group advocates deer hunting, there must be something to this solution.

I am even willing to accept his argument that, in this nation of meat-eaters, "to wring one's hands over them [dead deer], perhaps after polishing off a hamburger, is soggy sentimentality" (para. 14). According to Kristof, the present alternative to hunting deer is that we leave the deer to "die of disease and hunger" (para. 15). But what I am not convinced of is that there is no way to reduce the deer population other than by hunting. I don't think Kristof adequately explains why some sort of birth control is inadequate. In his eighth paragraph he makes a joke about controlling the birth of deer ("Liberals presumably support free condoms, while conservatives back abstinence education"), and the joke is funny, but it isn't an argument, it's just a joke. Why can't food containing some sort of sterilizing medicine be put out for the starving deer, food that will nourish them and yet make them unreproductive? In short, I don't think he has fairly informed his readers of alternatives to his own positions, and because he fails to look at counterproposals, he weakens his own proposal.

Although Kristof occasionally uses a word or phrase that suggests argument, such as "Granted" (para. 18), "So" (final paragraph), and "There's another reason" (para. 17), he relies chiefly on forceful writing rather than on reasoning. And the second of his two reasons for hunting seems utterly unconvincing to me. His first, as we have seen, is that the deer population (and apparently the bear population) is out of control. His second (para. 17) is that hunting "connects people with the outdoors and creates a broader constituency for wilderness preservation." I am not a hunter and I have never been one. Perhaps that's my misfortune, but I don't think I am missing anything. And when I hear Kristof say, in his final sentence—the climactic place in his essay—that "hunting is as natural as bird-watching," I rub my eyes in disbelief. If he had me at least half-convinced by his statistics and his citation of the Audubon Society, he now loses me when he argues that hunting is "natural." One might as well say that war is natural, rape is natural, bribery is natural—all these terrible things occur, but we ought to deplore them and we ought to make every effort to see that they disappear.

In short, I think that Kristof has written an engaging essay, and he may well have an important idea, but I think that in his glib final paragraph, where he tells us that "hunting is as natural as bird-watching," he utterly loses the reader's confidence.

AN ANALYSIS OF THE STUDENT'S ANALYSIS

Swinton's essay seems to us to be excellent, doubtless the product of a good deal of thoughtful revision. She does not cover every possible aspect of Kristof's essay—she concentrates on his reasoning and she says very little about his style—but we think that, given the limits of space (about 500 words), she does a good job. What makes this student's essay effective?

✓ A CHECKLIST FOR WRITING AN ANALYSIS
    OF AN ARGUMENT

Have I asked myself the following questions?

☐ Early in my essay have I accurately stated the writer's thesis (claim) and summarized his or her supporting reasons? Have I explained to my reader any disagreement about definitions of important terms?

☐ Have I, again fairly early in my essay, indicated where I will be taking my reader, i.e., have I indicated my general response to the essay I am analyzing?

☐ Have I called attention to the strengths, if any, and the weaknesses, if any, of the essay?

☐ Have I commented not only on the *logos* (logic, reasoning) but also on the *ethos* (character of the writer, as presented in the essay)? For instance, has the author convinced me that he or she is well-informed and is a person of goodwill? Or, on the other hand, does the writer seem to be chiefly concerned with ridiculing those who hold a different view?

☐ If there is an appeal to *pathos* (emotion, originally meaning "pity for suffering," but now interpreted more broadly to include appeals to patriotism, humor, or loyalty to family, for example), is it acceptable? If not, why not?

☐ Have I used occasional brief quotations to let my reader hear the author's tone and to ensure fairness and accuracy?

☐ Is my analysis effectively organized?

☐ Have I taken account of the author's audience(s)?

☐ Does my essay, perhaps in the concluding paragraphs, indicate my agreement or disagreement with the writer but also my view of the essay as a piece of argumentative writing?

☐ Is my tone appropriate?

- The essay has a title ("Tracking Kristof") that is of at least a little interest; it picks up Kristof's point about hunting, and it gives a hint of what is to come.

- The author promptly identifies her subject (she names the writer and the title of his essay) early.

- Early in the essay she gives us a hint of where she will be going (in her first paragraph she tells us that Kristof's essay is "engaging . . . *but* . . .").

- She recognizes Kristof's audience at the start, and she suggests that he may not have given thought to this matter of the audience.

- She uses a few brief quotations, to give us a feel for Kristof's essay and to let us hear the evidence for itself, but she does not pad her essay with long quotations.

- She takes up all of Kristof's main points.

- She gives her essay a reasonable organization, letting us hear Kristof's thesis, letting us know the degree to which she accepts it, and finally letting us know her specific reservations about the essay.

- She concludes without the formality of "in conclusion"; "in short" nicely does the trick.

- Notice, finally, that she sticks closely to Kristof's essay. She does not go off on a tangent about the virtues of vegetarianism or the dreadful politics of the *New York Times*, the newspaper that published Kristof's essay. She was asked to analyze the essay, and she has done so.

Exercise

Take one of the essays not yet discussed in class or an essay assigned now by your instructor, and in an essay of 500 words analyze and evaluate it, guided by the checklists and examples we have provided.

6

Developing an Argument of Your Own

The difficult part in an argument is not to defend one's opinion but to know what it is.

—ANDRÉ MAUROIS

Imagine that you enter a parlor. You come late. When you arrive, others have long preceded you, and they are engaged in a heated discussion, a discussion too heated for them to pause and tell you exactly what it is about. In fact, the discussion had already begun long before any of them got there, so that no one present is qualified to retrace for you all the steps that had gone before. You listen for a while, until you decide that you have caught the tenor of the argument; then you put in your oar. Someone answers; you answer him; another comes to your defense; another aligns himself against you, to either the embarrassment or gratification of your opponent, depending upon the quality of your ally's assistance. However, the discussion is interminable. The hour grows late, you must depart. And you do depart, with the discussion still vigorously in progress.

—KENNETH BURKE

No greater misfortune could happen to anyone than that of developing a dislike for argument.

—PLATO

PLANNING, DRAFTING, AND REVISING AN ARGUMENT

First, hear the wisdom of Mark Twain: "When the Lord finished the world, He pronounced it good. That is what I said about my first work, too. But Time, I tell you, Time takes the confidence out of these incautious early opinions."

All of us, teachers and students, have our moments of confidence, but for the most part we know that it takes considerable effort to write clear, thoughtful, seemingly effortless prose. In a conversation we can cover ourselves with such expressions as "Well, I don't know, but I sort of think . . . ," and we can always revise our position ("Oh, well, I didn't mean it that way"), but once we have handed in the final version of our writing, we are helpless. We are (putting it strongly) naked to our enemies.

Getting Ideas: Argument as an Instrument of Inquiry

In Chapter 1 we quoted Robert Frost, "To learn to write is to learn to have ideas," and we offered suggestions about getting ideas, a process traditionally called **invention**. A moment ago we said that we often improve our ideas when we try to explain them to someone else. Partly, of course, we are responding to questions or objections raised by our companion in the conversation. But partly we are responding to ourselves: Almost as soon as we hear what we have to say, we may find that it won't do, and, if we are lucky, we may find a better idea surfacing. One of the best ways of getting ideas is to talk things over.

The process of talking things over usually begins with the text that you are reading: Your notes, your summary, and your queries parenthetically incorporated within your summary are a kind of dialogue between you and the author you are reading. More obviously, when you talk with friends about your topic, you are trying out and developing ideas. You are arguing, but not chiefly to persuade; rather, you are using argument in order to find the truth. Finally, after reading, taking notes, and talking, you may feel that you now have clear ideas and need only put them into writing. And so you take a sheet of blank paper, and perhaps a paralyzing thought suddenly strikes: "I have ideas but just can't put them into words."

Despite what many people believe,

- Writing is not only a matter of putting one's ideas into words.
- Just as talking with others is a way of getting ideas, *writing is a way of getting and developing ideas*. Or, as we have already said, *argument* is an instrument of inquiry as well as of persuasion.

Writing, in short, can be an important part of critical thinking. One big reason we have trouble writing is our fear of putting ourselves on record, but another big reason is our fear that we have no ideas worth putting down. But by writing notes—or even free associations— and by writing a draft, however weak, we can help ourselves to think our way toward good ideas.

Freewriting   Writing for five or six minutes, nonstop, without censoring what you produce is one way of improving your thoughts. Some people who write on a computer find it useful to dim the screen so they won't be tempted to look up and fiddle too soon with what they have just written. Later they illuminate the screen, scroll back, and notice some keywords or passages that can be used later in drafting a paper. If you've kept notes on your blog or in a Google Doc, now is a good time to access them and to copy and paste some of your ideas.

Listing   Writing down keywords, just as you do when you make a shopping list, is another way of getting ideas. When you make a shopping list, you write *ketchup,* and the act of writing it reminds you that you also need hamburger rolls—and *that* in turn reminds you (who knows how or why?) that you also need a can of tuna fish. Similarly, when you prepare a list of ideas for a paper, just writing down one item will often generate another. Of course, when you look over the list, you will probably drop some of these ideas—the dinner menu will change—but you are making progress. If you have a smartphone, use it to write down thoughts. You can even e-mail these notes to yourself so you can access them later.

Diagramming   Sketching some sort of visual representation of an essay is a kind of listing. Three methods of diagramming are especially common:

- **Clustering**   Write, in the middle of a sheet of paper, a word or phrase summarizing your topic (for instance, *health care*; see diagram, p. 170), circle it, and then write down and circle

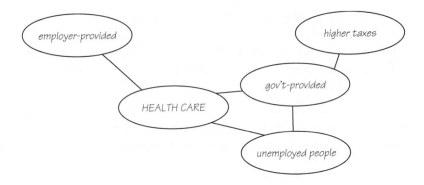

a related word (for example, *gov't-provided*). Perhaps this leads you to write *higher taxes,* and you then circle this phrase and connect it to *gov't-provided.* The next thing that occurs to you is *employer-provided*—and so you write this down and circle it. You will not connect this to *higher taxes,* but you will connect it to *health care* because it is a sort of parallel to *gov't-provided.* The next thing that occurs to you is *unemployed people.* This category does not connect easily with *employer-provided,* so you won't connect these two terms with a line, but you probably will connect *unemployed people* with *health care* and maybe also with *gov't-provided.* Keep going, jotting down ideas and making connections where possible, indicating relationships.

- **Branching**   Some writers find it useful to build a tree, moving from the central topic to the main branches (chief ideas) and then to the twigs (aspects of the chief ideas).

- **Comparing in columns**   Draw a line down the middle of the page, and then set up two columns showing oppositions. For instance, if you are concerned with health care, you might head one column *gov't-provided* and the other *employer-provided.* Under the first column, you might write *covers unemployed,* and under the second column, you might write *omits unemployed.* You might go on to write, under the first column, *higher taxes,* and under the second, *higher prices*—or whatever else relevant comes to mind.

All of these methods can, of course, be executed with pen and paper, but you may also be able to use them on your computer depending on the capabilities of your software.

Whether you are using a computer or a pen, you put down some words and almost immediately see that they need improvement, not simply a little polishing but a substantial overhaul. You write, "Race should be counted in college admissions for two reasons," and as soon as you write these words, a third reason comes to mind. Or perhaps one of those "two reasons" no longer seems very good. As E. M. Forster said, "How can I know what I think till I see what I say?" We have to see what we say, we have to get something down on paper, before we realize that we need to make it better.

Writing, then, is really **rewriting**—that is, **revising**—and a revision is a *re-vision*, a second look. The essay that you submit—whether a hard copy or on Blackboard—should be clear and may even seem effortless to the reader, but in all likelihood the clarity and apparent ease are the result of a struggle with yourself, a struggle during which you greatly improved your first thoughts. You begin by putting down your ideas, such as they are, perhaps even in the random order in which they occurred, but sooner or later comes the job of looking at them critically, developing what is useful in them and removing what is not. If you follow this procedure you will be in the company of Picasso, who said that he "advanced by means of destruction." Those passages that you cut or destroy can be kept in another file in case you want to revisit what you have removed. Sometimes, you end up restoring them.

Whether you advance bit by bit (writing a sentence, revising it, writing the next, and so on) or whether you write an entire first draft and then revise it and revise it again and again is chiefly a matter of temperament. Probably most people combine both approaches, backing up occasionally but trying to get to the end fairly soon so that they can see rather quickly what they know, or think they know, and can then start the real work of thinking, of converting their initial ideas into something substantial.

Asking Questions   Getting ideas, we said when we talked about **topics** and **invention** strategies in Chapter 1 (p. 18) is mostly a matter of asking (and then thinking about) questions. We append questions to the end of each argumentative essay in this book, not to torment you but to help you to think about the arguments—for instance, to turn your attention to especially important matters. If your instructor asks you to write an answer to one of these questions, you are lucky: Examining the question will stimulate your mind to work in a definite direction.

If a topic is not assigned, and you are asked to write an argumentative essay, you will find that some ideas (possibly poor ones, at this stage, but that doesn't matter because you will soon revise) will come to mind if you ask yourself questions. You can begin finding where you stand on an issue (**stasis**) by asking the following five basic questions:

1. What is *X*?
2. What is the value of *X*?
3. What are the causes (or the consequences) of *X*?
4. What should (or ought or must) we do about *X*?
5. What is the evidence for my claims about *X*?

Let's spend a moment looking at each of these questions.

1. **What is *X*?** We can hardly argue about the number of people sentenced to death in the United States in 2000 — a glance at the appropriate government report will give the answer — but we can argue about whether capital punishment as administered in the United States is discriminatory. Does the evidence, we can ask, support the view that in the United States the death penalty is unfair? Similarly, we can ask whether a human fetus is a human being (in saying what something is, must we take account of its potentiality?), and, even if we agree that a fetus is a human being, we can further ask about whether it is a person. In *Roe v. Wade* the U.S. Supreme Court ruled that even the "viable" unborn human fetus is not a "person" as that term is used in the Fifth and Fourteenth Amendments. Here the question is this: Is the essential fact about the fetus that it is a person?

An argument of this sort makes a claim — that is, it takes a stand, but notice that it does not also have to argue for an action. Thus, it may argue that the death penalty is administered unfairly — that's a big enough issue — but it need not go on to argue that the death penalty should be abolished. After all, another possibility is that the death penalty should be administered fairly. The writer of the essay may be doing enough if he or she establishes the truth of the claim and leaves to others the possible responses.

2. **What is the value of *X*?** College courses often call for literary judgments. No one can argue with you if you say you prefer the plays of Tennessee Williams to those of Arthur Miller. But academic papers are not mere declarations of preferences. As soon as you say that Williams is a better playwright than Miller, you have based your preference on implicit standards, and it is incumbent on

you to support your preference by giving evidence about the relative skill, insight, and accomplishments of Williams and of Miller. Your argument is an evaluation. The question now at issue is the merits of the two authors and the standards appropriate for such an appraisal.

In short, an essay offering an evaluation normally has two purposes:

- to set forth an assessment, and
- to convince the reader that the assessment is reasonable.

In writing an evaluation, you will have to rely on criteria, and these will vary depending on your topic. For instance, if you are comparing the artistic merit of the plays by Williams and by Miller, you may want to talk about the quality of the characterization, the importance of the theme, and so on. But if the topic is "Which playwright is more suitable to be taught in high school?" other criteria may be appropriate, such as

- the difficulty of the author's language,
- the sexual content of some scenes, and
- the presence of obscene words.

Or consider a nonliterary issue: On balance, are college fraternities and sororities good or bad? If good, how good? If bad, how bad? What criteria can we use in making our evaluation? Probably some or all of the following:

- testimony of authorities (for instance, persons who can offer firsthand testimony about the good or bad effects),
- inductive evidence (we can collect examples of good or bad effects),
- appeals to logic ("it follows, therefore, that . . ."), and
- appeals to emotion (for instance, an appeal to our sense of fairness).

3. **What are the causes (or the consequences) of *X*?** Why did the rate of auto theft increase during a specific period? If we abolish the death penalty, will that cause the rate of murder to increase? Notice, by the way, that such problems may be complex. The phenomena that people usually argue about—say, such things as inflation, war, suicide, crime—have many causes, and it

is therefore often a mistake to speak of *the* cause of *X*. A writer in
Time mentioned that the life expectancy of an average American
male is about sixty-seven years, a figure that compares unfavor-
ably with the life expectancy of males in Japan and Israel. The *Time*
writer suggested that an important cause of the relatively short life
span is "the pressure to perform well in business." Perhaps. But
the life expectancy of plumbers is no greater than that of managers and executives. Nutrition authority Jean Mayer, in an article
in *Life,* attributed the relatively poor longevity of American males
to a diet that is "rich in fat and poor in nutrients." Doubtless other
authorities propose other causes, and in all likelihood no one cause
accounts for the phenomenon.

Or take a second example of discussions of causality, this one
concerning the academic performance of girls in single-sex schools,
middle schools, and high schools. It is pretty much agreed (based
on statistical evidence) that the graduates of these schools do better,
as a group, than girls who graduate from co-educational schools.
Why do girls in single-sex schools tend, as a group, to do better?
What is the *cause*? The administrators of girls' schools usually attribute the success to the fact (we are admittedly putting the matter bluntly) that young women flourish better in an atmosphere
free from male intimidation: They allegedly gain confidence and
become more expressive when they are not threatened by males.
And this may be the answer, but skeptics have attributed the success to two other causes:

- Most single-sex schools require parents to pay tuition and it
  is a documented fact that the children of well-to-do parents
  do better, academically, than the children of poor parents.

- Further, most single-sex schools are private schools, and they
  select their students from a pool of candidates. Admissions
  officers naturally select those candidates who seem to be academically promising—that is, they select students who have
  already done well academically.[1]

In short, the girls who graduate from single-sex schools may owe
their later academic success not to the atmosphere inside the

[1]Until 2004 federal regulations discouraged public schools from separating boys
from girls. As of the time of this comment [2009] there are only ninety-five single-
sex public schools, twelve of which are in New York City. An article in the *New York
Times,* 11 March 2009, page A20, suggests that there is little evidence that girls do
better than boys in these schools. Indeed, in California a much-touted program in
which six public middle schools and high schools were turned into single-sex acad-
emies has been abandoned.

schools but to the fact that even at the time they were admitted to these schools they were academically stronger—we are, again, speaking of a cohort, not of individuals—than the girls who attend co-ed schools.

The lesson? Be cautious in attributing a cause. There may be several causes.

The kinds of support that usually accompany claims of cause include:

- factual data, especially statistics;
- analogies ("The Roman Empire declined because of X and Y," "Our society exhibits X and Y, and therefore . . ."); and
- inductive evidence.

4. **What should (or ought or must) we do about X?** Must we always obey the law? Should the law allow eighteen-year-olds to drink alcohol? Should eighteen-year-olds be drafted to do one year of social service? Should pornography be censored? Should steroid use by athletes be banned? Ought there to be Good Samaritan laws, making it a legal duty for a stranger to intervene to save a person from death or great bodily harm, when one might do so with little or no risk to oneself? These questions involve conduct and policy; how we answer them will reveal our values and principles.

An essay answering questions of this sort usually

- begins by explaining what the issue (the problem) is, then
- states why the reader should care about it, then
- offers the proposed solution, then
- considers alternative solutions, and finally
- reaffirms the merit of the proposed solution, especially in the light of the audience's interests and needs.

You will recall that throughout this book we have spoken about devices that help a writer to get ideas. If in drafting an essay concerned with policy you begin by writing down your thoughts on the five bulleted items we have just given, you will almost surely uncover ideas that you didn't know you had.

Support for claims of policy usually include

- statistics,
- appeals to common sense and to the reader's moral sense, and
- testimony of authorities.

5. **What is the evidence for my claims about *X*?** In commenting on the four previous topics, we have talked about the kinds of support that are commonly offered, but a few additional points can be made.

Critical reading, writing, and thinking depend essentially on identifying and evaluating the evidence for and against the claims one makes and encounters in the writings of others. It is not enough to have an *opinion* or belief one way or the other; you need to be able to support your opinions—the bare fact of your sincere belief in what you say or write is not itself any *evidence* that what you believe is true.

So what are good reasons for opinions, adequate evidence for one's beliefs? The answer, of course, depends on what kind of belief or opinion, assertion or hypothesis, claim or principle you want to assert. For example, there is good evidence that President John F. Kennedy was assassinated on November 22, 1963, because this is the date for his death reported in standard almanacs. You could further substantiate the date by checking the back issues of the *New York Times*. But a different kind of evidence is needed to support the proposition that the chemical composition of water is H_2O. And you will need still other kinds of evidence to support your beliefs about the likelihood of rain tomorrow, the probability that the Red Sox will win the pennant this year, the twelfth digit in the decimal expansion of pi, the average cumulative grades of the graduating seniors over the past three years in your college, the relative merits of *Hamlet* and *Death of a Salesman*, and the moral dimensions of sexual harassment. None of these issues is merely a matter of opinion; yet about some of them, educated and informed people may disagree over the reasons and the evidence and what they show. Your job as a critical thinker is to be alert to the relevant reasons and evidence and to make the most of them as you present your views.

Again, an argument may answer two or more of these five basic questions. Someone who argues that pornography should (or should not) be censored

- will have to mark out the territory of the discussion by defining pornography (our first question: What is *X*?). The argument probably

- will also need to examine the consequences of adopting the preferred policy (our third question) and

- may even have to argue about its value (our second question). Some people maintain that pornography produces crime, but others maintain that it provides a harmless outlet for impulses that otherwise might vent themselves in criminal behavior.

- Further, someone arguing about the wisdom of censoring pornography might have to face the objection that censorship, however desirable on account of some of its consequences, may be unconstitutional and that, even if censorship were constitutional, it would (or might) have undesirable side effects, such as repressing freedom of political opinion.

- And one will always have to keep asking oneself our fifth question, What is the evidence for my claims?

Thinking about one or more of these questions may get you going. For instance, thinking about the first question, What is *X*?, will require you to produce a definition, and as you work at producing a satisfactory definition, you may find new ideas arising. If a question seems relevant, start writing, even if you write only a fragmentary sentence. You'll probably find that one word leads to another and that ideas begin to appear. Even if these ideas seem weak as you write them, don't be discouraged; you have put something on paper, and returning to these words, perhaps in five minutes or perhaps the next day, you will probably find that some are not at all bad and that others will stimulate you to better ones.

It may be useful to record your ideas in a special notebook or in a private blog or a Google Doc reserved for the purpose. Such a **journal** can be a valuable resource when it comes time to write your paper. Many students find it easier to focus their thoughts on writing if during the period of gestation they have been jotting down relevant ideas on something more substantial than slips of paper or loose sheets. The very act of designating a notebook or blog as your journal for a course can be the first step in focusing your attention on the eventual need to write a paper.

Take advantage of the free tools at your disposal. Use the Internet and free Web tools, including RSS feeds, Google (Drive, sites, and others), Yahoo!, blogs, and wikis to help you organize your initial ideas and to solicit feedback. Talking with others can help, but sometimes we do not have time to chat about our ideas. By using an RSS feed on a Web site that you think will provide good information on your topic (or a topic you are thinking about), you can notify yourself via e-mail if the site has uploaded new material such as news links or op-eds. Posting a blog entry in a public space about your topic can also foster conversations about your topic and help you discover other opinions. Using the Internet to uncover and refine your topic is common, especially in the beginning of the research process.

If what we have just said does not sound convincing, and you know from experience that you often have trouble getting started with your writing, don't despair; first aid is at hand in a sure-fire method that we will now explain.

The Thesis or Main Point

Let's assume that you are writing an argumentative essay—perhaps an evaluation of an argument in this book—and you have what seems to be a pretty good draft or at least a bunch of notes that are the result of hard thinking. You really do have ideas now, and you want to present them effectively. How will you organize your essay? No one formula works best for every essayist and for every essay, but it is usually advisable to formulate a basic **thesis** (a claim, a central point, a chief position) and to state it early. Every essay that is any good, even a book-length one, has a thesis (a main point), which can be stated briefly, usually in a sentence. Remember Coolidge's remark on the preacher's sermon on sin: "He was against it." Don't confuse the **topic** (sin) with the thesis (sin is bad). The thesis is the argumentative theme, the author's primary claim or contention, the proposition that the rest of the essay will explain and defend. Of course, the thesis may sound commonplace, but the book or essay or sermon ought to develop it interestingly and convincingly.

Here are some sample theses:

- Smoking should be prohibited in all enclosed public places.
- Smoking should be limited to specific parts of enclosed public places and entirely prohibited in small spaces, such as elevators.

✓ A CHECKLIST FOR A THESIS STATEMENT

Consider the following questions:

- ☐ Does the statement make an arguable assertion rather than (a) merely assert an unarguable fact, (b) merely announce a topic, or (c) declare an unarguable opinion or belief?
- ☐ Is the statement broad enough to cover the entire argument that I will be presenting, and is it narrow enough for me to be able to cover the topic in the space allotted?

- Proprietors of public places such as restaurants and sports arenas should be free to determine whether they wish to prohibit, limit, or impose no limitations on smokers.

Imagining an Audience

Of course, the questions that you ask yourself to stimulate your thoughts will depend primarily on what you are writing about, but additional questions are always relevant:

- Who are my readers?
- What do they believe?
- What common ground do we share?
- What do I want my readers to believe?
- What do they need to know?
- Why should they care?

These questions require a little comment. The literal answer to the first probably is "my teacher," but (unless you are given instructions to the contrary) you should not write specifically for your teacher. Instead, you should write for an audience that is, generally speaking, like your classmates. In short, your imagined audience is literate, intelligent, and moderately well-informed, but it does not know everything that you know, and it does not know your response to the problem that you are addressing. It needs more information to make an intelligent decision.

The essays in this book are from many different sources, each with its own audience. An essay from the *New York Times* is addressed to the educated general reader; an essay from *Ms.* magazine is addressed to readers sympathetic to feminism. An essay from *Commonweal,* a Roman Catholic publication addressed to the nonspecialist, is likely to differ in point of view or tone from one in *Time,* even though both articles may advance approximately the same position. The writer of the article in *Commonweal* may, for example, effectively cite church fathers and distinguished Roman Catholic writers as authorities, whereas the writer of the *Time* article would probably cite few or even none of these figures because a non-Catholic audience might be unfamiliar with them or, even if familiar, might be unimpressed by their views.

The tone as well as the gist of the argument is in some degree shaped by the audience. For instance, popular journals, such as the *National Review* and *Ms.* magazine, are more likely to use ridicule than are journals chiefly addressed to, say, an academic audience.

The Audience as Collaborator

If you imagine an audience and keep asking yourself what this audience needs to be told and what it doesn't need to be told, you will find that material comes to mind, just as it comes to mind when a friend asks you what a film you saw was about, who was in it, and how you liked it.

Your readers do not have to be told that Thomas Jefferson was an American statesman in the early years of this country's history, but they do have to be told that Elizabeth Cady Stanton was a late-nineteenth-century American feminist. Why? You need to identify Stanton because it's your hunch that your classmates never heard of her, or even if they may have heard the name, they can't quite identify it. But what if your class has been assigned an essay by Stanton? In that case your imagined reader knows Stanton's name and knows at least a little about her, so you don't have to identify Stanton as an American of the nineteenth century. But you do still have to remind your reader about relevant aspects of her essay, and you do have to tell your reader about your responses to them.

After all, even if the instructor has assigned an essay by Stanton, you cannot assume that your classmates know the essay inside out. Obviously, you can't say, "Stanton's third reason is also unconvincing," without reminding the reader, by means of a brief summary, of her third reason. Again,

- Think of your classmates—people like you—as your imagined readers; and
- Be sure that your essay does not make unreasonable demands.

If you ask yourself,

- "What do my readers need to know?" and
- "What do I want them to believe?"

you will find some answers arising, and you will start writing.

We have said that you should imagine your audience as your classmates. But this is not the whole truth. In a sense, your argument is addressed not simply to your classmates but to the world interested in ideas. Even if you can reasonably assume that your classmates have read only one work by Stanton, you will not begin your essay by writing "Stanton's essay is deceptively easy." You will have to name the work; it is possible that a reader has read some other work by Stanton. And by precisely identifying your subject, you help to ease the reader into your essay.

Similarly, you won't begin by writing,

> The majority opinion in *Walker v. City of Birmingham* held that . . .

Rather, you'll write something like this:

> In *Walker v. City of Birmingham*, the U.S. Supreme Court ruled in 1966 that city authorities acted lawfully when they jailed Martin Luther King Jr. and other clergymen in 1963 for marching in Birmingham without a permit. Justice Potter Stewart delivered the majority opinion, which held that . . .

By the way, if you think you suffer from a writing block, the mere act of writing out such readily available facts will help you to get started. You will find that writing a few words, perhaps merely copying the essay's title or an interesting quotation from the essay, will stimulate you to write down thoughts that you didn't know you had in you.

Here, again, are the questions about audience. If you write on a computer, consider putting these questions into a file. For each assignment, copy the questions into the file you are currently working on, and then, as a way of generating ideas, *enter your responses, indented, under each question.*

1. Who are my readers?
2. What do they believe?
3. What common ground do we share?
4. What do I want my readers to believe?
5. What do they need to know?
6. Why should they care?

Thinking about your audience can help you to get started; even more important, it can help you to get ideas. Our second and third questions about the audience ("What do they believe?" and "How much common ground do we share?") will usually help you get ideas flowing.

- Presumably your imagined audience does not share your views, or at least does not fully share them. But why?

- How can these readers hold a position that to you seems unreasonable?

If you try to put yourself into your readers' shoes—and in your essay you will almost surely summarize the views that you are going to speak against—and if you think about what your audience knows or thinks it knows, you will find yourself getting ideas. Spend time online reviewing Web sites that are dedicated to your topic. What do they have to say, and why do the authors hold these views?

You do not believe (let's assume) that people should be allowed to smoke in enclosed public places, but you know that some people hold a different view. Why do they hold it? Try to state their view *in a way that would be satisfactory to them.* Having done so, you may come to perceive that your conclusions and theirs differ because they are based on different premises, perhaps different ideas about human rights. Examine the opposition's premises carefully, and explain, first to yourself and ultimately to your readers, why you find some premises unacceptable.

Possibly some facts are in dispute, such as whether nonsmokers may be harmed by exposure to tobacco. The thing to do, then, is to check the facts. If you find that harm to nonsmokers has not been proved, but you nevertheless believe that smoking should be prohibited in enclosed public places, of course you can't premise your argument on the wrongfulness of harming the innocent (in this case, the nonsmokers). You will have to develop arguments that take account of the facts, whatever they are.

Among the relevant facts there surely are some that your audience or your opponent will not dispute. The same is true of the values relevant to the discussion; the two of you are very likely to agree, if you stop to think about it, that you share belief in some of the same values (such as the principle mentioned above, that it is wrong to harm the innocent). These areas of shared agreement are crucial to effective persuasion in argument.

> **A RULE FOR WRITERS:** If you wish to persuade, you'll have to begin by finding premises you can share with your audience.

There are two good reasons why you should identify and isolate the areas of agreement:

- There is no point in disputing facts or values on which you and your readers really agree.

- It usually helps to establish goodwill between you and your opponent when you can point to beliefs, assumptions, facts, and values that the two of you share.

In a few moments we will return to the need to share some of the opposition's ideas.

Recall that in composing college papers it is usually best to write for a general audience, an audience rather like your classmates but without the specific knowledge that they all share as students enrolled in one course. If the topic is smoking in public places, the audience presumably consists of smokers and non-smokers. Thinking about our fifth question on page 181—"What do [readers] need to know?"—may prompt you to give statistics about the harmful effects of smoking. Or if you are arguing on behalf of smokers, it may prompt you to cite studies claiming that no evidence conclusively demonstrates that cigarette smoking is harmful to nonsmokers. If indeed you are writing for a general

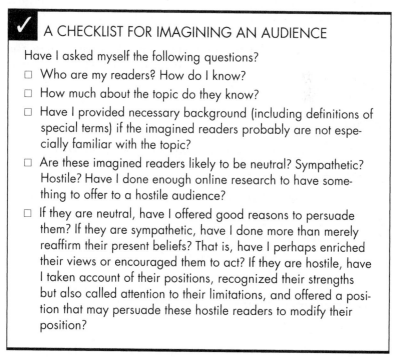

✓ A CHECKLIST FOR IMAGINING AN AUDIENCE

Have I asked myself the following questions?

☐ Who are my readers? How do I know?

☐ How much about the topic do they know?

☐ Have I provided necessary background (including definitions of special terms) if the imagined readers probably are not especially familiar with the topic?

☐ Are these imagined readers likely to be neutral? Sympathetic? Hostile? Have I done enough online research to have something to offer to a hostile audience?

☐ If they are neutral, have I offered good reasons to persuade them? If they are sympathetic, have I done more than merely reaffirm their present beliefs? That is, have I perhaps enriched their views or encouraged them to act? If they are hostile, have I taken account of their positions, recognized their strengths but also called attention to their limitations, and offered a position that may persuade these hostile readers to modify their position?

audience and you are not advancing a highly unfamiliar view, our second question ("What do they believe?") is less important here, but if the audience is specialized, such as an antismoking group, a group of restaurant owners who fear that antismoking regulations will interfere with their business, or a group of civil libertarians, an effective essay will have to address their special beliefs.

In addressing their beliefs (let's assume that you do not share them or do not share them fully), you must try to establish some common ground. If you advocate requiring restaurants to provide nonsmoking areas, you should at least recognize the possibility that this arrangement will result in inconvenience for the proprietor. But perhaps (the good news) the restaurant will regain some lost customers or will attract some new customers. This thought should prompt you to think of kinds of evidence, perhaps testimony or statistics.

When you formulate a thesis and ask questions about it, such as who the readers are, what do they believe, what do they know, and what do they need to know, you begin to get ideas about how to organize the material or at least to see that some sort of organization will have to be worked out. The thesis may be clear and simple, but the reasons (the argument) may take many pages. The thesis is the point; the argument sets forth the evidence that is offered to support the thesis.

The Title

It's not a bad idea to announce your thesis in your **title.** If you scan the table of contents of this book, you will notice that a fair number of essayists use the title to let the readers know, at least in a very general way, what position will be advocated. Here are a few examples of titles that take a position:

> Gay Marriages: Make Them Legal
>
> "Diversity" Is a Smoke Screen for Discrimination
>
> Why Handguns Must Be Outlawed

True, these titles are not especially engaging, but the reader welcomes them because they give some information about the writer's thesis.

Some titles do not announce the thesis, but they at least announce the topic:

Is All Discrimination Unfair?

On Racist Speech

Why Make Divorce Easy?

Although not clever or witty, these titles are informative.

Some titles seek to attract attention or to stimulate the imagination:

A First Amendment Junkie

A Crime of Compassion

Addicted to Health

All of these are effective, but a word of caution is appropriate here. In your effort to engage your reader's attention, be careful not to sound like a wise guy. You want to engage your readers, not turn them off.

Finally, be prepared to rethink your title *after* you have finished the last draft of your paper. A title somewhat different from your working title may be an improvement because the emphasis of your finished paper may have turned out to be rather different from what you expected when you first thought of a title.

The Opening Paragraphs

Opening paragraphs are difficult to write, so don't worry about writing an effective opening when you are drafting. Just get some words down on paper, and keep going. But when you revise your first draft—really a zero draft—you probably should begin to think seriously about the effect of your opening.

A good introduction arouses the reader's interest and helps prepare the reader for the rest of the paper. How? Opening paragraphs usually do at least one (and often all) of the following:

- attract the reader's interest (often with a bold statement of the thesis or with an interesting relevant statistic, quotation, or anecdote),
- prepare the reader's mind by giving some idea of the topic and often of the thesis,
- give the reader an idea of how the essay is organized, and
- define a key term.

You may not wish to announce your thesis in your title, but if you don't announce it there, you should set it forth early in the argument, in your introductory paragraph or paragraphs. In an essay called "Human Rights and Foreign Policy," Jeanne J. Kirkpatrick merely announces her topic (subject) as opposed to her thesis (point), but she begins to hint at the thesis in her first paragraph, by deprecating President Jimmy Carter's policy:

> In this paper I deal with three broad subjects: first, the content and consequences of the Carter administration's human rights policy; second, the prerequisites of a more adequate theory of human rights; and third, some characteristics of a more successful human rights policy.

Or consider this opening paragraph from Peter Singer's "Animal Liberation":

> We are familiar with Black Liberation, Gay Liberation, and a variety of other movements. With Women's Liberation some thought we had come to the end of the road. Discrimination on the basis of sex, it has been said, is the last form of discrimination that is universally accepted and practiced without pretense, even in those liberal circles which have long prided themselves on their freedom from racial discrimination. But one should always be wary of talking of "the last remaining form of discrimination." If we have learned anything from the liberation movements, we should have learned how difficult it is to be aware of the ways in which we discriminate until they are forcefully pointed out to us. A liberation movement demands an expansion of our moral horizons, so that practices that were previously regarded as natural and inevitable are now seen as intolerable.

Although Singer's introductory paragraph nowhere mentions animal liberation, in conjunction with the essay's title it gives us a good idea of what Singer is up to and where he is going. Singer knows that his audience will be skeptical, so he reminds them that in previous years many were skeptical of reforms now taken for granted. He adopts a strategy used fairly often by writers who advance unconventional theses: Rather than beginning with a bold announcement of a thesis that may turn off some of his readers because it sounds offensive or absurd, Singer warms up his audience, gaining their interest by cautioning them politely that although they may at first be skeptical of animal liberation, if they stay with his essay they may come to feel that they have expanded their horizons.

Notice, too, that Singer begins by establishing common ground with his readers; he assumes, probably correctly, that they share his view that other forms of discrimination (now seen to be unjust) were once widely practiced and were assumed to be acceptable and natural. In this paragraph, then, Singer is not only showing himself to be fair-minded but is also letting readers know that he will advance a daring idea. His opening wins their attention and goodwill. A writer can hardly hope to do more. (In a few pages we will talk a little more about winning the audience.)

In your introductory paragraphs:

- You may have to give some background information that your readers will need to keep in mind if they are to follow your essay.

- You may wish to define some terms that are unfamiliar or that you use in an unusual sense.

- If you are writing for an online publication (where your teacher or audience will encounter your argument on the Web), you might establish a context for your argument by linking to a news video that outlines your topic, or you might offer your thesis and then link to a news story that supports your claim. (Remember that using any videos, images, or links also requires a citation of some kind.) The beauty of publishing the piece in an online environment is that you can often link directly to your sources and use sources more easily than if you were submitting a hard copy.

After announcing the topic, giving the necessary background, and stating your position (and perhaps the opposition's) in as engaging a manner as possible, it is usually a good idea to give the reader an idea of *how* you will proceed—that is, what the organization will be. In other words, use the introduction to set up the organization of your essay. Your teachers may assign four- to six-page mini-research papers or they may assign ten- to fifteen-page research papers; if they assign an online venue, ask them about the approximate word count. Whatever the length, every paper needs to have a clear organization. The introduction is where you can

- hook your reader
- reveal your thesis and topic, and
- explain how you will organize your discussion of the topic—what you will do first, second, third, etc.

Look at Kirkpatrick's opening paragraph (p. 186) for an obvious illustration. She tells us she will deal with three subjects, and she names them. Her approach in the paragraph is concise, obvious, and effective.

A RULE FOR WRITERS: In writing or at least in revising these paragraphs, keep in mind this question: What do my readers need to know? Remember, your aim throughout is to write *reader-friendly* prose, and keeping the needs and interests of your audience constantly in mind will help you achieve this goal.

Similarly, you may, for instance, want to announce fairly early that there are four common objections to your thesis and that you will take them up one by one, beginning with the weakest (or most widely held, or whatever) and moving to the strongest (or least familiar), after which you will advance your own view in greater detail. Not every argument begins with refuting the other side, though many arguments do. The point to remember is that you usually ought to tell your readers where you will be taking them and by what route. In effect, you are giving them an outline.

Organizing and Revising the Body of the Essay

We begin with a wise remark by a newspaper columnist, Robert Cromier: "The beautiful part of writing is that you don't have to get it right the first time—unlike, say, a brain surgeon."

In drafting your essay you will of course begin with an organization that seems to you to make sense, but you may well find, in rereading the draft, that some other organization is better. Here, for a start, is an organization that is common in argumentative essays.

1. Statement of the problem or issue
2. Statement of the structure of the essay (its organization)
3. Statement of alternative solutions
4. Arguments in support of the proposed solution
5. Arguments answering possible objections
6. A summary, resolution, or conclusion

Let's look at each of these six steps.

1. **Statement of the problem or issue** Whether the problem is stated briefly or at length depends on the nature of the problem and the writer's audience. If you haven't already defined unfamiliar terms or terms you use in a special way, probably now is the time to do so. In any case, it is advisable here to state the problem objectively (thereby gaining the trust of the reader) and to indicate why the reader should care about the issue.

2. **Statement of the structure of the essay** After stating the problem at the appropriate length, the writer often briefly indicates the structure of the rest of the essay. The commonest structure is suggested below, in points 3 and 4.

3. **Statement of alternative (but less adequate) solutions** In addition to stating the alternatives fairly—let the readers know that you have done your homework—the writer probably conveys willingness to recognize not only the integrity of the proposals but also the (partial) merit of at least some of the alternative solutions.

The point made in the previous sentence is important and worth amplifying. Because it is important to convey your goodwill—your sense of fairness—to the reader, it is advisable to let your reader see that you are familiar with the opposition and that you recognize the integrity of those who hold that view. This you do by granting its merits as far as you can. (For more about this approach, see the essay by Carl R. Rogers on page 359.)

The next stage, which constitutes most of the body of the essay, usually is this:

4. **Arguments in support of the proposed solution**   The evidence offered will, of course, depend on the nature of the problem. Relevant statistics, authorities, examples, or analogies may come to mind or be available. This is usually the longest part of the essay.

5. **Arguments answering possible objections**   These arguments may suggest that

     a. The proposal won't work (perhaps it is alleged to be too expensive, to make unrealistic demands on human nature, or to fail to get to the heart of the problem).

     b. The proposed solution will create problems greater than the difficulty to be resolved. (A good example of a proposal that produced dreadful unexpected results is the law mandating a prison term for anyone over eighteen in possession of an illegal drug. Heroin dealers then began to use children as runners, and cocaine importers followed the practice.)

6. **A summary, resolution, or conclusion**   Here the writer may seek to accommodate the views of the opposition as far as possible but clearly suggest that the writer's own position makes good sense. A conclusion—the word comes from the Latin *claudere*, "to shut"—ought to provide a sense of closure, but it can be much more than a restatement of the writer's thesis. It can, for instance, make a quiet emotional appeal by suggesting that the issue is important and that the ball is now in the reader's court.

Of course not every essay will follow this six-step pattern, but let's assume that in the introductory paragraphs you have sketched the topic (and have shown or nicely said, or implied, that the reader doubtless is interested in it) and have fairly and courteously set forth the opposition's view, recognizing its merits ("I grant that," "admittedly," "it is true that") and indicating the degree to which you can share part of that view. You now want to set forth your arguments explaining why you differ on some essentials.

In setting forth your own position, you can begin either with your strongest reasons or your weakest. Each method of organization has advantages and disadvantages.

- If you begin with your strongest reason, the essay may seem to peter out.

- If you begin with your weakest reason, you build to a climax, but your readers may not still be with you because they may have felt at the start that the essay was frivolous.

The solution to this last possibility is to make sure that even your weakest argument is an argument of some strength. You can, moreover, assure your readers that stronger points will soon be offered and you offer this point first only because you want to show that you are aware of it and that, slight though it is, it deserves some attention. The body of the essay, then, is devoted to arguing a position, which means offering not only supporting reasons but also refutations of possible objections to these reasons.

Doubtless you will sometimes be uncertain, as you draft your essay, whether to present a given point before or after another point. When you write, and certainly when you revise, try to put yourself into your reader's shoes: Which point do you think the reader needs to know first? Which point *leads to* which further point? Your argument should not be a mere list of points, of course; rather, it should clearly integrate one point with another in order to develop an idea. But in all likelihood you won't have a strong sense of the best organization until you have written a draft and have reread it.

A RULE FOR WRITERS: When you revise, make sure that your organization is clear to your readers.

Checking Paragraphs   When you revise your draft, watch out also for short paragraphs. Although a paragraph of only two or three sentences (like some in this chapter) may occasionally be helpful as a transition between complicated points, most short paragraphs are undeveloped paragraphs. Newspaper editors favor very short paragraphs because they can be read rapidly when printed in the narrow columns typical of newspapers. Many of the essays reprinted in this book originally were published in newspapers, hence they consist of very short paragraphs, but they should *not* be regarded as models for your own writing. A second note about paragraphs: Writers for online venues often "chunk" (that is, they provide extra space for paragraph breaks) rather than write a continuous flow. These writers chunk their text for several reasons, but chiefly because breaking up paragraphs and adding space between them makes some types of writing "scannable": The screen is easier to navigate because it is not packed with text in a 12-pt font. The breaks in paragraphs also allow the reader to see a complete paragraph without having to scroll.

Checking Transitions   Make sure, too, in revising, that the reader can move easily from the beginning of a paragraph to the end and from one paragraph to the next. Transitions help the reader to perceive the connections between the units of the argument. For example ("For example" is a transition, of course, indicating that an illustration will follow), they may illustrate, establish a sequence, connect logically, amplify, compare, contrast, summarize, or concede (see Idea Prompt 6.1). Transitions serve as guideposts that enable your reader to move easily through your essay.

When writers revise an early draft, they chiefly

- **unify** the essay by eliminating irrelevancies;
- **organize** the essay by keeping in mind an imagined audience;
- **clarify** the essay by fleshing out thin paragraphs, by making certain that the transitions are adequate and by making certain that generalizations are adequately supported by concrete details and examples.

We are not talking about polish or elegance; we are talking about fundamental matters. Be especially careful not to abuse the logical connectives (*thus, as a result,* and so on). If you write several sentences followed by *therefore* or a similar word or phrase, be sure that what you write after the *therefore* really *does follow* from what has gone before. Logical connectives are not mere transitional devices used to link disconnected bits of prose. They are supposed to mark a real movement of thought—the essence of an argument.

The Ending

What about concluding paragraphs, in which you try to summarize the main points and reaffirm your position?

If you can look back over your essay and add something that enriches it and at the same time wraps it up, fine, but don't feel compelled to say, "Thus, in conclusion, I have argued *X, Y,* and *Z,* and I have refuted Jones." After all, *conclusion* can have two meanings: (1) ending, or finish, as the ending of a joke or a novel; or

IDEA PROMPT 6.1 USING TRANSITIONS IN ARGUMENT

Illustrate	*for example, for instance, consider this case*	"Many television crime dramas contain scenes of graphic violence. For example, in the episode of *Law and Order* titled . . ."
Establish a sequence	*a more important objection, a stronger example, the best reason*	"A stronger example of the ways that TV violence is susceptible to being mimicked is . . ."
Connect logically	*thus, as a result, therefore, so, it follows*	"Therefore, the Federal Communications Commission ought to consider more carefully regulating what types of violence they allow on the air."
Amplify	*further, in addition to, moreover*	"Further, fines for networks that violate these regulations should be steeper because . . ."
Compare	*similarly, in a like manner, just as, analogously*	"Just as the FCC regulates language and sexuality on broadcast TV . . ."
Contrast	*on the other hand, in contrast, however, but*	"On the other hand, studies have shown that violent television . . ."
Summarize	*in short, briefly*	"In short, the basic premise of his argument is . . ."
Concede	*admittedly, granted, to be sure*	"Admittedly, there are many points on which the author is correct."

(2) judgment or decision reached after deliberation. Your essay should finish effectively (the first sense), but it need not announce a judgment (the second).

If the essay is fairly short, so that a reader can more or less keep the whole thing in mind, you may not need to restate your view. Just make sure that you have covered the ground and that your last sentence is a good one. Notice that the student essay printed later in this chapter (p. 209) does not end with a formal conclusion, though it ends conclusively, with a note of finality.

By a note of finality we do *not* mean a triumphant crowing. It's usually far better to end with the suggestion that you hope you have by now indicated why those who hold a different view may want to modify it and accept yours.

If you study the essays in this book, or, for that matter, the editorials and op-ed pieces in a newspaper, you will notice that writers often provide a sense of closure by using one of the following devices:

- a return to something in the introduction,
- a glance at the wider implications of the issue (for example, if smoking is restricted, other liberties are threatened),
- an anecdote that engagingly illustrates the thesis,
- a suggestion that the reader can take some specific action, i.e., that the ball is now in the reader's court, or
- a brief summary (but this sort of ending may seem unnecessary and even tedious, especially if the paper is short and if the summary merely repeats what has already been said).

> **A RULE FOR WRITERS:** Emulate John Kenneth Galbraith, a distinguished writer on economics. Galbraith said that in his fifth draft he introduced the note of spontaneity for which his writing was famous.

Two Uses of an Outline

The Outline as a Preliminary Guide   Some writers find it useful to sketch an **outline** as soon as they think they know what they want to say, even before they write a first draft. This procedure can be helpful in planning a tentative organization, but remember that in revising a draft new ideas will arise, and the outline may have to be modified. A preliminary outline is chiefly useful as a means of getting going, not as a guide to the final essay.

The Outline as a Way of Checking a Draft   Whether or not you use a preliminary outline, we strongly suggest that after you have written what you hope is your last draft, you make an outline of it; there is no better way of finding out whether the essay is well organized.

Go through the draft and write down the chief points in the order in which you make them. That is, prepare a table of contents—perhaps a phrase for each paragraph. Next, examine your notes to see what kind of sequence they reveal in your paper:

- Is the sequence reasonable? Can it be improved?
- Are any passages irrelevant?
- Does something important seem to be missing?

If no coherent structure or reasonable sequence clearly appears in the outline, then the full prose version of your argument probably doesn't have any either. Therefore, produce another draft, moving things around, adding or subtracting paragraphs—cutting and pasting into a new sequence, with transitions as needed—and then make another outline to see if the sequence now is satisfactory.

You are probably familiar with the structure known as a **formal outline.** Major points are indicated by I, II, III; points within major points are indicated by A, B, C; divisions within A, B, C are indicated by 1, 2, 3; and so on. Thus,

I. Arguments for opening all Olympic sports to professionals
  A. Fairness
    1. Some Olympic sports are already open to professionals.
    2. Some athletes who really are not professionals are classified as professionals.
  B. Quality (achievements would be higher)

You may want to outline your draft according to this principle, or it may be enough if you simply write a phrase for each paragraph and indent the subdivisions. But keep these points in mind:

- It is not enough for the parts to be ordered reasonably.
- The order must be made clear to the reader, probably by means of transitions such as *for instance, on the other hand, we can now turn to an opposing view,* and so on.

Here is another way of thinking about an outline. For each paragraph, write

- what the paragraph *says,* and
- what the paragraph *does.*

An opening paragraph might be outlined thus:

- What the paragraph *says* is that the words "under God" in the Pledge of Allegiance should be omitted.

- What the paragraph *does* is, first, it informs the reader of the thesis, and second, it *provides some necessary background,* for instance, that the words were not in the original wording of the Pledge.

A dual outline of this sort will help you to see whether you have a final draft or a draft that needs refinement.

A Last Word about Outlines

Outlines may seem rigid to many writers, especially to writers who customarily compose online, where we are accustomed to cutting, copying, moving, and deleting as we draft. However, as we said earlier, an outline—whether you write it before you draft a single word or use it to evaluate the organization of something you have already written—is meant to be a guide rather than a straitjacket that confines you. Many writers who compose electronically find that the ability to keep banging out words—typing is so much easier than pushing a pen or pencil—and to cut and paste without actually reaching for scissors makes it easy to produce an essay that readers may find difficult to follow. (There is much truth in the proverb, "Easy writing makes hard reading.") If you compose electronically, and especially if you find yourself continually adding, deleting, and moving text around without a clear organizational goal in mind, be sure to read and outline your draft, and then examine the outline to see if indeed there is a reasonable organization.

Outlines are especially helpful for long essays, but even short ones benefit from a bit of advanced planning, a list of a few topics (drawn from notes already taken) that help to keep the writer moving in an orderly way. A longer work such as an honors or a master's thesis typically requires careful planning. An outline will be a great help in assuring that you will produce something that a reader can easily follow—but of course you may find, as you write, that the outline needs to be altered.

When readers finish reading, they should feel that the writer has brought them to a decisive point and now is not just abruptly and unexpectedly stopping.

Tone and the Writer's Persona

Although this book is chiefly about argument in the sense of rational discourse—the presentation of reasons in support of a thesis or conclusion—the appeal to reason is only one form of persuasion.

✓ A CHECKLIST FOR ORGANIZING AN ARGUMENT

- ☐ Does the introduction let the readers know where the author is taking them?
- ☐ Does the introduction state the problem or issue?
  - ☐ Does it state the claim (the thesis)?
  - ☐ Does it suggest the organization of the essay, thereby helping the reader to follow the argument?
- ☐ Do subsequent paragraphs support the claim?
  - ☐ Do they offer evidence?
  - ☐ Do they face objections to the claim and offer reasonable responses?
  - ☐ Do they indicate why the author's claim is preferable?
  - ☐ Do transitions (signposts such as "Furthermore," "On the other hand,"and "Consider as an example") guide the reader through the argument?
- ☐ Does the essay end effectively, with a paragraph (or at most two paragraphs) bringing a note of closure, for instance, by indicating that the proposed solution is relatively simple? By admitting that, although the proposed solution will be difficult to implement, it is certainly feasible? By reminding the reader of the urgency of the problem?

Another form is the appeal to emotion—to pity, for example. Aristotle saw, in addition to the appeal to reason and the appeal to emotion, a third form of persuasion, the appeal to the character of the speaker. He called it the **ethical appeal** (the Greek word for this kind of appeal is **ethos,** "character"). The idea is that effective speakers convey the suggestion that they are

- informed,
- intelligent,
- fair-minded (persons of goodwill), and
- honest.

Because they are perceived as trustworthy, their words inspire confidence in their listeners. It is, of course, a fact that when we read an argument we are often aware of the *person* or *voice* behind the words, and our assent to the argument depends partly on the extent to which we can share the speaker's assumptions, look at the matter from the speaker's point of view—in short, *identify* with this speaker.

How can a writer inspire the confidence that lets readers identify themselves with him or her? To begin with, the writer should possess the virtues Aristotle specified: intelligence or good sense, honesty, and benevolence or goodwill. As the Roman proverb puts it, "No one gives what he does not have." Still, possession of these qualities is not a guarantee that you will convey them in your writing. Like all other writers, you will have to revise your drafts so that these qualities become apparent, or, stated more moderately, you will have to revise so that nothing in the essay causes a reader to doubt your intelligence, honesty, and goodwill. A blunder in logic, a misleading quotation, a snide remark, even an error in spelling—all such slips can cause readers to withdraw their sympathy from the writer.

But of course all good argumentative essays do not sound exactly alike; they do not all reveal the same speaker. Each writer develops his or her own voice or (as literary critics and teachers call it) **persona.** In fact, one writer will have several voices or personae, depending on the topic and the audience. The president of the United States delivering an address on the State of the Union has one persona; chatting with a reporter at his summer home he has another. This change is not a matter of hypocrisy. Different circumstances call for different language. As a French writer put it, there is a time to speak of "Paris" and a time to speak of "the capital of the nation." When Lincoln spoke at Gettysburg, he didn't say "Eighty-seven years ago," but "Four score and seven years ago." We might say that just as some occasions required him to be the folksy Honest Abe, the occasion of the dedication of hallowed ground required him to be formal and solemn, and so the president of the United States appropriately used biblical language. The election campaigns called for one persona, and the dedication of a military cemetery—a different rhetorical situation—called for a different persona. For examples on how to vary tone, see Idea Prompt 6.2.

A RULE FOR WRITERS: Present yourself so that your readers see you as knowledgeable, honest, open-minded, and interested in helping them to think about an issue of significance.

IDEA PROMPT 6.2 VARYING TONE

Abraham Lincoln	*Four score and seven years ago our fathers brought forth on this continent a new nation, conceived in liberty, and dedicated to the proposition that all men are created equal.*	Invokes Biblical rhetoric ("Four score and seven years ago") in an appeal to national unity
More academic tone	*In 1776, America's Founding Fathers drafted and signed the Declaration of Independence, at the heart of which were the Enlightenment ideals of equality and individual liberty.*	Incorporates specific factual information and connects to overarching ideas
More informal tone	*Nearly a hundred years ago, the United States was founded in order to provide greater freedom and equality to its citizens.*	Is accurate but simplified, forgoing much detail
Too informal for most academic writing	*The US was created way back then so that everyone would be free.*	Mischaracterizes or oversimplifies the thought process

When we talk about a writer's persona, we mean the way in which the writer presents his or her attitudes

- toward *the self,*
- toward *the audience,* and
- toward *the subject.*

Thus, if a writer says,

> I have thought long and hard about this subject, and I can say with assurance that . . .

we may feel that we are listening to a self-satisfied ass who probably is simply mouthing other people's opinions. Certainly he is mouthing clichés: "long and hard," "say with assurance."

Let's look at a slightly subtler example of an utterance that reveals an attitude. When we read that

President Nixon was hounded out of office by journalists,

we hear a respectful attitude toward Nixon ("President Nixon") and a hostile attitude toward the press (they are beasts, curs who "hounded" our elected leader). If the writer's attitudes were reversed, she might have said something like this:

The press turned the searchlight on Tricky Dick's criminal shenanigans.

"Tricky Dick" and "criminal" are obvious enough, but notice that "shenanigans" also implies the writer's contempt for Nixon, and of course, "turned the searchlight" suggests that the press is a source of illumination, a source of truth. The original version and the opposite version both say that the press was responsible for Nixon's resignation, but the original version ("President Nixon was hounded") conveys indignation toward journalists, whereas the revision conveys contempt for Nixon.

These two versions suggest two speakers who differ not only in their view of Nixon but also in their manner, including the seriousness with which they take themselves. Although the passage is very short, it seems to us that the first speaker conveys righteous indignation ("hounded"), whereas the second conveys amused contempt ("shenanigans"). To our ears the tone, as well as the point, differs in the two versions.

We are talking about **loaded words,** words that convey the writer's attitude and that by their connotations are meant to win the reader to the writer's side. Compare the words in the left-hand column with those in the right:

freedom fighter	terrorist
pro-choice	pro-abortion
pro-life	antichoice
economic refugee	illegal alien
terrorist surveillance	domestic spying

The words in the left-hand column sound like good things; speakers who use these words are seeking to establish themselves as virtuous people who are supporting worthy causes. The **connotations** (associations, overtones) of these pairs of words differ, even though the **denotations** (explicit meanings, dictionary definitions) are the same, just as the connotations of *mother* and *female parent* differ, although the denotations are the same. Similarly, although Lincoln's "four score and seven" and "eighty-seven" both denote "thirteen less than one hundred," they differ in connotation.

Tone is not only a matter of connotations (*hounded out of office* versus, let's say, *compelled to resign*, or *pro-choice* versus *pro-abortion*); it is also a matter of such things as the selection and type of examples. A writer who offers many examples, especially ones drawn from ordinary life, conveys a persona different from that of a writer who offers no examples or only an occasional invented instance. The first of these probably is, one might say, friendlier, more down-to-earth.

Last Words on Tone   On the whole, when writing an argument, it is advisable to be courteous and respectful of your topic, of your audience, and of people who hold views you are arguing against. It is rarely good for one's own intellectual development to regard as villains or fools persons who hold views different from one's own, especially if some of them are in the audience. Keep in mind the story of the two strangers on a train who, striking up a conversation, found that both were clergymen, though of different faiths. Then one said to the other, "Well, why shouldn't we be friends? After all, we both serve God, you in your way and I in His."

Complacency is all right when telling a joke but not when offering an argument:

- Recognize opposing views.
- Assume they are held in good faith.
- State them fairly (if you don't, you do a disservice not only to the opposition but also to your own position because the perceptive reader will not take you seriously).
- Be temperate in arguing your own position: "If I understand their view correctly . . ."; "It seems reasonable to conclude that . . ."; "Perhaps, then, we can agree that . . ."
- Write calmly: If you become overly emotional your readers may interpret you as biased or unreasonable—even a bit nutty—and they may lose their confidence in you.

One way to practice thinking about tone and persona is in your professional e-mails. As a student you probably send many e-mails to your classmates and to your instructors or other offices on campus (the financial aid office, the parking/traffic office, your instructors, your advisor, etc.). As teachers, we are often surprised at how flippant and inattentive students are when e-mailing.

We, One, or I?

The use of *we* in the last sentence brings us to another point: May the first-person pronouns *I* and *we* be used? In this book, because two of us are writing, we often use *we* to mean the two authors. And we sometimes use *we* to mean the authors and the readers. This shifting use of one word can be troublesome, but we hope (clearly the *we* here refers only to the authors) that we have avoided any ambiguity. But can, or should, or must an individual use *we* instead of *I*? The short answer is no.

If you are simply speaking for yourself, use *I*. Attempts to avoid the first-person singular by saying things like "This writer thinks . . . ," and "It is thought that . . . ," and "One thinks that . . . ," are far more irritating (and wordy) than the use of *I*. The so-called editorial *we* is as odd-sounding in a student's argument as is the royal *we*. Mark Twain said that the only ones who can appropriately say *we* are kings, editors, and people with a tapeworm. And because one *one* leads to another, making the sentence sound (James Thurber's words) "like a trombone solo," it's best to admit that you are the author, and to use *I*. But there is no need to preface every sentence with "I think." The reader knows that the essay is yours; just write it, using *I* when you must, but not needlessly.

Often you will see *I* in journalistic writing and of course in autobiographical writing—and you will see it in some argumentative writing, too—but in most argumentative writing it is best to state the facts and (when drawing reasonable conclusions from them) to keep yourself in the background. Why? The more you use *I* in an essay, the more your readers will attach *you* directly to the argument and may regard your position as personal rather than as relevant to themselves.

Avoiding Sexist Language

Courtesy as well as common sense requires that you respect the feelings of your readers. Many people today find offensive the implicit sexism in the use of male pronouns to denote not only men but also women ("As the reader follows the argument, he will find . . ."). And sometimes the use of the male pronoun to denote all people is ridiculous: "An individual, no matter what his sex, . . ."

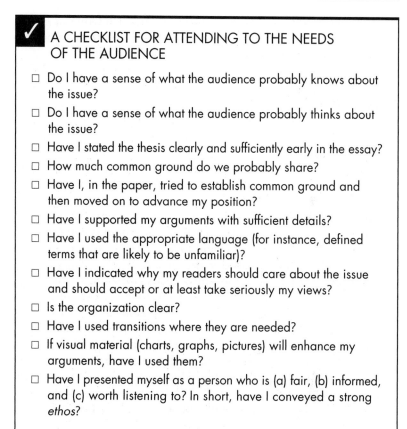

✓ A CHECKLIST FOR ATTENDING TO THE NEEDS
OF THE AUDIENCE

☐ Do I have a sense of what the audience probably knows about the issue?

☐ Do I have a sense of what the audience probably thinks about the issue?

☐ Have I stated the thesis clearly and sufficiently early in the essay?

☐ How much common ground do we probably share?

☐ Have I, in the paper, tried to establish common ground and then moved on to advance my position?

☐ Have I supported my arguments with sufficient details?

☐ Have I used the appropriate language (for instance, defined terms that are likely to be unfamiliar)?

☐ Have I indicated why my readers should care about the issue and should accept or at least take seriously my views?

☐ Is the organization clear?

☐ Have I used transitions where they are needed?

☐ If visual material (charts, graphs, pictures) will enhance my arguments, have I used them?

☐ Have I presented myself as a person who is (a) fair, (b) informed, and (c) worth listening to? In short, have I conveyed a strong *ethos*?

In most contexts there is no need to use gender-specific nouns or pronouns. One way to avoid using *he* when you mean any person is to use *he or she* (or *she or he*) instead of *he,* but the result is sometimes a bit cumbersome—although it is superior to the overly conspicuous *he/she* and to *s/he.*

Here are two simple ways to solve the problem:

• *Use the plural* ("As readers follow the argument, they will find . . ."), or

• *Recast the sentence* so that no pronoun is required ("Readers following the argument will find . . .").

Because *man* and *mankind* strike many readers as sexist when used in such expressions as "Man is a rational animal" and "Mankind has not yet solved this problem," consider using such words as *human being, person, people, humanity,* and *we.* (*Examples:* "Human beings are rational animals"; "We have not yet solved this problem.")

PEER REVIEW

Your instructor may suggest—or may even require—that you submit an early draft of your essay to a fellow student or small group of students for comment. Such a procedure benefits both author and readers: You get the responses of a reader and the student-reader gets experience in thinking about the problems of developing an argument, especially in thinking about such matters as the degree of detail that a writer needs to offer to a reader and the importance of keeping the organization evident to a reader.

Oral peer reviews allow for the give and take of discussion, but probably most students and most instructors find written peer reviews more helpful because reviewers think more carefully about their responses to the draft, and they help essayists to get beyond a knee-jerk response to criticism. Online reviews on a class Web site or through e-mail are especially helpful precisely because they are not face to face; the peer reviewer gets practice *writing,* and the essayist is not directly challenged. Sharing documents via Google Doc works well for peer review. You can copy and paste your essay into a Google Doc (if you did not compose it there) and then share it with a classmate who is sitting next to you.

A STUDENT'S ESSAY, FROM ROUGH NOTES TO FINAL VERSION

While we were revising this textbook, we asked the students in one of our classes to write a short essay (500–750 words) on some ethical problem that concerned them. Because this assignment was the first writing assignment in the course, we explained that a good way to get ideas is to ask oneself some questions, write down responses, question those responses, and write freely for ten minutes or so, not worrying about contradictions. We invited our students to hand in their initial notes along with the finished essay, so that we could get a sense of how they proceeded as writers. Not all of them chose to hand in their notes, but we were greatly encouraged by those who did. What was encouraging was the

A PEER REVIEW CHECKLIST FOR A DRAFT OF AN ARGUMENT

Read the draft through quickly. Then read it again, with the following questions in mind. Remember: You are reading a draft, a work in progress. You are expected to offer suggestions, and it is also expected that you will offer them courteously.

☐ In a sentence, indicate the degree to which the draft shows promise of fulfilling the assignment.

☐ Is the writer's tone appropriate? Who is the audience?

☐ Looking at the essay as a whole, what thesis (main idea) is advanced?

☐ Are the needs of the audience kept in mind? For instance, do some words need to be defined? Is the evidence (for instance, the examples and the testimony of authorities) clear and effective?

☐ Can I accept the assumptions? If not, why not?

☐ Is any obvious evidence (or counterevidence) overlooked?

☐ Is the writer proposing a solution? If so,

    ☐ Are other equally attractive solutions adequately examined?

    ☐ Has the writer overlooked some unattractive effects of the proposed solution?

☐ Looking at each paragraph separately,

    ☐ What is the basic point?

    ☐ How does each paragraph relate to the essay's main idea or to the previous paragraph?

    ☐ Should some paragraphs be deleted? Be divided into two or more paragraphs? Be combined? Be put elsewhere? (If you outline the essay by writing down the gist of each paragraph, you will get help in answering these questions.)

    ☐ Is each sentence clearly related to the sentence that precedes and to the sentence that follows? If not, in a sentence or two indicate examples of good and bad transitions.

    ☐ Is each paragraph adequately developed? Are there sufficient details, perhaps brief supporting quotations from the text?

    ☐ Are the introductory and concluding paragraphs effective?

☐ What are the paper's chief strengths?

☐ Make at least two specific suggestions that you think will assist the author to improve the paper.

confirmation of an old belief, the belief—we call it a fact—that students will hand in a thoughtful essay if before they prepare a final version they nag themselves, ask themselves *why* they think this or that, write down their responses, and are not afraid to change their minds as they proceed.

Here are the first notes of a student, Emily Andrews, who elected to write about whether to give money to street beggars. She simply put down ideas, one after the other.

Help the poor? Why do I (sometimes) do it?

I feel guilty, and think I should help them: poor, cold, hungry (but also some of them are thirsty for liquor, and will spend the money on liquor, not on food).

I also feel annoyed by them—most of them.

Where does the expression "the deserving poor" come from?

And "poor but honest"? Actually, that sounds a bit odd. Wouldn't "rich but honest" make more sense?

Why don't they work? Fellow with red beard, always by bus stop in front of florist's shop, always wants a handout. He is a regular, there all day every day, so I guess he is in a way "reliable," so why doesn't he put the same time in on a job?

Or why don't they get help? Don't they know they need it? They *must* know they need it.

Maybe that guy with the beard is just a con artist. Maybe he makes more money by panhandling than he would by working, and it's a lot easier!

Kinds of poor—how to classify??
    drunks, druggies, etc.
    mentally ill (maybe drunks belong here, too)
    decent people who have had terrible luck

Why private charity?

Doesn't it make sense to say we (fortunate individuals) should give something—an occasional handout—to people who have had terrible luck? (I suppose some people might say that there is no need for any of us to give anything — the government takes care of the truly needy — but I *do* believe in giving charity. A month ago a friend of the family passed away, and the woman's children suggested that people might want to make a donation in her name, to a shelter for battered women. I know my parents made a donation.)

BUT how can I tell who is who, which are which? Which of these people asking for "spare change" really need (deserve???) help, and which are phonies? Impossible to tell.

Possibilities:

> Give to no one
> Give to no one but make an annual donation, maybe to
> United Way
> Give a dollar to each person who asks. This would probably
> not cost me even a dollar a day
> Occasionally do without something — maybe a CD — or a meal
> in a restaurant — and give the money I save to people who
> seem worthy.

WORTHY? What am I saying? How can I, or anyone, tell? The neat-looking guy who says he just lost his job may be a phony, and the dirty bum — probably a drunk — may desperately need food. (OK, so what if he spends the money on liquor instead of food? At least he'll get a little pleasure in life. No! It's not all right if he spends it on drink.)

Other possibilities:

> Do some volunteer work?
> To tell the truth, I don't want to put in the time. I don't feel
> *that* guilty.

So what's the problem?

Is it, How I can help the very poor (handouts, or through an organization)? or

How I can feel less guilty about being lucky enough to be able to go to college, and to have a supportive family?

I can't quite bring myself to believe I should help every beggar
who approaches, but I also can't bring myself to believe that I
should do nothing, on the grounds that:

    a. it's probably their fault

    b. if they are deserving, they can get gov't help. No, I just
       can't believe that. Maybe some are too proud to look for
       government help, or don't know that they are entitled to it.

What to do?

On balance, it seems best to

    a. give to United Way

    b. maybe also give to an occasional individual, if I happen
       to be moved, without worrying about whether he or she is
       "deserving" (since it's probably impossible to know).

A day after making these notes Emily reviewed them, added
a few points, and then made a very brief selection from them to
serve as an outline for her first draft:

Opening para.: "poor but honest"? Deserve "spare change"?

Charity: private or through organizations?

        pros and cons

        guy at bus

        it wouldn't cost me much, but . . . better to give through
        organizations

Concluding para.: still feel guilty?

        maybe mention guy at bus again?

After writing and revising a draft, Emily Andrews submitted
her essay to a fellow student for peer review. She then revised her
work in light of the suggestions she received and in light of her
own further thinking.

On the next page we give the final essay. If after reading the
final version you reread the early notes, you will notice that some
of the notes never made it into the final version. But without the
notes, the essay probably could not have been as interesting as it
is. When the writer made the notes, she was not so much putting
down her ideas as *finding* ideas by the process of writing.

Andrews 1

Emily Andrews

Professor Barnet

English 102

January 15, 2010

Why I Don't Spare "Spare Change"

"Poor but honest." "The deserving poor." I don't know
the origin of these quotations, but they always come to mind
when I think of "the poor." But I also think of people who,
perhaps through alcohol or drugs, have ruined not only their
own lives but also the lives of others in order to indulge in
their own pleasure. Perhaps alcoholism and drug addiction really are "diseases," as many people say, but my own
feeling — based, of course, not on any serious study — is that
most alcoholics and drug addicts can be classified with the
"undeserving poor." And that is largely why I don't distribute
spare change to panhandlers.

But surely among the street people there are also some
who can rightly be called "deserving." Deserving what? My
spare change? Or simply the government's assistance? It
happens that I have been brought up to believe that it is
appropriate to make contributions to charity — let's say a
shelter for battered women — but if I give some change to a
panhandler, am I making a contribution to charity and thereby
helping someone, or, on the contrary, am I perhaps simply
encouraging someone not to get help? Or maybe even worse,
am I supporting a con artist?

If one believes in the value of private charity, one can
give either to needy individuals or to charitable organizations.

In giving to a panhandler one may indeed be helping a person who badly needs help, but one cannot be certain that one is giving to a needy individual. In giving to an organization such as the United Way, on the other hand, one can feel that one's money is likely to be used wisely. True, confronted by a beggar one may feel that *this* particular unfortunate individual needs help at *this* moment — a cup of coffee or a sandwich — and the need will not be met unless I put my hand in my pocket right now. But I have come to think that the beggars whom I encounter can get along without my spare change, and indeed perhaps they are actually better off for not having money to buy liquor or drugs.

It happens that in my neighborhood I encounter few panhandlers. There is one fellow who is always by the bus stop where I catch the bus to the college, and I never give him anything precisely because he is always there. He is such a regular that, I think, he ought to be able to hold a regular job. Putting him aside, I probably don't encounter more than three or four beggars in a week. (I'm not counting street musicians. These people seem quite able to work for a living. If they see their "work" as playing or singing, let persons who enjoy their performances pay them. I do not consider myself among their audience.) The truth of the matter is that, since I meet so few beggars, I could give each one a dollar and hardly feel the loss. At most, I might go without seeing a movie some week. But I know nothing about these people, and it's my impression — admittedly based on almost no evidence — that they simply prefer begging to working. I am not generalizing about street

Andrews 3

people, and certainly I am not talking about street people in the big urban centers. I am talking only about the people whom I actually encounter.

That's why I usually do not give "spare change," and I don't think I will in the future. These people will get along without me. Someone else will come up with money for their coffee or their liquor, or, at worst, they will just have to do without. I will continue to contribute occasionally to a charitable organization, not simply (I hope) to salve my conscience but because I believe that these organizations actually do good work. But I will not attempt to be a mini-charitable organization, distributing (probably to the unworthy) spare change.

THE ESSAY ANALYZED

Finally, here are a few comments about the essay:

The title is informative, alerting the reader to the topic and the author's position. (By the way, the student told us that in her next-to-last draft the title was "Is It Right to Spare 'Spare Change'?" This title, like the revision, introduces the topic but not the author's position.)

The opening paragraph holds a reader's interest, partly by alluding to the familiar phrase "the deserving poor" and partly by introducing the *un*familiar phrase "the *un*deserving poor." Notice, too, that this opening paragraph ends by clearly asserting the author's thesis. Writers need not always announce their thesis early, but it is usually advisable to do so.

Paragraph two begins by voicing what probably is the reader's somewhat uneasy—perhaps even negative—response to the first paragraph. That is, *the writer has a sense of her audience;* she knows how her reader feels, and she takes account of the feeling.

Paragraph three clearly sets forth the alternatives. A reader may disagree with the writer's attitude, but the alternatives seem to be stated fairly.

Paragraphs four and five are more personal than the earlier paragraphs. The writer, more or less having stated what she takes to be the facts, now is entitled to offer a highly personal response to them.

The final paragraph nicely wraps things up by means of the words "spare change," which go back to the title and to the end of the first paragraph. The reader thus experiences a sensation of completeness. The essayist, of course, has not solved the problem for all of us for all time, but she presents a thoughtful argument and ends the essay effectively.

EXERCISE

In a brief essay, state a claim and support it with evidence. Choose an issue in which you are genuinely interested and about which you already know something. You may want to interview a few experts and do some reading, but don't try to write a highly researched paper. Sample topics:

1. Students in laboratory courses should not be required to participate in the dissection of animals.

2. Washington, D.C., should be granted statehood.
3. Women should, in wartime, be exempted from serving in combat.
4. The annual Miss America contest is an insult to women.
5. The government should not offer financial support to the arts.
6. The chief fault of the curriculum in high school was . . .
7. No specific courses should be required in colleges or universities.

7

Using Sources

Research is formalized curiosity. It is poking and prying with a purpose.

—ZORA NEALE HURSTON

There is no way of exchanging information that does not involve an act of judgment.

—JACOB BRONOWSKI

For God's sake, stop researching for a while and begin to think.

—WALTER HAMILTON MOBERLY

A problem adequately stated is a problem on its way to being solved.

—R. BUCKMINSTER FULLER

I have yet to see any problem, however complicated, which, when you looked at it in the right way, did not become still more complicated.

—POUL ANDERSON

WHY USE SOURCES?

We have pointed out that one gets ideas by writing. In the exercise of writing a draft, ideas begin to form, and these ideas stimulate further ideas, especially when one questions—when one *thinks* about—what one has written. But of course in writing about complex, serious questions, nobody is expected to invent all the answers. On the contrary, a writer is expected to be familiar with the chief answers already produced by others and to make use of them through selective incorporation and criticism. In short, writers are not expected to reinvent the wheel; rather, they are expected to make good use of it and perhaps round it off a bit or replace a defective spoke. In order to think out your own views in writing, you are expected to do some preliminary research into the views of others.

When you are trying to understand an issue, high-quality sources will inform you of the various approaches others have taken and will help you establish what the facts are. Once you are informed enough to take a position, the sources you present to your readers will inform and persuade them, just as expert witnesses are sometimes brought in to inform and persuade a jury.

Research isn't limited to the world of professors and scientists. In one way or another, everyone does research at some point. If you want to persuade your city council to increase the number of bicycle lanes on city streets, you could bolster your argument with statistics on how much money the city could save if more people rode their bikes to work. If you decide to open your own business, you would do plenty of market research to persuade your bank that you could repay a loan. Sources (whether published information or data you gather yourself through interviews, surveys, or observation) are not only useful for background information; well-chosen and carefully analyzed sources are evidence for your readers that you know what you're talking about and that your interpretation is sound.

In Chapters 5 and 6 we discussed *ethos* as an appeal that establishes credibility with readers. When you do competent research and thereby let your audience see that you have done your homework, it increases your *ethos*; your audience will trust you because they see that you are well-informed, offering them not just your opinions but also an awareness of other opinions and of the relevant facts. Conducting thorough research not only helps you to develop your argument but it also shows respect for your audience.

Research is often misconstrued as the practice of transcribing information. In fact, it's a process of asking questions and gathering information that helps you come to conclusions about an issue. By using the information you find as evidence, you can develop an effective argument. But don't spend too much time searching and then waiting until the last minute to start writing. As you begin your search, write down observations and questions. When you find a useful source, take notes on what you think it means in your own words. This way, you won't find yourself with a pile of printouts and books and no idea what to say about them. What you have to say will flow naturally out of the prewriting you've already done—and that prewriting will help guide your search.

The process of research isn't always straightforward and neat. It involves scanning what other people have said about a topic and seeing what kinds of questions have been raised. As you poke and pry, you will learn more about the issue, and that, in turn, will help you develop a question to focus your efforts. Once you have a central idea—a thesis—you can sharpen your search to seek out the evidence that will make your readers sit up and take notice.

Consider arguments about whether athletes should be permitted to take anabolic steroids, drugs that supposedly build up muscle, restore energy, and enhance aggressiveness. A thoughtful argument on this subject will have to take account of information that the writer can gather only by doing some research.

- Do steroids really have the effects commonly attributed to them?
- Are they dangerous?
- If they are dangerous, how dangerous are they?

After all, competitive sports are inherently dangerous, some of them highly so. Many boxers, mixed martial arts fighters, jockeys, and football players have suffered severe injury, even death, from competing. Does anyone believe that anabolic steroids are more dangerous than the contests themselves? Obviously, again, a respectable argument about steroids will have to show awareness of what is known about them.

Or take this question:

Why did President Truman order that atomic bombs be dropped on Hiroshima and Nagasaki?

The most obvious answer is to end the war, but some historians believe he had a very different purpose. In their view, Japan's defeat was ensured before the bombs were dropped, and the Japanese were ready to surrender; the bombs were dropped not to save American (or Japanese) lives but to show Russia that the United States would not be pushed around. Scholars who hold this view, such as Gar Alperovitz in *Atomic Diplomacy* (1965), argue that Japanese civilians in Hiroshima and Nagasaki were incinerated not to save the lives of American soldiers who otherwise would have died in an invasion of Japan but to teach Stalin a lesson. Dropping the bombs, it is argued, marked not the end of the Pacific War but the beginning of the cold war.

One must ask: What evidence supports this argument or claim or thesis, which assumes that Truman could not have thought the bomb was needed to defeat the Japanese because the Japanese knew they were defeated and would soon surrender without a hard-fought defense that would cost hundreds of thousands of lives? What about the momentum that had built up to use the bomb? After all, years of effort and $2 billion had been expended to produce a weapon with the intention of using it to end the war against Germany. But Germany had been defeated without the use of the bomb. Meanwhile, the war in the Pacific continued unabated. If the argument we are considering is correct, all this background counted for little or nothing in Truman's decision, a decision purely diplomatic and coolly indifferent to human life. The task for the writer is to evaluate the evidence available and then to argue for or against the view that Truman's purpose in dropping the bomb was to impress the Soviet government.

A student writing on the topic will certainly want to consult the chief books on the subject (Alperovitz's, cited above, Martin Sherwin's *A World Destroyed* [1975], and John Toland's *The Rising Sun* [1970]) and perhaps reviews of them, especially the reviews in journals devoted to political science. (Reading a searching review of a serious scholarly book is a good way to identify quickly some of the book's main contributions and controversial claims.) Truman's letters and statements and books and articles about Truman are also clearly relevant, and doubtless important articles are to be found in recent issues of scholarly journals and electronic sources. In fact, even an essay on such a topic as whether Truman was morally justified in using the atomic bomb for *any* purpose will be a stronger essay if it is well-informed about such matters as the estimated loss of life that an invasion would have cost, the international rules governing weapons, and Truman's own statements about the issue.

How does one go about finding the material needed to write a well-informed argument? We will provide help, but first we want to offer a few words about choosing a topic.

CHOOSING A TOPIC

We will be brief. If a topic is not assigned, choose one that

- interests you and
- can be researched with reasonable thoroughness in the allotted time.

Topics such as censorship, the environment, and sexual harassment obviously impinge on our lives, and it may well be that one such topic is of especial interest to you. But the scope of these topics makes researching them potentially overwhelming. Type the word *censorship* into an **Internet** search engine, and you will be referred to millions of information sources.

This brings us to our second point—a manageable topic. Any of the previous topics would need to be narrowed substantially before you could begin searching in earnest. Similarly, a topic such as the causes of World War II can hardly be mastered in a few weeks or argued in a ten-page paper. It is simply too big.

You can, however, write a solid paper analyzing, evaluating, and arguing for or against General Eisenhower's views on atomic warfare. What were they, and when did he hold them? (In his books of 1948 and 1963 Eisenhower says that he opposed the use of the bomb before Hiroshima and that he argued with Secretary of War Henry Stimson against dropping it, but what evidence supports these claims? Was Eisenhower attempting to rewrite history in his books?) Eisenhower's own writings and books and other information sources on Eisenhower will, of course, be the major sources for a paper on this topic, but you will also want to look at books and articles about Stimson and at publications that contain information about the views of other generals, so that, for instance, you can compare Eisenhower's view with Marshall's or MacArthur's.

Spend a little time exploring a topic to see if it will be interesting and manageable by taking one or more of these approaches.

- Do a Web search on the topic. Though you may not use any of the sites that turn up, you can quickly put your finger on the pulse of popular approaches to the issue by scanning the first page or two of results to see what issues are getting the most attention.

- Plug the topic into one of the library's article databases. Again, just by scanning titles you can get a sense of what questions are being raised.

- Browse the library shelves where books on the topic are kept. A quick check of the tables of contents of recently published books may give you ideas of how to narrow the topic.

- Ask a librarian to show you where specialized reference books on your topic are found. Instead of general encyclopedias, try sources like these:

CQ Researcher
Encyclopedia of Applied Ethics
Encyclopedia of Bioethics
Encyclopedia of Crime and Justice
Encyclopedia of Science, Technology, and Ethics

- Talk to an expert. Members of the faculty who specialize in the area of your topic might be able to spell out some of the most significant controversies around a topic and may point you toward key sources.

FINDING MATERIAL

What strategy you use for finding good sources will depend on your topic. Researching a current issue in politics or popular culture may involve reading recent newspaper articles, scanning information on government Web sites, and locating current statistics. Other topics may be best tackled by seeking out books and scholarly journal articles that are less timely but more in-depth and analytical. You may want to supplement library and Web sources with your own fieldwork by conducting surveys or interviews.

Critical thinking is crucial to every step of the research process. Whatever strategy you use, remember that you will want to find material that is authoritative, represents a balanced approach to the issues, and is persuasive. As you choose your sources, bear in mind they will be serving as your "expert witnesses" as you make a case to your audience. Their quality and credibility are crucial to your argument.

If you find what seems to be an excellent source, look at some of the sources that this author repeatedly cites.

Finding Quality Information on the Web

The Web is a valuable source of information for many topics and less helpful for others. In general, if you're looking for information on public policy, popular culture, current events, legal affairs, or for any subject of interest to agencies of the federal or state government, the Web is likely to have useful material. If you're looking for literary criticism or scholarly analysis of historical or social issues, you will be better off using library databases, described later in this chapter.

To make good use of the Web, try these strategies.

- Use the most specific terms possible when using a general search engine; put phrases in quotes.

- Use the advanced search option to limit a search to a domain (e.g., *.gov* for government sites) or by date (such as Web sites updated in the past week or month).

- If you're not sure which sites might be good ones for research, try starting with one of the selective directories listed below instead of a general search engine.

- Consider which government agencies and organizations might be interested in your topic and go directly to their Web sites.

- Follow "about" links to see who is behind a Web site and why they put the information on the Web. If there is no "about" link, delete everything after the first slash in the URL to go to the parent site to see if it provides information.

- Use clues in URLs to see where sites originate. For example, URLs containing *.k12* are hosted at elementary and secondary schools, so may be intended for a young audience; those ending in *.gov* are government agencies, so they tend to provide official information.

- Always bear in mind that the sources you choose must be persuasive to your audience. Avoid sites that may be dismissed as unreliable or biased.

Some useful Web sites include the following:

Selective Web Site Directories
Infomine <http://infomine.ucr.edu/>
ipl2 <http://www.ipl.org>
Open Directory Project <http://www.dmoz.org>

Current News Sources
Google News <http://news.google.com>
Kidon Media-Link <http://www.kidon.com/media-link/index.php>

Digital Primary Sources
American Memory <http://memory.loc.gov>
American Rhetoric <http://www.americanrhetoric.com>
Avalon Project <http://avalon.law.yale.edu/default.asp>

Government Information
GPO Access <http://www.gpoaccess.gov>

Thomas (federal legislation) <http://thomas.loc.gov>
University of Michigan Documents Center <http://www.lib.umich
.edu/govdocs/>

Scholarly or Scientific Information
  Google Scholar <http://scholar.google.com>
  Scirus <http://www.scirus.com/>

Statistical Information
  American FactFinder <http://factfinder2.census.gov>
  Fedstats <http://www.fedstats.gov>
  Pew Global Attitudes Project <http://pewglobal.org>
  U.S. Census Bureau <http://www.census.gov>

A WORD ABOUT WIKIPEDIA

Links to Wikipedia (http://www.wikipedia.org) often rise to the top of Web search results. This vast and decentralized site provides over a million articles on a wide variety of topics. However, anyone can contribute to the online encyclopedia, so the accuracy of articles varies, and in some cases, the coverage of a controversial issue is one-sided or disputed. Even when the articles are accurate, they provide only basic information. Wikipedia's founder, Jimmy Wales, cautions students against using it as a source, except for obtaining general background knowledge: "You're in college; don't cite the encyclopedia."[1] Still, Wikipedia often provides valuable bibliographies that will help you to get going.

Finding Articles Using Library Databases

Your library has a wide range of general and specialized databases available through its Web site. Some databases provide references to articles (and perhaps abstracts or summaries) or may provide direct links to the entire text of articles. General and interdisciplinary databases include Academic Search Premier (produced by the EBSCO-host company) and Expanded Academic Index (from InfoTrac).

More specialized databases include PsycINFO (for psychology research) and ERIC (focused on topics in education). Others, such as JSTOR, are full-text digital archives of scholarly journals. You will likely have access to newspaper articles through LexisNexis

[1]"Wikipedia Founder Discourages Academic Use of His Creation," *Chronicle of Higher Education: The Wired Campus,* 12 June 2006, 16 Nov. 2006. http://chronicle.com /wiredcampus/article/1328/wikipedia-founder-discourages-academic-use-of-his-creation

FIGURE 7.1   AN ADVANCED WEB SEARCH

or Proquest Newsstand, particularly useful for articles that are not available for free on the Web. Look at your library's Web site to see what your options are, or stop by the reference desk for a quick personalized tutorial.

When using databases, first think through your topic using the listing and diagramming techniques described on pages 169–71. List synonyms for your key search terms. As you search, look at words used in titles and descriptors for alternative ideas and make use of the "advanced search" option so that you can easily combine multiple terms. Rarely will you find exactly what you're looking for right away. Try different search terms and different ways to narrow your topic.

Most databases have an advanced search option that offers forms for combining multiple terms. In Figure 7.1, a search on "anabolic steroids" retrieved far too many articles. In this advanced search, three concepts are being combined in a search: anabolic steroids, legal aspects of their use, and use of them by athletes. Related terms are combined with the word "or": *law* or *legal*. The last letters of a word have been replaced with an asterisk so that any ending will be included in the search. *Athlet** will search for *athlete, athletes,* or *athletics.* Options on both sides of the list of articles retrieved offer opportunities to refine a search by date of publication or to restrict the results to only academic journals, magazines, or newspapers.

As with a Web search, you'll need to make critical choices about which articles are worth pursuing. In this example, the first article may not be useful because it concerns German law. The second and third look fairly current and potentially useful. Only the third has a full text link, but the others may be available in another database. Many libraries have a program that will check other databases for you at the push of a button; in this case it's indicated by the "Find full text" button.

As you choose sources, keep track of them by selecting them. Then you can print off, save, or e-mail yourself the references you have selected. You may also have an option to export references to a citation management program such as RefWorks or EndNote. These programs allow you to create your own personal database of sources in which you can store your references and take notes. Later, when you're ready to create a bibliography, these programs will automatically format your references in MLA, APA, or another style. Ask a librarian if one of these programs is available to students on your campus.

Locating Books

The books that your library owns can be found through its online catalog. Typically, you can search by author or title or, if you don't have a specific book in mind, by keyword or subject. As with databases, think about different search terms to use, keeping an eye out for subject headings used for books that appear relevant. Take advantage of an "advanced search" option. You may, for example, be able to limit a search to books on a particular topic in English published within recent years. In addition to books, the catalog will also list DVDs, sound recordings, and other formats.

Unlike articles, books tend to cover broad topics, so be prepared to broaden your search terms. It may be that a book has a chapter or ten pages that are precisely what you need, but the catalog typically doesn't index the contents of books in detail. Think instead of what kind of book might contain the information you need.

Once you've found some promising books in the catalog, note down the call numbers, find them on the shelves, and then browse. Since books on the same topic are shelved together, you can quickly see what additional books are available by scanning the shelves. As you browse, be sure to look for books that have been published recently enough for your purposes. You do not have to read a book cover-to-cover to use it in your research. Instead, skim the introduction to see if it will be useful, then use its table of contents and index to pinpoint the sections of the book that are the most relevant.

If you have a very specific name or phrase you are searching for, you might try typing it into Google Book Search (http://books.google.com), which searches the contents of over 7 million scanned books. Though it tends to retrieve too many results for most topics, and you may only be able to see a snippet of context, it can help you locate a particular quote or identify which books might include an unusual name or phrase. There is a "find in a library" link that will help you determine whether the books are available in your library.

INTERVIEWING PEERS AND LOCAL AUTHORITIES

You ought to try to consult experts—for instance, members of the faculty or other local authorities on art, business, law, and so forth. You can also consult interested laypersons. Remember, however, that experts have their biases and that "ordinary" people may have knowledge that experts lack. When interviewing experts, keep in mind Picasso's comment: "You mustn't always believe what I say. Questions tempt you to tell lies, particularly when there is no answer."

If you are interviewing your peers, you will probably want to make an effort to get a representative sample. Of course, even within a group not all members share a single view—many African Americans favor affirmative action but not all do, and many gays favor legalizing gay marriage but, again, some don't. Make an effort to talk to a range of people who might be expected to offer varied opinions. You may learn some unexpected things.

Here we will concentrate, however, on interviews with experts.

1. **Finding subjects for interviews**   If you are looking for expert opinions, you may want to start with a faculty member on your campus. You may already know the instructor, or you may have to scan the catalog to see who teaches courses relevant to your topic. Department secretaries and college Web sites are good sources of information about the special interests of the faculty and also about lecturers who will be visiting the campus.

2. **Doing preliminary homework**   (a) In requesting the interview, make evident your interest in the topic and in the person. (If you know something about the person, you will be able to

indicate why you are asking him or her.) (b) Request the interview, preferably in writing, a week in advance, and ask for ample time—probably half an hour to an hour. Indicate whether the material will be confidential, and (if you want to use a recorder) ask if you may record the interview. (c) If the person accepts the invitation, ask if he or she recommends any preliminary reading, and establish a time and a suitable place, preferably not the cafeteria during lunchtime.

3. **Preparing thoroughly**   (a) If your interviewee recommended any reading or has written on the topic, read the material. (b) Tentatively formulate some questions, keeping in mind that (unless you are simply gathering material for a survey of opinions) you want more than yes or no answers. Questions beginning with *Why* and *How* will usually require the interviewee to go beyond yes and no.

Even if your subject has consented to let you bring a recorder, be prepared to take notes on points that strike you as especially significant; without written notes, you will have nothing if the recorder has malfunctioned. Further, by taking occasional notes you will give the interviewee some time to think and perhaps to rephrase or to amplify a remark.

4. **Conducting the interview**   (a) Begin by engaging in brief conversation, without taking notes. If the interviewee has agreed to let you use a recorder, settle on the place where you will put it. (b) Come prepared with an opening question or two, but as the interview proceeds, don't hesitate to ask questions that you had not anticipated asking. (c) Near the end (you and your subject have probably agreed on the length of the interview) ask the subject if he or she wishes to add anything, perhaps by way of clarifying some earlier comment. (d) Conclude by thanking the interviewee and by offering to provide a copy of the final version of your paper.

5. **Writing up the interview**   (a) As soon as possible— certainly within twenty-four hours after the interview—review your notes and clarify them. At this stage, you can still remember the meaning of your abbreviated notes and shorthand devices (maybe you have been using *n* to stand for *nurses* in clinics where abortions are performed), but if you wait even a whole day you may be puzzled by your own notes. If you have recorded the interview, you may want to transcribe all of it—the laboriousness of this task is one good reason why many interviewers do not use recorders—and you may then want to scan the whole and mark

the parts that now strike you as especially significant. If you have taken notes by hand, type them up, along with your own observations, for example, "Jones was very tentative on this matter, but she said she was inclined to believe that. . . ." (b) Be especially careful to indicate which words are direct quotations. If in doubt, check with the interviewee.

EVALUATING YOUR SOURCES

Each step of the way, you will be making choices about your sources. As your research proceeds, from selecting promising items in a database search to browsing the book collection, you will want to use the techniques for previewing and skimming detailed on pages 39–41 in order to make your first selection. Ask yourself some basic questions.

- Is this source relevant?
- Is it current enough?
- Does the title and/or abstract suggest it will address an important aspect of my topic?
- Am I choosing sources that represent a range of ideas, not simply ones that support my opinion?
- Do I have a reason to believe that these sources are trustworthy?

Once you have collected a number of likely sources, you will want to do further filtering. Examine each one with these questions in mind.

- *Is this source credible? Does it include information about the author and his or her credentials that can help me decide whether to rely on it?* In the case of books, you might check a database for book reviews for a second opinion. In the case of Web sites, find out where the site came from and why it has been posted on the Web. Don't use a Web source if you can't determine its authorship or purpose.
- *Will my audience find this source credible and persuasive?* Some publishers are more selective about which books they publish than others. University presses, for instance, have several experts read and comment on manuscripts before they decide which to publish. A story about U.S. politics from the

Washington Post, whose writers conduct firsthand reporting in the nation's capital, carries more clout than a story from a small-circulation newspaper that is drawing its information from a wire service. A scholarly source may be more impressive than a magazine article.

- *Am I using the best evidence available?* Quoting directly from a government report may be more effective than quoting a news story that summarizes the report. Finding evidence that supports your claims in a president's speeches or letters is more persuasive than drawing your conclusions from a page or two of a history textbook.

- *Am I being fair to all sides?* Make sure you are prepared to address alternate perspectives, even if you ultimately take a position. Avoid sources that clearly promote an agenda in favor of ones that your audience will consider balanced and reliable.

- *Can I corroborate my key claims in more than one source?* Compare your sources to ensure that you aren't relying on facts that can't be confirmed. If you're having trouble confirming a source, check with a librarian.

- *Do I really need this source?* It's tempting to use all the books and articles you have found, but if two sources say essentially the same thing, choose the one that is likely to carry the most weight with your audience.

The information you will look for as you evaluate a Web source is often the same as what you need to record in a citation. You can streamline the process of creating a list of works cited by identifying these elements as you evaluate a source.

In Figure 7.2 (see p. 228), the URL includes the ending *.gov*— meaning it is a government Web site, an official document that has been vetted. There is an "about" link that will explain the government agency's mission. The date is found at the bottom of the page: "revised 2006." This appears to be a high-quality source of basic information on the issue.

The information you need to cite this report is also on the page; make sure you keep track of where you found the source and when, since Web sites can change. One way to do this is by creating an account at a social bookmarking site such as Delicious (http://delicious.com) or Diigo (http://diigo.com) where you can store and annotate Web sites.

FIGURE 7.2   A HOMEPAGE FROM A GOVERNMENT WEB SITE

① URL—Site has a .gov domain.

② Sponsor

③ Author

④ Link will explain that this institute is a government agency.

⑤ Corporate author

⑥ Web site name

⑦ Title of page

⑧ Table of contents

⑨ Scanning list will give an idea of whether source is reliable and useful.

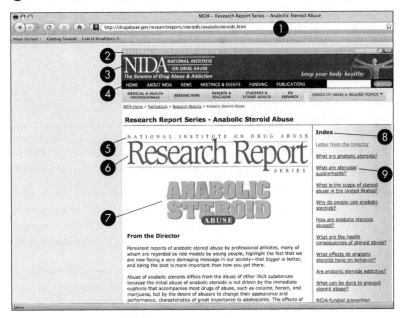

Figure 7.3 shows how the information on a Web page might lead you to reject it as a source. Clearly, though this site purports to provide educational information, its primary purpose is to sell products. The graphics emphasize the supposed benefits of these performance-enhancing drugs, a visual incentive to promote their use. The disclaimers about legal liability and age requirements send up a red flag.

FIGURE 7.3   A HOMEPAGE FROM A COMMERCIAL WEB SITE

This is a .com (commercial) site.

Table of contents looks useful, but . . .   Images seem to promote steriod use.

Disclaimers seem defensive.   Steroids are for sale.

TAKING NOTES

When it comes to taking notes, all researchers have their own habits that they swear by, and they can't imagine any other way of working. We still prefer to take notes on four-by-six-inch index cards, while others use a notebook or a computer for note taking. If you use a citation management program, such as RefWorks or EndNote, you can store your personal notes and commentary with the citations you have saved. Using the program's search function, you can easily pull together related notes and citations, or you can create project folders for your references so that you can easily review what you've collected.

Whatever method you use, the following techniques should help you maintain consistency and keep organized during the research process:

✓ A CHECKLIST FOR EVALUATING PRINT SOURCES

For Books:

☐ Is the book recent? If not, is the information I will be using from it likely or unlikely to change over time?

☐ What are the author's credentials?

☐ Is the book titled toward entertainment, or is it in-depth and even-handed?

☐ Is the book broad enough in its focus and written in a style I can understand?

☐ Does the book relate directly to my tentative thesis, or is it of only tangential interest?

☐ Do the arguments in the book seem sound, based on what I have learned about skillful critical reading and writing?

For Articles from Periodicals:

☐ Is the periodical recent?

☐ Is the author's name given? Does he or she seem a credible source?

☐ Does the article treat the topic superficially or in-depth? Does it take sides, or does it offer enough context so that you can make up your own mind?

☐ How directly does the article speak to my topic and tentative thesis?

☐ If the article is from a scholarly journal, am I sure I understand it?

1. If you use a notebook or cards, write in ink (pencil gets smudgy), and write on only one side of the card or paper. (Notes on the backs of cards tend to get lost, and writing on the back of paper will prevent you from later cutting up and rearranging your notes.) Consider using an online tool to keep up with your notes and ideas, for instance, a Google Doc, private blog, or wiki.

2. Summarize, for the most part, rather than quote at length.

3. Quote only passages in which the writing is especially effective or passages that are in some way crucial. These will be easy to access and use if kept in an online venue.

A CHECKLIST FOR EVALUATING ELECTRONIC SOURCES

An enormous amount of valuable material is available on the World Wide Web—but so is an enormous amount of junk. True, there is also plenty of junk in books and journals, but most printed material has been subjected to a review process: Book publishers and editors of journals send manuscripts to specialized readers who evaluate them and recommend whether the material should or should not be published. Publishing on the Web is quite different. Anyone can publish on the Web with no review process: All that is needed is sufficient access to the Internet. Ask yourself:

☐ What person or organization produced the site (a commercial entity, a nonprofit entity, a student, an expert)? Check the electronic address to get a clue about the authorship. If there is a link to the author's homepage, check it out to learn about the author. Does the author have an affiliation with a respectable institution?

☐ What is the purpose of the site? Is the site in effect an infomercial, or is it an attempt to contribute to a thoughtful discussion?

☐ Are the sources of information indicated and verifiable? If possible, check the sources.

☐ Is the site authoritative enough to use? (If it seems to contain review materials or class handouts, you probably don't want to take it too seriously.)

☐ When was the page made available? Is it out of date?

4. Make sure that all quotations are exact. Enclose quoted words within quotation marks, indicate omissions by ellipses (three spaced periods: . . .), and enclose within square brackets ([]) any insertions or other additions you make.

5. *Never* copy a passage, changing an occasional word. *Either* copy it word for word, with punctuation intact, and enclose it within quotation marks, *or* summarize it drastically. If you copy a passage but change a word here and there, you may later make the mistake of using your note verbatim in your essay, and you will be guilty of plagiarism.

6. Give the page number of your source, whether you summarize or quote. If a quotation you have copied runs in the original from the bottom of page 210 to the top of page 211,

in your notes put a diagonal line (/) after the last word on page 210, so that later, if in your paper you quote only the material from page 210, you will know that you must cite 210 and not 210–11.

7. Indicate the source. The author's last name is enough if you have consulted only one work by the author; but if you consult more than one work by an author, you need further identification, such as both the author's name and a short title.

8. Add your own comments about the substance of what you are recording. Such comments as "but contrast with Sherwin" or "seems illogical" or "evidence?" will ensure that you are thinking as well as writing and will be of value when you come to transform your notes into a draft. Be sure, however, to enclose such notes within double diagonals (//), or to mark them in some other way, so that later you will know they are yours and not your source's. If you use a computer for note taking, you may wish to write your comments in italics or in a different font.

9. In a separate computer file or notebook page or on separate index cards, write a bibliographic entry for each source. The information in each entry will vary, depending on whether the source is a book, a periodical, an electronic document, and so forth. The kind of information (for example, author and title) needed for each type of source can be found in the sections on MLA Format: The List of Works Cited (p. 253) or APA Format: The List of References (p. 267).

A NOTE ON PLAGIARIZING, PARAPHRASING, AND USING COMMON KNOWLEDGE

Plagiarism is the unacknowledged use of someone else's work. The word comes from a Latin word for "kidnapping," and plagiarism is indeed the stealing of something engendered by someone else. We won't deliver a sermon on the dishonesty (and folly) of plagiarism; we intend only to help you understand exactly what plagiarism is. The first thing to say is that plagiarism is not limited to the unacknowledged quotation of words.

A *paraphrase* is a sort of word-by-word or phrase-by-phrase translation of the author's language into your own language.

Unlike a summary, then, a paraphrase is approximately as long as the original. Why would anyone paraphrase something? There are two good reasons:

- You may, as a reader, want to paraphrase a passage in order to make certain that you are thinking carefully about each word in the original;
- You may, as a writer, want to paraphrase a difficult passage in order to help your reader.

Paraphrase thus has its uses, but it is often unnecessarily used, and students who overuse it may find themselves crossing the border into plagiarism. True, if you paraphrase you are using your own words, but

- you are also using someone else's ideas, and, equally important,
- you are using this other person's sequence of thoughts.

Even if you change every third word in your source, you are plagiarizing.

Here is an example of this sort of plagiarism, based on the previous sentence:

> Even if you alter every second or third word that your source gives, you still are plagiarizing.

Further, even if the writer of this paraphrase had cited a source after the paraphrase, he or she would still have been guilty of plagiarism. How, you may ask, can a writer who cites a source be guilty of plagiarism? Easy. Readers assume that only the gist of the idea is the source's and that the development of the idea—the way it is set forth—is the present writer's work. A paraphrase that runs to several sentences is in no significant way the writer's work: The writer is borrowing not only the idea but the shape of the presentation, the sentence structure. What the writer needs to do is to write something like this:

> Changing an occasional word does not free the writer from the obligation to cite a source.

And the source would still need to be cited, if the central idea were not a commonplace one.

The point that even if you cite a source for your paraphrase you are nevertheless plagiarizing—unless you clearly indicate that the entire passage is a paraphrase of the source—cannot be overemphasized.

You are plagiarizing if, without giving credit, you use some-one else's ideas—even if you put these ideas entirely into your own words. When you use another's ideas, you must indicate your indebtedness by saying something like "Alperovitz points out that . . ." or "Secretary of War Stimson, as Martin Sherwin notes, never expressed himself on this point." Alperovitz and Sherwin pointed out something that you had not thought of, and so you must give them credit if you want to use their findings.

Again, even if after a paraphrase you cite your source, you are plagiarizing. How, you may wonder, can you be guilty of plagiarism if you cite a source? Easy. A reader assumes that the citation refers to information or an opinion, *not* to the presentation or develop-ment of the idea; and of course, in a paraphrase you are not pre-senting or developing the material in your own way.

Now consider this question: *Why* paraphrase? Often there is no good answer. Since a paraphrase is as long as the original, you may as well quote the original, if you think that a passage of that length is worth quoting. Probably it is *not* worth quoting in full; prob-ably you should *not* paraphrase but rather should drastically *summarize* most of it, and perhaps quote a particularly effective phrase or two. As we explained on pages 45–52, the chief reason to paraphrase a passage is to clarify it—that is, to make certain that you and your readers understand a passage that—perhaps because it is badly written—is obscure.

Generally, what you should do is

- Take the idea and put it entirely into your own words, per-haps reducing a paragraph of a hundred words to a sentence of ten words, but you must still give credit for the idea.
- If you believe that the original hundred words are so per-fectly put that they cannot be transformed without great loss, you'll have to quote them in full and cite your source. You may in this case want to tell the reader *why* you are quoting at such great length.

In short, chiefly you will quote or you will summarize, and only rarely will you paraphrase, but in all cases you will cite your source. There is no point in paraphrasing an author's hundred words into a hundred of your own. Either quote or summarize, but cite the source.

Keep in mind, too, that almost all generalizations about human nature, no matter how common and familiar (for instance, "males are innately more aggressive than females") are not indisputable

---

✓ A CHECKLIST FOR AVOIDING PLAGIARISM

☐ In my notes did I *always* put quoted material within quotation marks?

☐ In my notes did I summarize *in my own words* and give credit to the source for the idea?

☐ In my notes did I avoid paraphrasing, that is, did I avoid copying, keeping the structure of the source's sentences but using some of my own words? (Paraphrases of this sort, even with a footnote citing the source, are *not* acceptable, since the reader incorrectly assumes that the writing is essentially yours.)

☐ If in my paper I set forth a borrowed idea, do I give credit, even though the words and the shape of the sentences are entirely my own?

☐ If in my paper I quote directly, do I put the words within quotation marks and cite the source?

☐ Do I *not* cite material that can be considered common knowledge (material that can be found in numerous reference works, such as the date of a public figure's birth or the population of San Francisco or the fact that *Hamlet* is regarded as a great tragedy)?

☐ If I have the slightest doubt about whether I should or should not cite a source, have I taken the safe course and cited the source?

---

facts; they are at best hypotheses on which people differ and therefore should either not be asserted at all or should be supported by some cited source or authority. Similarly, because nearly all statistics (whether on the intelligence of criminals or the accuracy of lie detectors) are the result of some particular research and may well have been superseded or challenged by other investigators, it is advisable to cite a source for any statistics you use unless you are convinced they are indisputable, such as the number of registered voters in Memphis in 1988.

On the other hand, there is something called **common knowledge,** and the sources for such information need not be cited. The term does not, however, mean exactly what it seems to. It is common knowledge, of course, that Ronald Reagan was an American president (so you don't cite a source when you make that statement), and under the conventional interpretation of this doctrine, it is also common knowledge that he was born in 1911. In fact, of course, few people other than Reagan's wife and children know this date. Still, information that can be found in many places and that is indisputable belongs to all of us; therefore, a writer need not cite her source when she says that Reagan was born in 1911. Probably she checked a dictionary or an encyclopedia for the date, but the source doesn't matter. Dozens of sources will give exactly the same information, and in fact, no reader wants to be bothered with a citation on such a point.

Some students have a little trouble developing a sense of what is and what is not common knowledge. Although, as we have just said, readers don't want to hear about the sources for information that is indisputable and can be documented in many places, if you are in doubt about whether to cite a source, cite it. Better risk boring the reader a bit than risk being accused of plagiarism.

Your college probably has issued a statement concerning plagiarism. If there is such a statement, be sure to read it carefully.

COMPILING AN ANNOTATED BIBLIOGRAPHY

When several sources have been identified and gathered, many researchers prepare an annotated bibliography. This is a list providing all relevant bibliographic information (just as it will appear in your Works Cited list or References list) as well as a brief descriptive and evaluative summary of each source—perhaps one to three sentences. Your instructor may ask you to provide an annotated bibliography for your research project.

An annotated bibliography serves four main purposes:

- First, constructing such a document helps you to master the material contained in any given source. To find the heart of the argument presented in an article or book, phrase it briefly, and comment on it, you must understand it fully.

- Second, creating an annotated bibliography helps you to think about how each portion of your research fits into the whole of your project, how you will use it, and how it relates to your topic and thesis.

- Third, an annotated bibliography helps your readers: They can quickly see which items may be especially helpful in their own research.

- Fourth, in constructing an annotated bibliography at this early stage, you will get some hands-on practice at bibliographic format, thereby easing the job of creating your final bibliography (the Works Cited list or References list for your paper).

Following are two examples of entries for an annotated bibliography in MLA (Modern Language Association) format for a project on the effect of violence in the media. The first is for a book, the second for an article from a periodical. Notice that each

- begins with a bibliographic entry—author (last name first), title, and so forth—and then

- provides information about the content of the work under consideration, suggesting how each may be of use to the final research paper.

Clover, Carol J. *Men, Women, and Chain Saws: Gender in the Modern Horror Film*. Princeton: Princeton UP, 1992. The author focuses on Hollywood horror movies of the 1970s and 1980s. She studies representations of women and girls in these movies and the responses of male viewers to female characters, suggesting that this relationship is more complex and less exploitative than the common wisdom claims.

Winerip, Michael. "Looking for an Eleven O'Clock Fix." *New York Times Magazine* 11 Jan. 1998: 30-40. The article focuses on the rising levels of violence on local television news and highlights a station in Orlando, Florida, that tried to reduce its depictions of violence and lost viewers as a result. Winerip suggests that people only claim to be against media violence, while their actions prove otherwise.

As you construct your annotated bibliography, consider posting your Word document in Google Drive for easy access and sharing.

A Rule for Writers: Citation Generators

There are many citation generators available online. These generators allow you to enter the information about your source, and, with a click, they will create Works Cited entries in APA or MLA format. But just as you cannot trust spell- and grammar-checkers in Microsoft Word, you cannot trust these generators. You can use them to cite works, but if you do, be sure to double-check what they produce before submitting your essay. Always remember that responsible writers take care to cite their sources properly and that failure to do so puts you at risk for accusations of plagiarism.

WRITING THE PAPER

Organizing Your Notes

If you have read thoughtfully, taken careful (and, again, thoughtful) notes on your reading, and then (yet again) thought about these notes, you are well on the way to writing a good paper. You have, in fact, already written some of it, in your notes. By now you should clearly have in mind the thesis you intend to argue. But you still have to organize the material, and, doubtless, even as you set about organizing it, you will find points that will require you to do some additional research and much additional thinking.

Divide your notes into clusters, each devoted to one theme or point (for instance, one cluster on the extent of use of steroids, another on evidence that steroids are harmful, yet another on arguments that even if harmful they should be permitted). If your notes are in a computer file, rearrange the notes into appropriate clusters. If you use index cards, simply sort them into packets. If you take notes in a notebook, either mark each note with a number or name indicating the cluster to which it belongs, or cut the notes apart and arrange them as you would cards. Put aside all notes that—however interesting—you now see are irrelevant to your paper.

Next, arrange the clusters or packets into a tentative sequence. In effect, you are preparing a **working outline.** At its simplest, say, you will give three arguments on behalf of *X* and then three counter-arguments. (Or you might decide that it is better to alternate material from the two sets of three clusters each, following each argument with an objection. At this stage, you can't be sure of the organization you will finally use, but you can make a tentative decision.)

The First Draft

Draft the essay, without worrying much about an elegant opening paragraph. Just write some sort of adequate opening that states the topic and your thesis. When you revise the whole later, you can put some effort into developing an effective opening. (Most experienced writers find that the opening paragraph in the final version is almost the last thing they write.)

If your notes are on cards or notebook paper, carefully copy into the draft all quotations that you plan to use. If your notes are in a computer, you may simply cut and paste them from one file to another. Do keep in mind, however, that rewriting or retyping quotations will make you think carefully about them and may result in a more focused and thoughtful paper. (In the next section of this chapter we will talk briefly about leading into quotations and about the form of quotations.) Be sure to include citations in your drafts so that if you must check a reference later it will be easy to do so.

Later Drafts

Give the draft, and yourself, a rest—perhaps for a day or two—and then go back to it. Read it over, make necessary revisions, and then **outline** it. That is, on a sheet of paper chart the organization and development, perhaps by jotting down a sentence summarizing each paragraph or each group of closely related paragraphs. Your outline or map may now show you that the paper obviously suffers from poor organization. For instance, it may reveal that you neglected to respond to one argument or that one point is needlessly treated in two places. It may also help you to see that if you gave three arguments and then three counterarguments, you probably should instead have followed each argument with its rebuttal. On the other hand, if you alternated arguments and objections, it may now seem better to use two main groups, all the arguments and then all the criticisms.

No one formula is always right. Much will depend on the complexity of the material. If the arguments are highly complex, it is better to respond to them one by one than to expect a reader to hold three complex arguments in mind before you get around to responding. If, however, the arguments can be stated briefly and clearly, it is effective to state all three and then to go on to the responses. If you write on a computer, you will find it easy, even fun, to move passages of text around. Even so, you will probably want to print out a hard copy from time to time to review the structure of your paper. Allow enough time to produce several drafts.

A Few More Words about Organization

There is a difference between

- a paper that *has* an organization and
- a paper that helpfully lets the reader know what the organization is.

Write papers of the second sort, but (there is always a "but") take care not to belabor the obvious. Inexperienced writers sometimes either hide the organization so thoroughly that a reader cannot find it or they so ploddingly lay out the structure ("Eighth, I will show . . .") that the reader becomes impatient. Yet it is better to be overly explicit than to be obscure.

The ideal, of course, is the middle route. Make the overall strategy of your organization evident by occasional explicit signs at the beginning of a paragraph ("We have seen . . . ," "It is time to consider the objections . . . ," "By far the most important . . ."); elsewhere make certain that the implicit structure is evident to the reader. When you reread your draft, if you try to imagine that you are one of your classmates, you will probably be able to sense exactly where explicit signs are needed and where they are not needed. Better still, exchange drafts with a classmate in order to exchange (tactful) advice.

Choosing a Tentative Title

By now a couple of tentative titles for your essay should have crossed your mind. If possible, choose a title that is both interesting and informative. Consider these three titles:

> Are Steroids Harmful?
>
> The Fuss over Steroids
>
> Steroids: A Dangerous Game

"Are Steroids Harmful?" is faintly interesting, and it lets the reader know the gist of the subject, but it gives no clue about the writer's thesis, the writer's contention or argument. "The Fuss over Steroids" is somewhat better, for it gives information about the writer's position. "Steroids: A Dangerous Game" is still better; it announces the subject ("steroids") and the thesis ("dangerous"), and it also displays a touch of wit because "game" glances at the world of athletics.

Don't try too hard, however; better a simple, direct, informative title than a strained, puzzling, or overly cute one. And remember to make sure that everything in your essay is relevant to your title. In fact, your title should help you to organize the essay and to delete irrelevant material.

The Final Draft

When at last you have a draft that is for the most part satisfactory, check to make sure that **transitions** from sentence to sentence and from paragraph to paragraph are clear ("Further evidence,"

"On the other hand," "A weakness, however, is apparent"), and then worry about your opening and your closing paragraphs. Your **opening paragraph** should be clear, interesting, and focused; if neither the title nor the first paragraph announces your thesis, the second paragraph probably should do so.

The **final paragraph** need not say, "In conclusion, I have shown that. . . ." It should effectively end the essay, but it need not summarize your conclusions. We have already offered a few words about final paragraphs (pp. 192–94), but the best way to learn how to write such paragraphs is to study the endings of some of the essays in this book and to adopt the strategies that appeal to you.

Be sure that all indebtedness is properly acknowledged. We have talked about plagiarism; now we will turn to the business of introducing quotations effectively.

QUOTING FROM SOURCES

Incorporating Your Reading into Your Thinking: The Art and Science of Synthesis

At the beginning of Chapter 6 we quoted a passage by Kenneth Burke (1887–1993), a college dropout who became one of America's most important twentieth-century students of rhetoric. It is worth repeating:

> Imagine that you enter a parlor. You come late. When you arrive, others have long preceded you, and they are engaged in a heated discussion, a discussion too heated for them to pause and tell you exactly what it is about. In fact, the discussion had already begun long before any of them got there, so that no one present is qualified to retrace for you all the steps that had gone before. You listen for a while, until you decide that you have caught the tenor of the argument; then you put in your oar. Someone answers; you answer him; another comes to your defense; another aligns himself against you, to either the embarrassment or gratification of your opponent, depending upon the quality of your ally's assistance. However, the discussion is interminable. The hour grows late, you must depart. And you do depart, with the discussion still vigorously in progress.

> —*The Philosophy of Literary Form* (Baton Rouge: Louisiana State University Press, 1941), 110–11.

Why do we quote this passage? Because it is your turn to join the unending conversation.

During the process of reading, and afterward, you will want to listen, think, say to yourself something like

- "No, no, I see things very differently; it seems to me that . . . " or
- "Yes, of course, but on one large issue I think I differ," or
- "Yes, sure, I agree, but I would go further and add . . ." or

- "Yes, I agree with your conclusion, but I hold this conclusion for reasons very different from the ones that you offer."

During your composition courses, at least (and we think during your entire life), you will be reading or listening and will sometimes want to put in your oar—you will sometimes want to respond in writing, for example in the form of a Letter to the Editor or in a memo at your place of employment. In the course of your response you almost surely will have to summarize very briefly the idea or ideas you are responding to, so that your readers will understand the context of your remarks. These ideas may not come from a single source; you may be responding to several sources. For instance, you may be responding to a report and also to some comments that the report evoked. In any case, you will state these ideas briefly and fairly and will then set forth your thoughtful responses, thereby giving the reader a statement that you hope represents an advance in the argument, even if only a tiny one. That is, you will **synthesize** sources, combining existing material into something new, drawing nourishment from what has already been said (giving credit, of course), and converting it into something new—a view that you think is worth considering.

Let's pause for a moment and consider this word **synthesis.** You probably are familiar with *photosynthesis*, the chemical process in green plants that produces carbohydrates from carbon dioxide and hydrogen. Synthesis, again, combines pre-existing elements and produces something new. In our use of the word *synthesis*, even a view that you utterly reject becomes a part of your new creation *because it helped to stimulate you to formulate your view*; without the idea that you reject, you might not have developed the view that you now hold. Consider the words of Francis Bacon, Shakespeare's contemporary:

> Some books are to be tasted, others to be swallowed, and some few to be chewed and digested.

Your instructor will expect you to digest your sources—this does not mean you need to accept them but only that you need to read them thoughtfully—and that, so to speak, you make them your own thoughts by refining them. Your readers will expect you to tell them *what you make out of your sources,* which means that you will go beyond writing a summary and will synthesize the material into your own contribution. *Your* view is what is wanted, and readers expect this view to be thoughtful—not mere summary and not mere tweeting.

> **A RULE FOR WRITERS:** In your final draft *you must give credit to all of your sources.* Let your reader know whether you are quoting (in this case, you will use quotation marks around all material directly quoted), or whether you are summarizing (you will explicitly say so), or whether you are paraphrasing (again, you will explicitly say so).

The Use and Abuse of Quotations

When is it necessary, or appropriate, to quote? Sometimes the reader must see the exact words of your source; the gist won't do. If you are arguing that Z's definition of *rights* is too inclusive, your readers have to know exactly how Z defined *rights.* Your brief summary of the definition may be unfair to Z; in fact, you want to convince your readers that you are being fair, and so you quote Z's definition, word for word. Moreover, if the passage is only a sentence or two long, or even if it runs to a paragraph, it may be so compactly stated that it defies summary. And to attempt to paraphrase it—substituting *natural* for *inalienable,* and so forth—saves no space and only introduces imprecision. There is nothing to do but to quote it, word for word.

Second, you may want to quote a passage that could be summarized but that is so effectively stated that you want your readers to have the pleasure of reading the original. Of course, readers will not give you credit for writing these words, but they will give you credit for your taste and for your effort to make especially pleasant the business of reading your paper.

In short, use (but don't overuse) quotations. Speaking roughly, quotations

- should occupy no more than 10 to 15 percent of your paper, and
- they may occupy much less.

Most of your paper should set forth your ideas, not other people's ideas.

How to Quote

Long and Short Quotations   **Long quotations** (more than four lines of typed prose or three or more lines of poetry) are set off from your text. To set off material, start on a new line, indent one inch from the left margin, and type the quotation double-spaced. Do not enclose quotations within quotation marks if you are setting them off.

Short quotations are treated differently. They are embedded within the text; they are enclosed within quotation marks, but otherwise they do not stand out.

All quotations, whether set off or embedded, must be exact. If you omit any words, you must indicate the ellipsis by substituting three spaced periods for the omission; if you insert any words or punctuation, you must indicate the addition by enclosing it within square brackets, not to be confused with parentheses.

Leading into a Quotation   Now for a less mechanical matter, the way in which a quotation is introduced. To say that it is "introduced" implies that one leads into it, though on rare occasions a quotation appears without an introduction, perhaps immediately after the title. Normally one leads into a quotation by giving

- the *name of the author* and (no less important)
- *clues signaling the content of the quotation and the purpose* it serves in the present essay. For example:

William James provides a clear answer to Huxley when he says that ". . ."

The writer has been writing about Huxley and now is signaling readers that they will be getting James's reply. The writer is also signaling (in "a clear answer") that the reply is satisfactory. If the writer believed that James's answer was not really acceptable, the lead-in might have run thus:

William James attempts to answer Huxley, but his response does not really meet the difficulty Huxley calls attention to. James writes, ". . ."

or thus:

William James provided what he took to be an answer to Huxley when he said that ". . ."

IDEA PROMPT 7.1 SIGNAL PHRASES

Think of your writing as a conversation between you and your sources. As in conversation, you want to be able to move smoothly between different, sometimes contrary, points of view. You also want to be able to set your thoughts apart from those of your sources. Signal phrases make it easy for your readers to know where your information came from and why it's trustworthy by including key facts about the source.

According to psychologist Stephen Ceci . . .

A report published by the U.S. Bureau of Justice Statistics concludes . . .

Feminist philosopher Sandra Harding argues . . .

To avoid repetitiveness, vary your sentence structure.

. . . claims Stephen Ceci.

. . . according to a report published by the U.S. Bureau of Statistics.

Useful verbs to introduce sources:

acknowledges	contends	points out
argues	denies	recommends
believes	disputes	reports
claims	observes	suggests

Note that papers written using MLA style refer to sources in the present tense. Papers written in APA style use the past tense (*acknowledged, argued, believed*).

 ## A CHECKLIST FOR USING QUOTATIONS RATHER THAN SUMMARIES

Ask yourself the following questions. If you cannot answer yes to at least one of the questions, consider *summarizing* the material rather than quoting it in full.

☐ Is the quotation given because it is necessary for the reader to see the exact wording of the original?

☐ Is the quotation given because the language is especially engaging?

☐ Is the quotation given because the author is a respected authority and the passage lends weight to my argument?

In this last example, clearly the words "what he took to be an answer" imply that the essayist will show, after the quotation from James, that the answer is in some degree inadequate. Or the essayist may wish to suggest the inadequacy even more strongly:

> William James provided what he took to be an answer to Huxley, but he used the word *religion* in a way that Huxley would not have allowed. James argues that ". . ."

If after reading something by Huxley the writer had merely given us "William James says . . . ," we wouldn't know whether we were getting confirmation, refutation, or something else. The essayist would have put a needless burden on the readers. Generally speaking, the more difficult the quotation, the more important is the introductory or explanatory lead-in, but even the simplest quotation profits from some sort of brief lead-in, such as "James reaffirms this point when he says . . ."

> **A RULE FOR WRITERS:** In introducing a quotation, it is usually advisable to signal the reader *why* you are using the quotation by means of a lead-in consisting of a verb or a verb and adverb, such as *claims*, or *convincingly shows*, or *admits*.

DOCUMENTATION

In the course of your essay, you will probably quote or summarize material derived from a source. You must give credit, and although there is no one form of documentation to which all scholarly fields subscribe, you will probably be asked to use one of two. One, established by the Modern Language Association (MLA), is used chiefly in the humanities; the other, established by the American Psychological Association (APA), is used chiefly in the social sciences.

We include two papers that use sources. "An Argument for Corporate Responsibility" (p. 273) uses the MLA format. "The Role of Spirituality and Religion in Mental Health" (p. 282) follows the APA format. (You may notice that various styles are illustrated in other selections we have included.)

In some online venues you can link directly to your sources. If your assignment is to write a blog or other online text, linking helps the reader to look at a note or citation or the direct source quickly and easily. For example, if you are describing or refer-encing a scene in a movie, you can link to reviews of the movie, or to a YouTube of the trailer, or to the exact scene that you are writing about. These kinds of links can help your audience get a clearer sense of your point. When formatting such a link in your text, make sure the link opens in a new window so that readers will not lose their place in the text they are reading. In a blog, linking to your sources usually is easy and helpful.

A Note on Footnotes (and Endnotes)

Before we discuss these two formats, a few words about footnotes are in order. Before the MLA and the APA developed their rules of style, citations commonly were given in footnotes. Although today footnotes are not so frequently used to give citations, they still may be useful for another purpose. (The MLA suggests end-notes rather than footnotes, but most readers seem to think that, in fact, footnotes are preferable to endnotes. After all, who wants to keep shifting from a page of text to a page of notes at the rear?) If you want to include some material that may seem intru-sive in the body of the paper, you may relegate it to a footnote. For example, in a footnote you might translate a quotation given in a foreign language, or you might demote from text to footnote a paragraph explaining why you are not taking account of such-and-such a point. By putting the matter in a footnote you are signaling the reader that it is dispensable; it is something relevant but not essential, something extra that you are, so to speak, toss-ing in. Don't make a habit of writing this sort of note, but there are times when it is appropriate.

MLA Format: Citations within the Text

Brief citations within the body of the essay give credit, in a highly abbreviated way, to the sources for material you quote, summarize, or make use of in any other way. These *in-text citations* are made clear by a list of sources, titled Works Cited, appended to the essay. Thus, in your essay you may say something like this:

> Commenting on the relative costs of capital punishment and life imprisonment, Ernest van den Haag says that he doubts "that capi-tal punishment really is more expensive" (33).

The **citation,** the number 33 in parentheses, means that the quoted words come from page 33 of a source (listed in the Works Cited) written by van den Haag. Without a Works Cited, a reader would have no way of knowing that you are quoting from page 33 of an article that appeared in the February 8, 1985, issue of the *National Review.*

Usually the parenthetic citation appears at the end of a sentence, as in the example just given, but it can appear elsewhere; its position will depend chiefly on your ear, your eye, and the context. You might, for example, write the sentence thus:

> Ernest van den Haag doubts that "capital punishment really is more expensive" than life imprisonment (33), but other writers have presented figures that contradict him.

Five points must be made about these examples:

1. **Quotation marks**   The closing quotation mark appears after the last word of the quotation, *not* after the parenthetic citation. Since the citation is not part of the quotation, the citation is not included within the quotation marks.

2. **Omission of words (ellipsis)**   If you are quoting a complete sentence or only a phrase, as in the examples given, you do not need to indicate (by three spaced periods) that you are omitting material before or after the quotation. But if for some reason you want to omit an interior part of the quotation, you must indicate the omission by inserting an *ellipsis,* the three spaced dots. To take a simple example, if you omit the word "really" from van den Haag's phrase, you must alert the reader to the omission:

> Ernest van den Haag doubts that "capital punishment . . . is more expensive" than life imprisonment (33).

Suppose you are quoting a sentence but wish to omit material from the end of the sentence. Suppose, also, that the quotation forms the end of your sentence. Write a lead-in phrase, quote what you need from your source, then type the bracketed ellipses for the omission, close the quotation, give the parenthetic citation, and finally type a fourth period to indicate the end of your sentence.

Here's an example. Suppose you want to quote the first part of a sentence that runs, "We could insist that the cost of capital punishment be reduced so as to diminish the differences." Your sentence would incorporate the desired extract as follows:

> Van den Haag says, "We could insist that the cost of capital pun-
> ishment be reduced . . ." (33).

3. **Punctuation with parenthetic citations**   In the preceding examples, the punctuation (a period or a comma in the
examples) *follows* the citation. If, however, the quotation ends with
a question mark, include the question mark *within* the quotation,
since it is part of the quotation, and put a period *after* the citation:

> Van den Haag asks, "Isn't it better — more just and more useful —
> that criminals, if they do not have the certainty of punishment, at
> least run the risk of suffering it?" (33).

But if the question mark is your own and not in the source, put it
after the citation, thus:

> What answer can be given to van den Haag's doubt that "capital
> punishment really is more expensive" (33)?

4. **Two or more works by an author**   If your list of Works
Cited includes two or more works by an author, you cannot, in
your essay, simply cite a page number because the reader will not
know which of the works you are referring to. You must give additional information. You can give it in your lead-in, thus:

> In "New Arguments against Capital Punishment," van den Haag ex-
> presses doubt "that capital punishment really is more expensive"
> than life imprisonment (33).

Or you can give the title, in a shortened form, within the citation:

> Van den Haag expresses doubt that "capital punishment really is
> more expensive" than life imprisonment ("New Arguments" 33).

5. **Citing even when you do not quote**   Even if you don't
quote a source directly, but use its point in a paraphrase or a summary, you will give a citation:

> Van den Haag thinks that life imprisonment costs more than capi-
> tal punishment (33).

Note that in all of the previous examples, the author's name is given in the text (rather than within the parenthetic citation). But there are several other ways of giving the citation, and we shall look at them now. (We have already seen, in the example given under number 4, that the title and the page number can be given within the citation.)

AUTHOR AND PAGE NUMBER IN PARENTHESES

It has been argued that life imprisonment is more costly than capital punishment (van den Haag 33).

AUTHOR, TITLE, AND PAGE NUMBER IN PARENTHESES

We have seen that if the Works Cited list includes two or more works by an author, you will have to give the title of the work on which you are drawing, either in your lead-in phrase or within the parenthetic citation. Similarly, if you are citing someone who is listed more than once in the Works Cited, and for some reason you do not mention the name of the author or the work in your lead-in, you must add the information in your citation:

Doubt has been expressed that capital punishment is as costly as life imprisonment (van den Haag, "New Arguments" 33).

A GOVERNMENT DOCUMENT OR A WORK
OF CORPORATE AUTHORSHIP

Treat the issuing body as the author. Thus, you will write something like this:

The Commission on Food Control, in *Food Resources Today*, concludes that there is no danger (37-38).

A WORK BY TWO OR MORE AUTHORS

If a work is by *two or three authors,* give the names of all authors, either in the parenthetic citation (the first example below) or in a lead-in (the second example below):

There is not a single example of the phenomenon (Smith, Dale, and Jones 182-83).

Smith, Dale, and Jones insist there is not a single example of the phenomenon (182-83).

If there are *more than three authors,* give the last name of the first author, followed by *et al.* (an abbreviation for *et alii,* Latin for "and others"), thus:

> Gittleman et al. argue (43) that . . .

or

> On average, the cost is even higher (Gittleman et al. 43).

PARENTHETIC CITATION OF AN INDIRECT SOURCE (CITATION OF MATERIAL THAT ITSELF WAS QUOTED OR SUMMARIZED IN YOUR SOURCE)

Suppose you are reading a book by Jones in which she quotes Smith and you wish to use Smith's material. Your citation must refer the reader to Jones—the source you are using—but of course, you cannot attribute the words to Jones. You will have to make it clear that you are quoting Smith, and so after a lead-in phrase like "Smith says," followed by the quotation, you will give a parenthetic citation along these lines:

> (qtd. in Jones 324-25).

PARENTHETIC CITATION OF TWO OR MORE WORKS

> The costs are simply too high (Smith 301; Jones 28).

Notice that a semicolon, followed by a space, separates the two sources.

A WORK IN MORE THAN ONE VOLUME

This is a bit tricky. If you have used only one volume, in the Works Cited you will specify the volume, and so in the parenthetic in-text citation you will not need to specify the volume. All that you need to include in the citation is a page number, as illustrated by most of the examples that we have given.

If you have used more than one volume, your parenthetic citation will have to specify the volume as well as the page, thus:

> Jackson points out that fewer than one hundred fifty people fit this description (2: 351).

The reference is to page 351 in volume 2 of a work by Jackson.

If, however, you are citing not a page but an entire volume—let's say volume 2—your parenthetic citation will look like this:

Jackson exhaustively studies this problem (vol. 2).

or

Jackson (vol. 2) exhaustively studies this problem.

Notice the following points:

- In citing a volume and page, the volume number, like the page number, is given in arabic (not roman) numerals, even if the original used roman numerals to indicate the volume number.
- The volume number is followed by a colon, then a space, then the page number.
- If you cite a volume number without a page number, as in the last example quoted, the abbreviation is *vol.* Otherwise do *not* use such abbreviations as *vol.* and *p.* and *pg.*

AN ANONYMOUS WORK

For an anonymous work, give the title in your lead-in, or give it in a shortened form in your parenthetic citation:

A Prisoner's View of Killing includes a poll taken of the inmates on death row (32).

or

A poll is available (*Prisoner's View* 32).

AN INTERVIEW

Probably you won't need a parenthetic citation because you'll say something like

Vivian Berger, in an interview, said . . .

or

According to Vivian Berger, in an interview . . .

and when your reader turns to the Works Cited, he or she will see that Berger is listed, along with the date of the interview. But if you do not mention the source's name in the lead-in, you will have to give it in the parentheses, thus:

> Contrary to popular belief, the death penalty is not reserved for se-
> rial killers and depraved murderers (Berger).

AN ELECTRONIC SOURCE

Electronic sources, such as those found on the Internet, are generally not divided into pages. Therefore, the in-text citation for such sources cites only the author's name (or, if a work is anonymous, the title):

> According to the World Wide Web site for the American Civil Liberties
> Union . . .

If the source does use pages or breaks down further into paragraphs or screens, insert the appropriate identifier or abbreviation (*p.* or *pp.* for page or pages; *par.* or *pars.* for paragraph or paragraphs; *screen* or *screens*) before the relevant number:

> The growth of day care has been called "a crime against posterity"
> by a spokesman for the Institute for the American Family
> (Terwilliger, screens 1-2).

MLA Format: The List of Works Cited

As the previous pages explain, parenthetic documentation consists of references that become clear when the reader consults the list titled Works Cited given at the end of an essay.

The list of Works Cited continues the pagination of the essay; if the last page of text is 10, then the Works Cited begins on its own page, in this case page 11. Type the page number in the upper right corner, a half inch from the top of the sheet and flush with the right margin. Next, type the heading Works Cited (*not* enclosed within quotation marks and not italic), centered, one inch from the top, and then double-space and type the first entry.

An Overview   Here are some general guidelines.

FORM ON THE PAGE

- Begin each entry flush with the left margin, but if an entry runs to more than one line, indent a half inch for each succeeding line of the entry. This is known as a hanging indent, and most word processing programs can achieve this effect easily.

- Double-space each entry, and double-space between entries.

- Italicize titles of works published independently—for instance, books, pamphlets, and journals. Enclose within quotation marks a work not published independently—for instance, an article in a journal or a short story.

- If you are citing a book that includes the title of another book, italicize the main title, but do *not* italicize the title mentioned. Example:

    A Study of Mill's On Liberty

- In the sample entries below, pay attention to the use of commas, colons, and the space after punctuation.

ALPHABETICAL ORDER

- Arrange the list alphabetically by author, with the author's last name first.

- For information about anonymous works, works with more than one author, and two or more works by one author, see below.

A Closer Look   Here is more detailed advice.

THE AUTHOR'S NAME

Notice that the last name is given first, but otherwise the name is given as on the title page. Do not substitute initials for names written out on the title page.

If your list includes two or more works by an author, do not repeat the author's name for the second title but represent it by three hyphens followed by a period. The sequence of the works is determined by the alphabetical order of the titles. Thus, Smith's book titled *Poverty* would be listed ahead of her book *Welfare*. See the example on page 256, listing two works by Roger Brown.

Anonymous works are listed under the first word of the title or the second word if the first is *A, An,* or *The* or a foreign equivalent. We discuss books by more than one author, government documents, and works of corporate authorship on pages 256–57.

THE TITLE

After the period following the author's name, allow one space and then give the title. Take the title from the title page, not from the cover or the spine, but disregard any unusual typography such as the use of all capital letters or the use of the ampersand (&) for *and*. Italicize the title and subtitle (separate them by a colon), but do not italicize the period that concludes this part of the entry.

- Capitalize the first word and the last word.

- Capitalize all nouns, pronouns, verbs, adjectives, adverbs, and subordinating conjunctions (for example, *although, if, because*).

- Do not capitalize (unless it's the first or last word of the title or the first word of the subtitle) articles (*a, an, the*), prepositions (for instance, *in, on, toward, under*), coordinating conjunctions (for instance, *and, but, or, for*), or the *to* in infinitives.

Examples:

The Death Penalty: A New View

On the Death Penalty: Toward a New View

On the Penalty of Death in a Democracy

PLACE OF PUBLICATION, PUBLISHER, DATE, AND MEDIUM OF PUBLICATION

For the place of publication, provide the name of the city; you can usually find it either on the title page or on the reverse of the title page. If a number of cities are listed, provide only the first. MLA does not require you to add a state or country name after the city, even in cases where cities are little known or may be confused with another city of the same name.

The name of the publisher is abbreviated. Usually the first word is enough (*Random House* becomes *Random*), but if the first word is a first name, such as in *Alfred A. Knopf*, the surname (*Knopf*) is used instead. University presses are abbreviated thus: *Yale UP, U of Chicago P, State U of New York P.*

The date of publication of a book is given when known; if no date appears on the book, write *n.d.* to indicate "no date."

Because you may find your sources in any number of places, each entry should end by indicating the medium of publication for each source ("Print" for books or periodicals, "Web," for sources found on the Internet, and so on).

SAMPLE ENTRIES Here are some examples illustrating the points we have covered thus far:

Brown, Roger. *Social Psychology*. New York: Free, 1965. Print.

- - - . *Words and Things*. Glencoe: Free, 1958. Print.

Douglas, Ann. *The Feminization of American Culture*. New York: Knopf, 1977. Print.

Hartman, Chester. *The Transformation of San Francisco*. Totowa: Rowman, 1984. Print.

Kellerman, Barbara. *The Political Presidency: Practice of Leadership from Kennedy through Reagan*. New York: Oxford UP, 1984. Print.

Notice that a period follows the author's name and another period follows the title. If a subtitle is given, as it is for Kellerman's book, it is separated from the title by a colon and a space. A colon follows the place of publication, a comma follows the publisher, and a period follows the date.

A BOOK BY MORE THAN ONE AUTHOR

The book is alphabetized under the last name of the first author named on the title page. If there are *two or three authors*, the names of these are given (after the first author's name) in the normal order, *first name first:*

Gilbert, Sandra M., and Susan Gubar. *The Madwoman in the Attic: The Woman Writer and the Nineteenth-Century Literary Imagination*. New Haven: Yale UP, 1979. Print.

Notice, again, that although the first author's name is given *last name first,* the second author's name is given in the normal order, first name first. Notice, too, that a comma is put after the first name of the first author, separating the authors.

If there are *more than three authors,* give the name only of the first and then add (but *not* enclosed within quotation marks and not italic) *et al.* (Latin for "and others").

Altshuler, Alan, et al. *The Future of the Automobile.* Cambridge: MIT
    P, 1984. Print.

GOVERNMENT DOCUMENTS

If the writer is not known, treat the government and the agency as the author. Most federal documents are issued by the Government Printing Office (abbreviated to *GPO*) in Washington, D.C.

United States. Office of Technology Assessment. *Computerized Manu-*
    facturing Automation: Employment, Education, and the Work-
    place. Washington: GPO, 1984. Print.

WORKS OF CORPORATE AUTHORSHIP

Begin the citation with the corporate author, even if the same body is also the publisher, as in the first example:

American Psychiatric Association. *Psychiatric Glossary.* Washington:
    American Psychiatric Association, 1984. Print.

Carnegie Council on Policy Studies in Higher Education. *Giving Youth*
    a Better Chance: Options for Education, Work, and Service. San
    Francisco: Jossey, 1980. Print.

A REPRINT (FOR INSTANCE, A PAPERBACK VERSION OF AN OLDER CLOTHBOUND BOOK)

After the title, give the date of original publication (it can usually be found on the reverse of the title page of the reprint you are using), then a period, and then the place, publisher, and date of the edition you are using. The example indicates that Gray's book was originally published in 1970 and that the student is using the Vintage reprint of 1971.

Gray, Francine du Plessix. *Divine Disobedience: Profiles in Catholic*
    Radicalism. 1970. New York: Vintage, 1971. Print.

A BOOK IN SEVERAL VOLUMES

If you have used more than one volume, in a citation within your essay you will (as explained on pp. 251–52) indicate a reference to, say, page 250 of volume 3 thus: (3: 250).

If, however, you have used only one volume of the set—let's say volume 3—in your entry in the Works Cited, specify which volume you used, as in the next example:

Friedel, Frank. *Franklin D. Roosevelt*. Vol. 3. Boston: Little, 1973.
   Print. 4 vols.

With such an entry in the Works Cited, the parenthetic citation within your essay would be to the page only, not to the volume and page, because a reader who consults the Works Cited will understand that you used only volume 3. In the Works Cited, you may specify volume 3 and not give the total number of volumes, or you may add the total number of volumes, as in the preceding example.

ONE BOOK WITH A SEPARATE TITLE IN A SET OF VOLUMES

Sometimes a set with a title makes use also of a separate title for each book in the set. If you are listing such a book, use the following form:

Churchill, Winston. *The Age of Revolution*. New York: Dodd, 1957.
   Vol. 3 of *History of the English-Speaking Peoples*. Print. 4 vols.
   1956-58.

A BOOK WITH AN AUTHOR AND AN EDITOR

Churchill, Winston, and Franklin D. Roosevelt. *The Complete Corre-
   spondence*. Ed. Warren F. Kimball. 3 vols. Princeton: Princeton
   UP, 1985. Print.

Kant, Immanuel. *The Philosophy of Kant: Immanuel Kant's Moral and
   Political Writings*. Ed. Carl J. Friedrich. New York: Modern, 1949.
   Print.

If you are making use of the editor's introduction or other editorial material rather than of the author's work, list the book under the name of the editor rather than of the author, as shown on page 259 under An Introduction, Foreword, or Afterword.

A REVISED EDITION OF A BOOK

Arendt, Hannah. *Eichmann in Jerusalem*. Rev. and enlarged ed. New
    York: Viking, 1965. Print.

Honour, Hugh, and John Fleming. *The Visual Arts: A History*. 5th ed.
    Englewood Cliffs: Prentice, 1999. Print.

A TRANSLATED BOOK

Franqui, Carlos. *Family Portrait with Fidel: A Memoir*. Trans. Alfred
    MacAdam. New York: Random, 1984. Print.

AN INTRODUCTION, FOREWORD, OR AFTERWORD

Goldberg, Arthur J. Foreword. *An Eye for an Eye? The Morality of Pun-
    ishing by Death*. By Stephen Nathanson. Totowa: Rowman, 1987.
    v-vi. Print.

Usually an introduction or comparable material is listed under
the name of the author of the book (here Nathanson) rather than
under the name of the writer of the foreword (here Goldberg), but
if you are referring to the apparatus rather than to the book itself,
use the form just given. The words *Introduction, Preface, Foreword,*
and *Afterword* are neither enclosed within quotation marks nor
italicized.

A BOOK WITH AN EDITOR BUT NO AUTHOR

Let's assume that you have used a book of essays written by
various people but collected by an editor (or editors), whose
name(s) appears on the collection.

LaValley, Albert J., ed. *Focus on Hitchcock*. Englewood Cliffs:
    Prentice, 1972. Print.

If the book has one editor, the abbreviation is *ed.;* if two or more
editors, *eds.*

A WORK WITHIN A VOLUME OF WORKS BY ONE AUTHOR

The following entry indicates that a short work by Susan Sontag,
an essay called "The Aesthetics of Silence," appears in a book by
Sontag titled *Styles of Radical Will*. Notice that the inclusive page

numbers of the short work are cited, not merely page numbers that you may happen to refer to but the page numbers of the entire piece.

> Sontag, Susan. "The Aesthetics of Silence." *Styles of Radical Will.*
>   New York: Farrar, 1969. 3-34. Print.

A BOOK REVIEW

Here is an example, citing Gerstein's review of Walker's book. Gerstein's review was published in a journal called *Ethics.*

> Gerstein, Robert S. Rev. of *Punishment, Danger and Stigma: The*
>   *Morality of Criminal Justice*, by Nigel Walker. *Ethics* 93 (1983):
>   408-10. Print.

If the review has a title, give the title between the period following the reviewer's name and *Rev.*

If a review is anonymous, list it under the first word of the title, or under the second word if the first is *A, An,* or *The.* If an anonymous review has no title, begin the entry with *Rev. of,* and then give the title of the work reviewed; alphabetize the entry under the title of the work reviewed.

AN ARTICLE OR ESSAY (NOT A REPRINT) IN A COLLECTION

A book may consist of a collection (edited by one or more persons) of new essays by several authors. Here is a reference to one essay in such a book. (The essay by Balmforth occupies pages 19 to 35 in a collection edited by Bevan.)

> Balmforth, Henry. "Science and Religion." *Steps to Christian Understand-*
>   *ing.* Ed. R. J. W. Bevan. London: Oxford UP, 1958. 19-35. Print.

AN ARTICLE OR ESSAY REPRINTED IN A COLLECTION

The previous example (Balmforth's essay in Bevan's collection) was for an essay written for a collection. But some collections reprint earlier material, such as essays from journals or chapters from books. The following example cites an essay that was originally printed in a book called *The Cinema of Alfred Hitchcock.* This essay has been reprinted in a later collection of essays on Hitchcock, edited by Albert J. LaValley, and it was LaValley's collection that the student used.

Bogdanovich, Peter. "Interviews with Alfred Hitchcock." *The Cinema of Alfred Hitchcock*. New York: Museum of Modern Art, 1963. 15-18. Rpt. in *Focus on Hitchcock*. Ed. Albert J. LaValley. Englewood Cliffs: Prentice, 1972. 28-31. Print.

The student has read Bogdanovich's essay or chapter, but not in Bogdanovich's book, where it occupied pages 15 to 18. The material was actually read on pages 28 to 31 in a collection of writings on Hitchcock edited by LaValley. Details of the original publication — title, date, page numbers, and so forth — were found in LaValley's collection. Almost all editors will include this information, either on the copyright page or at the foot of the reprinted essay, but sometimes they do not give the original page numbers. In such a case, you need not include the original numbers in your entry.

Notice that the entry begins with the author and the title of the work you are citing (here, Bogdanovich's interviews), not with the name of the editor of the collection or the title of the collection.

AN ENCYCLOPEDIA OR OTHER ALPHABETICALLY ARRANGED REFERENCE WORK

The publisher, place of publication, volume number, and page number do *not* have to be given. For such works, list only the edition (if it is given) and the date.

For a *signed* article, begin with the author's last name. (If the article is signed with initials, check elsewhere in the volume for a list of abbreviations, which will inform you who the initials stand for, and use the following form.)

Williams, Donald C. "Free Will and Determinism." *Encyclopedia Americana*. 1987 ed. Print.

For an *unsigned article*, begin with the title of the article:

"Automation." *The Business Reference Book*. 1977 ed. Print.

"Tobacco." *Encyclopaedia Britannica: Macropaedia*. 1988 ed. Print.

A TELEVISION OR RADIO PROGRAM

Be sure to include the title of the episode or segment (in quotation marks), the title of the show (italicized), the network, the call letters and city of the station, and the date of broadcast. Other information, such as performers, narrator, and so forth, may be included if pertinent.

> "Back to My Lai." *60 Minutes*. Narr. Mike Wallace. CBS. 29 Mar.
> 1998. Television.

> "Juvenile Justice." *Talk of the Nation*. Narr. Ray Suarez. Natl. Public
> Radio. WBUR, Boston. 15 Apr. 1998. Radio.

AN ARTICLE IN A SCHOLARLY JOURNAL   The title of the article is enclosed within quotation marks, and the title of the journal is italicized.

Some journals are paginated consecutively; the pagination of the second issue begins where the first issue leaves off. Other journals begin each issue with page 1.

A JOURNAL THAT IS PAGINATED CONSECUTIVELY

> Vilas, Carlos M. "Popular Insurgency and Social Revolution in Central
> America." *Latin American Perspectives* 15.1 (1988): 55-77. Print.

Vilas's article occupies pages 55 to 77 in volume 15, which was published in 1988. (Notice that the volume number is followed by a space, then by the year in parentheses, and then by a colon, a space, and the page numbers of the entire article.) When available, give the issue number.

A JOURNAL THAT BEGINS EACH ISSUE WITH PAGE 1

If the journal is, for instance, a quarterly, there will be four page 1's each year, so the issue number must be given. After the volume number, type a period and (without hitting the space bar) the issue number, as in the next example:

> Greenberg, Jack. "Civil Rights Enforcement Activity of the Depart-
> ment of Justice." *Black Law Journal* 8.1 (1983): 60-67. Print.

Greenberg's article appeared in the first issue of volume 8 of the *Black Law Journal.*

AN ARTICLE IN A WEEKLY, BIWEEKLY,
MONTHLY, OR BIMONTHLY PUBLICATION

Do not include volume or issue numbers, even if given.

Lamar, Jacob V. "The Immigration Mess." *Time* 27 Feb. 1989: 14-15.
Print.

Markowitz, Laura. "A Different Kind of Queer Marriage." *Utne
Reader* Sept.-Oct. 2000: 24-26. Print.

AN ARTICLE IN A NEWSPAPER

Because a newspaper usually consists of several sections, a
section number or a capital letter may precede the page number.
The example indicates that an article begins on page 1 of section 2
and is continued on a later page.

Chu, Harry. "Art Thief Defends Action." *New York Times* 8 Feb. 1989,
sec. 2: 1+. Print.

AN UNSIGNED EDITORIAL

"The Religious Tyranny Amendment." Editorial. *New York Times*
15 Mar. 1998, sec. 4: 16. Print.

A LETTER TO THE EDITOR

Lasken, Douglas. Letter. *New York Times* 15 Mar. 1998, sec. 4: 16. Print.

A PUBLISHED OR BROADCAST INTERVIEW

Give the name of the interview subject and the interviewer,
followed by the relevant publication or broadcast information, in the
following format:

Green, Al. Interview with Terry Gross. *Fresh Air*. Natl. Public Radio.
WFCR, Amherst. 16 Oct. 2000. Radio.

AN INTERVIEW YOU CONDUCT

Jevgrafovs, Alexandre L. Personal [or Telephone] interview. 14 Dec. 2003.

PERSONAL CORRESPONDENCE

Add "TS" for a typed letter, "MS" for a handwritten letter, or
"E-mail" to the end of the citation.

Paso, Robert. Letter [or Message, in the case of E-mail] to the author.
6 Jan. 2004. TS.

CD-ROM

Books on CD-ROMs are cited very much like their printed counterparts. Add the medium (*CD-ROM*) after the publication information. For articles, to the usual print citation information, add (1) the title of the database, italicized; (2) the medium (*CD-ROM*); (3) the vendor's name; and (4) the date of electronic publication.

> Louisberg, Margaret. *Charlie Brown Meets Godzilla: What Are Our Children Watching?* Urbana: ERIC Clearinghouse on Elementary and Early Childhood Education, 1990. CD-ROM.

> "Pornography." *The Oxford English Dictionary*. 2nd ed. CD-ROM. Oxford: Oxford UP, 1992.

A PERSONAL OR PROFESSIONAL WEB SITE

Include the following elements, separated by periods: the name of the person who created the site (omit if not given, as in Figure 7.4), site title (italicized), name of any sponsoring institution or organization; date of electronic publication or of the latest update (if given), the medium (*Web*), and the date of access.

> *Legal Guide for Bloggers*. Electronic Frontier Foundation. 11 Feb. 2009. Web. 30 May 2009.

AN ARTICLE IN AN ONLINE PERIODICAL

Give the same information as you would for a print article, plus the medium (*Web*) and the date of access. (See Figure 7.5 on p. 266.)

> Acocella, Joan. "In the Blood: Why Do Vampires Still Thrill?" *New Yorker* 16 Mar. 2009. Web. 30 May 2009.

AN ONLINE POSTING

The citation includes the author's name, subject line of posting, description *Online posting* if the posting has no title, name of the forum, date material was posted, the medium (*Web*), and date of access.

> Ricci, Paul. "Global Warming." Global Electronic Science Conference, 10 June 1996. Web. 22 Sept. 1997.

FIGURE 7.4 CITING A BLOG

1 Include the URL only if your instructor requires it.

2 Sponsor of Web site

3 No author given; start citation with the title

4 Title of Web page

5 Publication date

6 Include the medium (Web) and the date you retrieved it.

A DATABASE SOURCE

Treat material obtained from a computer service, such as Bibliographic Retrieval Service (BRS), like other printed material, but at the end of the entry add (if available) the title of the database (italicized), publication medium (*Web*), name of the computer service if known, and date of access.

Jackson, Morton. "A Look at Profits." *Harvard Business Review* 40
(1962): 106-13. *BRS*. Web. 23 Dec. 2006.

FIGURE 7.5   CITING AN ONLINE MAGAZINE

1 Include the URL only if your Instructor requires it.

2 Title of periodical

3 Title of article

4 Subtitle of article

5 Author

6 Publication date

7 Include the medium (Web) and the date you retrieved it.

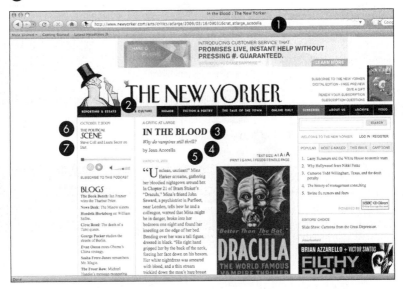

Caution: Although we have covered the most usual kinds of sources, it is entirely possible that you will come across a source that does not fit any of the categories that we have discussed. For approximately two hundred pages of explanations of these matters, covering the proper way to cite all sorts of troublesome and unbelievable (but real) sources, see *MLA Handbook for Writers of Research Papers,* Seventh Edition (New York: Modern Language Association of America, 2009).

APA Format: Citations within the Text

Your paper will conclude with a separate page headed References, on which you list all of your sources. If the last page of your essay is numbered 10, number the first page of the References 11.

The APA style emphasizes the date of publication; the date appears not only in the list of references at the end of the paper but also in the paper itself, when you give a brief parenthetic citation of a source that you have quoted or summarized or in any other way used. Here is an example:

Statistics are readily available (Smith, 1989, p. 20).

The title of Smith's book or article will be given at the end of your paper in the list titled References. We discuss the form of the material listed in the References after we look at some typical citations within the text of a student's essay.

A SUMMARY OF AN ENTIRE WORK

Smith (1988) holds the same view.

or

Similar views are held widely (Jones & Metz, 1990; Smith, 1988).

A REFERENCE TO A PAGE OR TO PAGES

Smith (1988) argues that "the death penalty is a lottery, and blacks usually are the losers" (p. 17).

A REFERENCE TO AN AUTHOR WHO HAS MORE THAN ONE WORK IN THE LIST OF REFERENCES

If in the References you list two or more works that an author published in the same year, the works are listed in alphabetical order, by the first letter of the title. The first work is labeled *a,* the second *b,* and so on. Here is a reference to the second work that Smith published in 1989:

Florida presents "a fair example" of how the death penalty is administered (Smith, 1989b, p. 18).

APA Format: The List of References

Your brief parenthetic citations are made clear when the reader consults the list you give in the References. Type this list on a separate page, continuing the pagination of your essay.

An Overview   Here are some general guidelines.

FORM ON THE PAGE

- Begin each entry flush with the left margin, but if an entry runs to more than one line, indent five spaces for each succeeding line of the entry.
- Double-space each entry, and double-space between entries.

ALPHABETICAL ORDER

- Arrange the list alphabetically by author.
- Give the author's last name first and then the initial of the first name and of the middle name (if any).
- If there is more than one author, name all of the authors up to seven, again inverting the name (last name first) and giving only initials for first and middle names. (But do not invert the editor's name when the entry begins with the name of an author who has written an article in an edited book.) When there are two or more authors, use an ampersand (&) before the name of the last author. Example (here, of an article in the tenth volume of a journal called *Developmental Psychology*):

Drabman, R. S., & Thomas, M. H. (1974). Does media violence increase children's tolerance of real-life aggression? *Developmental Psychology, 10,* 418-421.

- For eight or more authors, list the first six followed by three ellipses dots and then the last author. If you list more than one work by an author, do so in the order of publication, the earliest first. If two works by an author were published in the same year, give them in alphabetical order by the first letter of the title, disregarding *A, An,* or *The,* and their foreign equivalents. Designate the first work as *a,* the second as *b.* Repeat the author's name at the start of each entry.

Donnerstein, E. (1980a). Aggressive erotica and violence against women. *Journal of Personality and Social Psychology, 39,* 269-277.

Donnerstein, E. (1980b). Pornography and violence against women. *Annals of the New York Academy of Sciences, 347,* 227-288.

Donnerstein, E. (1983). Erotica and human aggression. In R. Green & E. Donnerstein (Eds.), *Aggression: Theoretical and empirical reviews* (pp. 87-103). New York, NY: Academic Press.

FORM OF TITLE

- In references to books, capitalize only the first letter of the first word of the title (and of the subtitle, if any) and capitalize proper nouns. Italicize the complete title (but not the period at the end).

- In references to articles in periodicals or in edited books, capitalize only the first letter of the first word of the article's title (and subtitle, if any) and all proper nouns. Do not put the title within quotation marks or italicize it. Type a period after the title of the article. For the title of the journal and the volume and page numbers, see the next instruction.

- In references to periodicals, give the volume number in arabic numerals, and italicize it. Do *not* use *vol.* before the number, and do not use *p.* or *pg.* before the page numbers.

Sample References   Here are some samples to follow.

A BOOK BY ONE AUTHOR

Pavlov, I. P. (1927). *Conditioned reflexes* (G. V. Anrep, Trans.). London, England: Oxford University Press.

A BOOK BY MORE THAN ONE AUTHOR

Belenky, M. F., Clinchy, B. M., Goldberger, N. R., & Torule, J. M. (1986). *Women's ways of knowing: The development of self, voice, and mind*. New York, NY: Basic Books.

A COLLECTION OF ESSAYS

Christ, C. P., & Plaskow, J. (Eds.). (1979). *Woman-spirit rising: A feminist reader in religion*. New York, NY: Harper & Row.

A WORK IN A COLLECTION OF ESSAYS

Fiorenza, E. (1979). Women in the early Christian movement. In C. P. Christ & J. Plaskow (Eds.), *Woman-spirit rising: A feminist reader in religion* (pp. 84-92). New York, NY: Harper & Row.

GOVERNMENT DOCUMENTS

If the writer is not known, treat the government and the agency as the author. Most federal documents are issued by the U.S.

Government Printing Office in Washington, D.C. If a document number has been assigned, insert that number in parentheses between the title and the following period.

> United States Congress. Office of Technology Assessment. (1984). *Computerized manufacturing automation: Employment, education, and the workplace*. Washington, DC: U.S. Government Printing Office.

AN ARTICLE IN A JOURNAL WITH CONTINUOUS PAGINATION

> Tversky, A., & Kahneman, D. (1981). The framing of decisions and the psychology of choice. *Science, 211*, 453-458.

AN ARTICLE IN A JOURNAL THAT PAGINATES EACH ISSUE SEPARATELY

> Foot, R. J. (1988-89). Nuclear coercion and the ending of the Korean conflict. *International Security, 13*(4), 92-112.

The reference informs us that the article appeared in issue number 4 of volume 13.

AN ARTICLE FROM A MONTHLY OR WEEKLY MAGAZINE

> Greenwald, J. (1989, February 27). Gimme shelter. *Time, 133*, 50-51.

> Maran, S. P. (1988, April). In our backyard, a star explodes. *Smithsonian, 19*, 46-57.

AN ARTICLE IN A NEWSPAPER

> Connell, R. (1989, February 6). Career concerns at heart of 1980s campus protests. *Los Angeles Times*, pp. 1, 3.

(*Note:* If no author is given, simply begin with the title followed by the date in parentheses.)

A BOOK REVIEW

> Daniels, N. (1984). Understanding physician power [Review of the book *The social transformation of American medicine*]. *Philosophy and Public Affairs, 13*, 347-356.

Daniels is the reviewer, not the author of the book. The book under review is called *The Social Transformation of American Medicine,* but the review, published in volume 13 of *Philosophy and Public Affairs,* had its own title, "Understanding Physician Power."

✓ A CHECKLIST FOR PAPERS USING SOURCES

Ask yourself the following questions:

☐ Are all borrowed words and ideas credited, including those from Internet sources?

☐ Are all summaries and paraphrases acknowledged as such?

☐ Are quotations and summaries not too long?

☐ Are quotations accurate? Are omissions of words indicated by three spaced periods? Are additions of words enclosed within square brackets?

☐ Are quotations provided with helpful lead-ins?

☐ Is documentation in proper form?

And of course, you will also ask yourself the questions that you would ask of a paper that did not use sources, such as:

☐ Is the topic sufficiently narrowed?

☐ Is the thesis (to be advanced or refuted) stated early and clearly, perhaps even in the title?

☐ Is the audience kept in mind? Are opposing views stated fairly and as sympathetically as possible? Are controversial terms defined?

☐ Are assumptions likely to be shared by readers? If not, are they argued rather than merely asserted?

☐ Is the focus clear (evaluation, recommendation of policy)?

☐ Is evidence (examples, testimony, statistics) adequate and sound?

☐ Are inferences valid?

☐ Is the organization clear (effective opening, coherent sequence of arguments, unpretentious ending)?

☐ Is all worthy opposition faced?

☐ Is the tone appropriate?

☐ Has the paper been carefully proofread?

☐ Is the title effective?

☐ Is the introduction effective?

☐ Is the structure reader-friendly?

☐ Is the ending effective?

If the review does not have a title, retain the square brackets, and use the material within as the title. Proceed as in the example just given.

A WEB SITE

American Psychological Association. (1995). Lesbian and gay parenting. Retrieved June 12, 2000, from http://www.apa.org/pi/parent.html

AN ARTICLE IN AN ONLINE PERIODICAL

Carpenter, S. (2000, October). Biology and social environments jointly influence gender development. *Monitor on Psychology 31*(9). Retrieved from http://www.apa.org/monitor/

For a full account of the APA method of dealing with all sorts of unusual citations, see the sixth edition (2010) of the APA manual, *Publication Manual of the American Psychological Association*.

AN ANNOTATED STUDENT RESEARCH PAPER IN MLA FORMAT

The following argument makes good use of sources. Early in the semester the students were asked to choose one topic from a list of ten and to write a documented argument of 750 to 1,250 words (three to five pages of double-spaced typing). The completed paper was due two weeks after the topics were distributed. The assignment, a prelude to working on a research paper of 2,500 to 3,000 words, was in part designed to give students practice in finding and in using sources. Citations are given in the MLA form.

Timmerman 1

Lesley Timmerman

Professor Jennifer Wilson

English 102

15 August 2012

An Argument for Corporate Responsibility

Opponents of corporate social responsibility (CSR) argue

that a company's sole duty is to generate profits. According

to them, by acting for the public good, corporations are

neglecting their primary obligation to make money. However,

as people are becoming more and more conscious of corporate

impacts on society and the environment, separating profits

from company practices and ethics does not make sense.

Employees want to work for institutions that share their values,

and consumers want to buy products from companies that are

making an impact and improving people's lives. Furthermore,

businesses exist in an interdependent world where the health of

the environment and the well-being of society really do matter.

For these reasons, corporations have to take responsibility for

their actions, beyond making money for shareholders. For their

own benefit as well as the public's, companies must strive to be

socially responsible.

In his article "The Case against Corporate Responsibility,"

Wall Street Journal writer Aneel Karnani argues that CSR will never

be able to solve the world's problems. Thinking it can, Karnani

says, is a dangerous illusion. He recommends that instead of

expecting corporate managers to act in the public interest, we

should rely on philanthropy and government regulation. Karnani

maintains that "Managers who sacrifice profit for the common

Title is focused and announces the thesis.

Double-space between the title and first paragraph—and throughout the essay.

Brief statement of one side of the issue.

Summary of the opposing view.

Lead-in to quotation.

Timmerman 2

good [. . .] are in effect imposing a tax on their shareholders and
arbitrarily deciding how that money should be spent." In other
words, according to Karnani, corporations should not be determining what constitutes socially responsible behavior; individual
donors and the government should. Certainly, individuals should
continue to make charitable gifts, and governments should maintain laws and regulations to protect the public interest. However,
Karnani's reasoning for why corporations should be exempt from
social responsibility is flawed. With very few exceptions, corporations' socially responsible actions are not arbitrary and do not
sacrifice long-term profits.

In fact, corporations have already proven that they can
contribute profitably and meaningfully to solving significant
global problems by integrating CSR into their standard practices
and long-term visions. Rather than focusing on shareholders'
short-term profits, many companies have begun measuring their
success by "profit, planet and people"—what is known as the
"triple bottom line." Businesses operating under this principle
consider their environmental and social impacts, as well as their
financial impacts, and make responsible and compassionate
decisions. For example, such businesses use resources efficiently,
create healthy products, choose suppliers who share their
ethics, and improve economic opportunities for people in the
communities they serve. By doing so, companies often save
money. They also contribute to the sustainability of life on earth
and ensure the sustainability of their own businesses. In their
book *The Triple Bottom Line: How Today's Best-Run Companies
Are Achieving Economic, Social, and Environmental Success,*

Timmerman 3

coauthors Savitz and Weber demonstrate that corporations need to become sustainable, in all ways. They argue that "the only way to succeed in today's interdependent world is to embrace sustainability" (xi). The authors go on to show that, for the vast majority of companies, a broad commitment to sustainability enhances profitability (Savitz and Weber 39).

For example, PepsiCo has been able to meet the financial expectations of its shareholders while demonstrating its commitment to the triple bottom line. In addition to donating over $16 million to help victims of natural disasters, Pepsi has woven concerns for people and for the planet into its company practices and culture (Bejou 4). For instance, because of a recent water shortage in an area of India where Pepsi runs a plant, the company began a project to build community wells (Savitz and Weber 160). Though Pepsi did not cause the water shortage nor was its manufacturing threatened by it, "Pepsi realizes that the well-being of the community is part of the company's responsibility" (Savitz and Weber 161). Ultimately, Pepsi chose to look beyond the goal of maximizing short-term profits. By doing so, the company improved its relationship with this Indian community, improved people's daily lives and opportunities, and improved its own reputation. In other words, Pepsi embraced CSR and ensured a more sustainable future for everyone involved.

Another example of a wide-reaching company that is working toward greater sustainability on all fronts is Walmart. The corporation has issued a CSR policy that includes three ambitious goals: "to be fully supplied by renewable energy, to create zero waste and to sell products that sustain people and the environment" ("From Fringe to Mainstream"). As Dr. Doug Guthrie, dean of George Washington University's School of Business, noted in a recent lecture, if a company as powerful as Walmart were to succeed in these goals, the impact would be huge. To illustrate Walmart's potential influence, Dr. Guthrie pointed out that the corporation's exports from China to the United States are equal to Mexico's total exports to the United States. In committing to CSR, the company's leaders are acknowledging how much their power depends on the earth's natural resources, as well as the communities who produce, distribute, sell, and purchase Walmart's products. The company is also well aware that achieving its goals will "ultimately save the company a great deal of money" ("From Fringe to Mainstream"). For good reason, Walmart, like other companies around the world, is choosing to act in *everyone's* best interest.

Author now introduces statistical evidence that, if introduced earlier, might have turned the reader off.

Recent research on employees' and consumers' social consciousness offers companies further reason to take corporate responsibility seriously. For example, studies show that workers care about making a difference (Meister). In many cases, workers would even take a pay cut to work for a more responsible, sustainable company. In fact, 45 percent of workers said they would take a 15 percent reduction in pay "for a job that makes a social or environmental impact" (Meister). Even more said they would take a 15 percent cut in pay to work for a company with values that match their own (Meister). The numbers are most significant amongst Millennials (those born between, approximately, 1980 and the early 2000s). Eighty percent of

Millennials said they "wanted to work for a company that cares about how it impacts and contributes to society," and over half said they would not work for an "irresponsible company" (Meister). Given this more socially conscious generation, companies are going to find it harder and harder to ignore CSR. To recruit and retain employees, employers will need to earn the admiration, respect, and loyalty of their workers by becoming "good corporate citizen[s]" (qtd. in "From Fringe to Mainstream").

Similarly, studies clearly show that CSR matters to today's consumers. According to an independent report, 80 percent of Americans say they would switch brands to support a social cause (Cone Communications 6). Eighty-eight percent say they approve of companies' using social or environmental issues in their marketing (Cone Communications 5). And 83 percent say they "wish more of the products, services and retailers would support causes" (Cone Communications 5). Other independent surveys corroborate these results, confirming that today's customers, especially Millennials, care about more than just price ("From Fringe to Mainstream"). Furthermore, plenty of companies have seen what happens when they assume that consumers do not care about CSR. For example, in 1997, when Nike customers discovered that their shoes were manufactured by child laborers in Indonesia, the company took a huge financial hit (Guthrie). Today, Information-Age customers are even more likely to educate themselves about companies' labor practices and environmental records. Smart corporations will listen to consumer preferences, provide transparency, and commit to integrating CSR into their long-term business plans.

Author argues that it is to the *companies'* interest to be socially responsible.

Timmerman 6

In this increasingly interdependent world, the case against CSR is becoming more and more difficult to defend. Exempting corporations and relying on government to be the world's conscience does not make good social, environmental, or economic sense. Contributors to a recent article in the online journal *Knowledge@Wharton,* published by the Wharton School of Business, agree. Professor Eric Orts maintains that "it is an out-moded view to say that one must rely only on the government and regulation to police business responsibilities. What we need is re-conception of what the purpose of business is" (qtd. in "From Fringe to Mainstream"). The question is, what should the purpose of a business be in today's world? Professor of Business Administration David Bejou of Elizabeth City State University has a thoughtful and sensible answer to that question. He writes,

> . . . it is clear that the sole purpose of a business is not merely that of generating profits for its owners. Instead, because compassion provides the necessary equilibrium between a company's purpose and the needs of its communities, it should be the new philosophy of business. (Bejou 1)

As Bejou implies, the days of allowing corporations to act in their own financial self-interest with little or no regard for their effects on others are over. None of us can afford such a narrow view of business. The world is far too interconnected. A seemingly small corporate decision — to buy coffee beans directly from local growers or to install solar panels — can affect the lives and livelihoods of many people and determine the environmental health of whole regions. A business, just

Author's lead-in to the quotation guides the reader's response to the quotation.

Timmerman 7

like a government or an individual, therefore has an ethical
responsibility to act with compassion for the public good.

Fortunately, corporations have many incentives to
act responsibly. Customer loyalty, employee satisfaction,
overall cost-saving, and long-term viability are just some of
the advantages businesses can expect to gain by embracing
comprehensive CSR policies. Meanwhile, companies have very
little to lose by embracing a socially conscious view. These
days, compassion is profitable. Corporations would be wise to
recognize the enormous power, opportunity, and responsibility
they have to effect positive change.

Upbeat
ending.

Timmerman 8

Works Cited

Bejou, David. "Compassion as the New Philosophy of Business."
Journal of Relationship Marketing 10.1 (2011): 1-6.
Business Source Complete. Web. 15 Aug. 2012.

Cone Communications. *2010 Cone Cause Evolution Study*. Cone,
Inc., 2010. Web. 15 Aug. 2012.

"From Fringe to Mainstream: Companies Integrate CSR Initia-
tives into Everyday Business." *Knowledge@Wharton*. The
Wharton School of the University of Pennsylvania,
23 May 2012. Web. 14 Aug. 2012.

Guthrie, Doug. Keynote address. *Promoting a Comprehensive
Approach to Corporate Social Responsibility (CSR)*. *YouTube*.
YouTube, 22 May 2012. Web. 11 Aug. 2012.

Karnani, Aneel. "The Case against Corporate Social Responsibility."
The Wall Street Journal. Dow Jones & Co., Inc., 14 June
2012. Web. 12 Aug. 2012.

Meister, Jeanne. "Corporate Social Responsibility: A Lever for
Employee Attraction & Engagement." *Forbes*. Forbes.com,
7 June 2012. Web. 12 Aug. 2012.

Savitz, Andrew W., with Karl Weber. *The Triple Bottom Line:
How Today's Best-Run Companies Are Achieving Economic,
Social, and Environmental Success*. San Francisco: Jossey-
Bass, 2006. Print.

Alphabetical by author's last name.

Hanging indent ½".

An article on a blog without a known author.

A clip from YouTube.

AN ANNOTATED STUDENT RESEARCH PAPER IN APA FORMAT

The following paper is an example of a student paper that uses APA format.

Running Head: RELIGION IN MENTAL HEALTH   1

The APA-style
cover page
gives title,
author, and
course
information.

The Role of Spirituality and Religion

in Mental Health

Laura DeVeau

English 102

Professor Gardner

April 12, 2010

The Role of Spirituality and Religion

in Mental Health

It has been called "a vestige of the childhood of mankind," "the feeling of something true, total and absolute," "an otherworldly answer as regards the meaning of life" (Amaro, 1998; Jones, 1991, p. 1; Kristeva, 1987, p. 27). It has been compared to medicine, described as a psychological cure for mental illness, and also referred to as the cause of a dangerous fanaticism. With so many differing opinions on the impact of religion in people's lives, where would one begin a search for the truth? Who has the answer: Christians, humanists, objectivists, atheists, psychoanalysts, Buddhists, philosophers, cults? This was my dilemma at the advent of my research into how religion and spirituality affect the mental health of society as a whole.

In this paper, I explore the claims, widely accepted by professionals in the field of psychology, that religious and spiritual practices have a negative impact on mental health. In addition, though, I cannot help but reflect on how this exploration has changed my beliefs as well. Religion is such a personal experience that one cannot be dispassionate in reporting it. One can, however, subject the evidence provided by those who have studied the issue to critical scrutiny. Having done so, I find myself in disagreement with those who claim religious feelings are incompatible with sound mental health. There is a nearly limitless number of beliefs regarding spirituality. Some are organized and involve rituals like mass or worship. Many are centered around the existence of a higher

---

Short form of title and page number as running head.

Citation of multiple works from references.

Acknowledgment of opposing viewpoints.

being, while others focus on the self. I have attempted to uncover the perfect set of values that lead to a better lifestyle, but my research has pointed me in an entirely different direction, where no single belief seems to be adequate but where spiritual belief in general should be valued more highly than it is currently in mental health circles.

Thesis explicitly introduced.

I grew up in a moderately devout Catholic family. Like many young people raised in a household where one religion is practiced by both parents, it never occurred to me to question those beliefs. I went through a spiritual cycle, which I believe much of Western society also experiences. I attended religious services because I had to. I possessed a blind, unquestioning acceptance of what I was being taught because the adults I trusted said it was so. Like many adolescents and young adults, though, I stopped going to church when I was old enough to decide because I thought I had better things to do. At this stage, we reach a point when we begin searching for a meaning to our existence. For some, this search is brought on by a major crisis or a feeling of emptiness in their daily lives, while for others it is simply a part of growing up. This is where we begin to make personal choices, but with the barrage of options, where do we turn?

Beginning with the holistic health movement in the eighties, there has been a mass shift from traditional religions to less structured spiritual practices such as meditation, yoga, the Cabala, and mysticism (Beyerman, 1989). They venture beyond the realm of conventional dogmatism and into the new wave of spirituality. Many of these practices are based on the notion that

Author and date cited for summary or paraphrase.

health of the mind and spirit equals health of the body. Associated
with this movement is a proliferation of retreats offering a chance
to get in touch with the beauty and silence of nature and seminars
where we can take "a break from our everyday environment
where our brains are bustling and our bodies are exhausting
themselves" ("Psychological benefits," 1999). A major concept
of the spiritual new wave is that it focuses inward toward the
individual psyche, rather than outward toward another being
like a god. Practitioners do not deny the existence of this
being, but they believe that to fully love another, we must first
understand ourselves. Many find this a preferable alternative
to religions where the individual is seen as a walking dispenser
of sin who is very fortunate to have a forgiving creator. It is also
a relief from the scare tactics like damnation used by traditional
religions to make people behave. Many, therefore, praise the
potential psychological benefits of such spirituality.

  While I believe strongly in the benefits of the new wave,
I am not willing to do away with structured religion, for I find
that it also has its benefits. Without the existence of churches
and temples, it would be harder to expose the public to values
beneficial to mental stability. It is much more difficult to hand
a child a copy of the Cabala and say "Read this, and then get
back to me on it" than it is to bring a child to a service where
the ideas are represented with concrete examples. My religious
upbringing presented me with a set of useful morals and values,
and it does the same for millions of others who are brought up in
this manner. Many people, including some followers of the new
wave, are bitter toward Christianity because of events in history

Anonymous
source
cited by title
and date.

Clear
transition
refers to
previous
paragraph.

like the Crusades, the Inquisition, the Salem witch trials, and countless other horrific acts supposedly committed in the name of God. But these events were based not on biblical teachings but on pure human greed and lust for power. We should not reject the benevolent possibilities of organized religion on the basis of historical atrocities any more than we should abandon public education because a few teachers are known to mistreat children.

Another factor contributing to the reluctance concerning religion is the existence of cults that seduce people into following their extreme teachings. The victims are often at vulnerable times in their lives, and the leaders are usually very charming, charismatic, and sometimes also psychotic or otherwise mentally unstable. Many argue that if we acknowledge these groups as dangerous cults, then we must do the same for traditional religions such as Christianity and Islam, which are likewise founded on the teachings of charismatic leaders. Again, though, critics are too quick to conflate all religious and spiritual practice; we must distinguish between those who pray and attend services and those who commit group suicide because they think that aliens are coming to take over the world. Cults have provided many psychologists, who are eager to discount religion as a factor in improving mental health, with an easy target. Ellis (1993), the founder of rational-emotive therapy, cites many extreme examples of religious commitment, such as cults and antiabortion killings, to show that commitment is hazardous to one's sanity. Anomalies like these should not be used to speak of religion as a whole, though. Religion is clearly the least of these people's mental problems.

When the author's name appears in text, only the date is cited in parentheses.

Besides Ellis, there are many others in the field of psychology who do not recognize religion as a potential aid for improving the condition of the psyche. Actually, fewer than 45 percent of the members of the American Psychiatric Association even believe in God. The general American public has more than twice that percentage of religious devotees (Larson, 1998). Going back to the days of Freud, many psychologists have held atheist views. The father of psychoanalysis himself called religion a "universal obsessional neurosis." Psychologists have long rejected research that demonstrates the benefits of spirituality by saying that this research is biased. They claim that such studies are out to prove that religion helps because the conductors are religious people who need to justify their beliefs.

While this may be true in some instances, there is also some quite empirical research available to support the claims of those who promote religion and spirituality. The *Journal for the Scientific Study of Religion* has conducted many studies examining the effects of religion on individuals and groups. In one example, the relationship between religious coping methods and positive recovery after major stressful events was observed. The results indicated not only that spirituality was not harmful to the mind but that "the positive religious coping pattern was tied to benevolent outcomes, including fewer symptoms of psychological distress, [and] reports of psychological and spiritual growth as a result of the stressor" (Pargament et al., 1998, p. 721). Clearly, the benefits of piety can, in fact, be examined empirically, and in some cases the results point to a positive correlation between religion and mental health.

Bracketed word in quotation not in original source.

Author, date, and page number are cited for a direct quotation.

RELIGION IN MENTAL HEALTH   7

But let us get away from statistics and studies. If religion is both useless and dangerous, as so many psychologists claim, we must ask why has it remained so vital a part of humanity for so long. Even if it can be reduced to a mere coping method that humans use to justify their existence and explain incomprehensible events, is it futile? I would suggest that this alone represents a clear benefit to society. Should religion, if it cannot be proven as "true," be eliminated and life based on scientific fact alone? Surely many would find this a pointless existence. With all the conflicting knowledge I have gained about spirituality during my personal journey and my research, one idea is clear. It is not the depth of devotion, the time of life when one turns to religion, or even the particular combination of beliefs one chooses to adopt that will improve the quality of life. There is no right or wrong answer when it comes to self-fulfillment. It is whatever works for the individual, even if that means holding no religious or spiritual beliefs at all. But clearly there *are* benefits to be gained, at least for some individuals, and mental health professionals need to begin acknowledging this fact in their daily practice.

Conclusion restates and strengthens thesis.

References

Amaro, J. (1998). Psychology, psychoanalysis and religious

faith. *Nielsen's psychology of religion pages*. Retrieved

from http://www.psywww.com/psyrelig/amaro.html

Beyerman A. K. (1989). *The holistic health movement.*

Tuscaloosa, AL: Alabama University Press.

Ellis, A. (1993). Dogmatic devotion doesn't help, it hurts. In

B. Slife (Ed.), *Taking sides: Clashing views on controver-*

sial psychological issues (pp. 297-301). New York, NY:

Scribner.

Jones, J. W. (1991). *Contemporary psychoanalysis and religion:*

Transference and transcendence. New Haven, CT: Yale

University Press.

Kristeva, J. (1987). *In the beginning was love: Psychoanalysis*

and faith. New York, NY: Columbia University Press.

Larson, D. (1998). Does religious commitment improve mental

health? In B. Slife (Ed.), *Taking sides: Clashing views on*

controversial psychological issues (pp. 292-296). New

York, NY: Scribner.

Pargament, K. I., Smith, B. W., Koening, H. G., & Perez, L.

(1998). Patterns of positive and negative religious cop-

ing with major life stressors. *Journal for the Scientific*

Study of Religion, 37, 710-724.

"Psychological benefits." (1999). *Walking the labyrinth.*

Retrieved April 3, 2000, from http://www.labyrinthway

.com/html/benefits.html

References
begin on a
new page.

An online
source.

A book.

An article or
a chapter in a
book.

An article in a
journal.

Anonymous
source alpha-
betized by title.

PART TWO

FURTHER VIEWS
on ARGUMENT

8

A Philosopher's View: The Toulmin Model

All my ideas hold together, but I cannot elaborate them all at once.
——JEAN-JACQUES ROUSSEAU

Clarity has been said to be not enough. But perhaps it will be time to go into that when we are within measurable distance of achieving clarity on some matter.
——J. L. AUSTIN

[Philosophy is] a peculiarly stubborn effort to think clearly.
——WILLIAM JAMES

Philosophy is like trying to open a safe with a combination lock: Each little adjustment of the dials seems to achieve nothing, only when everything is in place does the door open.
——LUDWIG WITTGENSTEIN

In Chapter 3, we explained the contrast between making *deductive* and *inductive* arguments, the two main methods people use to reason. Either:

- we make explicit something concealed in what we already accept (**deduction**), or
- we use what we have observed as a basis for asserting or proposing something new (**induction**).

These two types of reasoning share some structural features, as we also noticed. Both deductive and inductive reasoning seek to establish a **thesis** (or conclusion) by offering **reasons** for accepting

293

the conclusion. Thus every argument contains both a thesis and one or more supportive reasons.

After a little scrutiny, we can in fact point to several features shared by all arguments, whether deductive or inductive, good or bad. We use the vocabulary popularized by Stephen Toulmin, Richard Rieke, and Allan Janik in their book *An Introduction to Reasoning* (1979; second edition 1984) to explore the various elements of argument. Once these elements are understood, it is possible to analyze an argument using their approach and their vocabulary in what has come to be known as "The Toulmin Method."

THE CLAIM

Every argument has a purpose, goal, or aim—namely, to establish a **claim** (*conclusion* or *thesis*). Suppose you are arguing in favor of equal rights for women. You might state your thesis or claim as follows:

> Men and women ought to have equal rights.

A more precise formulation of the claim might be

> Men and women ought to have equal legal rights.

A still more precise formulation might be

> Equal legal rights for men and women ought to be protected by our Constitution.

The third version of this claim states what the controversy in the 1970s over the Equal Rights Amendment was all about. (Both houses of Congress passed it in 1972, but the number of state legislatures that needed to ratify it before the Amendment could be added to the Constitution failed to do so before Congress's mandated deadline of June 30, 1982.)

In other words, the *claim* being made in an argument is the whole point of making the argument in the first place. Consequently, when you read or analyze someone else's argument, the first questions you should ask are these:

- What is the argument intended to prove or establish?
- *What claim is it making?*
- Has this claim been clearly and precisely formulated, so that it unambiguously asserts what its advocate wants it to assert?

GROUNDS

Once we have the argument's purpose or point clearly in mind and thus know what the arguer is aiming to establish, then we can look for the evidence, reasons, support—in short, for the **grounds**—on which that claim is based. In a *deductive* argument, these grounds are the premises from which the claim is deduced; in an *inductive* argument, the grounds are the evidence—which could be based on a sample, an observation, or an experiment—that makes the claim plausible or probable.

Not every kind of claim can be supported by every kind of ground, and, conversely, not every kind of ground gives equally good support for every kind of claim. Suppose, for instance, that I claim half the students in the classroom are women. I can establish the *ground* for this claim in any of several ways. For example:

1. I can count all the women and all the men. Suppose the total equals fifty. If the number of women is twenty-five and the number of men is twenty-five, I have vindicated my claim.
2. I can count a sample of ten students—perhaps the first ten to walk into the classroom—and find that in the sample five of the students are women. I thus have inductive—plausible but not conclusive—grounds for my claim.
3. I can point out that the students in the college divide equally into men and women and then claim that this class is a representative sample of the whole college.

Clearly, ground 1 is stronger than ground 2, and 2 is much stronger than 3.

Up to this point, we have merely restated points about premises and conclusions that were covered in Chapter 3. We want now to consider four additional features of arguments.

WARRANTS

Once we have the claim or the point of an argument fixed in mind and have isolated the evidence or reasons offered in its support, the next question you need to ask is this:

Exactly how do the reasons offered in support of the conclusion work? In other words, what kind of guarantee—**warrant**—is provided to demonstrate that the reasons proffered actually do support the claim or lead to the conclusion? (A *warrant* in this context is like the *warranty* you get when you buy something.)

In ordinary and straightforward *deductive* arguments, warrants take different forms. In the simplest cases, we can point to the way in which the *meanings* of the key terms are really equivalent. Thus, if John is taller than Bill, then Bill must be shorter than John. We know this because we know what "is shorter than" and "is taller than" mean. If A is taller than B, it must be the case that B is shorter than A; those are the meanings of the phrases being used here. Of course everyone involved does have to know the language well enough to understand the relationship between "is taller than" and "is shorter than." The *warrant* in this case is the common understanding of what those two phrases mean.

In other cases, we may need to be more resourceful. A reliable tactic is to think up a simple *parallel argument*, an argument exactly parallel in form and structure to the argument we are trying to defend. If the two arguments really do have the same form and structure, and we are ready to accept the simpler one, then we can point out that the more complex argument must be accepted—because the two arguments have exactly the same structure. For example, if we want to argue that it is reasonable for FedEx to charge more for their delivery services than the U.S. Postal Service (USPS) does, we could point out that, since it seems entirely reasonable to pay higher costs for special services from the USPS such as overnight delivery promised by a certain time (depending on factors such as location), then it is reasonable to pay even higher fees for similar overnight delivery by FedEx because that service includes sending someone to pick up what you want delivered.

In simple *inductive* arguments, we are likely to point to the way in which observations or sets of data constitute a *representative sample* of a whole population, even if not every member of the sample is strictly in evidence. For instance, when scattered information is plotted on a graph, the trend line does not have to touch each (or even any) of the data points as long as they are scattered above and below the line in roughly equal numbers in pairs that are roughly equidistant from the trend line. We can defend this projection on the grounds that it takes all of the points into account in the least complicated way. In such a case, the warrant is this combination of *inclusiveness* and *simplicity*.

Establishing the warrants for our reasoning—that is, explaining why our grounds really do support our claims—can quickly become a highly technical and exacting procedure that goes far beyond the aims of this book. Even so, developing a "feel" for why reasons or grounds are or are not relevant to what they are alleged to support is important. "That's just my view" is *not* a convincing warrant for any argument. Even without formal training, however, one can sense that something is wrong with many bad arguments. Here is one example: British professor C. E. M. Joad found himself standing on a station platform, annoyed because he had just missed his train. Then another train, making an unscheduled stop, pulled up to the platform in front of him. Joad decided to jump aboard, only to hear the conductor say, "I'm afraid you'll have to get off, Sir. This train doesn't stop here." "In that case," replied the professor, "don't worry. I'm not on it."

BACKING

A really solid argument may need even further support, especially if what is being argued is complicated. *Warrants*, remember, explain the way our *grounds* support our *claims*. The next task, however, is to be able to show that we can back up what we have claimed by showing that the reasons we have given for a claim are good reasons. To establish that kind of further support for an argument is to provide **backing.**

What is appropriate backing for one kind of argument might be quite inappropriate for another kind of argument. For example, the kinds of reasons relevant to support an amendment to the Constitution are completely different from the kinds appropriate to settle the question of what caused the defeat of Napoleon's invasion of Russia. Arguments for the amendment might be rooted in an appeal to fairness, whereas arguments about the military defeat might be rooted in letters and other documents in French and Russian archives. The *canons* (established conventions) of good argument in two such dramatically different cases have to do with the means that scholarly communities in law and history, respectively, have developed over the years to support, defend, challenge, and undermine a given kind of argument.

Another way of stating this point is to recognize that once you have given reasons for a claim, you are then likely to be challenged to explain why your reasons are good reasons—why, that is, anyone should believe your reasons rather than regard them skeptically. They have to be the right kinds of reasons, given the field you are arguing about. Why (to give a simple example) should we accept the testimony of Dr. *X* when Dr. *Y*, equally renowned, supports the opposite side? What more do we need to know before "expert testimony" is appropriately invoked? For a different kind of case: When and why is it safe to rest a prediction on a small though admittedly carefully selected sample? And still another: Why is it legitimate to argue that (1) if I dream I am the King of France, then I must exist, whereas it is illegitimate to argue that (2) if I dream I am the King of France, then the King of France must exist?

To answer challenges of these sorts is to back up one's reasons, to give them legitimate *backing*. No argument is any better than its backing.

MODAL QUALIFIERS

As we have seen, all arguments are made up of assertions or propositions that can be sorted into four categories:

- the *claim* (conclusion, thesis to be established),
- the *grounds* (explicit reasons advanced),
- the *warrant* (guarantee, evidence, or principle that legitimates the ground by connecting it to the claim), and
- the *backing* (relevant support, implicit assumptions).

All of the kinds of propositions that emerge when we assert something in an argument have what philosophers call a **modality**. This means that propositions generally indicate—explicitly or tacitly—the *character* and *scope* of what is believed to be their likely truth.

Character has to do with the nature of the claim being made, the extent of an argument's presumed reach. Both making and evaluating arguments require being clear about whether they are *necessary, probable, plausible,* or *possible.* Consider, for example, a claim that it is to the advantage of a college to have a racially diverse student body. Is that *necessarily* or only *probably* true? What about an argument that a runner who easily wins a 100-meter race should also be able to win at 200 meters? Is this *plausible*—or only *possible*? Indicating the *character* with which an assertion is advanced is crucial to any argument for or against it. Furthermore, if there is more than one reason for making a claim, and all of those reasons are *good*, it is still possible that one of those good reasons may be *better* than the others. If so, the better reason should be stressed.

Indicating the *scope* of an assertion is equally crucial to how an argument plays out. *Scope* entails such considerations as whether the proposition is thought to be true *always* or just *sometimes*. Further, is the claim being made supposed to apply in *all* instances or just in *some?* Assertions are usually clearer, as well as more likely to be true, if they are explicitly *quantified* and *qualified*. Suppose, for example, that you are arguing against smoking, and the ground for your claim is this:

Heavy smokers cut short their life span.

In this case, there are three obvious alternative quantifications to choose among: *all* smokers cut short their life span, *most* do, or only *some* do. Until the assertion is quantified in one of these ways, we really do not know what is being asserted—and so we do not know what degree and kind of evidence or counterevidence is relevant. Other quantifiers include *few, rarely, often, sometimes, perhaps, usually, more or less, regularly, occasionally*.

Scope also has to do with the fact that empirical generalizations are typically *contingent* on various factors. Indicating such contingencies clearly is an important way to protect a generalization against obvious counterexamples. Thus, consider this empirical generalization:

Students do best on final examinations if they study hard for them.

Are we really to believe that students who cram ("study hard" in that concentrated sense) for an exam will do better than those who do the work diligently throughout the whole course ("study hard" in that broader sense) and therefore do not need to cram for the final? Probably not; what is really meant is that *all other things being equal* (in Latin, *ceteris paribus*), concentrated study just before an exam will yield good results. Alluding in this way to the contingencies—the things that might derail the argument—shows that the writer is aware of possible exceptions and is conceding them from the start.

In sum, sensitivity to both character and (especially) scope—paying attention to the role played by quantifiers, qualifiers, and contingencies and making sure you use appropriate ones for each of your assertions—will strengthen your arguments enormously. Not least of the benefits is that you will reduce the peculiar vulnerabilities of an argument that is undermined by exaggeration and other misguided generalizations.

REBUTTALS

Very few arguments of any interest are beyond dispute, conclusively knockdown affairs. Only very rarely is the claim of an argument so rigidly tied to its grounds, warrants, and backing—and with its quantifiers and qualifiers argued in so precise a manner—that it proves its conclusion beyond any possibility of doubt. On the contrary, most arguments have many counterarguments, and sometimes one of these counterarguments is more convincing than the original argument.

Suppose someone has taken a sample that appears to be random: An interviewer on your campus accosts the first ten students she encounters, and seven of them are fraternity or sorority members. She is now ready to argue that seven-tenths of enrolled students belong to Greek organizations.

You believe, however, that the Greeks are in the minority and point out that she happens to have conducted her interview around the corner from the Panhellenic Society's office just off Sorority Row. Her random sample is anything but. The ball is now back in her court as you await her response to your rebuttal.

As this example illustrates, it is safe to say that we do not understand our own arguments very well until we have tried to get a grip on the places in which they are vulnerable to criticism, counterattack, or refutation. We have already, in Chapter 3, quoted Edmund Burke—but the passage is worth repeating: "He that wrestles with us strengthens our nerves, and sharpens our skill. Our antagonist is our helper."

To be sure, in everyday conversation we may not enjoy being in the company of people who interrupt to ask what are our grounds, warrants, backing, and so forth. The poet T. S. Eliot amusingly characterized himself as such a person:

How Unpleasant to Meet Mr. Eliot!

How unpleasant to meet Mr. Eliot!
With his features of clerical cut.
And his brow so grim
And his mouth so prim
And his conversation, so nicely
Restricted to What Precisely
And If and Perhaps and But . . .
How unpleasant to meet Mr. Eliot!
(Whether his mouth be open or shut.)

Still, if we wish to make serious progress in thinking and arguing about significant issues, cultivating alertness to possible weak spots in arguments—our own arguments as well as the arguments of others—and incorporating thoughtful responses to anticipated criticisms will always be helpful.

IDEA PROMPT 8.1 CONSTRUCTING A TOULMIN ARGUMENT

Claim	*What is your argument?*	"Driving while texting should be made illegal."
Grounds	*What is your evidence?*	"A 2011 study shows an increase in accidents due to drivers who drive and text."
Warrant	*What reasoning connects your evidence to your argument?*	"We should pass laws that promote safer roads."
Backing	*Why should the reader agree with your grounds?*	"We all use the roads, and we have a duty to make our shared roads as safe as possible."
Rebuttal	*What are the objections to this argument?*	"Many people would ignore this law just as they ignore laws about seatbelts, thereby making it ineffective, so why pass it in the first place?"
Qualifier	*What are the limits of your argument?*	"A ban on texting and driving might save some lives, even if it doesn't fix the whole problem."
One possible Toulmin argument	"In light of a 2011 study that shows that texting while driving has contributed to an increase in deadly automobile accidents, texting while driving should be banned. As a community, we have a responsibility to address such serious threats to our safety. Although many people would continue to text while driving, creating penalties for texting while driving may deter some drivers from engaging in such unsafe behavior."	

PUTTING THE TOULMIN METHOD TO WORK:
Responding to an Argument

Let's take a look at another argument—it happens to be on why buying directly from farmers near you won't save the planet—and see how the Toulmin method can be applied. The checklist on page 304 can help you focus your thoughts as you read.

James E. McWilliams

James E. McWilliams, the author of Just Food, *is an associate professor of history at Texas State University. This piece first appeared in* Forbes Magazine *on August 3, 2009.*

The Locavore Myth: Why Buying from Nearby Farmers Won't Save the Planet

Buy local, shrink the distance food travels, save the planet. The locavore movement has captured a lot of fans. To their credit, they are highlighting the problems with industrialized food. But a lot of them are making a big mistake. By focusing on transportation, they overlook other energy-hogging factors in food production.

Take lamb. A 2006 academic study (funded by the New Zealand government) discovered that it made more environmental sense for a Londoner to buy lamb shipped from New Zealand than to buy lamb raised in the U.K. This finding is counterintuitive—if you're only counting food miles. But New Zealand lamb is raised on pastures with a small carbon footprint, whereas most English lamb is produced under intensive factory-like conditions with a big carbon footprint. This disparity overwhelms domestic lamb's advantage in transportation energy.

New Zealand lamb is not exceptional. Take a close look at water usage, fertilizer types, processing methods, and packaging techniques and you discover that factors other than shipping far outweigh the energy it takes to transport food. One analysis, by Rich Pirog of the Leopold Center for Sustainable Agriculture, showed that transportation accounts for only 11 percent of food's carbon footprint. A fourth of the energy required to produce food is expended in the consumer's kitchen. Still more energy is consumed per meal in a restaurant, since restaurants throw away most of their leftovers.

Locavores argue that buying local food supports an area's farmers and, in turn, strengthens the community. Fair enough. Left unacknowledged, however, is the fact that it also hurts farmers in other parts of the world. The U.K. buys most of its green beans from Kenya. While it's true that the beans almost always arrive in airplanes — the form of transportation that consumes the most energy — it's also true that a campaign to shame English consumers with small airplane stickers affixed to flown-in produce threatens the livelihood of 1.5 million sub-Saharan farmers.

Another chink in the locavores' armor involves the way food miles are calculated. To choose a locally grown apple over an apple trucked in from across the country might seem easy. But this decision ignores economies of scale. To take an extreme example, a shipper sending a truck with 2,000 apples over 2,000 miles would consume the same amount of fuel per apple as a local farmer who takes a pickup 50 miles to sell 50 apples at his stall at the green market. The critical measure here is not food miles but apples per gallon.

The one big problem with thinking beyond food miles is that it's hard to get the information you need. Ethically concerned consumers know very little about processing practices, water availability, packaging waste, and fertilizer application. This is an opportunity for watchdog groups. They should make life-cycle carbon counts available to shoppers.

Until our food system becomes more transparent, there is one thing you can do to shrink the carbon footprint of your dinner: Take the meat off your plate. No matter how you slice it, it takes more energy to bring meat, as opposed to plants, to the table. It takes 6 pounds of grain to make a pound of chicken and 10 to 16 pounds to make a pound of beef. That difference translates into big differences in inputs. It requires 2,400 liters of water to make a burger and only 13 liters to grow a tomato. A majority of the water in the American West goes toward the production of pigs, chickens, and cattle.

The average American eats 273 pounds of meat a year. Give up red meat once a week and you'll save as much energy as if the only food miles in your diet were the distance to the nearest truck farmer.

If you want to make a statement, ride your bike to the farmer's market. If you want to reduce greenhouse gases, become a vegetarian.

✓ A CHECKLIST FOR USING THE TOULMIN METHOD

Have I asked the following questions?
- ☐ What claim does the argument make?
- ☐ What grounds are offered for the claim?
- ☐ What warrants the inferences from the grounds to the claim?
- ☐ What backing supports the claim?
- ☐ With what modalities are the claim and grounds asserted?
- ☐ To what rebuttals are the claim, grounds, and backing vulnerable?

See *Re:Writing*
bedfordstmartins.com/rewriting
for links related to the Toulmin model.

THINKING WITH TOULMIN'S METHOD

Remember to make use of the checklist above as you work to find the claim(s), grounds, and warrant(s) that McWilliams puts forward in this short essay.

- First and foremost, what is the **claim** being made by the author? Is it in his title? The opening sentence? Or is it buried in the first paragraph?

McWilliams really gives away his game in his title, even though he opens the essay itself in a way that might make the reader think he is about to launch into a defense of the locavore movement. He even goes out of his way to praise its members ("To their credit . . ."). The signal that his claim really appears already in the title and that he is *not* going to defend the locavore movement is the way he begins the fourth sentence. Notice that, although you may have been told that starting a sentence with *But* is not the best way to write, McWilliams here does so to good effect. Not only does he dramatically counter what he said just prior to that; he also sets up the final sentence of the paragraph, which turns out to be crucial. In this way, he draws sharp attention to his *claim*. How would you state his claim?

- Second, what are the **grounds,** the evidence or reasons, that the author advances in support of his claim?

As it turns out, McWilliams spells out only one example as evidence for his claim. What is it? Is it convincing? Should he have provided more evidence or reasons at this point? It turns out that he does have other grounds to offer—but he mentions them only later. What are those other pieces of evidence?

- Third, what **warrants** does McWilliams offer to show why we should accept his grounds? What authority does he cite? How effective and convincing is this way of trying to get us to accept the grounds he offered in support of his claim?

The essence of the Toulmin method lies in these three elements: the claim(s), the grounds, and the warrant(s). If you have extracted these from McWilliams's essay, you are well on the way to being able to identify the argument he is putting forward. So far, so good. Further probing, however—looking for the other three elements of the Toulmin method (the backing, the modal qualifiers and quantifiers, and the rebuttal)—is essential before you are in a position to actually evaluate the argument. So let's go on.

- Fourth, what **backing** does McWilliams provide? What reasons does he give that might persuade us to accept his argument? Look for what he claimed came out of the analysis that was his basic *warrant*. He certainly seems to be using factual information—but what if you challenged him? Has he provided adequate reasons for us to believe him? What could he (or would he have to be able to) tell us if we challenged him with questions like "How do you know . . . ?" or "Why do you believe . . . ?" In other words, has he provided adequate backing? Or does he want us to just accept his statement of the facts?

- Fifth, does McWilliams use **modal qualifiers**? Can you find phrases like "in most cases" or "generally it is true that . . . "? Or does he write so boldly—with little in the way of qualifiers or quantifiers—that one is left uncertain about whether to accept his position? Where might he have effectively used qualifiers?

- Finally, does McWilliams use **rebuttals**, the reasons given in anticipation of someone rejecting the author's claim, or conceding the claim but rejecting the grounds? Does McWilliams anticipate rejections and prepare rebuttals? Does he offer anything to forestall criticisms? If so, what is it that he does? If not, what could or should he have done?

Just how good an argument has McWilliams made? Is he convincing? If you identified weak points in his argument, what are they? Can you help strengthen the argument?

9

A Logician's View:
Deduction, Induction,
Fallacies

Logic is the anatomy of thought.

—JOHN LOCKE

Logic takes care of itself; all we have to do is to look and see how it does it.

—LUDWIG WITTGENSTEIN

In Chapter 3 we introduced the terms *deduction, induction,* and *fallacy*. Here we discuss them in greater detail.

DEDUCTION

The basic aim of deductive reasoning is to start with some assumption or premise and extract from it a conclusion—a logical consequence—that is concealed but implicit in it. Thus, taking the simplest case, if I assert as a premise

1a. Nuclear power poses more risks of harm to the environment than fossil fuels.

then it is a matter of simple deduction to infer the conclusion that

1b. Fossil fuels pose fewer risks of harm to the environment than nuclear power.

Anyone who understands English would grant that 1b follows 1a—or equivalently, that 1b can be validly deduced from 1a—because whatever two objects, *A* and *B*, you choose, if *A* does *more things than B*, then *B* must do *fewer things than A*.

Thus, in this and all other cases of valid deductive reasoning, we can say not only that we are entitled to *infer* the conclusion from the premise—in this case, infer 1b from 1a—but that the premise *implies* the conclusion. Remember, too, the conclusion (1b) that fossil fuels pose fewer risks than nuclear power—inferred or deduced from the statement (1a) that nuclear power poses more risks—does not depend on the truth of the statement that nuclear power poses more risks. If the speaker (falsely) asserts that nuclear power poses more risks, then the hearer validly (that is to say, logically) concludes that fossil fuels pose fewer risks. Thus, 1b follows from 1a whether or not 1a is true; consequently, if 1a is true, then so is 1b; but if 1a is false, then 1b must be false also.

Let's take another example—more interesting but comparably simple:

2a. President Truman was underrated by his critics.

Given 2a, a claim amply verified by events of the 1950s, one is entitled to infer

2b. His critics underrated President Truman.

On what basis can we argue that 2a implies 2b? The two propositions are equivalent because a rule of English grammar assures us that we can convert the position of subject and predicate phrases in a sentence by shifting from the passive to the active voice (or vice versa) without any change in the conditions that make the proposition true (or false).

Both pairs of examples illustrate that in deductive reasoning, our aim is to transform, reformulate, or restate in our conclusion some (or, as in the two examples above, all) of the information contained in our premises.

Remember, even though a proposition or statement follows from a previous proposition or statement, the statements need not be true. We can see why if we consider another example. Suppose someone asserts or claims that

3a. The Gettysburg Address is longer than the Declaration of Independence.

As every student of American history knows, 3a is false. But false or not, we can validly deduce from it that

   3b. The Declaration of Independence is shorter than the Gettysburg Address.

This inference is valid (even though the conclusion is untrue) because the conclusion follows logically (more precisely, deductively) from 3a: In English, as we know, the meaning of "*A* is shorter than *B*," which appears in 3b, is simply the converse of "*B* is longer than *A*," which appears in 3a.

The deductive relation between 3a and 3b reminds us again that the idea of validity, which is so crucial to deduction, is not the same as the idea of truth. False propositions have implications—logical consequences—too, just as true propositions do.

In the three pairs of examples so far, what can we point to as the warrant for our claims? Well, look at the reasoning in each case; the arguments rely on rules of ordinary English, on the accepted meanings of words like *on, under,* and *underrated.*

In many cases, of course, the deductive inference or pattern of reasoning is much more complex than that which we have seen in the examples so far. When we introduced the idea of deduction in Chapter 3, we gave as our primary example the *syllogism.* Here is another example:

   4. Texas is larger than California; California is larger than Arizona; therefore, Texas is larger than Arizona.

The conclusion in this syllogism is derivable from the two premises; that is, anyone who asserts the two premises is committed to accepting the conclusion as well, whether or not one thinks of it.

Notice again that the *truth* of the conclusion is not established merely by validity of the inference. The conclusion in this syllogism happens to be true. And the premises of this syllogism imply the conclusion. But the argument establishes the conclusion only because both of the premises on which the conclusion depends are true. Even a Californian admits that Texas is larger than California, which in turn is larger than Arizona. In other words, argument 4 is a *sound* argument because (as we explained in Chapter 3) it is valid and all its premises are true. All—and only—arguments that *prove* their conclusions have these two traits.

How might we present the warrant for the argument in 4? Short of a crash course in formal logic, either of two strategies might suffice. One is to argue from the fact that the validity of the inference depends on the meaning of a key concept, *being larger than*. This concept has the property of *transitivity,* a property that many concepts share (for example, *is equal to, is to the right of, is smarter than*—all are transitive concepts). Consequently, whatever *A, B,* and *C* are, if *A* is larger than *B,* and *B* is larger than *C,* then *A* will be larger than *C.* The final step is to substitute "Texas," "California," and "Arizona" for *A, B,* and *C,* respectively.

A second strategy, less abstract and more graphic, is to think of representing Texas, California, and Arizona by nested circles. Thus, the first premise in argument 4 would look like this:

The second premise would look like this:

The conclusion would look like this:

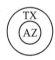

We can see that this conclusion follows from the premises because it amounts to nothing more than what one gets by superimposing the two premises on each other. Thus, the whole argument can be represented like this:

$$\left(\text{TX} \left(\text{CA}\right)\right) + \left(\text{CA} \left(\text{AZ}\right)\right) = \left(\text{TX} \left(\text{AZ}\right)\right)$$

The so-called middle term in the argument—California—disappears from the conclusion; its role is confined to be the link between the other two terms, Texas and Arizona, in the premises. (This is an adaptation of the technique used in elementary formal logic known as Venn diagrams.) In this manner one can give graphic display to the important fact that the conclusion follows from the premises because one can literally *see* the conclusion represented by nothing more than a representation of the premises.

Both of these strategies bring out the fact that validity of deductive inference is a purely *formal* property of argument. Each strategy abstracts the form from the content of the propositions involved to show how the concepts in the premises are related to the concepts in the conclusion.

For the sake of illustration, here is another syllogistic argument with the same logical features as argument 4. (A nice exercise is to restate argument 5 using diagrams in the manner of argument 4.)

5. African American slaves were treated worse than white indentured servants. Indentured white servants were treated worse than free white labor. Therefore, African American slaves were treated worse than free white labor.

Not all deductive reasoning occurs in syllogisms, however, or at least not in syllogisms like the ones in 4 and 5. (The term *syllogism* is sometimes used to refer to any deductive argument of whatever form, provided only that it has two premises.) In fact, syllogisms such as 4 are not the commonest form of our deductive reasoning at all. Nor are they the simplest (and of course, not the most complex). For an argument that is even simpler, consider this:

6. If a youth is an African American slave, he is probably treated worse than a youth in indentured service. This youth is an African American slave. Therefore, he is probably treated worse than if he had been an indentured servant.

Here the pattern of reasoning has the form: If *A*, then *B*; *A*; therefore, *B*. Notice that the content of the assertions represented by *A* and *B* do not matter; any set of expressions having the same form or structure will do equally well, including assertions built out of meaningless terms, as in this example:

7. If the slithy toves, then the gyres gimble. The slithy toves. Therefore, the gyres gimble.

Argument 7 has the form: If *A*, then *B*; *A*; therefore *B*. As a piece of deductive inference it is every bit as good as argument 6. Unlike 6, however, 7 is of no interest to us because none of its assertions make any sense (unless you are a reader of Lewis Carroll's "Jabberwocky," and even then the sense of 7 is doubtful). You cannot, in short, use a valid deductive argument to prove anything unless the premises and the conclusion are *true*, but they can't be true unless they *mean* something in the first place.

This parallel between arguments 6 and 7 shows once again that deductive validity in an argument rests on the *form* or structure of the argument, and not on its content or meaning. If all one can say about an argument is that it is valid—that is, its conclusion follows from the premises—one has not given a sufficient reason for accepting the argument's conclusion. It has been said that the Devil can quote Scripture; similarly, an argument can be deductively valid and of no further interest or value whatever because valid (but false) conclusions can be drawn from false or even meaningless assumptions. For example,

> 8. New York's Metropolitan Museum of Art has the finest collection of abstract impressionist painting in the world. The finest collection of abstract impressionist paintings includes dozens of canvases by Winslow Homer. Therefore, the Metropolitan Museum of Art has dozens of paintings by Winslow Homer.

Here, the conclusion follows validly from the premises, even though all three propositions are false. Nevertheless, although validity by itself is not enough, it is a necessary condition of any deductive argument that purports to establish its conclusion.

Now let us consider another argument with the same form as 8, only more interesting.

> 9. If President Truman knew the Japanese were about to surrender, then it was immoral of him to order that atom bombs be dropped on Hiroshima and Nagasaki. Truman knew the Japanese were about to surrender. Therefore, it was immoral of him to order dropping those bombs.

As in the two previous examples, anyone who assents to the premises in argument 9 must assent to the conclusion; the form of arguments 8 and 9 is identical. But do the premises of argument 9 *prove* the conclusion? That depends on whether both premises are true. Well, are they? This turns on a number of considerations, and it is worthwhile pausing to examine this argument closely to illustrate the kinds of things that are involved in answering this question.

Let us begin by examining the second (minor) premise. Its truth is controversial even to this day. Autobiography, memoranda, other documentary evidence—all are needed to assemble the evidence to back up the grounds for the thesis or claim made in the conclusion of this valid argument. Evaluating this material effectively will probably involve not only further deductions but inductive reasoning as well.

Now consider the first (major) premise in argument 9. Its truth doesn't depend on what history shows but on the moral principles one accepts. The major premise has the form of a hypothetical proposition ("if . . . then . . .") and asserts a connection between two very different kinds of things. The antecedent of the hypothetical (the clause following "if") mentions facts about Truman's *knowledge,* and the consequent of the hypothetical (the clause following "then") mentions facts about the *morality* of his conduct in light of such knowledge. The major premise as a whole can thus be seen as expressing *a principle of moral responsibility.*

Such principles can, of course, be controversial. In this case, for instance, is the principle peculiarly relevant to the knowledge and conduct of a president of the United States? Probably not; it is far more likely that this principle is merely a special case of a more general proposition about anyone's moral responsibility. (After all, we know a great deal more about the conditions of our own moral responsibility than we do about those of high government officials.) We might express this more general principle in this way: If we have knowledge that would make our violent conduct unnecessary, then we are immoral if we deliberately act violently anyway. Thus, accepting this general principle can serve as a basis for defending the major premise of argument 9.

We have examined this argument in some detail because it illustrates the kinds of considerations needed to test whether a given argument is not only valid but whether its premises are true—that is, whether its premises really prove the conclusion.

The great value of the form of argument known as hypothetical syllogism, exemplified by arguments 6 and 7, is that the structure of the argument is so simple and so universally applicable in reasoning that it is often both easy and worthwhile to formulate one's claims so that they can be grounded by an argument of this sort.

Before leaving the subject of deductive inference, consider three other forms of argument, each of which can be found in actual use elsewhere in the readings in this volume. The simplest of these is **disjunctive syllogism,** so called because its major premise is a **disjunction.** For example,

10. Either censorship of television shows is overdue, or our society is indifferent to the education of its youth. Our society is not indifferent to the education of its youth. Therefore, censorship of television is overdue.

Notice, by the way, that the validity of an argument, as in this case, does not turn on pedantic repetition of every word or phrase as the argument moves along; nonessential elements can be dropped, or equivalent expressions substituted for variety without adverse effect on the reasoning. Thus, in conversation or in writing, the argument in 10 might actually be presented like this:

11. Either censorship of television is overdue, or our society is indifferent to the education of its youth. But, of course, we aren't indifferent; it's censorship that's overdue.

The key feature of disjunctive syllogism, as example 11 suggests, is that the conclusion is whichever of the disjuncts is left over after the others have been negated in the minor premise. Thus, we could easily have a very complex disjunctive syllogism, with a dozen disjuncts in the major premise, and seven of them denied in the minor premise, leaving a conclusion of the remaining five. Usually, however, a disjunctive argument is formulated in this manner: Assert a disjunction with two or more disjuncts in the major premise; then *deny all but one* in the minor premise; and infer validly the remaining disjunct as the conclusion. That was the form of argument 11.

Another type of argument, especially favored by orators and rhetoricians, is the **dilemma.** Ordinarily we use the term *dilemma* in the sense of an awkward predicament, as when we say, "His dilemma was that he didn't have enough money to pay the waiter." But when logicians refer to a dilemma, they mean a forced choice between two or more equally unattractive alternatives. For example, the predicament of the U.S. government during the mid-1980s as it faced the crisis brought on by terrorist attacks on American civilian targets, which were believed, during that time, to be inspired and supported by the Libyan government, can be formulated in a dilemma:

12. If the United States bombs targets in Libya, innocent people will be killed, and the Arab world will be angered. If the United States doesn't bomb Libyan targets, then terrorists will go unpunished, and the United States will lose respect among other governments. Either the United States bombs

Libyan targets, or it doesn't. Therefore, in either case unattractive consequences will follow: The innocent will be killed, or terrorists will go unpunished.

Notice first the structure of the argument: two conditional propositions asserted as premises, followed by another premise that states a **necessary truth.** (The premise, that either we bomb the Libyans or we don't, is a disjunction; since its two alternatives are exhaustive, one of the two alternatives must be true. Such a statement is often called analytically true, or a *tautology*.) No doubt the conclusion of this dilemma follows from its premises.

But does the argument prove, as it purports to do, that whatever the U.S. government does, it will suffer "unattractive consequences"? It is customary to speak of "the horns of the dilemma," as though the challenge posed by the dilemma were like a bull ready to gore you whichever direction you turn. But if the two conditional premises failed to exhaust the possibilities, then one can escape from the dilemma by going "between the horns," that is, by finding a third alternative. If (as in this case) that is not possible, one can still ask whether both of the main premises are true. (In this argument, it should be clear that neither of these main premises spells out all or even most of the consequences that could be foreseen.) Even so, in cases where both these conditional premises are true, it may be that the consequences of one alternative are nowhere nearly so bad as those of the other. If that is true, but our reasoning stops before evaluating that fact, we may be guilty of failing to distinguish between the greater and the lesser of two admitted evils. The logic of the dilemma itself cannot decide this choice for us. Instead, we must bring to bear empirical inquiry and imagination to the evaluation of the grounds of the dilemma itself.

Writers commonly use the term *dilemma* without explicitly formulating the dilemma to which they refer, leaving it for the readers to do. And sometimes, what is called a dilemma really isn't one. (Remember the dog's tail? Calling it a leg doesn't make it a leg.) As an example, consider the plight of Sophie in William Styron's novel, *Sophie's Choice*. The scene is Birkenau, the main Nazi extermination camp during World War II. Among the thousands arriving at the prison gates are Sophie and her two children, Jan and Eva. On the train platform they are confronted by a Nazi SS medical officer. He will decide which are the lucky ones; they will live to work in the camp. The rest will go to their death in the gas chambers. When Sophie insists she is Polish but not Jewish, the officer says she may choose one of her children to be saved. Which of the two ought to be saved? On what basis ought Sophie resolve her dilemma? It looks as if she has only two alternatives, each of which presents her with an agonizing outcome. Or is there a third way out?

Finally, one of the most powerful and dramatic forms of argument is **reductio ad absurdum** (from the Latin, meaning "reduction to absurdity"). The idea of a reductio argument is to disprove a proposition by showing the absurdity of its inevitable conclusion. It is used, of course, to refute your opponent's position and prove your own. For example, in Plato's *Republic,* Socrates asks an old gentleman, Cephalus, to define what right conduct is. Cephalus says that it consists of paying your debts and keeping your word. Socrates rejects this answer by showing that it leads to a contradiction. He argues that Cephalus cannot have given the correct answer because if we believe that he did, we will be quickly led into contradictions; in some cases when you keep your word you will nonetheless be doing the wrong thing. For suppose, says Socrates, that you borrowed a weapon from a man, promising to return it when he asks for it. One day he comes to your door, demanding his weapon and swearing angrily that he intends to murder a neighbor. Keeping your word under those circumstances is absurd, Socrates implies, and the reader of the dialogue is left to infer that Cephalus's definition, which led to this result, is refuted.

Let's take a closer look at another example. Suppose you are opposed to any form of gun control, whereas I am in favor of gun control. I might try to refute your position by attacking it with a reductio argument. To do that, I start out by assuming the very opposite of what I believe or favor and try to establish a contradiction that results from following out the consequences of this initial assumption. My argument might look like this:

13. Let's assume your position—namely, that there ought to be no legal restrictions whatever on the sale and ownership of guns. That means that you'd permit having every neighborhood hardware store sell pistols and rifles to whoever walks in the door. But that's not all. You apparently also would permit selling machine guns to children, antitank weapons to lunatics, small-bore cannons to the nearsighted, as well as guns and the ammunition to go with them to anyone with a criminal record. But this is utterly preposterous. No one could favor such a dangerous policy. So the only question worth debating is what kind of gun control is necessary.

Now in this example, my reductio of your position on gun control is not based on claiming to show that you have strictly contradicted yourself, for there is no purely logical contradiction in opposing all forms of gun control. Instead, what I have tried to do is to show that there is a contradiction between what you profess—no gun controls whatever—and what you probably really believe, if only you will stop to think about it—no lunatic should be allowed to buy a loaded machine gun.

My refutation of your position rests on whether I succeed in establishing an inconsistency among your own beliefs. If it turns out that you really believe lunatics should be free to purchase guns and ammunition, then my attempted refutation fails.

In explaining reductio ad absurdum, we have had to rely on another idea fundamental to logic, that of **contradiction,** or inconsistency. (We used this idea, remember, to define validity in Chapter 3. A deductive argument is valid if and only if affirming the premises and denying the conclusion results in a contradiction.) The opposite of contradiction is **consistency,** a notion of hardly less importance to good reasoning than validity. These concepts deserve a few words of further explanation and illustration. Consider this pair of assertions:

14. Abortion is homicide.
15. Racism is unfair.

No one would plausibly claim that we can infer or deduce 15 from 14, or, for that matter, 14 from 15. This almost goes without saying because there is no evident connection between these two assertions. They are unrelated assertions; logically speaking, they are *independent* of each other. In such cases the two assertions are mutually *consistent;* that is, both could be true—or both could be false. But now consider another proposition:

16. Euthanasia is not murder.

Could a person assert 14 (*Abortion is homicide*) and also assert 16 (*Euthanasia is not murder*) and be consistent? This question is equivalent to asking whether one could assert the **conjunction** of these two propositions—namely,

17. Abortion is homicide, and euthanasia is not murder.

It is not so easy to say whether 17 is consistent or inconsistent. The kinds of moral scruples that might lead a person to assert one of these conjuncts (that is, one of the two initial propositions, *Abortion is homicide* and *Euthanasia is not murder*) might lead to the belief that the other one must be false and thus to the conclusion that 17 is inconsistent. (Notice that if 14 were the assertion that *Abortion is murder*, instead of *Abortion is homicide*, the problem of asserting consistently both 14 and 16 would be more acute.) Yet if we think again, we might imagine someone being convinced that there is no inconsistency in asserting that *Abortion is homicide*, say, and that *Euthanasia is not murder*, or even the reverse. (For instance, suppose you believed that the unborn deserve a chance to live and that putting elderly persons to death in a painless manner and with their consent confers a benefit on them.)

Let us generalize: We can say of any set of propositions that they are *consistent* if and only if *all could be true together.* (Notice that it follows from this definition that propositions mutually imply each other, as do *Seabiscuit was America's fastest racehorse* and *America's fastest racehorse was Seabiscuit.*) Remember that, once again, the truth of the assertions in question does not matter. Two propositions can be consistent or not, quite apart from whether they are true. Not so with falsehood: It follows from our definition of consistency that an *inconsistent* proposition must be *false.* (We have relied on this idea in explaining how a reductio ad absurdum works.)

Assertions or claims that are not consistent can take either of two forms. Suppose you assert proposition 14, that abortion is homicide, early in an essay you are writing, but later you assert that

18. Abortion is harmless.

You have now asserted a position on abortion that is strictly contrary to the one with which you began; contrary in the sense that both assertions 14 and 18 cannot be true. It is simply not true that, if an abortion involves killing a human being (which is what *homicide* strictly means), then it causes no one any harm (killing a person always causes harm—even if it is excusable, justifiable, not wrong, the best thing to do in the circumstances, and so on). Notice that although 14 and 18 cannot both be true, they can both be false. In fact, many people who are perplexed about the morality of abortion believe precisely this. They concede that abortion does harm the fetus, so 18 must be false; but they also believe that abortion doesn't kill a person, so 14 must also be false.

Or consider another, simpler case. If you describe the glass as half empty and I describe it as half full, both of us can be right; the two assertions are consistent, even though they sound vaguely incompatible. (This is the reason that disputing over whether the glass is half full or half empty has become the popular paradigm of a futile, purely *verbal disagreement.*) But if I describe the glass as half empty whereas you insist that it is two-thirds empty, then we have a real disagreement; your description and mine are strictly contrary, in that both cannot be true—although both can be false. (Both are false if the glass is only one-quarter full.)

This, by the way, enables us to define the difference between a pair of **contradictory** propositions and a pair of **contrary** propositions. Two propositions are contrary if and only if both cannot be true (though both can be false); two propositions are contradictory if and only if they are such that if one is true the other must be false, and vice versa. Thus, if Jack says that Alice Walker's *The Color Purple* is a better novel than Mark Twain's *Huckleberry Finn*, and Jill says, "No, *Huckleberry Finn* is better than *The Color Purple*," she is contradicting Jack. If what either one of them says is true, then what the other says must be false.

A more subtle case of contradiction arises when two or more of one's own beliefs implicitly contradict each other. We may find ourselves saying "Travel is broadening," and saying an hour later, "People don't really change." Just beneath the surface of these two beliefs lies a self-contradiction: How can travel broaden us unless it influences—and changes—our beliefs, values, and outlook? But if we can't really change ourselves, then traveling to new places won't change us, either. (Indeed, there is a Roman saying to the effect that travelers change the skies above them, not their hearts.) "Travel is broadening" and "People don't change" collide with each other; something has to give.

Our point, of course, is not that you must never say today something that contradicts something you said yesterday. Far from it; if you think you were mistaken yesterday, of course you will take a different position today. But what you want to avoid is what George Orwell called *doublethink* in his novel *1984*: "*Doublethink* means the power of holding two contradictory beliefs in one's mind simultaneously, and accepting them both."

Genuine contradiction, and not merely contrary assertion, is the situation we should expect to find in some disputes. Someone advances a thesis—such as the assertion in 14, *Abortion is homicide*—and someone else flatly contradicts it by the simple expedient of negating it, thus:

19. Abortion is not homicide.

If we can trust public opinion polls, many of us are not sure whether to agree with 14 or with 19. But we should agree that whichever is true, *both* cannot be true, and *both* cannot be false. The two assertions, between them, exclude all other possibilities; they pose a forced choice for our belief. (Again, we have met this idea, too, in a reductio ad absurdum.)

Now it is one thing for Jack and Jill in a dispute or argument to contradict each other. It is quite another matter for Jack to contradict himself. One wants (or should want) to avoid self-contradiction because of the embarrassing position in which one then finds oneself. Once I have contradicted myself, what are others to believe I really believe? What, indeed, *do* I believe, for that matter?

It may be, as Emerson observed, that a "foolish consistency is the hobgoblin of little minds"—that is, it may be shortsighted to purchase a consistency in one's beliefs at the expense of flying in the face of common sense. But making an effort to avoid a foolish inconsistency is the hallmark of serious thinking.

While we are speaking of inconsistency, we should spend a moment on **paradox.** The word refers to two different things:

- an assertion that is essentially self-contradictory and therefore cannot be true and
- a seemingly contradictory assertion that nevertheless may be true.

An example of the first might be, "Evaluations concerning quality in literature are all a matter of personal judgment, but Shakespeare is the world's greatest writer." It is hard to make any sense out of this assertion. Contrast it with a paradox of the second sort, a *seeming* contradiction that may make sense, such as "The longest way round is the shortest way home," or "Work is more fun than fun," or "The best way to find happiness is not to look for it." Here we have assertions that are striking because as soon as we hear them we realize that, although they seem inconsistent and self-defeating, they contain (or may contain) profound truths. Paradoxes of this second sort are especially common in religious texts, where they may imply a mysterious reality concealed by a world of contradictory appearances. Examples are "Some who are last shall be first, and some who are first shall be last" (Jesus, quoted in Luke 13:30), and "Death, thou shalt die" (the poet John Donne, alluding to the idea that the person who has faith in Jesus dies to this world but lives eternally). If you use the word *paradox* in your own writing—for instance, to characterize an argument that you are reading—be sure that your reader will understand in which sense you are using the word. (And, of course, you will not want to write paradoxes of the first, self-contradictory sort.)

INDUCTION

Deduction involves logical thinking that applies to any assertion or claim whatever—because every possible statement, true or false, has its deductive logical consequences. Induction is relevant to one kind of assertion only; namely, to **empirical** or *factual* claims. Other kinds of assertions (such as definitions, mathematical equations, and moral or legal norms) simply are not the product of inductive reasoning and cannot serve as a basis for further inductive thinking.

And so, in studying the methods of induction, we are exploring tactics and strategies useful in gathering and then using **evidence**—empirical, observational, experimental—in support of a belief as its ground. Modern scientific knowledge is the product of these methods, and they differ somewhat from one science to another because they depend on the theories and technology appropriate to each of the sciences. Here, all we can do is discuss generally the more abstract features common to inductive inquiry generally. For fuller details, you must eventually consult your local physicist, chemist, geologist, or their colleagues and counterparts in other scientific fields.

Observation and Inference

Let us begin with a simple example. Suppose we have evidence (actually we don't, but that will not matter for our purposes) in support of the claim that

1. In a sample of 500 smokers, 230 persons observed have cardiovascular disease.

The basis for asserting 1—the evidence or ground—would be, presumably, straightforward physical examination of the 500 persons in the sample, one by one.

With this claim in hand, we can think of the purpose and methods of induction as being pointed in both of two opposite directions: toward establishing the basis or ground of the very empirical proposition with which we start (in this example, the observation stated in 1) or toward understanding what that observation indicates or suggests as a more general, inclusive, or fundamental fact of nature.

In each case, we start from something we *do* know (or take for granted and treat as a sound starting point) — some fact of nature, perhaps a striking or commonplace event that we have observed and recorded — and then go on to something we do *not* fully know and perhaps cannot directly observe. In example 1, only the second of these two orientations is of any interest, and so let us concentrate exclusively on it. Let us also generously treat as a *method* of induction any regular pattern or style of nondeductive reasoning that we could use to support a claim such as that in 1.

Anyone truly interested in the observed fact that *230 of 500 smokers have cardiovascular disease* is likely to start speculating about, and thus be interested in finding out, whether any or all of several other propositions are also true. For example, one might wonder whether

> 2. *All* smokers have cardiovascular disease or will develop it during their lifetimes.

This claim is a straightforward generalization of the original observation as reported in claim 1. When we think inductively about the linkage between 1 and 2, we are reasoning from an observed sample (some smokers — that is, 230 of the 500 *observed*) to the entire membership of a more inclusive class (*all* smokers, whether observed or not). The fundamental question raised by reasoning from the narrower claim 1 to the broader claim 2 is whether we have any ground for believing that what is true of *some* members of a class is true of them *all*. So the difference between 1 and 2 is that of *quantity* or scope.

We can also think inductively about the *relation* between the factors mentioned in 1. Having observed data as reported in 1, we may be tempted to assert a different and profounder kind of claim:

> 3. Smoking *causes* cardiovascular disease.

Here our interest is not merely in generalizing from a sample to a whole class; it is the far more important one of *explaining* the observation with which we began in claim 1. Certainly the preferred, even if not the only, mode of explanation for a natural phenomenon is a *causal* explanation. In proposition 3, we propose to explain the presence of one phenomenon (cardiovascular disease) by the prior occurrence of an independent phenomenon (smoking). The observation reported in 1 is now being used as evidence or support for this new conjecture stated in 3.

Our original claim in 1 asserted no causal relation between anything and anything else; whatever the cause of cardiovascular disease may be, that cause is not observed, mentioned, or assumed in assertion 1. Similarly, the observation asserted in claim 1 is consistent with many explanations. For example, the explanation of 1 might not be 3, but some other, undetected, carcinogenic factor unrelated to smoking—for instance, exposure to high levels of radon. The question one now faces is what can be added to 1, or teased out of it, to produce an adequate ground for claiming 3. (We shall return to this example for closer scrutiny.)

But there is a third way to go beyond 1. Instead of a straight-forward generalization, as we had in 2, or a pronouncement on the cause of a phenomenon, as in 3, we might have a somewhat more complex and cautious further claim in mind, such as this:

4. Smoking is a factor in the causation of cardiovascular disease in some persons.

This proposition, like 3, advances a claim about causation. But 4 is obviously a weaker claim than 3. That is, other observations, theories, or evidence that would require us to reject 3 might be consistent with 4; evidence that would support 4 could easily fail to be enough to support 3. Consequently, it is even possible that 4 is true although 3 is false, because 4 allows for other (unmentioned) factors in the causation of cardiovascular disease (genetic or dietary factors, for example) that may not be found in all smokers.

Propositions 2, 3, and 4 differ from proposition 1 in an important respect. We began by assuming that 1 states an empirical fact based on direct observation, whereas these others do not. Instead, they state empirical *hypotheses* or conjectures—tentative generalizations not fully confirmed—each of which goes beyond the observed facts asserted in 1. Each of 2, 3, and 4 can be regarded as an *inductive inference* from 1. We can also say that 2, 3, and 4 are hypotheses relative to 1, even if relative to some other starting point (such as all the information that scientists today really have about smoking and cardiovascular disease) they are not.

Probability

Another way of formulating the last point is to say that whereas proposition 1, a statement of observed fact (*230 out of 500 smokers have cardiovascular disease*), has a **probability** of 1.0—that is, it is absolutely certain—the probability of each of the hypotheses stated in 2, 3, and 4, *relative* to 1 is smaller than 1.0. (We need not worry here about how much smaller than 1.0 the probabilities are, nor about how to calculate these probabilities precisely.) Relative to some starting point other than 1, however, the probability of these same three hypotheses might be quite different. Of course, it still would not be 1.0, absolute certainty. But it takes only a moment's reflection to realize that, whatever may be the probability of 2 or 3 or 4 relative to 1, those probabilities in each case will be quite different relative to different information, such as this:

> 5. Ten persons observed in a sample of 500 smokers have cardiovascular disease.

The idea that a *given proposition can have different probabilities* relative to different bases is fundamental to all inductive reasoning. It can be convincingly illustrated by the following example. Suppose we want to consider the probability of this proposition being true:

> 6. Susanne Smith will live to be eighty.

Taken as an abstract question of fact, we cannot even guess what the probability is with any assurance. But we can do better than guess; we can in fact even calculate the answer, if we are given some further information. Thus, suppose we are told that

> 7. Susanne Smith is seventy-nine.

Our original question then becomes one of determining the probability that 6 is true given 7; that is, relative to the evidence contained in proposition 7. No doubt, if Susanne Smith really is seventy-nine, then the probability that she will live to be eighty is greater than if we know only that

> 8. Susanne Smith is more than nine years old.

Obviously, a lot can happen to Susanne in the seventy years between nine and seventy-nine that is not very likely to happen to her in the one year between seventy-nine and eighty. And so, proposition 6 is more probable relative to proposition 7 than it is relative to proposition 8.

Let us suppose for the sake of the argument that the following is true:

9. Ninety percent of the women alive at seventy-nine live to be eighty.

Given this additional information, and the information that Susanne is seventy-nine, we now have a basis for answering our original question about proposition 6 with some precision. But suppose, in addition to 8, we are also told that

10. Susanne Smith is suffering from inoperable cancer.

and also that

11. The survival rate for women suffering from inoperable cancer is 0.6 years (that is, the average life span for women after a diagnosis of inoperable cancer is about seven months).

With this new information, the probability that 6 will be true has dropped significantly, all because we can now estimate the probability in relation to a new body of evidence.

The probability of an event, thus, is not a fixed number but one that varies because it is always relative to some evidence—and given different evidence, one and the same event can have different probabilities. In other words, the probability of any event is always relative to how much is known (assumed, believed), and because different persons may know different things about a given event, or the same person may know different things at different times, one and the same event can have two or more probabilities. This conclusion is not a paradox but a logical consequence of the concept of what it is for an event to have (that is, to be assigned) a probability.

If we shift to the *calculation* of probabilities, we find that generally we have two ways to calculate them. One way to proceed is by the method of **a priori** or **equal probabilities**—that is, by reference to the relevant possibilities taken abstractly and apart from any other information. Thus, in an election contest with only two candidates, Smith and Jones, each of the candidates has a fifty-fifty chance of winning (whereas in a three-candidate race, each candidate would have one chance in three of winning). Therefore, the probability that Smith will win is 0.5, and the probability that Jones will win is also 0.5. (The sum of the probabilities of all possible independent outcomes must always equal 1.0, which is obvious enough if you think about it.)

But in politics the probabilities are not reasonably calculated so abstractly. We know that many empirical factors affect the outcome of an election and that a calculation of probabilities in ignorance of those factors is likely to be drastically misleading. In our example of the two-candidate election, suppose Smith has strong party support and is the incumbent, whereas Jones represents a party long out of power and is further handicapped by being relatively unknown. No one who knows anything about electoral politics would give Jones the same chance of winning as Smith. The two events are not equiprobable in relation to all the information available.

Not only that, a given event can have more than one probability. This happens whenever we calculate a probability by relying on different bodies of data that report how often the event in question has been observed to happen. Probabilities calculated in this way are **relative frequencies.** Our earlier hypothetical example of Susanne Smith provides an illustration. If she is a smoker and we have observed that 100 out of a random set of 500 smokers are observed to have cardiovascular disease, we have a basis for claiming that she has a probability of 100 in 500, or 0.2 (one-fifth), of having this disease. However, if we had other data showing that 250 out of 500 women smokers ages eighty or older have cardiovascular disease, we have a basis for believing that there is a probability of 250 in 500, or 0.5 (one-half), that she has this disease. Notice, of course, that in both calculations we assume that Susanne Smith is not among the persons we have examined. In both cases we infer the probability with which she has this disease from observing its frequency in populations that exclude her.

Both methods of calculating probabilities are legitimate; in each case the calculation is relative to observed circumstances. But as the examples show, it is most reasonable to have recourse to the method of equiprobabilities only when few or no other factors affecting possible outcomes are known.

Mill's Methods

Let us return to our earlier discussion of smoking and cardiovascular disease and consider in greater detail the question of a causal connection between the two phenomena. We began thus:

1. In a sample of 500 smokers, 230 persons observed have cardiovascular disease.

We regarded 1 as an observed fact, though in truth, of course, it is mere supposition. Our question now is, how might we augment this information so as to strengthen our confidence that

   3. Smoking *causes* cardiovascular disease.

or at least

   4. Smoking is a factor in the causation of cardiovascular disease in some persons.

Suppose further examination showed that

   12. In the sample of 230 smokers with cardiovascular disease, no other suspected factor (such as genetic predisposition, lack of physical exercise, age over fifty) was also observed.

Such an observation would encourage us to believe 3 or 4 is true. Why? We are encouraged to believe it because we are inclined to believe also that whatever the cause of a phenomenon is, it must *always* be present when its effect is present. Thus, the inference from 1 to 3 or 4 is supported by 12, using **Mill's Method of Agreement,** named after the British philosopher, John Stuart Mill (1806–1873), who first formulated it. It is called a method of agreement because of the way in which the inference relies on *agreement* among the observed phenomena where a presumed cause is thought to be *present.*

   Let us now suppose that in our search for evidence to support 3 or 4 we conduct additional research and discover that

   13. In a sample of 500 nonsmokers, selected to be representative of both sexes, different ages, dietary habits, exercise patterns, and so on, none is observed to have cardiovascular disease.

This observation would further encourage us to believe that we had obtained significant additional confirmation of 3 or 4. Why? Because we now know that factors present (such as male sex, lack of exercise, family history of cardiovascular disease) in cases where the effect is absent (no cardiovascular disease observed) cannot be the cause. This is an example of **Mill's Method of Difference,** so called because the cause or causal factor of an effect must be *different* from whatever the factors are that are present when the effect is *absent.*

Suppose now that, increasingly confident we have found the cause of cardiovascular disease, we study our first sample of 230 smokers ill with the disease, and discover this:

14. Those who smoke two or more packs of cigarettes daily for ten or more years have cardiovascular disease either much younger or much more severely than those who smoke less.

This is an application of **Mill's Method of Concomitant Variation,** perhaps the most convincing of the three methods. Here we deal not merely with the presence of the conjectured cause (smoking) or the absence of the effect we are studying (cardiovascular disease), as we were previously, but with the more interesting and subtler matter of the *degree and regularity of the correlation* of the supposed cause and effect. According to the observations reported in 14, it strongly appears that the more we have of the "cause" (smoking), the sooner or the more intense the onset of the "effect" (cardiovascular disease).

Notice, however, what happens to our confirmation of 3 and 4 if, instead of the observation reported in 14, we had observed

15. In a representative sample of 500 nonsmokers, cardiovascular disease was observed in 34 cases.

(Let us not pause here to explain what makes a sample more or less representative of a population, although the representativeness of samples is vital to all statistical reasoning.) Such an observation would lead us almost immediately to suspect some other or additional causal factor: Smoking might indeed be *a* factor in causing cardiovascular disease, but it can hardly be *the* cause because (using Mill's Method of Difference) we cannot have the effect, as we do in the observed sample reported in 15, unless we also have the cause.

An observation such as the one in 15, however, is likely to lead us to think our hypothesis that *smoking causes cardiovascular disease* has been disconfirmed. But we have a fallback position ready; we can still defend a weaker hypothesis, namely 4, *Smoking is a factor in the causation of cardiovascular disease in some persons.* Even if 3 stumbles over the evidence in 15, 4 does not. It is still quite possible that smoking is a factor in causing this disease, even if it is not the *only* factor—and if it is, then 4 is true.

Confirmation, Mechanism, and Theory

Notice that in the discussion so far, we have spoken of the *confirmation* of a hypothesis, such as our causal claim in 4, but not of its *verification*. (Similarly, we have imagined very different evidence, such as that stated in 15, leading us to speak of the *dis*confirmation of 3, though not of its *falsi*fication.) Confirmation (getting some evidence for) is weaker than verification (getting sufficient evidence to regard as true), and our (imaginary) evidence so far in favor of 4 falls well short of conclusive support. Further research—the study of more representative or much larger samples, for example—might yield very different observations. It might lead us to conclude that although initial research had confirmed our hypothesis about smoking as the cause of cardiovascular disease, the additional information obtained subsequently disconfirmed the hypothesis. For most interesting hypotheses, both in detective stories and in modern science, there is both confirming and disconfirming evidence simultaneously. The challenge is to evaluate the hypothesis by considering such conflicting evidence.

As long as we confine our observations to *correlations* of the sort reported in our several (imaginary) observations, such as proposition 1, *230 smokers in a group of 500 have cardiovascular disease*, or 12, *230 smokers with the disease share no other suspected factors*, such as lack of exercise, any defense of a *causal* hypothesis such as claim 3, *Smoking causes cardiovascular disease*, or claim 4, *Smoking is a factor in causing the disease*, is not likely to convince the skeptic or lead those with beliefs alternative to 3 and 4 to abandon them and agree with us. Why is that? It is because a causal hypothesis without any account of the *underlying mechanism* by means of which the (alleged) cause produces the effect will seem superficial. Only when we can specify in detail *how* the (alleged) cause produces the effect will the causal hypothesis be convincing.

In other cases, in which no mechanism can be found, we seek instead to embed the causal hypothesis in a larger *theory*, one that rules out as incompatible any causal hypothesis except the favored one. (That is, we appeal to the test of consistency and thereby bring deductive reasoning to bear on our problem.) Thus, perhaps we cannot specify any mechanism—any underlying structure that generates a regular sequence of events, one of which is the effect we are studying—to explain why, for example, the gravitational mass of a body causes it to attract other bodies. But we can embed this claim in a larger body of physical theory that rules out as inconsistent any alternative causal explanation. To do that convincingly in regard to any given causal hypothesis, as this example suggests, requires detailed knowledge of the current state of the relevant body of scientific theory, something far beyond our aim or need to consider in further detail here.

FALLACIES

The straight road on which sound reasoning proceeds gives little latitude for cruising about. Irrationality, carelessness, passionate attachment to one's unexamined beliefs, and the sheer complexity of some issues occasionally spoil the reasoning of even the best of us. Although in this book we reprint many varied voices and arguments, we hope we have reprinted no readings that exhibit the most flagrant errors or commit the graver abuses against the canons of good reasoning. Nevertheless, an inventory of those abuses and their close examination can be an instructive (as well as an amusing) exercise—instructive because the diagnosis and repair of error helps to fix more clearly the principles of sound reasoning on which such remedial labors depend; amusing because we are so constituted that our perception of the nonsense of others can stimulate our mind, warm our heart, and give us comforting feelings of superiority.

The discussion that follows, then, is a quick tour through the twisting lanes, mudflats, forests, and quicksands of the faults that one sometimes encounters in reading arguments that stray from the highway of clear thinking.

Fallacies of Ambiguity

Ambiguity   Near the center of the town of Concord, Massachusetts, is an empty field with a sign reading "Old Calf Pasture." Hmm. A pasture in former times in which calves grazed? A pasture now in use for old calves? An erstwhile pasture for old calves? These alternative readings arise because of **ambiguity;** brevity in the sign has produced a group of words that give rise to more than one possible interpretation, confusing the reader and (presumably) frustrating the sign writer's intentions.

Consider a more complex example. Suppose someone asserts *People have equal rights* and also *Everyone has a right to property.* Many people believe both these claims, but their combination involves an ambiguity. According to one interpretation, the two claims entail that everyone has an *equal right* to property. (That is, you and I each have an equal right to whatever property we have.) But the two claims can also be interpreted to mean that everyone has a *right to equal property*. (That is, whatever property you have a right to, I have a right to the same, or at least equivalent, property.) The latter interpretation is revolutionary, whereas the former is not. Arguments over equal rights often involve this ambiguity.

Division   In the Bible, we are told that the apostles of Jesus were twelve and that Matthew was an apostle. Does it follow that Matthew was twelve? No. To argue in this way from a property of a group to a property of a member of that group is to commit the **fallacy of division.** The example of the apostles may not be a very tempting instance of this error; here is a classic version that is a bit more interesting. If it is true that the average American family has 1.8 children, does it follow that your brother and sister-in-law are likely to have 1.8 children? If you think it does, you have committed the fallacy of division.

Composition   Could an all-star team of professional basketball players beat the Boston Celtics in their heyday—say, the team of 1985 to 1986? Perhaps in one game or two, but probably not in seven out of a dozen games in a row. As students of the game know, teamwork is an indispensable part of outstanding performance, and the 1985 to 1986 Celtics were famous for their self-sacrificing style of play.

The **fallacy of composition** can be convincingly illustrated, therefore, in this argument: *A team of five NBA all-stars is the best team in basketball if each of the five players is the best at his position.* The fallacy is called composition because the reasoning commits the error of arguing from the true premise that each member of a group has a certain property to the not necessarily true conclusion that the group (the composition) itself has the property. (That is, because A is the best player at forward, B is the best center, and so on, therefore, the team of A, B, . . . is the best team.)

Equivocation   In a delightful passage in Lewis Carroll's *Through the Looking-Glass*, the king asks his messenger, "Who did you pass on the road?" and the messenger replies, "Nobody." This prompts the king to observe, "Of course, Nobody walks slower than you," provoking the messenger's sullen response: "I do my best. I'm sure nobody walks much faster than I do." At this the king remarks with surprise, "He can't do that or else he'd have been here first!" (This, by the way, is the classic predecessor of the famous comic dialogue "Who's on First?" between the comedians Bud Abbott and Lou Costello.) The king and the messenger are equivocating on the term *nobody*. The messenger uses it in the normal way as an indefinite pronoun equivalent to "not anyone." But the king uses the word as though it were a proper noun, *Nobody*, the rather odd name of some person. No wonder the king and the messenger talk right past each other.

Equivocation (from the Latin for "equal voice" — that is, giving utterance to two meanings at the same time in one word or phrase) can ruin otherwise good reasoning, as in this example: *Euthanasia is a good death; one dies a good death when one dies peacefully in old age; therefore, euthanasia is dying peacefully in old age.* The etymology of *euthanasia* is literally "a good death," and so the first premise is true. And the second premise is certainly plausible. But the conclusion of this syllogism is false. Euthanasia cannot be defined as a peaceful death in one's old age, for two reasons. First, euthanasia requires the intervention of another person who kills someone (or lets the person die); second, even a very young person can be euthanized. The problem arises because "a good death" is used in the second premise in a manner that does not apply to euthanasia. Both meanings of "a good death" are legitimate, but when used together, they constitute an equivocation that spoils the argument.

The fallacy of equivocation takes us from the discussion of confusions in individual claims or grounds to the more troublesome fallacies that infect the linkages between the claims we make and the grounds (or reasons) for them. These are the fallacies that occur in statements that, following the vocabulary of the Toulmin method, are called the *warrant* of reasoning. Each fallacy is an example of reasoning that involves a **non sequitur** (Latin for "It does not follow"). That is, the *claim* (the conclusion) does not follow from the *grounds* (the premises).

For a start, here is an obvious non sequitur: "He went to the movies on three consecutive nights, so he must love movies." Why doesn't the claim ("He must love movies") follow from the grounds ("He went to the movies on three consecutive nights")? Perhaps the person was just fulfilling an assignment in a film course (maybe he even hated movies so much that he had postponed three assignments to see films and now had to see them all in quick succession), or maybe he went with a girlfriend who was a movie buff, or maybe . . .—well, one can think of any number of other possible reasons.

Fallacies of Presumption

Distorting the Facts   Facts can be distorted either intentionally (to deceive or mislead) or unintentionally, and in either case usually (but not invariably) to the benefit of whoever is doing the distortion. Consider this not entirely hypothetical case. A pharmaceutical company spends millions of dollars to develop a new drug that will help pregnant women avoid spontaneous abortion. The company reports its findings, but it does not also report that it has learned from its researchers of a serious downside for this drug in many cases, resulting in deformed limbs in the neonate. Had the company informed the public of this fact, the drug would not have been certified for use.

Here is another case. Half a century ago the surgeon general reported that smoking cigarettes increased the likelihood that smokers would eventually suffer from lung cancer. The cigarette manufacturers vigorously protested that the surgeon general relied on inconclusive research and was badly misleading the public about the health risks of smoking. It later turned out that the tobacco companies knew that smoking increased the risk of lung cancer—a fact established by the company's own laboratories but concealed from the public. Today, thanks to public access to all the facts, it is commonplace knowledge that inhaled smoke—including secondhand smoke—is a risk factor for many illnesses.

Post Hoc, Ergo Propter Hoc   One of the most tempting errors in reasoning is to ground a claim about causation on an observed temporal sequence; that is, to argue "after this, therefore because of this" (which is what the phrase *post hoc, ergo propter hoc* means in Latin). In 1964, when the medical community first announced that smoking tobacco caused lung cancer, advocates for the tobacco industry replied that doctors were guilty of this fallacy.

These industry advocates argued that medical researchers had merely noticed that in some people, lung cancer developed *after* considerable smoking, indeed, years after; but (they insisted) this correlation was not at all the same as a causal relation between smoking and lung cancer. True enough. The claim that *A causes B* is not the same as the claim that *B* comes after *A*. After all, it was possible that smokers as a group had some other common trait and that this factor was the true cause of their cancer.

As the long controversy over the truth about the causation of lung cancer shows, to avoid the appearance of fallacious *post hoc* reasoning one needs to find some way to link the observed phenomena (the correlation of smoking and the onset of lung cancer). This step requires some further theory and preferably some experimental evidence for the exact sequence or physical mechanism, in full detail, of how ingestion of tobacco smoke is a crucial factor—and is not merely an accidental or happenstance prior event—in the subsequent development of the cancer.

Many Questions   The old saw, "When did you stop beating your wife?" illustrates the **fallacy of many questions.** This question, as one can readily see, is unanswerable unless all three of its implicit presuppositions are true. The questioner presupposes that (1) the addressee has or had a wife, (2) he has beaten her, and (3) he has stopped beating her. If any of these presuppositions is false, then the question is pointless; it cannot be answered strictly and simply with a date.

Hasty Generalization   From a logical point of view, **hasty generalization** is the precipitous move from true assertions about *one* or a *few* instances to dubious or even false assertions about *all*. For example, while it may be true, based on your personal experience, that the only native Hungarians you personally know do not speak English very well, that is no basis for asserting that all Hungarians do not speak English very well. Or if the clothes you recently ordered online turn out not to fit very well, it doesn't follow that *all* online clothes turn out to be too large or too small. A hasty generalization usually lies behind a **stereotype**—that is, a person or event treated as typical of a whole class. Thus, in 1914, after the German invasion of Belgium, during which some atrocities were committed by the invaders, the German troops were quickly stereotyped by the Allies as brutal savages who skewered helpless babies on their bayonets.

The Slippery Slope   One of the most familiar arguments against any type of government regulation is that if it is allowed, then it will be just the first step down the path that leads to ruinous interference, overregulation, and totalitarian control. Fairly often we encounter this mode of argument in the public debates over handgun control, the censorship of pornography, and physician-assisted suicide. The argument is called the **slippery slope argument** (or the **wedge argument,** from the way we use the thin end of a wedge to split solid things apart; it is also called, rather colorfully, "letting the camel's nose under the tent"). The fallacy here is in implying that the first step necessarily leads to the second, and so on down the slope to disaster, when in fact there is no necessary slide from the first step to the second. (Would handgun registration lead to a police state? Well, it hasn't in Switzerland.) Sometimes the argument takes the form of claiming that a seemingly innocent or even attractive principle that is being applied in a given case (censorship of pornography, to avoid promoting sexual violence) requires one for the sake of consistency to apply the same principle in other cases, only with absurd and catastrophic results (censorship of everything in print, to avoid hurting anyone's feelings).

Here's an extreme example of this fallacy in action:

> Automobiles cause more deaths than handguns do. If you oppose handguns on the ground that doing so would save lives of the innocent, you'll soon find yourself wanting to outlaw the automobile.

Does opposition to handguns have this consequence? Not necessarily. Most people accept without dispute the right of society to regulate the operation of motor vehicles by requiring drivers to have a license, a greater restriction than many states impose on gun ownership. Besides, a gun is a lethal weapon designed to kill, whereas an automobile or truck is a vehicle designed for transportation. Private ownership and use in both cases entail risks of death to the innocent. But there is no inconsistency in a society's refusal to tolerate this risk in the case of guns and its willingness to do so in the case of automobiles.

Closely related to the slippery slope is what lawyers call a **parade of horrors,** an array of examples of terrible consequences that will or might follow if we travel down a certain path. A good example appears in Justice William Brennan's opinion for the Supreme Court in *Texas v. Johnson* (1989), concerned with a Texas law against burning the American flag in political protest. If this law is allowed to stand, Brennan suggests, we may next find laws against burning the presidential seal, state flags, and the Constitution.

False Analogy   Argument by analogy, as we point out in Chapter 3 and as many of the selections in this book show, is a familiar and even indispensable mode of argument. But it can be treacherous because it runs the risk of the **fallacy of false analogy.** Unfortunately, we have no simple or foolproof way of distinguishing between the useful, legitimate analogies and the others. The key question to ask yourself is this: Do the two things put into analogy differ in any essential and relevant respect, or are they different only in unimportant and irrelevant aspects?

In a famous example from his discussion in support of suicide, philosopher David Hume rhetorically asked: "It would be no crime in me to divert the Nile or Danube from its course, were I able to effect such purposes. Where then is the crime of turning a few ounces of blood from their natural channel?" This is a striking analogy, except that it rests on a false assumption. No one has the right to divert the Nile or the Danube or any other major international watercourse; it would be a catastrophic crime to do so without the full consent of people living in the region, their government, and so forth. Therefore, arguing by analogy, one might well say that no one has the right to take his or her own life, either. Thus, Hume's own analogy can be used to argue against his thesis that suicide is no crime. But let us ignore the way in which his example can be turned against him. The analogy is a terrible one in any case. Isn't it obvious that the Nile, whatever its exact course, would continue to nourish Egypt and the Sudan, whereas the blood flowing out of someone's veins will soon leave that person dead? The fact that the blood is the same blood, whether in one's body or in a pool on the floor (just as the water of the Nile is the same body of water whatever path it follows to the sea) is, of course, irrelevant to the question of whether one has the right to commit suicide.

Let us look at a more complex example. During the 1960s, when the United States was convulsed over the purpose and scope of its military involvement in Southeast Asia, advocates of more vigorous U.S. military participation appealed to the so-called domino effect, supposedly inspired by a passing remark from President Eisenhower in the 1950s. The analogy refers to the way in which a row of standing dominoes will collapse, one after the other, if the first one is pushed. If Vietnam turns Communist, according to this analogy, so too will its neighbors, Laos and Cambodia, followed by Thailand and then Burma, until the whole region is as communist as China to the north. The domino analogy (or metaphor) provided, no doubt, a vivid illustration and effectively portrayed the worry of many anti-Communists. But did it really shed any light on the likely pattern of political and military developments in the region? The history of events there during the 1970s and 1980s did not bear out the domino analogy.

Straw Man It is often tempting to reframe or report your opponent's thesis to make it easier to attack and perhaps refute it. If you do this in the course of an argument, you are creating a straw man, a thing of no substance and easily blown away. The straw man you've constructed is usually a radically conservative or extremely liberal thesis, which few if any would want to defend. That is why it is easier to refute than the view your opponent actually holds. "So you defend the death penalty—and all the horrible things done in its name. No one in his right mind would hold such a view." It's highly unlikely that your friend supports *everything* that has been done in the name of capital punishment—crucifixion and beheading, for example, or execution of the children of the guilty offender.

Special Pleading We all have our favorites—relatives, friends, and neighbors—and we are all too likely to show that favoritism in unacceptable ways. How about this: "Yes, I know Billy hit Sally first, but he's my son. He's a good boy, and I know he must have had a good reason." Or this: "True, she's late for work again—the third time this week!—but her uncle's my friend, and it will be embarrassing to me if she is fired, so we'll just ignore it." Special pleading inevitably leads to unmerited advantages, as illustrated above.

Begging the Question The argument over whether the death penalty is a deterrent illustrates another fallacy. From the fact that you live in a death-penalty state and were not murdered yesterday, we cannot infer that the death penalty was a deterrent. Yet it is tempting to make this inference, perhaps because—all unawares—we are relying on the **fallacy of begging the question.** If someone tacitly assumes from the start that the death penalty is an effective deterrent, then the fact that you weren't murdered yesterday certainly looks like evidence for the truth of that assumption. But it isn't, so long as there are competing but unexamined alternative explanations, as in this case. (The fallacy is called "begging the question," *petitio principii* in Latin, because the conclusion of the argument is hidden among its assumptions—and so the conclusion, not surprisingly, follows from the premises.)

Of course, the fact that you weren't murdered is *consistent* with the claim that the death penalty is an effective deterrent, just as someone else's being murdered is also consistent with that claim (for an effective deterrent need not be a *perfect* deterrent). In general, from the fact that two propositions are consistent with each other, we cannot infer that either is evidence for the other.

Note: The term "begging the question" is often wrongly used to mean "raises the question," as in "His action of burning the flag begs the question, What drove him to do such a thing?"

False Dichotomy   Sometimes oversimplification takes a more complex form, in which contrary possibilities are wrongly presented as though they were exhaustive and exclusive. "Either we get tough with drug users, or we must surrender and legalize all drugs." Really? What about doing neither and instead offering education and counseling, detoxification programs, and incentives to "Say no"? A favorite of debaters, **either/or** reasoning always runs the risk of ignoring a third (or fourth) possibility. Some disjunctions are indeed exhaustive: "Either we get tough with drug users, or we do not." This proposition, though vague (what does "get tough" really mean?), is a tautology; it cannot be false, and there is no third alternative. But most disjunctions do not express a pair of *contradictory* alternatives: They offer only a pair of *contrary* alternatives, and mere contraries do not exhaust the possibilities (recall our discussion of contraries versus contradictories on page 319).

A writer would be guilty of creating a false dichotomy if, for example, in an argument in favor of flogging his entire discussion was built on the relative superiority of whipping over imprisonment, as though there was no alternative punishment worth considering. But of course, there is, notably community service (especially for non-violent, juvenile, or many first offenders).

Oversimplification   "Poverty causes crime," "Taxation is unfair," "Truth is stranger than fiction"—these are examples of generalizations that exaggerate and therefore oversimplify the truth. Poverty as such can't be the sole cause of crime because many poor people do not break the law. Some taxes may be unfairly high, others unfairly low—but there is no reason to believe that *every* tax is unfair to all those who have to pay it. Some true stories do amaze us as much as or more than some fictional stories, but the reverse is true, too. (In the language of the Toulmin method, **oversimplification** is the result of a failure to use suitable modal qualifiers in formulating one's claims or grounds or backing.)

Red Herring   The fallacy of **red herring,** less colorfully named irrelevant thesis, occurs when one tries to distract one's audience by invoking a consideration that is irrelevant to the topic under discussion. (This fallacy probably gets its name from the fact that a rotten herring, or a cured herring, which is reddish, will throw pursuing hounds off the right track.) Consider this case. Some critics, seeking to defend our government's refusal to sign the Kyoto accords to reduce global warming, argue that signing is supported mainly by left-leaning scientists. This argument supposedly shows that global warming—if there is such a thing—is not a serious, urgent issue. But claiming that the supporters of these accords are left-inclined is a red herring, an irrelevant thesis. By raising doubts about the political views of the advocates of signing, it distracts attention from the scientific question (Is there global warming?) and also from the separate political question (Ought the United States sign these accords?). The refusal of a government to sign these accords does not show there is no such thing as global warming. And even if all of the advocates of signing were left-leaning (they aren't), this fact (if it were a fact, but it isn't) would not show that worries about global warming are exaggerated.

Fallacies of Relevance

Tu Quoque The Romans had a word for it: *Tu quoque* means "you, too." Consider this: "You're a fine one, trying to persuade me to give up smoking when you indulge yourself with a pipe and a cigar from time to time. Maybe I should quit, but then so should you. As things stand now, however, it's hypocritical of you to complain about my smoking when you persist in the same habit." The fallacy is this: The merit of a person's argument has nothing to do with the person's character or behavior. Here, the assertion that smoking is bad for one's health is *not* weakened by the fact that a smoker offers the argument.

The Genetic Fallacy A member of the family of fallacies that includes poisoning the well and ad hominem is the **genetic fallacy.** Here the error takes the form of arguing against some claim by pointing out that its origin (genesis) is tainted or that it was invented by someone deserving our contempt. Thus, one might attack the ideas of the Declaration of Independence by pointing out that its principal author, Thomas Jefferson, was a slaveholder. Assuming that it is not anachronistic and inappropriate to criticize a public figure of two centuries ago for practicing slavery, and conceding that slavery is morally outrageous, it is nonetheless fallacious to attack the ideas or even the sincerity of the Declaration by attempting to impeach the credentials of its author. Jefferson's moral faults do not by themselves falsify, make improbable, or constitute counterevidence to the truth or other merits of the claims made in his writings. At most, one's faults cast doubt on one's integrity or sincerity if one makes claims at odds with one's practice.

The genetic fallacy can take other forms less closely allied to ad hominem argument. For example, an opponent of the death penalty might argue,

> Capital punishment arose in barbarous times; but we claim to be civilized; therefore, we should discard this relic of the past.

Such reasoning shouldn't be persuasive because the question of the death penalty for our society must be decided by the degree to which it serves our purposes—justice and defense against crime, presumably—to which its historic origins are irrelevant. The practices of beer- and wine-making are as old as human civilization, but their origin in antiquity is no reason to outlaw them in our time. The curious circumstances in which something originates usually play no role whatever in its validity. Anyone who would argue that nothing good could possibly come from molds and fungi is refuted by Sir Alexander Fleming's discovery of penicillin in 1928.

Poisoning the Well   During the 1970s some critics of the Equal Rights Amendment (ERA) argued against it by pointing out that Marx and Engels, in their *Communist Manifesto*, favored equality of women and men—and therefore the ERA was immoral, undesirable, and perhaps even a Communist plot. This kind of reasoning is an attempt to **poison the well;** that is, an attempt to shift attention from the merits of the argument—the validity of the reasoning, the truth of the claims—to the source or origin of the argument. Such criticism deflects attention from the real issue; namely, whether the view in question is true and what the quality of evidence is in its support. The mere fact that Marx (or Hitler, for that matter) believed something does not show that the belief is false or immoral; just because some scoundrel believes the world is round, that is no reason for you to believe it is flat.

Appeal to Ignorance   In the controversy over the death penalty, the issues of deterrence and executing the innocent are bound to be raised. Because no one knows how many innocent persons have been convicted for murder and wrongfully executed, it is tempting for abolitionists to argue that the death penalty is too risky. It is equally tempting for the proponent of the death penalty to argue that since no one knows how many people have been deterred from murder by the threat of execution, we abolish it at our peril.

Each of these arguments suffers from the same flaw: the **fallacy of appeal to ignorance.** Each argument invites the audience to draw an inference from a premise that is unquestionably true—but what is that premise? It asserts that there is something "we don't know." But what we *don't* know cannot be *evidence* for (or against) anything. Our ignorance is no reason for believing anything, except perhaps that we ought to try to undertake an appropriate investigation in order to reduce our ignorance and replace it with reliable information.

Ad Hominem   Closely allied to poisoning the well is another fallacy, **ad hominem** argument (from the Latin for "against the person"). A critic can easily yield to the temptation to attack an argument or theory by trying to impeach or undercut the credentials of its advocates.

Example: Jones is arguing that prayer should not be permitted in public schools, and Smith responds by pointing out that Jones has twice been convicted of assaulting members of the clergy. Jones's behavior doubtless is reprehensible, but the issue is not Jones, it is prayer in school, and what must be scrutinized is Jones's argument, not his police record or his character.

Appeal to Authority   The example of Jefferson given to illustrate the genetic fallacy can be turned around to illustrate another fallacy. One might easily imagine someone from the South in 1860 defending the slave-owning society of that day by appealing to the fact that no less a person than Jefferson—a brilliant public figure, thinker, and leader by any measure—owned slaves. Or today one might defend capital punishment on the ground that Abraham Lincoln, surely one of the nation's greatest presidents, signed many death warrants during the Civil War, authorizing the execution of Union soldiers. No doubt the esteem in which such figures as Jefferson and Lincoln are deservedly held amounts to impressive endorsement for whatever acts and practices, policies and institutions, they supported. But the **authority** of these figures in itself is not evidence for the truth of their views, and so their authority cannot be a reason for anyone to agree with them. Obviously, Jefferson and Lincoln themselves could not support their beliefs by pointing to the fact that they held them. Because their own authority is no reason for them to believe what they believe, it is no reason for anyone else, either.

Sometimes the appeal to authority is fallacious because the authoritative person is not an expert on the issue in dispute. The fact that a high-energy physicist has won the Nobel Prize is no reason for attaching any special weight to her views on the causes of cancer, the reduction of traffic accidents, or the legalization of marijuana. On the other hand, one would be well advised to attend to her views on the advisability of ballistic missile-defense systems, for there may be a connection between the kind of research for which she received the prize and the defense research projects.

All of us depend heavily on the knowledge of various experts and authorities, and so we tend not to ignore their views. Conversely, we should resist the temptation to accord their views on diverse subjects the same respect that we grant them in the area of their expertise.

Appeal to Fear   The Romans called this fallacy *ad baculum*, "resorting to violence" (*baculum* means "stick," or "club"). Trying to persuade people to agree with you by threatening them with painful consequences is obviously an appeal that no rational person would contemplate. The violence need not be physical; if you threaten someone with the loss of a job, for instance, you are still using a stick. Violence or the threat of harmful consequences in the course of an argument is beyond reason and always shows the haste or impatience of those who appeal to it. It is also an indication that the argument on its merits would be unpersuasive, inconclusive, or worse. President Teddy Roosevelt's epigrammatic doctrine for the kind of foreign policy he favored—"Speak softly but carry a big stick"—illustrates an attempt to have it both ways, an appeal to reason for starters but a recourse to coercion, or the threat of coercion, as a backup if needed.

Finally, we add two fallacies, not easily embraced by Engel's three categories that have served us well thus far (ambiguity, erroneous presumption, and irrelevance): death by a thousand qualifications and protecting the hypothesis.

Death by a Thousand Qualifications   In a letter of recommendation sent in support of an applicant for a job on your newspaper, you find this sentence: "Young Smith was the best student I've ever taught in an English course." Pretty strong endorsement, you think, except that you do not know, because you have not been told, the letter writer is a very junior faculty member, has been teaching for only two years, is an instructor in the history department, taught a section of freshman English as a courtesy for a sick colleague, and had only eight students enrolled in the course. Thanks to these implicit qualifications, the letter writer did not lie or exaggerate in his praise; but the effect of his sentence on you, the unwitting reader, is quite misleading. The explicit claim in the letter, and its impact on you, is quite different from the tacitly qualified claim in the mind of the writer.

Death by a thousand qualifications gets its name from the ancient torture of death by a thousand small cuts. Thus, a bold assertion can be virtually killed, its true content reduced to nothing, bit by bit, as all the appropriate or necessary qualifications are added to it. Consider another example. Suppose you hear a politician describing another country (let's call it Ruritania so as not to offend anyone) as a "democracy"—except it turns out that Ruritania doesn't have regular elections, lacks a written constitution, has no independent judiciary, prohibits religious worship except of the state-designated deity, and so forth. So what is left of the original claim that Ruritania is a democracy is little or nothing. The qualifications have taken all the content out of the original description.

Protecting the Hypothesis   In Chapter 3, we contrasted *reasoning* and *rationalization* (or the finding of bad reasons for what one intends to believe anyway). Rationalization can take subtle forms, as the following example indicates. Suppose you're standing with a friend on the shore or on a pier, and you watch as a ship heads out to sea. As it reaches the horizon, it slowly disappears—first the hull, then the upper decks, and finally the tip of the mast. Because the ship (you both assume) isn't sinking, it occurs to you that you have in this sequence of observations convincing evidence that the earth's surface is curved. Nonsense, says your companion. Light waves sag, or bend down, over distances of a few miles, and so a flat surface (such as the ocean) can intercept them. Hence the ship, which appears to be going "over" the horizon, really isn't: It's just moving steadily farther and farther away in a straight line. Your friend, you discover to your amazement, is a card-carrying member of the Flat Earth Society (yes, there really is such an organization). Now most of us would regard the idea that light rays bend down in the manner required by the Flat Earther's argument as a rationalization whose sole purpose is to protect the flat-earth doctrine against counterevidence. We would be convinced it was a rationalization, and not a very good one at that, if the Flat Earther held to it despite a patient and thorough explanation from a physicist that showed modern optical theory to be quite incompatible with the view that light waves sag.

✓   A CHECKLIST FOR EVALUATING AN ARGUMENT
    FROM A LOGICAL POINT OF VIEW

☐ Is the argument purely deductive, purely inductive, or a mixture of the two?

☐ If it is deductive, is it valid?

☐ If it is valid, are all its premises and assumptions true?

☐ If it is not valid, what fallacy does it commit?

☐ If it is not valid, are the claims at least consistent with each other?

☐ If it is not valid, can you think of additional plausible assumptions that would make it valid?

☐ If the argument is inductive, on what observations is it based?

☐ If the argument is deductive, how probable are its premises and its conclusion?

☐ In any case, can you think of evidence that would further confirm the conclusion? Disconfirm the conclusion?

This example illustrates two important points about the *backing* of arguments. First, it is always possible to protect a hypothesis by abandoning adjacent or connected hypotheses; this is the tactic our Flat Earth friend has used. This maneuver is possible, however, only because—and this is the second point—whenever we test a hypothesis, we do so by taking for granted (usually quite unconsciously) many other hypotheses as well. So the evidence for the hypothesis we think we are confirming is impossible to separate entirely from the adequacy of the connected hypotheses. As long as we have no reason to doubt that light rays travel in straight lines (at least over distances of a few miles), our Flat Earth friend's argument is unconvincing. But once that hypothesis is itself put in doubt, the idea that looked at first to be a pathetic rationalization takes on an even more troublesome character.

There are, then, not one but two fallacies exposed by this example. The first and perhaps graver is in rigging your hypothesis so that *no matter what* observations are brought against it, you will count nothing as falsifying it. The second and subtler is in thinking that as you test one hypothesis, all of your other background beliefs are left safely to one side, immaculate and uninvolved. On the contrary, our beliefs form a corporate structure, intertwined and connected to each other with great complexity, and no one of them can ever be singled out for unique and isolated application, confirmation, or disconfirmation, to the world around us.

EXERCISE: FALLACIES — OR NOT?

Here, for diversion and practice, are some fallacies in action. Some of these statements, however, are not fallacies. Can you tell which is which? Can you detect *what* has gone wrong in the cases where something has gone wrong? Please explain your reasoning.

1. Abortion is murder—and it doesn't matter whether we're talking about killing a human embryo or a human fetus.
2. Euthanasia is not a good thing, it's murder—and it doesn't matter how painful one's dying may be.
3. Never loan a tool to a friend. I did once and never got it back.
4. If the neighbors don't like our loud music, that's just too bad. After all, we have a right to listen to the music we like when and where we want to play it.
5. The Good Samaritan in the Bible was pretty foolish; he was taking grave risks with no benefits for him in sight.
6. "Shoot first and ask questions afterward" is a good epigram for the kind of foreign policy we need.
7. "You can fool some of the people all of the time, and you can fool all the people some of the time, but you can't fool all the people all of the time." That's what Abraham Lincoln said, and he was right.
8. It doesn't matter whether Shakespeare wrote the plays attributed to him. What matters is whether the plays are any good.
9. The Golden Gate Bridge in San Francisco ought to be closed down. After all, just look at all the suicides that have occurred there.
10. Reparations for African Americans are way overdue; it's just another version of the reparations eventually paid to the Japanese Americans who were wrongly interned in 1942 during World War II.
11. Animals don't have rights any more than do trees or stones. They don't have desires, either. What they have are feelings and needs.
12. The average American family is said to have 2.1 children. This is absurd—did you ever meet 2.1 children?
13. My marriage was a failure, which just proves my point: Don't ever get married in the first place.
14. The Red Queen in *Alice in Wonderland* was right: Verdict first, evidence later.
15. Not until astronauts sailed through space around the moon and could see its back side for themselves did we have adequate reason to believe that the moon even had a back side.

16. If you start out with a bottle of beer a day and then go on to a glass or two of wine on the weekends, you're well on your way to becoming a hopeless drunk.

17. Two Indians are sitting on a fence. The small Indian is the son of the big Indian, but the big Indian is not the small Indian's father. How is that possible?

18. If you toss a coin five times and each time it comes up heads, is it more likely than not that on the sixth throw you'll come up heads again—or is it more likely that you'll come up tails? Or is neither more likely?

19. Going to church on a regular basis is bad for your health. Instead of sitting in a pew for an hour each Sunday you'd be better off taking an hour's brisk walk.

20. You can't trust anything he says. When he was young he was an avid Communist.

21. Since 9/11 we've tried and convicted few terrorists, so our defense systems must be working.

22. We can trust the White House in its press releases because it's a reliable source of information.

23. Intelligent design must be true because the theory of evolution can't explain how life began.

24. Andreas Serrano's notorious photograph called *Piss Christ* (1989), showing a small plastic crucifix submerged in a glass of urine, never should have been put on public display, let alone financed by public funds.

25. Doubting Thomas was right—you need more than somebody's say-so to support a claim of resurrection.

26. You are a professional baseball player and you have a good-luck charm. When you wear it the team wins. When you don't wear it the team loses. What do you infer?

27. Resolve the following dilemma: When it rains you can't fix the hole in the roof. When it's not raining there is no need to mend the roof. Conclusion: Leave the roof as it is.

28. You are at the beach and you watch a ship steaming toward the horizon. Bit by bit it disappears from view—first the masts, then the upper deck, then the main deck, then the stern, and then it's gone. Why would it be wrong to infer that the ship is sinking?

29. How can it be true that "it's the exception that proves the rule"? If anything, isn't it the exception that *dis*proves the rule?

30. How come herbivores don't eat herbs?

31. In the 1930s it was commonplace to see ads announcing "More Doctors Smoke Camels." What do you make of such an ad?

32. Suppose the only way you could save five innocent people was by killing one of them. Would you do it? Suppose the only way you could save one innocent person was by killing five others. Would you do it?

Max Shulman

Having read about proper and improper arguments, you are now well equipped to read a short story on the topic.

    Max Shulman (1919–1988) began his career as a writer when he was a journalism student at the University of Minnesota. Later he wrote humorous novels, stories, and plays. One of his novels, Barefoot Boy with Cheek *(1943), was made into a musical, and another,* Rally Round the Flag, Boys! *(1957), was made into a film starring Paul Newman and Joanne Woodward.* The Tender Trap *(1954), a play he wrote with Robert Paul Smith, still retains its popularity with theater groups.*

    "Love Is a Fallacy" was first published in 1951, when demeaning stereotypes about women and minorities were widely accepted in the marketplace as well as the home. Thus, jokes about domineering mothers-in-law or about dumb blondes routinely met with no objection.

Love Is a Fallacy

Cool was I and logical. Keen, calculating, perspicacious, acute, and astute—I was all of these. My brain was as powerful as a dynamo, as precise as a chemist's scales, as penetrating as a scalpel. And—think of it!—I was only eighteen.

It is not often that one so young has such a giant intellect. Take, for example, Petey Bellows, my roommate at the university. Same age, same background, but dumb as an ox. A nice enough fellow, you understand, but nothing upstairs. Emotional type. Unstable. Impressionable. Worst of all, a faddist. Fads, I submit, are the very negation of reason. To be swept up in every new craze that comes along, to surrender yourself to idiocy just because everybody else is doing it—this, to me, is the acme of mindlessness. Not, however, to Petey.

One afternoon I found Petey lying on his bed with an expression of such distress on his face that I immediately diagnosed appendicitis. "Don't move," I said. "Don't take a laxative. I'll call a doctor."

"Raccoon," he mumbled thickly.

"Raccoon?" I said, pausing in my flight.

"I want a raccoon coat," he wailed.

I perceived that his trouble was not physical, but mental. "Why do you want a raccoon coat?"

"I should have known it," he cried, pounding his temples. "I should have known they'd come back when the Charleston came back. Like a fool I spent all my money for textbooks, and now I can't get a raccoon coat."

"Can you mean," I said incredulously, "that people are actually wearing raccoon coats again?"

"All the Big Men on Campus are wearing them. Where've you been?" 10

"In the library," I said, naming a place not frequented by Big Men on Campus.

He leaped from the bed and paced the room. "I've got to have a raccoon coat," he said passionately. "I've got to!"

"Petey, why? Look at it rationally. Raccoon coats are unsanitary. They shed. They smell bad. They weigh too much. They're unsightly. They——"

"You don't understand," he interrupted impatiently. "It's the thing to do. Don't you want to be in the swim?"

"No," I said truthfully. 15

"Well, I do," he declared. "I'd give anything for a raccoon coat. Anything!"

My brain, that precision instrument, slipped into high gear. "Anything?" I asked, looking at him narrowly.

"Anything," he affirmed in ringing tones.

I stroked my chin thoughtfully. It so happened that I knew where to get my hands on a raccoon coat. My father had had one in his undergraduate days; it lay now in a trunk in the attic back home. It also happened that Petey had something I wanted. He didn't *have* it exactly, but at least he had first rights on it. I refer to his girl, Polly Espy.

I had long coveted Polly Espy. Let me emphasize that my 20 desire for this young woman was not emotional in nature. She was, to be sure, a girl who excited the emotions, but I was not one to let my heart rule my head. I wanted Polly for a shrewdly calculated, entirely cerebral reason.

I was a freshman in law school. In a few years I would be out in practice. I was well aware of the importance of the right kind of wife in furthering a lawyer's career. The successful lawyers I had observed were, almost without exception, married to beautiful, gracious, intelligent women. With one omission, Polly fitted these specifications perfectly.

Beautiful she was. She was not yet of pin-up proportions, but I felt sure that time would supply the lack. She already had the makings.

Gracious she was. By gracious I mean full of graces. She had an erectness of carriage, an ease of bearing, a poise that clearly indicated the best of breeding. At table her manners were exquisite. I had seen her at the Kozy Kampus Korner eating the specialty of the house—a sandwich that contained scraps of pot roast, gravy, chopped nuts, and a dipper of sauerkraut—without even getting her fingers moist.

Intelligent she was not. In fact, she veered in the opposite direction. But I believed that under my guidance she would smarten up. At any rate, it was worth a try. It is, after all, easier to make a beautiful dumb girl smart than to make an ugly smart girl beautiful.

"Petey," I said, "are you in love with Polly Espy?"   25

"I think she's a keen kid," he replied, "but I don't know if you'd call it love. Why?"

"Do you," I asked, "have any kind of formal arrangement with her? I mean are you going steady or anything like that?"

"No. We see each other quite a bit, but we both have other dates. Why?"

"Is there," I asked, "any other man for whom she has a particular fondness?"

"Not that I know of. Why?"   30

I nodded with satisfaction. "In other words, if you were out of the picture, the field would be open. Is that right?"

"I guess so. What are you getting at?"

"Nothing, nothing," I said innocently, and took my suitcase out of the closet.

"Where you going?" asked Petey.

"Home for the week end." I threw a few things into the bag.   35

"Listen," he said, clutching my arm eagerly, "while you're home, you couldn't get some money from your old man, could you, and lend it to me so I can buy a raccoon coat?"

"I may do better than that," I said with a mysterious wink and closed my bag and left.

"Look," I said to Petey when I got back Monday morning. I threw open the suitcase and revealed the huge, hairy, gamy object that my father had worn in his Stutz Bearcat in 1925.

"Holy Toledo!" said Petey reverently. He plunged his hands into the raccoon coat and then his face. "Holy Toledo!" he repeated fifteen or twenty times.

"Would you like it?" I asked.   40

"Oh yes!" he cried, clutching the greasy pelt to him. Then a canny look came into his eyes. "What do you want for it?"

"Your girl," I said, mincing no words.

"Polly?" he said in a horrified whisper. "You want Polly?"

"That's right."

He flung the coat from him. "Never," he said stoutly.   45

I shrugged. "Okay. If you don't want to be in the swim, I guess it's your business."

I sat down in a chair and pretended to read a book, but out of the corner of my eye I kept watching Petey. He was a torn man. First he looked at the coat with the expression of a waif at a bakery window. Then he turned away and set his jaw resolutely. Then he looked back at the coat, with even more longing in his face. Then he turned away, but with not so much resolution this time. Back and forth his head swiveled, desire waxing, resolution waning. Finally he didn't turn away at all; he just stood and stared with mad lust at the coat.

"It isn't as though I was in love with Polly," he said thickly. "Or going steady or anything like that."

"That's right," I murmured.

"What's Polly to me, or me to Polly?"   50

"Not a thing," said I.

"It's just been a casual kick—just a few laughs, that's all."

"Try on the coat," said I.

He complied. The coat bunched high over his ears and dropped all the way down to his shoe tops. He looked like a mound of dead raccoons. "Fits fine," he said happily.

I rose from my chair. "Is it a deal?" I asked, extending my hand. 55

He swallowed. "It's a deal," he said and shook my hand.

I had my first date with Polly the following evening. This was in the nature of a survey; I wanted to find out just how much work I had to do to get her mind up to the standard I required. I took her first to dinner. "Gee, that was a delish dinner," she said as we left the restaurant. Then I took her to a movie. "Gee, that was a marvy movie," she said as we left the theater. And then I took her home. "Gee, I had a sensaysh time," she said as she bade me good night.

I went back to my room with a heavy heart. I had gravely underestimated the size of my task. This girl's lack of information was terrifying. Nor would it be enough merely to supply her with information. First she had to be taught to *think*. This loomed as a project of no small dimensions, and at first I was tempted to give her back to Petey. But then I got to thinking about her abundant physical charms and about the way she entered a room and the way she handled a knife and fork, and I decided to make an effort.

I went about it, as in all things, systematically. I gave her a course in logic. It happened that I, as a law student, was taking a course in logic myself, so I had all the facts at my fingertips. "Polly," I said to her when I picked her up on our next date, "tonight we are going over to the Knoll and talk."

"Oo, terrif," she replied. One thing I will say for this girl: You 60
would go far to find another so agreeable.

We went to the Knoll, the campus trysting place, and we sat
down under an old oak, and she looked at me expectantly: "What
are we going to talk about?" she asked.

"Logic."

She thought this over for a minute and decided she liked it.
"Magnif," she said.

"Logic," I said, clearing my throat, "is the science of thinking.
Before we can think correctly, we must first learn to recognize the
common fallacies of logic. These we will take up tonight."

"Wow-dow!" she cried, clapping her hands delightedly.   65

I winced, but went bravely on. "First let us examine the fallacy
called Dicto Simpliciter."

"By all means," she urged, batting her lashes eagerly.

"Dicto Simpliciter means an argument based on an unqualified
generalization. For example: Exercise is good. Therefore everybody
should exercise."

"I agree," said Polly earnestly. "I mean exercise is wonderful. I
mean it builds the body and everything."

"Polly," I said gently, "the argument is a fallacy. *Exercise is good* 70
is an unqualified generalization. For instance, if you have heart disease, exercise is bad, not good. Many people are ordered by their
doctors *not* to exercise. You must *qualify* the generalization. You
must say exercise is *usually* good, or exercise is good *for most people.*
Otherwise you have committed a Dicto Simpliciter. Do you see?"

"No," she confessed. "But this is marvy. Do more! Do more!"

"It will be better if you stop tugging at my sleeve," I told her, and
when she desisted, I continued. "Next we take up a fallacy called Hasty
Generalization. Listen carefully: You can't speak French. I can't speak
French. Petey Bellows can't speak French. I must therefore conclude
that nobody at the University of Minnesota can speak French."

"Really?" said Polly, amazed. "*Nobody?*"

I hid my exasperation. "Polly, it's a fallacy. The generalization
is reached too hastily. There are too few instances to support such a
conclusion."

"Know any more fallacies?" she asked breathlessly. "This is 75
more fun than dancing even."

I fought off a wave of despair. I was getting nowhere with this
girl, absolutely nowhere. Still, I am nothing if not persistent. I continued. "Next comes Post Hoc. Listen to this: Let's not take Bill on
our picnic. Every time we take him out with us, it rains."

352 9 / A LOGICIAN'S VIEW: DEDUCTION, INDUCTION, FALLACIES

"I know somebody just like that," she exclaimed. "A girl back home—Eula Becker, her name is. It never fails. Every single time we take her on a picnic——"

"Polly," I said sharply, "it's a fallacy. Eula Becker doesn't *cause* the rain. She has no connection with the rain. You are guilty of Post Hoc if you blame Eula Becker."

"I'll never do it again," she promised contritely. "Are you mad at me?"

I sighed. "No, Polly, I'm not mad."   80

"Then tell me some more fallacies."

"All right. Let's try Contradictory Premises."

"Yes, let's," she chirped, blinking her eyes happily.

I frowned, but plunged ahead. "Here's an example of Contradictory Premises: If God can do anything, can He make a stone so heavy that He won't be able to lift it?"

"Of course," she replied promptly.   85

"But if He can do anything, He can lift the stone," I pointed out.

"Yeah," she said thoughtfully. "Well, then I guess He can't make the stone."

"But He can do anything," I reminded her.

She scratched her pretty, empty head. "I'm all confused," she admitted.

"Of course you are. Because when the premises of an argu-   90
ment contradict each other, there can be no argument. If there is an irresistible force, there can be no immovable object. If there is an immovable object, there can be no irresistible force. Get it?"

"Tell me some more of this keen stuff," she said eagerly.

I consulted my watch. "I think we'd better call it a night. I'll take you home now, and you go over all the things you've learned. We'll have another session tomorrow night."

I deposited her at the girls' dormitory, where she assured me that she had had a perfectly terrif evening, and I went glumly home to my room. Petey lay snoring in his bed, the raccoon coat huddled like a great hairy beast at his feet. For a moment I considered waking him and telling him that he could have his girl back. It seemed clear that my project was doomed to failure. The girl simply had a logic-proof head.

But then I reconsidered. I had wasted one evening; I might as well waste another. Who knew? Maybe somewhere in the extinct crater of her mind a few embers still smoldered. Maybe somehow I could fan them into flame. Admittedly it was not a prospect fraught with hope, but I decided to give it one more try.

Seated under the oak the next evening I said, "Our first fallacy   95
tonight is called Ad Misericordiam."

She quivered with delight.

"Listen closely," I said. "A man applies for a job. When the boss
asks him what his qualifications are, he replies that he has a wife and
six children at home, the wife is a helpless cripple, the children have
nothing to eat, no clothes to wear, no shoes on their feet, there are
no beds in the house, no coal in the cellar, and winter is coming."

A tear rolled down each of Polly's pink cheeks. "Oh, this is
awful, awful," she sobbed.

"Yes, it's awful," I agreed, "but it's no argument. The man never
answered the boss's question about his qualifications. Instead he
appealed to the boss's sympathy. He committed the fallacy of Ad
Misericordiam. Do you understand?"

"Have you got a handkerchief?" she blubbered.   100

I handed her a handkerchief and tried to keep from screaming
while she wiped her eyes. "Next," I said in a carefully controlled
tone, "we will discuss False Analogy. Here is an example: Students
should be allowed to look at their textbooks during examinations.
After all, surgeons have X rays to guide them during an operation,
lawyers have briefs to guide them during a trial, carpenters have
blueprints to guide them when they are building a house. Why,
then, shouldn't students be allowed to look at their textbooks during an examination?"

"There now," she said enthusiastically, "is the most marvy idea
I've heard in years."

"Polly," I said testily, "the argument is all wrong. Doctors, lawyers, and carpenters aren't taking a test to see how much they have
learned, but students are. The situations are altogether different,
and you can't make an analogy between them."

"I still think it's a good idea," said Polly.

"Nuts," I muttered. Doggedly I pressed on. "Next we'll try   105
Hypothesis Contrary to Fact."

"Sounds yummy," was Polly's reaction.

"Listen: If Madame Curie had not happened to leave a photo-
graphic plate in a drawer with a chunk of pitchblende, the world
today would not know about radium."

"True, true," said Polly, nodding her head. "Did you see the
movie? Oh, it just knocked me out. That Walter Pidgeon is so
dreamy. I mean he fractures me."

"If you can forget Mr. Pidgeon for a moment," I said coldly,
"I would like to point out that the statement is a fallacy. Maybe

Madame Curie would have discovered radium at some later date. Maybe somebody else would have discovered it. Maybe any number of things would have happened. You can't start with a hypothesis that is not true and then draw any supportable conclusions from it."

"They ought to put Walter Pidgeon in more pictures," said Polly. "I hardly ever see him any more." 110

One more chance, I decided. But just one more. There is a limit to what flesh and blood can bear. "The next fallacy is called Poisoning the Well."

"How cute!" she gurgled.

"Two men are having a debate. The first one gets up and says, 'My opponent is a notorious liar. You can't believe a word that he is going to say.' . . . Now, Polly, think. Think hard. What's wrong?"

I watched her closely as she knit her creamy brow in concentration. Suddenly a glimmer of intelligence—the first I had seen—came into her eyes. "It's not fair," she said with indignation. "It's not a bit fair. What chance has the second man got if the first man calls him a liar before he even begins talking?"

"Right!" I cried exultantly. "One hundred percent right. It's not fair. The first man has *poisoned the well* before anybody could drink from it. He has hamstrung his opponent before he could even start. . . . Polly, I'm proud of you." 115

"Pshaw," she murmured, blushing with pleasure.

"You see, my dear, these things aren't so hard. All you have to do is concentrate. Think—examine—evaluate. Come now, let's review everything we have learned."

"Fire away," she said with an airy wave of her hand.

Heartened by the knowledge that Polly was not altogether a cretin, I began a long, patient review of all I had told her. Over and over and over again I cited instances, pointed out flaws, kept hammering away without letup. It was like digging a tunnel. At first everything was work, sweat, and darkness. I had no idea when I would reach the light, or even *if* I would. But I persisted. I pounded and clawed and scraped, and finally I was rewarded. I saw a chink of light. And then the chink got bigger and the sun came pouring in and all was bright.

Five grueling nights this took, but it was worth it. I had made a logician out of Polly; I had taught her to think. My job was done. She was worthy of me at last. She was a fit wife for me, a proper hostess for my many mansions, a suitable mother for my well-heeled children. 120

It must not be thought that I was without love for this girl. Quite the contrary. Just as Pygmalion loved the perfect woman he had fashioned, so I loved mine. I decided to acquaint her with my feelings at our very next meeting. The time had come to change our relationship from academic to romantic.

"Polly," I said when next we sat beneath our oak, "tonight we will not discuss fallacies."

"Aw, gee," she said, disappointed.

"My dear," I said, favoring her with a smile, "we have now spent five evenings together. We have gotten along splendidly. It is clear that we are well matched."

"Hasty Generalization," said Polly brightly.   125

"I beg your pardon," said I.

"Hasty Generalization," she repeated. "How can you say that we are well matched on the basis of only five dates?"

I chuckled with amusement. The dear child had learned her lessons well. "My dear," I said, patting her hand in a tolerant manner, "five dates is plenty. After all, you don't have to eat a whole cake to know that it's good."

"False Analogy," said Polly promptly. "I'm not a cake. I'm a girl."

I chuckled with somewhat less amusement. The dear child   130 had learned her lesson perhaps too well. I decided to change tactics. Obviously the best approach was a simple, strong, direct declaration of love. I paused for a moment while my massive brain chose the proper words. Then I began:

"Polly, I love you. You are the whole world to me, and the moon and the stars and the constellations of outer space. Please, my darling, say that you will go steady with me, for if you will not, life will be meaningless. I will languish. I will refuse my meals. I will wander the face of the earth, a shambling, hollow-eyed hulk."

There, I thought, folding my arms, that ought to do it.

"Ad Misericordiam," said Polly.

I ground my teeth. I was not Pygmalion; I was Frankenstein, and my monster had me by the throat. Frantically I fought back the tide of panic surging through me. At all costs I had to keep cool.

"Well, Polly," I said, forcing a smile, "you certainly have   135 learned your fallacies."

"You're darn right," she said with a vigorous nod.

"And who taught them to you, Polly?"

"You did."

"That's right. So you do owe me something, don't you, my dear? If I hadn't come along you never would have learned about fallacies."

"Hypothesis Contrary to Fact," she said instantly.   140

I dashed perspiration from my brow. "Polly," I croaked, "you mustn't take all these things so literally. I mean this is just class-room stuff. You know that the things you learn in school don't have anything to do with life."

"Dicto Simpliciter," she said, wagging her finger at me playfully.

That did it. I leaped to my feet, bellowing like a bull. "Will you or will you not go steady with me?"

"I will not," she replied.

"Why not?" I demanded.   145

"Because this afternoon I promised Petey Bellows that I would go steady with him."

I reeled back, overcome with the infamy of it. After he prom-ised, after he made a deal, after he shook my hand! "That rat!" I shrieked, kicking up great chunks of turf. "You can't go with him, Polly. He's a liar. He's a cheat. He's a rat."

"Poisoning the Well," said Polly, "and stop shouting. I think shouting must be a fallacy too."

With an immense effort of will, I modulated my voice. "All right," I said. "You're a logician. Let's look at this thing logically. How could you choose Petey Bellows over me? Look at me — a brilliant student, a tremendous intellectual, a man with an assured future. Look at Petey — a knothead, a jitterbug, a guy who'll never know where his next meal is coming from. Can you give me one logical reason why you should go steady with Petey Bellows?"

"I certainly can," declared Polly. "He's got a raccoon coat."   150

TOPIC FOR CRITICAL THINKING AND WRITING

After you have finished reading "Love Is a Fallacy," you may want to write an argumentative essay of 500 to 750 words on one of the follow-ing topics: (1) the story, rightly understood, is not antiwoman; (2) if the story is antiwoman, it is equally antiman; (3) the story is antiwoman but nevertheless belongs in this book; or (4) the story is antiwoman and does not belong in the book.

See *Re:Writing*
bedfordstmartins.com/rewriting
for a series of brain teasers and links related to
the logical point of view in argument.

10

A Psychologist's View: Rogerian Argument

Real communication occurs . . . when we listen with understanding.

— CARL ROGERS

The first duty of a wise advocate is to convince his opponents that he understands their arguments, and sympathizes with their just feelings.

— SAMUEL TAYLOR COLERIDGE

ROGERIAN ARGUMENT: AN INTRODUCTION

Carl R. Rogers (1902–1987), perhaps best known for his book entitled *On Becoming a Person* (1961), was a psychotherapist, not a teacher of writing. This short essay by Rogers has, however, exerted much influence on instructors who teach argument. Written in the 1950s, this essay reflects the political climate of the cold war between the United States and the Soviet Union, which dominated headlines for more than forty years (1947–1989). Several of Rogers's examples of bias and frustrated communication allude to the tensions of that era.

On the surface, many arguments seem to show *A* arguing with *B*, presumably seeking to change *B*'s mind; but *A*'s argument is really directed not to *B* but to *C*. This attempt to persuade a nonparticipant is evident in the courtroom, where neither the prosecutor (*A*) nor the defense lawyer (*B*) is really trying to convince the opponent. Rather, both are trying to convince a third party, the jury (*C*). Prosecutors do not care whether they convince defense lawyers; they don't even mind infuriating defense lawyers because their only real goal is to convince the jury. Similarly, the writer of a letter to a newspaper, taking issue with an editorial, does not expect to change the paper's policy. Rather, the writer hopes to convince a third party, the reader of the newspaper.

But suppose *A* really does want to bring *B* around to *A*'s point of view. Suppose Mary really wants to persuade the teacher to allow her little lamb to stay in the classroom. Rogers points out that when we engage in an argument, if we feel our integrity or our identity is threatened, we will stiffen our position. (The teacher may feel that his or her dignity is compromised by the presence of the lamb and will scarcely attend to Mary's argument.) The sense of threat may be so great that we are unable to consider the alternative views being offered, and we therefore remain unpersuaded. Threatened, we may defend ourselves rather than our argument, and little communication takes place. Of course, a third party might say that we or our opponent presented the more convincing case, but we, and perhaps the opponent, have scarcely listened to each other, and so the two of us remain apart.

Rogers suggests, therefore, that a writer who wishes to communicate with someone (as opposed to convincing a third party) needs to reduce the threat. In a sense, the participants in the argument need to become partners rather than adversaries. Rogers writes, "Mutual communication tends to be pointed toward solving a problem rather than toward attacking a person or group." Thus, an essay on whether schools should test students for use of drugs, need not—and probably should not—see the issue as black or white, *either/or*. Such an essay might indicate that testing is undesirable because it may have bad effects, *but in some circumstances* it may be acceptable. This qualification does not mean that one must compromise. Thus, the essayist might argue that the potential danger to liberty is so great that no circumstances justify testing students for drugs. But even such an essayist should recognize the merit (however limited) of the opposition and should grant that the position being advanced itself entails great difficulties and dangers.

A writer who wishes to reduce the psychological threat to the opposition and thus facilitate the partnership in the study of some issue can do several things:

- one can show sympathetic understanding of the opposing argument,
- one can recognize what is valid in it, and
- one can recognize and demonstrate that those who take the other side are nonetheless persons of goodwill.

Advocates of Rogerian argument are likely to contrast it with Aristotelian argument, saying that the style of argument associated with Aristotle (384–322 B.C., Greek philosopher and rhetorician)

- is adversarial, seeking to refute other views; and
- sees the listener as wrong, someone who now must be overwhelmed by evidence.

In contrast to the confrontational Aristotelian style, which allegedly seeks to present an airtight case that compels belief, Rogerian argument (it is said)

- is nonconfrontational, collegial, and friendly;
- respects other views and allows for plural truths; and
- seeks to achieve some degree of assent rather than convince utterly.

Thus a writer who takes Rogers seriously will, usually, in the first part of an argumentative essay

1. state the problem,
2. give the opponent's position, and
3. grant whatever validity the writer finds in that position—for instance, will recognize the circumstances in which the position would indeed be acceptable.

Next, the writer will, if possible,

4. attempt to show how the opposing position will be improved if the writer's own position is accepted.

Sometimes, of course, the differing positions may be so far apart that no reconciliation can be proposed, in which case the writer will probably seek to show how the problem can best be solved by adopting the writer's own position. We have discussed these matters in Chapter 6, but not from the point of view of a psychotherapist, and so we reprint Rogers's essay here.

Carl R. Rogers

Communication: Its Blocking and Its Facilitation

It may seem curious that a person whose whole professional effort is devoted to psychotherapy should be interested in problems of communication. What relationship is there between

providing therapeutic help to individuals with emotional malad-
justments and the concern of this conference with obstacles to
communication? Actually the relationship is very close indeed.
The whole task of psychotherapy is the task of dealing with a failure in communication. The emotionally maladjusted person, the
"neurotic," is in difficulty first because communication within
himself has broken down, and second because as a result of this
his communication with others has been damaged. If this sounds
somewhat strange, then let me put it in other terms. In the "neurotic" individual, parts of himself which have been termed uncon-
scious, or repressed, or denied to awareness, become blocked off
so that they no longer communicate themselves to the conscious
or managing part of himself. As long as this is true, there are distortions in the way he communicates himself to others, and so
he suffers both within himself, and in his interpersonal relations.
The task of psychotherapy is to help the person achieve, through a
special relationship with a therapist, good communication within
himself. Once this is achieved he can communicate more freely
and more effectively with others. We may say then that psychotherapy is good communication, within and between men. We
may also turn that statement around and it will still be true. Good
communication, free communication, within or between men, is
always therapeutic.

It is, then, from a background of experience with communication in counseling and psychotherapy that I want to present here
two ideas. I wish to state what I believe is one of the major factors
in blocking or impeding communication, and then I wish to present
what in our experience has proven to be a very important way to
improving or facilitating communication.

I would like to propose, as an hypothesis for consideration,
that the major barrier to mutual interpersonal communication is
our very natural tendency to judge, to evaluate, to approve or dis-
approve, the statement of the person, or the other group. Let me
illustrate my meaning with some very simple examples. As you
leave the meeting tonight, one of the statements you are likely to
hear is, "I didn't like that man's talk." Now what do you respond?
Almost invariably your reply will be either approval or disapproval
of the attitude expressed. Either you respond, "I didn't either. I
thought it was terrible," or else you tend to reply, "Oh, I thought it
was really good." In other words, your primary reaction is to evaluate what has just been said to you, to evaluate it from *your* point of
view, your own frame of reference.

Or take another example. Suppose I say with some feeling, "I think the Republicans are behaving in ways that show a lot of good sound sense these days," what is the response that arises in your mind as you listen? The overwhelming likelihood is that it will be evaluative. You will find yourself agreeing, or disagreeing, or making some judgment about me such as "He must be a conservative," or "He seems solid in his thinking." Or let us take an illustration from the international scene. Russia says vehemently, "The treaty with Japan is a war plot on the part of the United States." We rise as one person to say "That's a lie!"

This last illustration brings in another element connected with 5 my hypothesis. Although the tendency to make evaluations is common in almost all interchange of language, it is very much heightened in those situations where feelings and emotions are deeply involved. So the stronger our feelings, the more likely it is that there will be no mutual element in the communication. There will be just two ideas, two feelings, two judgments, missing each other in psychological space. I'm sure you recognize this from your own experience. When you have not been emotionally involved yourself, and have listened to a heated discussion, you often go away thinking, "Well, they actually weren't talking about the same thing." And they were not. Each was making a judgment, an evaluation, from his own frame of reference. There was really nothing which could be called communication in any genuine sense. This tendency to react to any emotionally meaningful statement by forming an evaluation of it from our own point of view, is, I repeat, the major barrier to interpersonal communication.

But is there any way of solving this problem, of avoiding this barrier? I feel that we are making exciting progress toward this goal and I would like to present it as simply as I can. Real communication occurs, and this evaluative tendency is avoided, when we listen with understanding. What does that mean? It means *to see the expressed idea and attitude from the other person's point of view, to sense how it feels to him, to achieve his frame of reference in regard to the thing he is talking about.*

Stated so briefly, this may sound absurdly simple, but it is not. It is an approach which we have found extremely potent in the field of psychotherapy. It is the most effective agent we know for altering the basic personality structure of an individual, and improving his relationships and his communications with others. If I can listen to what he can tell me, if I can understand how it seems to him, if I can see its personal meaning for him, if I can sense the emotional flavor which it has for him, then I will be releasing potent forces of change in him. If I can really understand how he hates his father, or hates the university, or hates communists—if I can catch the flavor of his fear of insanity, or his fear of atom bombs, or of Russia—it will be of the greatest help to him in altering those very hatreds and fears, and in establishing realistic and harmonious relationships with the very people and situations toward which he has felt hatred and fear. We know from our research that such empathic understanding—understanding *with* a person, not *about* him—is such an effective approach that it can bring about major changes in personality.

Some of you may be feeling that you listen well to people, and that you have never seen such results. The chances are very great indeed that your listening has not been of the type I have described. Fortunately I can suggest a little laboratory experiment which you can try to test the quality of your understanding. The next time you get into an argument with your wife, or your friend, or with a small group of friends, just stop the discussion for a moment and for an experiment, institute this rule. "Each person can speak up for himself only *after* he has first restated the ideas and feelings of the previous speaker accurately, and to that speaker's satisfaction." You see what this would mean. It would simply mean that before presenting your own point of view, it would be necessary for you to really achieve the other speaker's frame of reference—to understand his thoughts and feelings so well that you could summarize them for him. Sounds simple, doesn't it? But if you try it you will discover it one of the most difficult things you have ever tried to do. However, once you have been able to see the other's point of view, your own comments will have to be drastically revised. You will also find the emotion going out of the discussion, the differences being reduced, and those differences which remain being of a rational and understandable sort.

Can you imagine what this kind of an approach would mean if it were projected into larger areas? What would happen to a labor-management dispute if it was conducted in such a way that labor, without necessarily agreeing, could accurately state management's point of view in a way that management could accept; and management, without approving labor's stand, could state labor's case in a way that labor agreed was accurate? It would mean that real communication was established, and one could practically guarantee that some reasonable solution would be reached.

If then this way of approach is an effective avenue to good communication and good relationships, as I am quite sure you will agree if you try the experiment I have mentioned, why is it not more widely tried and used? I will try to list the difficulties which keep it from being utilized.

In the first place it takes courage, a quality which is not too widespread. I am indebted to Dr. S. I. Hayakawa, the semanticist, for pointing out that to carry on psychotherapy in this fashion is to take a very real risk, and that courage is required. If you really understand another person in this way, if you are willing to enter his private world and see the way life appears to him, without any attempt to make evaluative judgments, you run the risk of being changed yourself. You might see it his way, you might find yourself influenced in your attitudes or your personality. This risk of being changed is one of the most frightening prospects most of us can face. If I enter, as fully as I am able, into the private world of a neurotic or psychotic individual, isn't there a risk that I might become lost in that world? Most of us are afraid to take that risk. Or if we had a Russian communist speaker here tonight, or Senator Joe McCarthy, how many of us would dare to try to see the world from each of these points of view? The great majority of us could not *listen;* we would find ourselves compelled to *evaluate,* because listening would seem too dangerous. So the first requirement is courage, and we do not always have it.

But there is a second obstacle. It is just when emotions are strongest that it is most difficult to achieve the frame of reference of the other person or group. Yet it is the time the attitude is most needed, if communication is to be established. We have not found this to be an insuperable obstacle in our experience in psychotherapy. A third party, who is able to lay aside his own feelings and evaluations, can assist greatly by listening with understanding to each person or group and clarifying the views and attitudes each holds. We have found this very effective in small groups in which contradictory or antagonistic attitudes exist. When the parties to a dispute realize that they are being understood, that someone sees how the situation seems to them, the statements grow less exaggerated and less defensive, and it is no longer necessary to maintain the attitude, "I am 100 percent right and you are 100 percent wrong." The influence of such an understanding catalyst in the group permits the members to come closer and closer to the objective truth involved in the relationship. In this way mutual communication is established and some type of agreement becomes much more possible. So we may say that though heightened emotions make it much more difficult to understand *with* an opponent, our experience makes it clear that a neutral, understanding, catalyst type of leader or therapist can overcome this obstacle in a small group.

This last phrase, however, suggests another obstacle to utilizing the approach I have described. Thus far all our experience has been with small face-to-face groups—groups exhibiting industrial tensions, religious tensions, racial tensions, and therapy groups in which many personal tensions are present. In these small groups our experience, confirmed by a limited amount of research, shows that this basic approach leads to improved communication, to greater acceptance of others and by others, and to attitudes which are more positive and more problem-solving in nature. There is a decrease in defensiveness, in exaggerated statements, in evaluative and critical behavior. But these findings are from small groups. What about trying to achieve understanding between larger groups that are geographically remote? Or between face-to-face groups who are not speaking for themselves, but simply as representatives of others, like the delegates at Kaesong?[1] Frankly we do not know the answers to these questions. I believe the situation might be put this way. As social scientists we have a tentative test-tube solution of the problem of breakdown in communication. But to confirm the validity of this test-tube solution, and to adapt it to the enormous problems of communication breakdown between classes, groups, and nations, would involve additional funds, much more research, and creative thinking of a high order.

Even with our present limited knowledge we can see some steps which might be taken, even in large groups, to increase the amount of listening *with,* and to decrease the amount of evaluation *about.* To be imaginative for a moment, let us suppose that a therapeutically oriented international group went to the Russian leaders and said, "We want to achieve a genuine understanding of your views and even more important, of your attitudes and feelings, toward the United States. We will summarize and resummarize the views and feelings if necessary, until you agree that our description represents the situation as it seems to you." Then suppose they did the same thing with the leaders in our own country. If they then gave the widest possible distribution to these two views, with the feelings clearly described but not expressed in name-calling, might not the effect be very great? It would not guarantee the type of understanding I have been describing, but it would make it much more possible. We can understand the feelings of a person

---

[1]**the delegates at Kaesong** Representatives of North and South Korea met at the border town of Kaesong to arrange terms for an armistice to hostilities during the Korean War (1950–1953). [All notes are the editors'.]

who hates us much more readily when his attitudes are accurately described to us by a neutral third party, than we can when he is shaking his fist at us.

But even to describe such a first step is to suggest another obsta- 15 cle to this approach of understanding. Our civilization does not yet have enough faith in the social sciences to utilize their findings. The opposite is true of the physical sciences. During the war[2] when a test-tube solution was found to the problem of synthetic rubber, millions of dollars and an army of talent was turned loose on the problem of using that finding. If synthetic rubber could be made in milligrams, it could and would be made in the thousands of tons. And it was. But in the social science realm, if a way is found of facilitating communication and mutual understanding in small groups, there is no guarantee that the finding will be utilized. It may be a generation or more before the money and the brains will be turned loose to exploit that finding.

In closing, I would like to summarize this small-scale solution to the problem of barriers in communication, and to point out certain of its characteristics.

I have said that our research and experience to date would make it appear that breakdowns in communication, and the evaluative tendency which is the major barrier to communication, can be avoided. The solution is provided by creating a situation in which each of the different parties come to understand the other from the *other's* point of view. This has been achieved, in practice, even when feelings run high, by the influence of a person who is willing to understand each point of view empathically, and who thus acts as a catalyst to precipitate further understanding.

This procedure has important characteristics. It can be initiated by one party, without waiting for the other to be ready. It can even be initiated by a neutral third person, providing he can gain a minimum of cooperation from one of the parties.

This procedure can deal with the insincerities, the defensive exaggerations, the lies, the "false fronts" which characterize almost every failure in communication. These defensive distortions drop away with astonishing speed as people find that the only intent is to understand, not judge.

This approach leads steadily and rapidly toward the discovery 20 of the truth, toward a realistic appraisal of the objective barriers to

[2]**the war** World War II.

communication. The dropping of some defensiveness by one party leads to further dropping of defensiveness by the other party, and truth is thus approached.

This procedure gradually achieves mutual communication. Mutual communication tends to be pointed toward solving a problem rather than toward attacking a person or group. It leads to a situation in which I see how the problem appears to you, as well as to me, and you see how it appears to me, as well as to you. Thus accurately and realistically defined, the problem is almost certain to yield to intelligent attack, or if it is in part insoluble, it will be comfortably accepted as such.

This then appears to be a test-tube solution to the breakdown of communication as it occurs in small groups. Can we take this small-scale answer, investigate it further, refine it; develop it and apply it to the tragic and well-nigh fatal failures of communication which threaten the very existence of our modern world? It seems to me that this is a possibility and a challenge which we should explore.

✓ A CHECKLIST FOR ANALYZING ROGERIAN ARGUMENT

☐ Have I stated the problem and indicated that a dialogue is possible?

☐ Have I stated at least one other point of view in a way that would satisfy its proponents?

☐ Have I been courteous to those who hold views other than mine?

☐ Have I enlarged my own understanding to the extent that I can grant validity, at least in some circumstances, to at least some aspects of other positions?

☐ Have I stated my position and indicated the contexts in which I believe it is valid?

☐ Have I pointed out the ground that we share?

☐ Have I shown how other positions will be strengthened by accepting some aspects of my position?

See *Re:Writing*
bedfordstmartins.com/rewriting
for links related to Rogerian argument.

Edward O. Wilson

Edward O. Wilson, born in in Birmingham, Alabama, in 1929, is an emeritus professor of evolutionary biology at Harvard University. A distinguished writer as well as a researcher and teacher, Wilson has twice won the Pulitzer Prize for General Non-Fiction. We reprint a piece first published in 2006.

Letter to a Southern Baptist Minister

Dear Pastor:

We have not met, yet I feel I know you well enough to call you friend. First of all, we grew up in the same faith. As a boy I too answered the altar call; I went under the water. Although I no longer belong to that faith, I am confident that if we met and spoke privately of our deepest beliefs, it would be in a spirit of mutual respect and good will. I know we share many precepts of moral behavior. Perhaps it also matters that we are both Americans and, insofar as it might still affect civility and good manners, we are both Southerners.

I write to you now for your counsel and help. Of course, in doing so, I see no way to avoid the fundamental differences in our respective worldviews. You are a literalist interpreter of Christian Holy Scripture. You reject the conclusion of science that mankind evolved from lower forms. You believe that each person's soul is immortal, making this planet a way station to a second, eternal life. Salvation is assured those who are redeemed in Christ.

I am a secular humanist. I think existence is what we make of it as individuals. There is no guarantee of life after death, and heaven and hell are what we create for ourselves, on this planet. There is no other home. Humanity originated here by evolution from lower forms over millions of years. And yes, I will speak plain, our ancestors were apelike animals. The human species has adapted physically and mentally to life on Earth and no place else. Ethics is the code of behavior we share on the basis of reason, law, honor, and an inborn sense of decency, even as some ascribe it to God's will.

For you, the glory of an unseen divinity; for me, the glory of the universe revealed at last. For you, the belief in God made flesh to save mankind; for me, the belief in Promethean fire seized to set men free. You have found your final truth; I am still searching. I may be wrong, you may be wrong. We may both be partly right.

Does this difference in worldview separate us in all things? It 5 does not. You and I and every other human being strive for the same imperatives of security, freedom of choice, personal dignity, and a cause to believe in that is larger than ourselves.

Let us see, then, if we can, and you are willing, to meet on the near side of metaphysics in order to deal with the real world we share. I put it this way because you have the power to help solve a great problem about which I care deeply. I hope you have the same concern. I suggest that we set aside our differences in order to save the Creation. The defense of living Nature is a universal value. It doesn't rise from, nor does it promote, any religious or ideological dogma. Rather, it serves without discrimination the interests of all humanity.

Pastor, we need your help. The Creation—living Nature—is in deep trouble. Scientists estimate that if habitat conversion and other destructive human activities continue at their present rates, half the species of plants and animals on Earth could be either gone or at least fated for early extinction by the end of the century. A full quarter will drop to this level during the next half century as a result of climate change alone. The ongoing extinction rate is calculated in the most conservative estimates to be about a hundred times above that prevailing before humans appeared on Earth, and it is expected to rise to at least a thousand times greater or more in the next few decades. If this rise continues unabated, the cost to humanity, in wealth, environmental security, and quality of life, will be catastrophic.

Surely we can agree that each species, however inconspicuous and humble it may seem to us at this moment, is a masterpiece of biology, and well worth saving. Each species possesses a unique combination of genetic traits that fits it more or less precisely to a particular part of the environment. Prudence alone dictates that we act quickly to prevent the extinction of species and, with it, the pauperization of Earth's ecosystems—hence of the Creation.

You may well ask at this point, Why me? Because religion and science are the two most powerful forces in the world today, including especially the United States. If religion and science could be united on the common ground of biological conservation, the problem would soon be solved. If there is any moral precept shared by people of all beliefs, it is that we owe ourselves and future generations a beautiful, rich, and healthful environment.

I am puzzled that so many religious leaders, who spiritually 10 represent a large majority of people around the world, have hesitated to make protection of the Creation an important part of their magisterium. Do they believe that human-centered ethics and preparation for the afterlife are the only things that matter? Even more perplexing is the widespread conviction among Christians that the Second Coming is imminent, and that therefore the condition of the planet is of little consequence. Sixty percent of Americans, according to a 2004 poll, believe that the prophecies of the book of Revelation are accurate. Many of these, numbering in the millions, think the End of Time will occur within the life span of those now living. Jesus will return to Earth, and those redeemed by Christian faith will be transported bodily to heaven, while those left behind will struggle through severe hard times and, when they die, suffer eternal damnation. The condemned will remain in hell, like those already consigned in the generations before them, for a trillion trillion years, enough for the universe to expand to its own, entropic death, time enough for countless universes like it afterward to be born, expand, and likewise die away. And that is just the beginning of how long condemned souls will suffer in hell—all for a mistake they made in choice of religion during the infinitesimally small time they inhabited Earth.

For those who believe this form of Christianity, the fate of 10 million other life forms indeed does not matter. This and other similar doctrines are not gospels of hope and compassion. They are gospels of cruelty and despair. They were not born of the heart of Christianity. Pastor, tell me I am wrong!

However you will respond, let me here venture an alternative ethic. The great challenge of the twenty-first century is to raise people everywhere to a decent standard of living while preserving as much of the rest of life as possible. Science has provided this part of the argument for the ethic: the more we learn about the biosphere, the more complex and beautiful it turns out to be. Knowledge of it is a magic well: the more you draw from it, the more there is to draw. Earth, and especially the razor-thin film of life enveloping it, is our home, our wellspring, our physical and much of our spiritual sustenance.

I know that science and environmentalism are linked in the minds of many with evolution, Darwin, and secularism. Let me postpone disentangling all this (I will come back to it later) and stress again: to protect the beauty of Earth and of its prodigious variety of life forms should be a common goal, regardless of differences in our metaphysical beliefs.

To make the point in good Gospel manner, let me tell the story of a young man, newly trained for the ministry, and so fixed in his Christian faith that he referred all questions of morality to readings from the Bible. When he visited the cathedral-like Atlantic rainforest of Brazil, he saw the manifest hand of God and in his notebook wrote, "It is not possible to give an adequate idea of the higher feelings of wonder, admiration, and devotion which fill and elevate the mind."

That was Charles Darwin in 1832, early into the voyage of 15 HMS *Beagle*, before he had given any thought to evolution.

And here is Darwin, concluding *On the Origin of Species* in 1859, having first abandoned Christian dogma and then, with his newfound intellectual freedom, formulated the theory of evolution by natural selection: "There is grandeur in this view of life, with its several powers, having been originally breathed into a few forms or into one; and that, whilst this planet has gone cycling on according to the fixed law of gravity, from so simple a beginning endless forms most beautiful and most wonderful have been, and are being, evolved."

Darwin's reverence for life remained the same as he crossed the seismic divide that divided his spiritual life. And so it can be for the divide that today separates scientific humanism from mainstream religion. And separates you and me.

You are well prepared to present the theological and moral arguments for saving the Creation. I am heartened by the movement growing within Christian denominations to support global conservation. The stream of thought has arisen from many sources, from evangelical to unitarian. Today it is but a rivulet. Tomorrow it will be a flood.

I already know much of the religious argument on behalf of the Creation, and would like to learn more. I will now lay before you and others who may wish to hear it the scientific argument. You will not agree with all that I say about the origins of life — science and religion do not easily mix in such matters — but I like to think that in this one life-and-death issue we have a common purpose.

Topics for Critical Thinking and Writing

1. Wilson claims to be a "secular humanist" (para. 3). How would you define that term? Are you a secular humanist? Why, or why not?

2. What does Wilson mean by "metaphysics" (para. 6)? Which if any of his views qualify as metaphysical?

3. Wilson obviously seeks to present his views in a fashion that makes them as palatable as possible. Do you think he succeeds in this endeavor? Write an essay of 500 words arguing for or against his achievement in this regard.

11

A Rhetorician's View: Rhetorical Analysis of Nontraditional Texts[1]

The media work us over completely. They are so pervasive in their personal, political, economic, aesthetic, psychological, moral, ethical, and social consequences that they leave no part of us untouched, unaffected, unaltered. The medium is the massage.

——MARSHALL MCLUHAN

We not only interpret the character of events . . . we may also interpret our interpretations.

——KENNETH BURKE

A twenty-first-century rhetorician must now consider not only print and traditional texts but also the kinds and types of technologies used to compose and design those texts. Chapters 4, 5, and 6 discussed both reading and analyzing arguments as well as making them, partly in the light of Aristotle's ideas of *ethos* (the character of the speaker or writer), *pathos* (appeals to the emotions), and *logos* (appeals to reason, notably the use of induction and deduction, but also the testimony of authorities and the display of evidence). Aristotle (384–322 B.C.E.), writing almost two thousand years before Gutenberg's invention of movable type and the printing press, was talking chiefly about *oral* arguments, though the Greeks did have written arguments also, in the form of words handwritten

---

[1]This section was contributed by Anthony Atkins, associate professor of English and composition coordinator at the University of North Carolina Wilmington.

on scrolls. Relatively soon after the introduction of movable type and the printing press in the mid-fifteenth century, *written* arguments—books—largely displaced oral arguments, though oral arguments of course remain important even today, notably in courts and classrooms. Nor should we forget political oratory, in Congress and other political arenas, including televised debates between the candidates for the presidency of the United States.

Compared with Aristotle's chiefly oral world, or even compared with the print world of our parents, today we work with a much more diverse range of texts—for instance, Web sites, Twitter, Facebook, and memes. Nevertheless, we can engage rhetorically with these new texts just as we would with oral texts and with traditional print texts. Furthermore, we engage with these technologic texts for the same reasons that the ancients engaged with their texts. In the world of classical Greece, teachers of rhetoric (at least the best of them) hoped that their teaching would create ethical citizens—effective speakers promoting good causes. Today, rhetoric is an established discipline of study that seeks both to record how people communicate and to teach students how to clearly and responsibly connect their messages with society at large.

> **A RULE FOR WRITERS:** Although the word *rhetoric* today is frequently used with unfavorable connotations, as in *empty rhetoric* and *mere rhetoric*, the traditional meaning of rhetoric (and the meaning in this essay) is the study of language in use, language in real-life situations.

While we still use the Aristotelian strategies of traditional rhetoric, we must acknowledge that even Aristotle, wise though he was, did not envision the rise of the Internet and social and mass media, and the impact those modes of communication would have on our day-to-day communications. Instead of witnessing live speeches in the town square, today we witness and experience Tweets, status updates, online journals and magazines, blogs, and interactive news and sports and entertainment Web sites. Today's town squares exist online, and they are highly interactive; we can instantly respond in detail to most of what we encounter on the Internet, whereas persons listening in the actual physical presence of the speaker cannot do much more than mutter, or, at most boo, hiss, or applaud. The new ways in which we communicate, share ideas, and conduct our private and work lives depend on using digital technologies. Because digital technologies are becoming the backbone of information exchange, rhetoricians have to develop new modes of studying writing and receiving (i.e., interpreting) arguments in a digital age. The New London Group, an association of ten scholars in media, rhetoric, and communication, says:

> [P]rivate lives are being made more public as everything becomes a potential subject of media discussion, resulting in what we refer to as a "conversationalization" of public language. Discourses that were once the domain of the private—the intricacies of the sexual lives of public figures, discussion of repressed memories of child abuse—are now made unashamedly public.

About the ways in which our work lives are changing, the group says:

> With a new worklife comes a new language. A good deal of this change is the result of new technologies, such as the iconographic, text, and screen-based modes of interacting with automated machinery; "user-friendly" interfaces operate with more subtle levels of cultural embeddedness than interfaces based on abstract commands. But much of the change is also the result of the new social relationships of work.

Along with these massive but sometimes subtle changes, rhetoric shifts its focus from the traditional concern with writer, message, and audience to a concern with the context surrounding publication or distribution, which requires us to ask three additional questions:

- Who is publishing the message?
- In what medium (e.g., print, blog, television) is it published?
- How has the message been adapted to suit the medium in which it is published?

You may be familiar with the sentence, "The medium is the message," coined by Marshall McLuhan in 1964. McLuhan's point was that the *medium*—a book versus television, for instance—itself is a message. The idea that each medium is in itself a unique kind of stimulus underlies a pun McLuhan also made, "The medium is the massage."

For a simple example of how technology shapes the message, consider a presidential debate. Ordinarily the candidates stand at podiums several yards apart; viewers in the auditorium look chiefly at whichever person is speaking and pay little attention to the silent candidate. But television directors now commonly use a split screen, bringing the two figures next to each other, and viewers inevitably see not only the speaker but also the immediate reactions of the silent opponent—the raised eyebrows, the frowns, the rolling eyes. In short, the viewers at home, watching the debate on television, experience—because of the medium—a debate that is somewhat different from the debate witnessed by persons in the auditorium, and the home viewer also experiences a debate that is very different from the printed text of the debate a reader encounters in a newspaper.

The three bulleted questions ("Who," "In what medium," "How") influence not only how we read and analyze arguments, but also how we create them. Suppose, for example, you want to make an argument about an aspect of reality TV (as Michelle Dean does on page 384). You may feel that print is not sufficient for your argument; you may decide that you can make a stronger argument by using a blog that allows you to embed clips from the show or links to additional reading.

HOW RHETORICIANS ANALYZE ARGUMENTS

When we interact with texts, we automatically make judgments about them. We come out of a movie theater grumbling that the movie wasn't worth the cost of the ticket, or, on the other hand, perhaps we tell our companion that we are going to recommend this film to our parents. Or we see an ad on TV, and we admire or hate it. Such responses are often the root of rhetorical analysis. When we begin by considering *why* we dislike or like something, we are then in a position to go on—first explaining to ourselves and then to others what the *reasons* are for our judgments. The most important thing for you to do in your role as a rhetorician is to use evidence from your text—whatever the medium—to support your judgments. Nontraditional texts—that is, nonprint texts—can be slightly more difficult to analyze, but you can get a good start by thinking about what evidence from the text you can use to support your opinion. Exactly which aspects of the movie make it not worth the cost of the ticket? What aspect of that television show makes it "the best show on TV"? Why does that commercial make you feel as if you can't live another day without the product it is promoting? When you review the text for evidence, you are clarifying your own initial thoughts; you are searching for truth, and when you think you have found it, you will then try to communicate it to your audience.

You are familiar with analyzing an argument on the basis of its authorship, content, purpose, and audience, and you are familiar with applying the principles of *ethos, pathos,* and *logos.* Although you almost surely will consider these traditional principles when analyzing arguments put forward in emerging media, digital texts may call for additional points of analysis. New technologies require that we continue to rethink what counts as an argument. For example, would you consider a Twitter post an argument? Suppose a politician running for office has used Twitter to criticize an opponent's stance on taxing the wealthy. You could analyze the substance of the tweet and decide that this candidate is arguing that we should raise taxes on people who make above a certain amount each year, and you may be correct. But your analysis shouldn't stop there, because you haven't yet considered how the politician has adapted his argument so that it is uniquely suitable to Twitter, which takes advantage of social media tools that traditional texts cannot. Suppose the politician had tagged the tweet with the hashtag #payyourshare. Adding a hashtag would share that tweet with anyone following that tag rather than sharing the tweet only with people who follow the politician. Your analysis would require you to consider how the politician chose a tag that might connect with a new, perhaps sympathetic, audience because a hashtag, while it may seem like a simple tool, is also a critical part of the text.

Blogs, text messages, tweets, and Facebook status updates are significant texts and may well contain genuine arguments. They deserve the same close analysis that we give to traditional print essays, images, and videos. The increasing presence of visual communication in our lives also forces us to contend with and consider just what effect the visual can have on the meaning of a message. For better, or worse, we live in a world where technology increasingly blurs the line between what counts as print and what counts as visual.

Facebook, for example, requires that we post and share our private lives with the public. Facebook users connect, share, and interact with each other by posting, forwarding, liking, and commenting. Facebook contains elements common to print and to visual media, but it is also interactive in a way traditional print and visual media are not. If you have a Facebook account, but you aren't posting or sharing, are you really using Facebook? One way we might think about rhetoric in the twenty-first century, then, is to think about Facebook, Twitter, and most other free Web applications as new categories of media. The application is carrying information to you or from you, and it therefore becomes the vehicle with which you interact with others, with which you convey and receive information.

PRODUCTION, DISTRIBUTION, AND CONSUMPTION: PERFORMING A RHETORICAL ANALYSIS

When you analyze a traditional print argument, you focus much of your analysis on the author's words. Nontraditional texts, however, have proven that arguments do not necessarily rely on words. On a daily basis, you probably interact with complex texts that mix written, visual, and aural elements far more frequently than you do with traditional print. These texts require more than an analysis of their words. If you want to analyze a music video, for example, and you focus your analysis on only the song's lyrics, your analysis is notably incomplete; you have ignored the music and the visuals.

One way to analyze a text, whether print or other, involves thinking about it not as a solitary piece but as part of a social process, that is, considering its function in society and how it incorporates social rules as part of its argument. You might at first think, for example, that a music video is not an argument, but if you consider that a music video is likely to communicate a point of view about what good music is or what it means to be young, then you begin to see a music video in a new light. In order to analyze a cultural artifact, you must consider who produces the text, where it is distributed, and who consumes that text (and how). Put it this way: You want to

- investigate who is making/developing/creating/producing the text you are analyzing;
- explore where that text is displayed/shown/viewed/distributed; and
- think critically about how you/we consume/think about that text.

In the scheme that we describe below, we explain the key words and concepts needed to perform the analysis; we also explain production, distribution, and consumption.

When you analyze the **producer** of a text, consider what cultural values are present in the text, whether they are stated explicitly or implicitly. These values can be examined in the form of **cultural codes,** that is, as statements of an ideal, such as "The ideal X should (be/do/have) Y." Cultural codes are perhaps easiest to see in advertisements. For example, when you watch a commercial for running shoes, the producer of the commercial may seek to entice you to buy these shoes by including footage of athletic people. In this case, the text is telling you, "The ideal healthy body should be sculpted and lean."

When you have decided what text you will be analyzing, brainstorm as many cultural codes (i.e., intended effects) as you can from it. Remember to phrase them in the form of codes: "The ideal X should (be/do/have) Y." The more codes you can generate, the easier it will be to find the most important ones and critique them on the basis of your own experience. Here are some examples of cultural codes:

> *Gender:* Women should be glamorous. (*Sex in the City*)
>
> *Gender:* Men should be rugged. (an ad for Eddie Bauer)
>
> *Ethnicity:* Beautiful people have exotic features. (*Elle*)
>
> *Economic class:* The American dream is to be famous and live a raucous lifestyle. (*US Weekly*)
>
> *Age:* The elderly are active and vital. (*Betty White's Off Their Rockers*)

As you can see, cultural codes construct *ideal* images (the ideal X should be/do/have Y), and they are adapted to particular media/ ideologies.

In the preceding examples, cultural codes are arranged according to cultural categories (gender, ethnicity, class, political and national identity, age, etc.) as represented in assorted media/ideologies. When you analyze a text, ask yourself whether it endorses one or more of these cultural codes. What evidence from the text can you point to that illustrates the ideal?

Distribution is where (the location) the audience encounters the produced effects (the cultural codes). For example, you are likely to encounter codes related to ideals of beauty in magazines such as *Vogue*. Thus distribution refers to the point of intersection between those who produce cultural artifacts (and the cultural codes associated with them) and those who consume and interact with these artifacts and codes. Today, the spread of technology has assured that points of distribution are more diverse than ever. Cultural codes are conveyed in different ways through different media. Every medium of distribution—from TV shows like *Snapped* and *TMZ* to magazines like *Sports Illustrated* to radio shock jocks like Howard Stern to Web sites like the *Huffington Post*—has a different feel to it, a different *technology* and a different *ideology*. The twenty-first-century rhetorician has to pay careful attention to the particular medium of distribution. Is the artifact distributed via a blog or some other online tool or application? What impact will its distribution have on how the message is promoted and on how it is consumed? Consider, for example, that the *New York Times* is published both in print and in an iPad edition. You may read the print edition from front to back, or skim each page, but if you are an iPad subscriber, the app may recommend stories to you based on what topics have interested you in the past, or those stories may include videos or interactive graphics that change the way you interact with an article. The method of distribution matters, then, in how the *New York Times* reaches different consumers and attracts different audiences.

When we think about **consumption**, we consider the impact cultural codes have on us as *consumers,* people who come into contact with the cultural codes produced by certain artifacts and texts through the media that distribute these artifacts. As consumers (whether readers, viewers, or hearers), we often *accommodate* (passively accept) the cultural codes promoted in the media. For example, in our earlier example concerning the commercial for running shoes, you might accept the producer's communicated ideal that "The ideal healthy body is sculpted and lean." When we accommodate cultural codes without understanding them critically, we allow the media that perpetuate these codes to interpret our worlds for us. That is, we accept their interpretations without questioning the social and cultural values implicit in their assumptions, many of which may run counter to our own social and cultural values.

Suppose, for instance, you have just watched a viral video that promotes environmentalism by showing someone driving a Hummer that is spewing toxic fumes into the air. You could say that this argument relies on the code, "The ideal environmentalist does not drive a Hummer." You could react to this code in one of three ways:

- If you agree that Hummers are terrible for the environment, you are **accommodating** the idea of the video.

- If you deny that global warming is an established scientific fact, or even if you grant that it is a scientific fact but you deny that science has proven that global warming results from combustion of carbon-based fuels, and you further deny that decreased use of these fuels will stop global warming—and therefore you see nothing wrong with buying a Hummer (except maybe the high price)—you are **resisting** the video.

- If you think there is indeed something sound in the anti-Hummer advertisement but you have a wife and four children and two dogs, and, further, you spend a lot of time working "off-road," you might carefully analyze the fuel-consumption of competing vehicles before you make your purchase, in which case you are **negotiating** the anti-Hummer video.

Negotiation, the most useful mode of consumption, involves a process of revision, a process of changing the conditions that give rise to negative aspects of cultural codes. Negotiation also necessitates practical intervention into the processes that construct oppressive social formations, for without intervention, there can be no revision, no positive social or cultural change. We *negotiate* cultural codes when

- we understand their underlying messages and accept the general cultural implications of these codes
- but we acknowledge that there are specific circumstances to which the general codes do not apply.

Using this scheme will help you analyze diverse kinds of texts as well as develop more nuanced arguments about the messages these texts send. In the next section, we'll walk through the analysis of a public service announcement about bullying.

A SAMPLE ANALYSIS: PUBLIC SERVICE ANNOUNCEMENT

Consider the following public service announcement (PSA) on bullying. Public service announcements are usually intended to advise or warn the general public or to facilitate proper civic engagement or participation within a community.

Production

Let's begin our analysis by thinking about the intended audience and cultural codes the PSA produces. We immediately know who the ideal audience is: parents. How do we know this? The evidence is in the artifact/text: "Teach your kids how to be more than a bystander." This is a PSA from StopBullying.gov, a government Web site. What codes can we generate from this simple message?

Class: Ideal parents have access to technologies that distribute PSA announcements.

Class: Ideal parents regardless of class should "teach" their kids how to handle bullying.

Age: Ideal parents are out of high school.

Political Orientation: Ideal parents should have jobs and occupations.

Ideal parents should recognize the government as a resource for parenting help.

Ideal parents should trust the government.

Ideal parents believe that bullying can be controlled or stopped.

Ideal parents should be involved with their kids' school.

Along with the cultural codes that we have generated, we want to think about what else we know about the text's production, distribution, and consumption. We also know that this text can be found both online and in print. There is a link on the text, so if we take this piece seriously we ought to visit the site to get more information.

This text is produced by the federal government. Evidence from the text tells us that this announcement is from StopBullying. gov. The fact that we know this helps us understand the context and the nature of the text. When we visit this site, we find out very quickly that October is Bullying Prevention Month. Furthermore, we learn that calling October "Bullying Prevention Month" is not new. In fact, it started in 2006, when it was initiated by PACER's (Parent Advocacy Coalition for Education Rights) National Bullying Prevention Center. Every October, this site presents activities and resources on bullying. We also learn something by looking at who is partnering with StopBullying.gov: The National Education Association, National PTA, American Federation for Teachers, and the National Coalition for Parent Involvement. We also find out that October 10 is designated as Unity Day, a day when people across the country are encouraged to wear orange as a show of support for students who have been bullied. The goal at StopBullying .gov is to help prevent bullying. It aims to send a message around the world to prevent the bullying of students. Given the partners involved, we can infer that much of the interest in this cause comes from parents and teachers.

At this point, you may be wondering why you are being told all this stuff about the background. Well, now that we have done a little research on this text and what it stands for, we are in a better position to think about two of the arguments the text might be making:

- what role the government should play in not only helping to stop bullying but in providing parents and teachers with resources to work to that end and

- what the producers of the text consider to be an ideal family.

For example, the Web site and the PSA are directly targeted to parents who are out of high school. Together, the PSA and the Web site also tell us that parents should trust the government, be involved with their kids' school, and have jobs or occupations. When the text says, "You don't see bullying like this every day. Your kids do," this assertion rests on an assumption that parents do not see bullying because they are not in school or not at school. Presumably, parents have jobs and other grown-up things to do, so would not notice, witness, or see the kinds of bullying that their kids do. Based on the number and kinds of organizations that partner with StopBullying.gov, we also know that the main source of concern is from parents and teachers and presupposes that most bullying occurs at school.

Distribution

This PSA, designed to appear in a magazine, is a *print text*, but PSAs are typically distributed as widely as possible. We may see them on television, hear them on the radio, or read them on billboards at the side of the road; nowadays, we also see them online as we surf various Web sites. Thinking about the distribution for PSAs matters: particular consumers may not come into contact with billboards (lack of car), may not hear radio announcements (no radio), may not see ads on television (no television), or may not find banners online (no Internet access). In thinking about the distribution of this PSA, we have to acknowledge that economic class plays a significant role in the distribution and accessibility of information in multiple venues. And, in fact, if you visit StopBullying.gov, you will see that this PSA is accompanied by additional ones designed for distribution to different media. How do those vary from this one?

Consumption

As we think more about the PSA on bullying, our minds are bound to turn to the question of how we consume the message. If we *accommodate* it, we could focus our argument on what a good job the government is doing to help protect kids from bullying. We might say, for example, that the government is helping parents, schools, teachers, and students have a better educational experience, free from bullying. The large headline "Everybody hates you" grabs the attention of anyone who sees the announcement. We could also argue that it is a good use of tax dollars because the PSA is an effort on the part of the government to protect its citizens — in particular, America's children.

If we *resist* this PSA, we could argue that the government is not responsible for helping parents raise their kids or even that government help of this sort is another example of the government meddling in the lives of citizens. We might also argue that bullying cannot be stopped because the psychological makeup of some students makes bullying inevitable. Some kids just are more aggressive than others, and they always have been. The PSA does not consider what medical or psychological issues might cause bullying. We might continue by arguing that the government should focus its energies and finances on other more serious causes where there was more reason to expect success.

If we decide to *negotiate* the PSA, we might argue that, yes, the PSA does consider a number of reasons for why someone bullies another but the announcement also serves as a reminder that grown-ups, parents, and teachers should pay closer attention to behaviors in the classroom, that we should do a better job of helping kids and students get along and become productive citizens of the community. The PSA, targeted at parents and teachers, also speaks to those without children when it pleads for the reader or viewer of the announcement not to be a "bystander." Although we may not think the government is the best resource for helping to raise our children, we recognize the efforts being made to keep kids as safe and protected as possible. In short, we would recognize in our argument the ways that the PSA is productive and helpful to its audience, but we would also point out its weaknesses.

✓ A CHECKLIST FOR CULTURAL ANALYSIS

☐ What sort of text are you analyzing? A Web site (what kind of Web site?), a printed text, an image, an advertisement, a song or an album, an artifact (for instance a toy, a grocery item, a magazine), a Twitter feed? The kind of text you are analyzing will determine your approach.

☐ Have you thought about the cultural codes of your text: The ideal X should be/do/have Y?

☐ Have you described the codes and—*using evidence from the text*—have you explained how you reached your conclusion?

☐ Have you thought about where your text is distributed and where people come into contact with your text? Is it online, on television, in a newspaper, a film, etc.?

☐ Have you thought about whether you accommodate, resist, or negotiate the cultural codes illustrated by the text? Do you explain *why* you feel the way you do?

☐ Who is the main audience for the text you are analyzing? How can you tell? Who might be the main audience for the essay or project that you are composing?

☐ What should readers or viewers of your essay or project take away about the text you have analyzed, and what value can others get from it?

A SAMPLE CULTURAL ANALYSIS

Michelle Dean

The following essay, a rhetorical analysis of the reality TV phenomenon Here Comes Honey Boo Boo, *was originally published online at* Slate *on August 24, 2012. It was written by Michelle Dean, a lawyer who now writes about class, gender, and television. As you read the essay, think about how Dean constructs an analysis that considers audience, production, distribution, and consumption.*

Here Comes the Hillbilly, Again

Somehow America always goes a little off the rails in the allegedly slow month of August, and this year's party is as wild as any. Republicans can't figure out how babies are made; cutting-and-pasting an article from *The New Yorker* into your *Time* column is no longer a fireable offense; and all the way down in McIntyre, Ga., there is a mother who feeds her child a Mountain Dew-and-Red Bull concoction before the six-year-old gets onstage at beauty pageants. June Shannon, who stars with her daughter Alana "Honey Boo Boo Child" Thompson in TLC's controversial hit *Here Comes Honey Boo Boo*, would have provoked a firestorm even if what she calls "go-go juice" were the only sin she was broadcasting all over Christendom. All that caffeine, pop-culture commentators everywhere clucked, and all that sugar.

Lost in the outrage is just how squarely "go-go juice" fits into America's long tradition of "white trash" entertainment, which for decades has elevated characters like Honey Boo Boo into the nation's objects of fun. The Pepsi Co. borrowed the Mountain Dew brand-name from slang for moonshine; in the 1960s, it was explicitly advertised as a "hillbilly" drink. The campaign's entertaining TV ads, which you can watch on YouTube, were scored by twangy banjos and errant buckshot and plotted around a "stone-hearted gal" who will open her heart to you if you only take a swig. Watching these old videos after an episode or two of *Honey Boo Boo* makes at least one thing clear: The hillbilly has regained the spotlight in American culture.

As Anthony Harkins observes in *Hillbilly: A Cultural History of an American Icon*, one of the hillbilly's signature moves is to peak, popularity-wise, just when Americans sense that things in general are headed south. Its first true zenith came in the depressed 1930s, a handmaiden to the birth of commercial country music. Another arrived in the turbulent 1960s, when *The Beverly Hillbillies* and *Green Acres* and *Hee Haw* were in their prime. (Those are hardly the only examples, of course: It also popped up in the Ma and Pa Kettle films of the 1940s and 1950s and Paul Webb's 1930s *Esquire* cartoons about "The Mountain Boys," among other places.)

Though the term first referred to mountaineers in the Appalachians and the Ozarks, the hillbilly trope spread to cover pretty much all nonurban territory in America, joined by its cousins in cultural iconography, the "redneck" and "white trash." Today, people even apply that last term to residents of certain New Jersey beach-fronts, for instance. Yet, as Harkins points out, no matter where an alleged country bumpkin comes from, he will be derided for his crass behavior. And such ridicule has always been politically coded: The hillbilly figure allows middle-class white people to offload the venality and sin of the nation onto some other constituency, people who live somewhere—anywhere—else. The hillbilly's backwardness highlights the progress more upstanding Americans in the cities or the suburbs have made. These fools haven't crawled out of the muck, the story goes, because they don't want to.

This idea that the hillbilly's poverty is a choice allows more upscale Americans to feel comfortable while laughing at the antics before them. It also pushes some people to embrace the stereotype as a badge of honor. "Guitars, Cadillacs, hillbilly music / It's the only thing that keeps me hangin' on," Dwight Yoakam once sang. For more contemporary examples of reappropriation, you can attend any number of Tea Party rallies. The classist term "redneck," originally coined to indicate those who worked so hard and so long in the sun that they sported sunburns in the designated anatomical location, likewise has been adopted in the name of all that's good and holy. What's more American than a hard day's work?

June Shannon is a reappropriator par excellence. One of her signature phrases on *Here Comes Honey Boo Boo* is a call to, as she puts it, "redneck-ognize." And yet all the cultural chatter that's attended *Honey Boo Boo* has been less than affectionate. The word of the day across the media is "apocalypse"—that is, the show is a sign of it. It's not just the caffeine highs, either. It's a family of six chopping up a roadkill deer for dinner, belly-flopping in the mud, and—those with delicate constitutions may want to avert their eyes for this next part—farting in public. Even critics who enjoy the show do so from a crouched, defensive posture. People seem to think this has all gone a little too far. Even the *Today Show* is starting to wonder if reality television just might be "exploitative."

I'm not a *Toddlers & Tiaras* fan, so I missed out on Alana's big splash on that show earlier this year. Beauty pageants in general are foreign and noxious to me: I can barely muster the energy to put on lip gloss and mascara. But I watched *Honey Boo Boo* out of curiosity about the fuss, and found myself, somewhat surprisingly, relating to Alana and her milieu. I have fond memories of that Dwight Yoakam song playing softly on my parents' radio as we drove home through the dark from a visit to my grandparents' house in rural Quebec. My family isn't from the South—we're not even from the United States—but I know enough of the land Honey Boo Boo lives in to be dubious of simple accusations of bad parenting and worse morals.

The practices are different, of course, and no, I'm not wild about the caffeine and sugar thing, either. Alana's little-girl gran-diosity must become exhausting when experienced in more than thirty-minute increments. But the people raising her are clearly aware of your disdain. Shannon can be delightfully funny when she self-consciously plays with her hillbilly image, warning the audience that she's about to "scratch her bugs," or speaking of her beauty routine: "Granted, I ain't the most beautimous out the box, but a little paint on this barn, shine it back to its original condition. 'Cause it shines up like it's brand new."

That's not to say the humor is always comfortable or even funny. Alana's trademark phrases and mannerisms—"a dollar makes me holler," a particular head swivel she does—are informed by racist stereotypes of black women. This ambiguous borrowing from black culture has always been part of the hillbilly trope as well. Early commercial country music borrowed liberally from black folk music. (Hank Williams learned to play guitar, he said, from a black street performer.) And this borrowing often turned into racist mim-icry: The Grand Ole Opry included minstrelsy shows in the 1920s and 1930s. Interestingly, the term "white trash" may have been coined by black slaves in the early nineteenth century to describe poor white people in the South; American attitudes toward poor white people have long been tangled up with "the race problem."

And hillbilly stereotypes have always made it easier for middle- 10 class whites to presume that racism is the exclusive province of "that kind" of person. As Ta-Nehisi Coates has written, "It is comforting to think of racism as species of misanthropy, or akin to child molestation, thus exonerating all those who bear no real hatred in their heart. It's much more troubling to think of it as it's always been—a means of political organization and power distribution."

As that distribution of power becomes more and more unequal, it's no surprise to see the hillbilly here again—on *Here Comes Honey Boo Boo*, on Jersey Shore, on MTV's *16 & Pregnant* and *Teen Mom* franchises. These shows reassure us that our struggle is worth it, all economic evidence to the contrary—if only because we would never belly-flop into the mud on cable television. *Here Comes Honey Boo Boo* casts this socioeconomic divide in especially sharp relief, since the show is rooted partly in beauty pageant culture, which, in its own idiosyncratic way, indulges the American belief that you can work and spend your way to greatness. If you can afford the entry fees, the glitter, the makeup, the coach, and the stylists, you will be the Ultimate Supreme, as they say in the business. You'll have the sash to prove it.

But tiny, six-year-old Alana is too crass and happy to get it. She is a terrible pageant queen. Her wigs are always askew, her daisy-dukes ill-fitting, and sometimes she grinds her fake teeth. Those rhinestone-studded bootstraps simply can't pull her up the way she needs them to.

TOPICS FOR CRITICAL THINKING AND WRITING

1. What would you say was Dean's main argument? Support your reasoning with examples.

2. What cultural codes does Dean see as present both in *Here Comes Honey Boo Boo* and in the ensuing criticism of it?

3. *Here Comes Honey Boo Boo* is a reality TV show. How does Dean characterize this medium of distribution?

4. Visit slate.com, where Dean's essay was originally published. With respect to distribution, how would you characterize the technology and ideology of *Slate*? Is it the kind of site where you would expect to find an essay defending *Here Comes Honey Boo Boo*? Why, or why not?

5. Would you say that Dean's essay accommodates, resists, or negotiates the codes imposed by *Here Comes Honey Boo Boo*?

6. Write an essay (about 500 words) in which you analyze a nontraditional text—perhaps a popular cultural artifact (such as a magazine, toy, or product), a Web site, a smartphone application, a commercial, television show, or anything else, preferably a text with which you have regular contact and to which you have easy access. Get a copy of the text you plan to analyze (you will submit a copy of it when you turn in your final critical essay). Your essay should follow the general structure discussed in this chapter (production, distribution, consumption); you may wish to use Dean's essay as a model. Your essay should have a strong introduction, in which you introduce your text and lay out your basic points of analysis, and a strong conclusion. Within the body of your analysis, make sure you do the following: Discuss who the audience for your text is, what codes the text produces, how the codes are distributed and whether this distribution is effective, and how this text targets you as a consumer, including whether you accommodate, resist, or negotiate the cultural codes you have found within the text. Make certain to use evidence from the text to support your claims.

Text Credits

Harlan Coben, "The Undercover Parent" from the *New York Times* March 16, 2008. Copyright © 2008 by The New York Times. Reprinted by permission. All rights reserved. Used by permission and protected by the Copyright Laws of the United States. The printing, copying, redistribution, or retransmission of this Content without express written permission is prohibited.

Michelle Dean, "Here Comes the Hillbilly, Again" from *Slate*, Aug. 24, 2012, copyright © 2012 The Slate Group. All rights reserved. Used by permission and protected by the Copyright Laws of the United States. The printing, copying, redistribution, or retransmission of the Material without express written permission is prohibited.

Susan Jacoby, "A First Amendment Junkie" by Susan Jacoby. Copyright © 1978 by Susan Jacoby. Originally appeared in the *New York Times* (January 26, 1978). Reprinted by permission of Georges Borchardt, Inc. on behalf of the author.

Nicholas Kristof, "For Environmental Balance, Pick Up a Rifle," from the *New York Times*, December 14, 2005. Copyright © 2005 by the New York Times. All rights reserved. Used by permission and protected by the Copyright Laws of the United States. The printing, copying, redistribution, or retransmission of this Content without express written permission is prohibited.

Jena McGregor, "Military Women in Combat: Why Making It Official Matters" from the *Washington Post*, May 25, 2012 issue. Copyright © 2012 the Washington Post. All rights reserved. Used by permission and protected by the Copyright Laws of the United States. The printing, copying, redistribution, or retransmission of the Material without express written permission is prohibited.

James E. McWilliams, "The Locavore Myth" from *Forbes*, Aug. 3, 2009. Copyright © 2009 by Forbes. All rights reserved. Used by permission and protected by the Copyright Laws of the United States. The printing, copying, redistribution, or retransmission of this Content without express written permission is prohibited.

Carl Rogers, "Communication: Its Blocking and Its Facilitation." Copyright © Natalie Rogers. Reprinted by permission of the Natalie Rogers Trust.

Zachary B. Shemtob and David Lat, "Executions Should Be Televised" from the *New York Times*, July 29, 2011 issue. Copyright © 2011 by the New York Times. All rights reserved. Used by permission and protected by the Copyright Laws of the United States. The printing, copying, redistribution, or retransmission of this Content without express written permission is prohibited.

Max Shulman, "Love Is a Fallacy," copyright © 1951 by Max Shulman, renewed 1979. Reprinted by permission of the Harold Matson Co., Inc.

Carol Weston, Letter in response to Harlan Coben's Op-Ed "The Undercover Parent" from the *New York Times*, March 16, 2008. Letter reprinted by permission of Carol Weston, author of *Girltalk, The Diary of Melanie Martin*, and other titles. See her website carolweston.com.

George F. Will, "Being Green at Ben & Jerry's" from *Newsweek*, May 5, 2002. Copyright © 2002 by Newsweek/Daily Beast Company LLC. All rights reserved. Used by permission and protected by the Copyright Laws of the United States. The printing, copying, redistribution, or retransmission of the Material without express written permission is prohibited.

Edward O. Wilson, from *The Creation: An Appeal to Save Life on Earth* by Edward O. Wilson. Copyright © 2006 by Edward O. Wilson. Used by permission of W.W. Norton & Company, Inc.

Art Credits

"He saves all his critical thinking for my behavior," Cartoon Bank/Kaplan: Bruce Eric Kaplan/The New York Collection/www.cartoonbank.com.

Index of Terms

■ Directory to Documentation Models in MLA Format

IN-TEXT OR PARENTHETICAL CITATIONS, 247

LIST OF WORKS CITED, 253

■ Idea Prompts

Below is an index to the Idea Prompts that appear in this book. Idea Prompts provide models and strategies for: